BOOKS

BURMESE
VOCABULARY

FOR ENGLISH SPEAKERS

ENGLISH-BURMESE

The most useful words
To expand your lexicon and sharpen
your language skills

9000 words

Burmese vocabulary for English speakers - 9000 words

By Andrey Taranov

T&P Books vocabularies are intended for helping you learn, memorize and review foreign words. The dictionary is divided into themes, covering all major spheres of everyday activities, business, science, culture, etc.

The process of learning words using T&P Books' theme-based dictionaries gives you the following advantages:

- Correctly grouped source information predetermines success at subsequent stages of word memorization
- Availability of words derived from the same root allowing memorization of word units (rather than separate words)
- Small units of words facilitate the process of establishing associative links needed for consolidation of vocabulary
- Level of language knowledge can be estimated by the number of learned words

Copyright © 2019 T&P Books Publishing

All rights reserved. No part of this book may be reproduced or utilized in any form or by any means, electronic or mechanical, including photocopying, recording or by information storage and retrieval system, without permission in writing from the publishers.

T&P Books Publishing
www.tpbooks.com

ISBN: 978-1-78767-996-2

This book is also available in E-book formats.
Please visit www.tpbooks.com or the major online bookstores.

BURMESE VOCABULARY
for English speakers

T&P Books vocabularies are intended to help you learn, memorize, and review foreign words. The vocabulary contains over 9000 commonly used words arranged thematically.

- Vocabulary contains the most commonly used words
- Recommended as an addition to any language course
- Meets the needs of beginners and advanced learners of foreign languages
- Convenient for daily use, revision sessions, and self-testing activities
- Allows you to assess your vocabulary

Special features of the vocabulary

- Words are organized according to their meaning, not alphabetically
- Words are presented in three columns to facilitate the reviewing and self-testing processes
- Words in groups are divided into small blocks to facilitate the learning process
- The vocabulary offers a convenient and simple transcription of each foreign word

The vocabulary has 256 topics including:

Basic Concepts, Numbers, Colors, Months, Seasons, Units of Measurement, Clothing & Accessories, Food & Nutrition, Restaurant, Family Members, Relatives, Character, Feelings, Emotions, Diseases, City, Town, Sightseeing, Shopping, Money, House, Home, Office, Working in the Office, Import & Export, Marketing, Job Search, Sports, Education, Computer, Internet, Tools, Nature, Countries, Nationalities and more ...

TABLE OF CONTENTS

Pronunciation guide 12
Abbreviations 13

BASIC CONCEPTS 14
Basic concepts. Part 1 14

1. Pronouns 14
2. Greetings. Salutations. Farewells 14
3. How to address 15
4. Cardinal numbers. Part 1 15
5. Cardinal numbers. Part 2 17
6. Ordinal numbers 17
7. Numbers. Fractions 17
8. Numbers. Basic operations 18
9. Numbers. Miscellaneous 18
10. The most important verbs. Part 1 19
11. The most important verbs. Part 2 20
12. The most important verbs. Part 3 21
13. The most important verbs. Part 4 21
14. Colors 23
15. Questions 23
16. Prepositions 24
17. Function words. Adverbs. Part 1 24
18. Function words. Adverbs. Part 2 26

Basic concepts. Part 2 28

19. Opposites 28
20. Weekdays 30
21. Hours. Day and night 30
22. Months. Seasons 31
23. Time. Miscellaneous 33
24. Lines and shapes 34
25. Units of measurement 35
26. Containers 36
27. Materials 37
28. Metals 37

HUMAN BEING   39
Human being. The body   39

29.	Humans. Basic concepts	39
30.	Human anatomy	39
31.	Head	40
32.	Human body	41

Clothing & Accessories   42

33.	Outerwear. Coats	42
34.	Men's & women's clothing	42
35.	Clothing. Underwear	43
36.	Headwear	43
37.	Footwear	43
38.	Textile. Fabrics	44
39.	Personal accessories	45
40.	Clothing. Miscellaneous	45
41.	Personal care. Cosmetics	46
42.	Jewelry	47
43.	Watches. Clocks	47

Food. Nutricion   49

44.	Food	49
45.	Drinks	51
46.	Vegetables	52
47.	Fruits. Nuts	52
48.	Bread. Candy	53
49.	Cooked dishes	54
50.	Spices	55
51.	Meals	55
52.	Table setting	56
53.	Restaurant	57

Family, relatives and friends   58

54.	Personal information. Forms	58
55.	Family members. Relatives	58
56.	Friends. Coworkers	60
57.	Man. Woman	60
58.	Age	61
59.	Children	61
60.	Married couples. Family life	62

Character. Feelings. Emotions   64

61. Feelings. Emotions   64
62. Character. Personality   65
63. Sleep. Dreams   66
64. Humour. Laughter. Gladness   67
65. Discussion, conversation. Part 1   68
66. Discussion, conversation. Part 2   69
67. Discussion, conversation. Part 3   70
68. Agreement. Refusal   71
69. Success. Good luck. Failure   72
70. Quarrels. Negative emotions   72

Medicine   75

71. Diseases   75
72. Symptoms. Treatments. Part 1   77
73. Symptoms. Treatments. Part 2   78
74. Symptoms. Treatments. Part 3   79
75. Doctors   79
76. Medicine. Drugs. Accessories   80
77. Smoking. Tobacco products   81

HUMAN HABITAT   82
City   82

78. City. Life in the city   82
79. Urban institutions   83
80. Signs   85
81. Urban transportation   86
82. Sightseeing   87
83. Shopping   87
84. Money   88
85. Post. Postal service   89

Dwelling. House. Home   91

86. House. Dwelling   91
87. House. Entrance. Lift   92
88. House. Electricity   92
89. House. Doors. Locks   92
90. Country house   93
91. Villa. Mansion   94
92. Castle. Palace   94
93. Apartment   95
94. Apartment. Cleaning   95

95.	Furniture. Interior	96
96.	Bedding	96
97.	Kitchen	97
98.	Bathroom	98
99.	Household appliances	99
100.	Repairs. Renovation	99
101.	Plumbing	100
102.	Fire. Conflagration	100

HUMAN ACTIVITIES 103
Job. Business. Part 1 103

103.	Office. Working in the office	103
104.	Business processes. Part 1	104
105.	Business processes. Part 2	105
106.	Production. Works	106
107.	Contract. Agreement	108
108.	Import & Export	108
109.	Finances	109
110.	Marketing	110
111.	Advertising	110
112.	Banking	111
113.	Telephone. Phone conversation	112
114.	Cell phone	113
115.	Stationery	113
116.	Various kinds of documents	114
117.	Kinds of business	115

Job. Business. Part 2 118

118.	Show. Exhibition	118
119.	Mass Media	119
120.	Agriculture	120
121.	Building. Building process	121
122.	Science. Research. Scientists	122

Professions and occupations 124

123.	Job search. Dismissal	124
124.	Business people	124
125.	Service professions	126
126.	Military professions and ranks	127
127.	Officials. Priests	127
128.	Agricultural professions	128
129.	Art professions	128
130.	Various professions	129
131.	Occupations. Social status	130

Sports   132

132. Kinds of sports. Sportspersons   132
133. Kinds of sports. Miscellaneous   133
134. Gym   134
135. Hockey   134
136. Soccer   135
137. Alpine skiing   136
138. Tennis. Golf   137
139. Chess   137
140. Boxing   138
141. Sports. Miscellaneous   138

Education   140

142. School   140
143. College. University   141
144. Sciences. Disciplines   142
145. Writing system. Orthography   142
146. Foreign languages   144
147. Fairy tale characters   145
148. Zodiac Signs   145

Arts   147

149. Theater   147
150. Cinema   148
151. Painting   149
152. Literature & Poetry   150
153. Circus   151
154. Music. Pop music   152

Rest. Entertainment. Travel   154

155. Trip. Travel   154
156. Hotel   155
157. Books. Reading   155
158. Hunting. Fishing   157
159. Games. Billiards   158
160. Games. Playing cards   158
161. Casino. Roulette   159
162. Rest. Games. Miscellaneous   159
163. Photography   160
164. Beach. Swimming   161

TECHNICAL EQUIPMENT. TRANSPORTATION   163
Technical equipment   163

165. Computer   163
166. Internet. E-mail   164
167. Electricity   165
168. Tools   166

Transportation   169

169. Airplane   169
170. Train   170
171. Ship   171
172. Airport   173
173. Bicycle. Motorcycle   174

Cars   175

174. Types of cars   175
175. Cars. Bodywork   175
176. Cars. Passenger compartment   177
177. Cars. Engine   177
178. Cars. Crash. Repair   178
179. Cars. Road   179
180. Traffic signs   180

PEOPLE. LIFE EVENTS   182
Life events   182

181. Holidays. Event   182
182. Funerals. Burial   183
183. War. Soldiers   184
184. War. Military actions. Part 1   185
185. War. Military actions. Part 2   186
186. Weapons   188
187. Ancient people   189
188. Middle Ages   190
189. Leader. Chief. Authorities   192
190. Road. Way. Directions   193
191. Breaking the law. Criminals. Part 1   194
192. Breaking the law. Criminals. Part 2   196
193. Police. Law. Part 1   197
194. Police. Law. Part 2   198

NATURE
The Earth. Part 1

195. Outer space
196. The Earth
197. Cardinal directions
198. Sea. Ocean
199. Seas' and Oceans' names
200. Mountains
201. Mountains names
202. Rivers
203. Rivers' names
204. Forest
205. Natural resources

200
200

200
201
202
202
204
204
205
206
206
207
208

The Earth. Part 2

210

206. Weather
207. Severe weather. Natural disasters
208. Noises. Sounds
209. Winter

210
211
212
212

Fauna

214

210. Mammals. Predators
211. Wild animals
212. Domestic animals
213. Dogs. Dog breeds
214. Sounds made by animals
215. Young animals
216. Birds
217. Birds. Singing and sounds
218. Fish. Marine animals
219. Amphibians. Reptiles
220. Insects
221. Animals. Body parts
222. Actions of animals
223. Animals. Habitats
224. Animal care
225. Animals. Miscellaneous
226. Horses

214
214
216
217
217
218
218
220
220
221
221
222
223
223
224
225
225

Flora

227

227. Trees
228. Shrubs
229. Mushrooms

227
228
228

230. Fruits. Berries   228
231. Flowers. Plants   229
232. Cereals, grains   231
233. Vegetables. Greens   231

REGIONAL GEOGRAPHY   233
Countries. Nationalities   233

234. Western Europe   233
235. Central and Eastern Europe   235
236. Former USSR countries   237
237. Asia   238
238. North America   240
239. Central and South America   240
240. Africa   241
241. Australia. Oceania   242
242. Cities   242
243. Politics. Government. Part 1   244
244. Politics. Government. Part 2   245
245. Countries. Miscellaneous   246
246. Major religious groups. Confessions   247
247. Religions. Priests   249
248. Faith. Christianity. Islam   249

MISCELLANEOUS   253

249. Various useful words   253
250. Modifiers. Adjectives. Part 1   254
251. Modifiers. Adjectives. Part 2   257

MAIN 500 VERBS   260

252. Verbs A-C   260
253. Verbs D-G   263
254. Verbs H-M   265
255. Verbs N-R   267
256. Verbs S-W   269

PRONUNCIATION GUIDE

Comments

Transcription used in this book - the Myanmar Language Commission Transcription System (MLCTS)
A description of this system can be found here:
https://en.wiktionary.org/wiki/Wiktionary:Burmese_transliteration
https://en.wikipedia.org/wiki/MLC_Transcription_System

ABBREVIATIONS
used in the vocabulary

English abbreviations

ab.	-	about
adj	-	adjective
adv	-	adverb
anim.	-	animate
as adj	-	attributive noun used as adjective
e.g.	-	for example
etc.	-	et cetera
fam.	-	familiar
fem.	-	feminine
form.	-	formal
inanim.	-	inanimate
masc.	-	masculine
math	-	mathematics
mil.	-	military
n	-	noun
pl	-	plural
pron.	-	pronoun
sb	-	somebody
sing.	-	singular
sth	-	something
v aux	-	auxiliary verb
vi	-	intransitive verb
vi, vt	-	intransitive, transitive verb
vt	-	transitive verb

BASIC CONCEPTS

Basic concepts. Part 1

1. Pronouns

I, me	ကျွန်ုပ်	kjunou'
you	သင်	thin
he	သူ	thu
she	သူမ	thu ma.
it	၎င်း	jin:
we	ကျွန်ုပ်တို့	kjunou' tou.
we (masc.)	ကျွန်တော်တို့	kjun do. dou.
we (fem.)	ကျွန်မတို့	kjun ma. tou.
you (to a group)	သင်တို့	thin dou.
you (polite, sing.)	သင်	thin
you (polite, pl)	သင်တို့	thin dou.
they (masc.)	သူတို့	thu dou.
they (fem.)	သူမတို့	thu ma. dou.

2. Greetings. Salutations. Farewells

Hello! (fam.)	မင်္ဂလာပါ	min ga. la ba
Hello! (form.)	မင်္ဂလာပါ	min ga. la ba
Good morning!	မင်္ဂလာနံနက်ခင်းပါ	min ga. la nan ne' gin: ba
Good afternoon!	မင်္ဂလာနေ့လယ်ခင်းပါ	min ga. la nei. le gin: ba
Good evening!	မင်္ဂလာညနေခင်းပါ	min ga. la nja nei gin: ba
to say hello	နှုတ်ဆက်သည်	hnou' hsei' te
Hi! (hello)	ဟိုင်း	hain:
greeting (n)	ဟာလို	ha. lou
to greet (vt)	နှုတ်ဆက်သည်	hnou' hsei' te
How are you?	နေကောင်းလား	nei gaun: la:
How are you? (form.)	နေကောင်းပါသလား	nei gaun: ba dha la:
How are you? (fam.)	အဆင်ပြေလား	ahsin bjei la:
What's new?	ဘာထူးသေးလဲ	ba du: dei: le:
Bye-Bye! Goodbye!	နောက်မှတွေ့ကြမယ်	nau' hma. dwei. gja. me
Goodbye!	ဝတ်တိုင်	gu' bain
Bye!	တာ့တာ	ta. da

See you soon!	မကြာခင်ပြန် ဆုံကြမယ်	ma gja. gin bjan zoun gja. me
Farewell!	နုတ်ဆက်ပါတယ်	hnou' hsei' pa de
to say goodbye	နုတ်ဆက်သည်	hnou' hsei' te
So long!	တာ့တာ	ta. da
Thank you!	ကျေးဇူးတင်ပါတယ်	kjei: zu: din ba de
Thank you very much!	ကျေးဇူးအများ ကြီးတင်ပါတယ်	kjei: zu: amja: kji: din ba de
You're welcome	ရပါတယ်	ja. ba de
Don't mention it!	ကိစ္စမရှိပါဘူး	kei: sa ma. shi. ba bu:
It was nothing	ရပါတယ်	ja. ba de
Excuse me! (fam.)	ေဆာရီးနော်	hso: ji: no:
Excuse me! (form.)	တောင်းပန်ပါတယ်	thaun: ban ba de
to excuse (forgive)	ခွင့်လွှတ်သည်	khwin. hlu' te
to apologize (vi)	တောင်းပန်သည်	thaun: ban de
My apologies	တောင်းပန်ပါတယ်	thaun: ban ba de
I'm sorry!	ခွင့်လွှတ်ပါ	khwin. hlu' pa
to forgive (vt)	ခွင့်လွှတ်သည်	khwin. hlu' te
It's okay! (that's all right)	ကိစ္စမရှိပါဘူး	kei: sa ma. shi. ba bu:
please (adv)	ကျေးဇူးပြု၍	kjei: zu: pju. i.
Don't forget!	မမေ့ပါနဲ့	ma. mei. ba ne.
Certainly!	ရတာပေါ့	ja. da bo.
Of course not!	မဟုတ်တာသေချာတယ်	ma hou' ta dhei gja de
Okay! (I agree)	သဘောတူတယ်	dhabo: tu de
That's enough!	တော်ပြီ	to bji

3. How to address

Excuse me, …	ခွင့်ပြုပါ	khwin. bju. ba
mister, sir	ဦး	u:
ma'am	ဒေါ်	do
miss	မိန်းကလေး	mein: ga. lei:
young man	လူငယ်	lu nge
young man (little boy, kid)	ကောင်ကလေး	keaagkle:
miss (little girl)	ကောင်မလေး	kaun ma. lei:

4. Cardinal numbers. Part 1

0 zero	သုည	thoun nja.
1 one	တစ်	ti'
2 two	နှစ်	hni'
3 three	သုံး	thoun:
4 four	လေး	lei:
5 five	ငါး	nga:

6 six	ခြောက်	chau'
7 seven	ခုနစ်	khun hni'
8 eight	ရှစ်	shi'
9 nine	ကိုး	kou:
10 ten	တစ်ဆယ်	ti' hse
11 eleven	တစ်ဆယ့်တစ်	ti' hse. ti'
12 twelve	တစ်ဆယ့်နှစ်	ti' hse. hni'
13 thirteen	တစ်ဆယ့်သုံး	ti' hse. thoun:
14 fourteen	တစ်ဆယ့်လေး	ti' hse. lei:
15 fifteen	တစ်ဆယ့်ငါး	ti' hse. nga:
16 sixteen	တစ်ဆယ့်ခြောက်	ti' hse. khau'
17 seventeen	တစ်ဆယ့်ခုနှစ်	ti' hse. khu ni'
18 eighteen	တစ်ဆယ့်ရှစ်	ti' hse. shi'
19 nineteen	တစ်ဆယ့်ကိုး	ti' hse. gou:
20 twenty	နှစ်ဆယ်	hni' hse
21 twenty-one	နှစ်ဆယ့်တစ်	hni' hse. ti'
22 twenty-two	နှစ်ဆယ့်နှစ်	hni' hse. hni'
23 twenty-three	နှစ်ဆယ့်သုံး	hni' hse. thuan:
30 thirty	သုံးဆယ်	thoun: ze
31 thirty-one	သုံးဆယ့်တစ်	thoun: ze. di'
32 thirty-two	သုံးဆယ့်နှစ်	thoun: ze. hni'
33 thirty-three	သုံးဆယ့်သုံး	thoun: ze. dhoun:
40 forty	လေးဆယ်	lei: hse
41 forty-one	လေးဆယ့်တစ်	lei: hse. ti'
42 forty-two	လေးဆယ့်နှစ်	lei: hse. hni'
43 forty-three	လေးဆယ့်သုံး	lei: hse. thaun:
50 fifty	ငါးဆယ်	nga: ze
51 fifty-one	ငါးဆယ့်တစ်	nga: ze di'
52 fifty-two	ငါးဆယ့်နှစ်	nga: ze hni'
53 fifty-three	ငါးဆယ့်သုံး	nga: ze dhoun:
60 sixty	ခြောက်ဆယ်	chau' hse
61 sixty-one	ခြောက်ဆယ့်တစ်	chau' hse. di'
62 sixty-two	ခြောက်ဆယ့်နှစ်	chau' hse. hni'
63 sixty-three	ခြောက်ဆယ့်သုံး	chau' hse. dhoun:
70 seventy	ခုနှစ်ဆယ်	khun hni' hse.
71 seventy-one	ခုနှစ်ဆယ့်တစ်	qunxcy•tx
72 seventy-two	ခုနှစ်ဆယ့်နှစ်	khun hni' hse. hni
73 seventy-three	ခုနှစ်ဆယ့်သုံး	khu. ni' hse. dhoun:
80 eighty	ရှစ်ဆယ်	shi' hse
81 eighty-one	ရှစ်ဆယ့်တစ်	shi' hse. ti'
82 eighty-two	ရှစ်ဆယ့်နှစ်	shi' hse. hni'
83 eighty-three	ရှစ်ဆယ့်သုံး	shi' hse. dhun:
90 ninety	ကိုးဆယ်	kou: hse

91 ninety-one	ကိုးဆယ့်တစ်	kou: hse. ti'
92 ninety-two	ကိုးဆယ့်နှစ်	kou: hse. hni'
93 ninety-three	ကိုးဆယ့်သုံး	kou: hse. dhaun:

5. Cardinal numbers. Part 2

100 one hundred	တစ်ရာ	ti' ja
200 two hundred	နှစ်ရာ	hni' ja
300 three hundred	သုံးရာ	thoun: ja
400 four hundred	လေးရာ	lei: ja
500 five hundred	ငါးရာ	nga: ja

600 six hundred	ခြောက်ရာ	chau' ja
700 seven hundred	ခုနှစ်ရာ	khun hni' ja
800 eight hundred	ရှစ်ရာ	shi' ja
900 nine hundred	ကိုးရာ	kou: ja

1000 one thousand	တစ်ထောင်	ti' htaun
2000 two thousand	နှစ်ထောင်	hni' taun
3000 three thousand	သုံးထောင်	thoun: daun
10000 ten thousand	တစ်သောင်း	ti' thaun:
one hundred thousand	တစ်သိန်း	ti' thein:
million	တစ်သန်း	ti' than:
billion	ဘီလီယံ	bi li jan

6. Ordinal numbers

first (adj)	ပထမ	pahtama.
second (adj)	ဒုတိယ	du. di. ja.
third (adj)	တတိယ	tati. ja.
fourth (adj)	စတုတ္ထ	zadou' hta.
fifth (adj)	ပဉ္စမ	pjin sama.

sixth (adj)	ဆဋ္ဌမ	hsa. htama.
seventh (adj)	သတ္တမ	tha' tama.
eighth (adj)	အဋ္ဌမ	a' htama.
ninth (adj)	နဝမ	na. wa. ma.
tenth (adj)	ဒသမ	da dha ma

7. Numbers. Fractions

fraction	အပိုင်းကိန်း	apain: gein:
one half	နှစ်ပိုင်းတစ်ပိုင်း	hni' bain: di' bain:
one third	သုံးပိုင်းတစ်ပိုင်း	thoun: bain: di' bain:
one quarter	လေးပိုင်းတစ်ပိုင်း	lei: bain: ti' pain:
one eighth	ရှစ်ပိုင်းတစ်ပိုင်း	shi' bain: di' bain:

one tenth	ဆယ်ပိုင်းတစ်ပိုင်း	hse bain: da' bain:
two thirds	သုံးပိုင်းနှစ်ပိုင်း	thoun: bain: hni' bain:
three quarters	လေးပိုင်းသုံးပိုင်း	lei: bain: dhoun: bain:

8. Numbers. Basic operations

subtraction	နုတ်ခြင်း	nou' khjin:
to subtract (vi, vt)	နုတ်သည်	nou' te
division	စားခြင်း	sa: gjin:
to divide (vt)	စားသည်	sa: de

addition	ပေါင်းခြင်း	paun: gjin:
to add up (vt)	ပေါင်းသည်	paun: de
to add (vi, vt)	ထပ်ပေါင်းသည်	hta' paun: de
multiplication	မြှောက်ခြင်း	hmjau' chin:
to multiply (vt)	မြှောက်သည်	hmjau' de

9. Numbers. Miscellaneous

digit, figure	ကိန်းဂဏန်း	kein: ga nan:
number	ကိန်း	kein:
numeral	ဂဏန်းအက္ခရာ	ganan: e' kha ja
minus sign	အနုတ်	ahnou'
plus sign	အပေါင်း	apaun:
formula	ပုံသေနည်း	poun dhei ne:

calculation	တွက်ချက်ခြင်း	twe' che' chin:
to count (vi, vt)	ရေတွက်သည်	jei dwe' te
to count up	ရေတွက်သည်	jei dwe' te
to compare (vt)	နှိုင်းယှဉ်သည်	hnain: shin de

| How much? | ဘယ်လောက်လဲ | be lau' le: |
| How many? | ဘယ်လောက်လဲ | be lau' le: |

sum, total	ပေါင်းလဒ်	paun: la'
result	ရလဒ်	jala'
remainder	အကြွင်း	akjwin:

a few (e.g., ~ years ago)	အချို့	achou.
little (I had ~ time)	အနည်းငယ်	ane: nge
few (I have ~ friends)	အနည်းငယ်	ane: nge
a little (~ water)	အနည်းငယ်	ane: nge
the rest	ကျန်သော	kjan de.
one and a half	တစ်ခုခွဲ	ti' khu. khwe:
dozen	ဒါဇင်	da zin

| in half (adv) | တစ်ဝက်စီ | ti' we' si |
| equally (evenly) | ညီတူညီမျှ | nji du nji hmja. |

half	တစ်ဝက်	ti' we'
time (three ~s)	ကြိမ်	kjein

10. The most important verbs. Part 1

to advise (vt)	အကြံပေးသည်	akjan bei: de
to agree (say yes)	သဘောတူသည်	dhabo: tu de
to answer (vi, vt)	ဖြေသည်	hpjei de
to apologize (vi)	တောင်းပန်သည်	thaun: ban de
to arrive (vi)	ရောက်သည်	jau' te
to ask (~ oneself)	မေးသည်	mei: de
to ask (~ sb to do sth)	တောင်းဆိုသည်	taun: hsou: de
to be (~ a teacher)	ဖြစ်သည်	hpji' te
to be (~ on a diet)	ဖြစ်နေသည်	hpji' nei de
to be afraid	ကြောက်သည်	kjau' te
to be hungry	ဗိုက်ဆာသည်	bai' hsa de
to be interested in …	စိတ်ဝင်စားသည်	sei' win za: de
to be needed	အလိုရှိသည်	alou' shi. de
to be surprised	အံ့ဩသည်	an. o. de
to be thirsty	ရေဆာသည်	jei za de
to begin (vt)	စတင်သည်	sa. tin de
to belong to …	ပိုင်ဆိုင်သည်	pain zain de
to boast (vi)	ကြွားသည်	kjwa: de
to break (split into pieces)	ဖျက်ဆီးသည်	hpje' hsi: de
to call (~ for help)	ခေါ်သည်	kho de
can (v aux)	တတ်နိုင်သည်	ta' nain de
to catch (vt)	ဖမ်းသည်	hpan: de
to change (vt)	ပြောင်းလဲသည်	pjaun: le: de
to choose (select)	ရွေးသည်	jwei: de
to come down (the stairs)	ဆင်းသည်	hsin: de
to compare (vt)	နှိုင်းယှဉ်သည်	hnain: shin de
to complain (vi, vt)	တိုင်ပြောသည်	tain bjo: de
to confuse (mix up)	ရောထွေးသည်	jo: dwei: de
to continue (vt)	ဆက်လုပ်သည်	hse' lou' te
to control (vt)	ထိန်းချုပ်သည်	htein: gjou' te
to cook (dinner)	ချက်ပြုတ်သည်	che' pjou' te
to cost (vt)	ကုန်ကျသည်	koun kja de
to count (add up)	ရေတွက်သည်	jei dwe' te
to count on …	အားကိုးသည်	a: kou: de
to create (vt)	ဖန်တီးသည်	hpan di: de
to cry (weep)	ငိုသည်	ngou de

11. The most important verbs. Part 2

to deceive (vi, vt)	လိမ်ပြောသည်	lain bjo: de
to decorate (tree, street)	အလှဆင်သည်	ahla. zin dhe
to defend (a country, etc.)	ကာကွယ်သည်	ka gwe de
to demand (request firmly)	တိုက်တွန်းသည်	tai' tun: de
to dig (vt)	တူးသည်	tu: de
to discuss (vt)	ဆွေးနွေးသည်	hswe: nwe: de
to do (vt)	ပြုလုပ်သည်	pju. lou' te
to doubt (have doubts)	သံသယဖြစ်သည်	than thaja. bji' te
to drop (let fall)	ဖြုတ်ချသည်	hpjou' cha. de
to enter (room, house, etc.)	ဝင်သည်	win de
to excuse (forgive)	ခွင့်လွှတ်သည်	khwin. hlu' te
to exist (vi)	တည်ရှိသည်	ti shi. de
to expect (foresee)	ကြိုမြင်သည်	kjou mjin de
to explain (vt)	ရှင်းပြသည်	shin: bja. de
to fall (vi)	ကျဆင်းသည်	kja zin: de
to find (vt)	ရှာတွေ့သည်	sha dwei. de
to finish (vt)	ပြီးသည်	pji: de
to fly (vi)	ပျံသန်းသည်	pjan dan: de
to follow ... (come after)	လိုက်သည်	lai' te
to forget (vi, vt)	မေ့သည်	mei. de
to forgive (vt)	ခွင့်လွှတ်သည်	khwin. hlu' te
to give (vt)	ပေးသည်	pei: de
to give a hint	အရိပ်အမြွက်ပေးသည်	aji' ajmwe' pei: de
to go (on foot)	သွားသည်	thwa: de
to go for a swim	ရေကူးသည်	jei ku: de
to go out (for dinner, etc.)	ထွက်သည်	htwe' te
to guess (the answer)	မှန်းဆသည်	hman za de
to have (vt)	ရှိသည်	shi. de
to have breakfast	နံနက်စာစားသည်	nan ne' za za: de
to have dinner	ညစာစားသည်	nja. za za: de
to have lunch	နေ့လယ်စာစားသည်	nei. le za za de
to hear (vt)	ကြားသည်	ka: de
to help (vt)	ကူညီသည်	ku nji de
to hide (vt)	ဖုံးကွယ်သည်	hpoun: gwe de
to hope (vi, vt)	မျှော်လင့်သည်	hmjo. lin. de
to hunt (vi, vt)	အမဲလိုက်သည်	ame: lai' de
to hurry (vi)	လောသည်	lo de

12. The most important verbs. Part 3

to inform (vt)	အကြောင်းကြားသည်	akjaun: kja: de
to insist (vi, vt)	တိုက်တွန်းပြောဆိုသည်	tou' tun: bjo: zou de
to insult (vt)	စော်ကားသည်	so ga: de
to invite (vt)	ဖိတ်သည်	hpi' de
to joke (vi)	စနောက်သည်	sanau' te
to keep (vt)	ထိန်းထားသည်	htein: da: de
to keep silent, to hush	နှုတ်ဆိတ်သည်	hnou' hsei' te
to kill (vt)	သတ်သည်	tha' te
to know (sb)	သိသည်	thi. de
to know (sth)	သိသည်	thi. de
to laugh (vi)	ရယ်သည်	je de
to liberate (city, etc.)	လွတ်မြောက်စေသည်	lu' mjau' sei de
to like (I like …)	ကြိုက်သည်	kjai' de
to look for … (search)	ရှာသည်	sha de
to love (sb)	ချစ်သည်	chi' te
to make a mistake	မှားသည်	hma: de
to manage, to run	ညွှန့်ကြားသည်	hnjun gja: de
to mean (signify)	ဆိုလိုသည်	hsou lou de
to mention (talk about)	ဖော်ပြသည်	hpjo bja. de
to miss (school, etc.)	ပျက်ကွက်သည်	pje' kwe' te
to notice (see)	သတိထားမိသည်	dhadi. da: mi. de
to object (vi, vt)	ငြင်းသည်	njin: de
to observe (see)	စောင့်ကြည့်သည်	saun. gji. de
to open (vt)	ဖွင့်သည်	hpwin. de
to order (meal, etc.)	မှာသည်	hma de
to order (mil.)	အမိန့်ပေးသည်	amin. bei: de
to own (possess)	ပိုင်ဆိုင်သည်	pain zain de
to participate (vi)	ပါဝင်သည်	pa win de
to pay (vi, vt)	ပေးချေသည်	pei: gjei de
to permit (vt)	ခွင့်ပြုသည်	khwin bju. de
to plan (vt)	စီစဉ်သည်	si zin de
to play (children)	ကစားသည်	gaza: de
to pray (vi, vt)	ရှိခိုးသည်	shi. gou: de
to prefer (vt)	ပိုကြိုက်သည်	pou gjai' te
to promise (vt)	ကတိပေးသည်	gadi pei: de
to pronounce (vt)	အသံထွက်သည်	athan dwe' te
to propose (vt)	အဆိုပြုသည်	ahsou bju. de
to punish (vt)	အပြစ်ပေးသည်	apja' pei: de

13. The most important verbs. Part 4

to read (vi, vt)	ဖတ်သည်	hpa' te
to recommend (vt)	အကြံပြုထောက်ခံသည်	akjan pju htau' khan de

to refuse (vi, vt)	ငြင်းဆန်သည်	njin: zan de
to regret (be sorry)	နောင်တရသည်	naun da. ja. de
to rent (sth from sb)	ငှားသည်	hnga: de
to repeat (say again)	ထပ်လုပ်သည်	hta' lou' te
to reserve, to book	မှာသည်	hma de
to run (vi)	ပြေးသည်	pjei: de
to save (rescue)	ကယ်ဆယ်သည်	ke ze de
to say (~ thank you)	ပြောသည်	pjo: de
to scold (vt)	ဆူသည်	hsu. de
to see (vt)	မြင်သည်	mjin de
to sell (vt)	ရောင်းသည်	jaun: de
to send (vt)	ပို့သည်	pou. de
to shoot (vi)	ပစ်သည်	pi' te
to shout (vi)	အော်သည်	o de
to show (vt)	ပြသည်	pja. de
to sign (document)	လက်မှတ်ထိုးသည်	le' hma' htou: de
to sit down (vi)	ထိုင်သည်	htain de
to smile (vi)	ပြုံးသည်	pjoun: de
to speak (vi, vt)	ပြောသည်	pjo: de
to steal (money, etc.)	ခိုးသည်	khou: de
to stop (for pause, etc.)	ရပ်သည်	ja' te
to stop (please ~ calling me)	ရပ်သည်	ja' te
to study (vt)	သင်ယူလေ့လာသည်	thin ju lei. la de
to swim (vi)	ရေကူးသည်	jei ku: de
to take (vt)	ယူသည်	ju de
to think (vi, vt)	ထင်သည်	htin de
to threaten (vt)	ခြိမ်းခြောက်သည်	chein: gjau' te
to touch (with hands)	ကိုင်သည်	kain de
to translate (vt)	ဘာသာပြန်သည်	ba dha bjan de
to trust (vt)	ယုံကြည်သည်	joun kji de
to try (attempt)	စမ်းကြည့်သည်	san: kji. de
to turn (e.g., ~ left)	ကွေ့သည်	kwei. de
to underestimate (vt)	လျှော့တွက်သည်	sho. dwe' de
to understand (vt)	နားလည်သည်	na: le de
to unite (vt)	ပေါင်းစည်းသည်	paun: ze: de
to wait (vt)	စောင့်သည်	saun. de
to want (wish, desire)	လိုချင်သည်	lou gjin de
to warn (vt)	သတိပေးသည်	dhadi. pei: de
to work (vi)	အလုပ်လုပ်သည်	alou' lou' te
to write (vt)	ရေးသည်	jei: de
to write down	ရေးထားသည်	jei: da: de

14. Colors

color	အရောင်	ajaun
shade (tint)	အသွေးအဆင်း	athwei: ahsin:
hue	အရောင်အသွေး	ajaun athwei:
rainbow	သက်တံ	the' tan
white (adj)	အဖြူရောင်	ahpju jaun
black (adj)	အနက်ရောင်	ane' jaun
gray (adj)	မိုးရောင်	khe: jaun
green (adj)	အစိမ်းရောင်	asain: jaun
yellow (adj)	အဝါရောင်	awa jaun
red (adj)	အနီရောင်	ani jaun
blue (adj)	အပြာရောင်	apja jaun
light blue (adj)	အပြာနုရောင်	apja nu. jaun
pink (adj)	ပန်းရောင်	pan: jaun
orange (adj)	လိမ္မော်ရောင်	limmo jaun
violet (adj)	ခရမ်းရောင်	khajan: jaun
brown (adj)	အညိုရောင်	anjou jaun
golden (adj)	ရွှေရောင်	shwei jaun
silvery (adj)	ငွေရောင်	ngwei jaun
beige (adj)	ဝါညိုနုရောင်	wa njou nu. jaun
cream (adj)	နို့ဆီရောင်	nou. hni' jaun
turquoise (adj)	စိမ်းပြာရောင်	sein: bja jaun
cherry red (adj)	ချယ်ရီရောင်	che ji jaun
lilac (adj)	ခရမ်းဖျော့ရောင်	khajan: bjo. jaun
crimson (adj)	ကြက်သွေးရောင်	kje' thwei: jaun
light (adj)	အရောင်ဖျော့သော	ajaun bjo. de.
dark (adj)	အရောင်ရင့်သော	ajaun jin. de.
bright, vivid (adj)	တောက်ပသော	tau' pa. de.
colored (pencils)	အရောင်ရှိသော	ajaun shi. de.
color (e.g., ~ film)	ရောင်စုံ	jau' soun
black-and-white (adj)	အဖြူအမည်း	ahpju ame:
plain (one-colored)	တစ်ရောင်တည်းရှိသော	ti' jaun te: shi. de.
multicolored (adj)	အရောင်စုံသော	ajaun zoun de.

15. Questions

Who?	ဘယ်သူလဲ	be dhu le:
What?	ဘာလဲ	ba le:
Where? (at, in)	ဘယ်မှာလဲ	be hma le:
Where (to)?	ဘယ်ကိုလဲ	be gou le:
From where?	ဘယ်ကလဲ	be ga. le:

When?	ဘယ်တော့လဲ	be do. le:
Why? (What for?)	ဘာအတွက်လဲ	ba atwe' le:
Why? (~ are you crying?)	ဘာကြောင့်လဲ	ba gjaun. le:
What for?	ဘာအတွက်လဲ	ba atwe' le:
How? (in what way)	ဘယ်လိုလဲ	be lau le:
What? (What kind of …?)	ဘယ်လိုမျိုးလဲ	be lau mjou: le:
Which?	ဘယ်ဟာလဲ	be ha le:
To whom?	ဘယ်သူ့ကိုလဲ	be dhu. gou le:
About whom?	ဘယ်သူ့အကြောင်းလဲ	be dhu. kjaun: le:
About what?	ဘာအကြောင်းလဲ	ba akjain: le:
With whom?	ဘယ်သူနဲ့လဲ	be dhu ne. le:
How many? How much?	ဘယ်လောက်လဲ	be lau' le:
Whose?	ဘယ်သူ့	be dhu.

16. Prepositions

with (accompanied by)	နဲ့အတူ	ne. atu
without	မပါဘဲ	ma. ba be:
to (indicating direction)	သို့	thou.
about (talking ~ …)	အကြောင်း	akjaun:
before (in time)	မတိုင်မီ	ma. dain mi
in front of …	ရှေ့မှာ	shei. hma
under (beneath, below)	အောက်မှာ	au' hma
above (over)	အပေါ်မှာ	apo hma
on (atop)	အပေါ်	apo
from (off, out of)	မှ	hma.
of (made from)	ဖြင့်	hpjin.
in (e.g., ~ ten minutes)	နောက်	nau'
over (across the top of)	ဖြတ်လျက်	hpja' lje'

17. Function words. Adverbs. Part 1

Where? (at, in)	ဘယ်မှာလဲ	be hma le:
here (adv)	ဒီမှာ	di hma
there (adv)	ဟိုမှာ	hou hma.
somewhere (to be)	တစ်နေရာရာမှာ	ti' nei ja ja hma
nowhere (not in any place)	ဘယ်မှာမှ	be hma hma.
by (near, beside)	နားမှာ	na: hma
by the window	ပြတင်းပေါက်နားမှာ	badin: pau' hna: hma
Where (to)?	ဘယ်ကိုလဲ	be gou le:
here (e.g., come ~!)	ဒီဘက်ကို	di be' kou

there (e.g., to go ~)	ဟိုဘက်ကို	hou be' kou
from here (adv)	ဒီဘက်မှ	di be' hma
from there (adv)	ဟိုဘက်မှ	hou be' hma.

| close (adv) | နီးသည် | ni: de |
| far (adv) | အဝေးမှာ | awei: hma |

near (e.g., ~ Paris)	နားမှာ	na: hma
nearby (adv)	ဘေးမှာ	bei: hma
not far (adv)	မနီးမဝေး	ma. ni ma. wei:

left (adj)	ဘယ်	be
on the left	ဘယ်ဘက်မှာ	be be' hma
to the left	ဘယ်ဘက်	be be'

right (adj)	ညာဘက်	nja be'
on the right	ညာဘက်မှာ	nja be' hma
to the right	ညာဘက်	nja be'

in front (adv)	ရှေ့မှာ	shei. hma
front (as adj)	ရှေ့	shei.
ahead (the kids ran ~)	ရှေ့	shei.

behind (adv)	နောက်မှာ	nau' hma
from behind	နောက်က	nau' ka.
back (towards the rear)	နောက်	nau'

| middle | အလယ် | ale |
| in the middle | အလယ်မှာ | ale hma |

at the side	ဘေးမှာ	bei: hma
everywhere (adv)	နေရာတိုင်းမှာ	nei ja dain: hma
around (in all directions)	ပတ်လည်မှာ	pa' le hma

from inside	အထဲမှ	a hte: hma.
somewhere (to go)	တစ်နေရာရာကို	ti' nei ja ja gou
straight (directly)	တိုက်ရိုက်	tai' jai'
back (e.g., come ~)	အပြန်	apjan

| from anywhere | တစ်နေရာရာမှ | ti' nei ja ja hma. |
| from somewhere | တစ်နေရာရာမှ | ti' nei ja ja hma. |

firstly (adv)	ပထမအနေဖြင့်	pahtama. anei gjin.
secondly (adv)	ဒုတိယအနေဖြင့်	du. di. ja. anei bjin.
thirdly (adv)	တတိယအနေဖြင့်	tati. ja. anei bjin.

suddenly (adv)	မတော်တဆ	ma. do da. za.
at first (in the beginning)	အစမှာ	asa. hma
for the first time	ပထမဆုံး	pahtama. zoun:
long before ...	မတိုင်ခင် အတော်	ma. dain gin ato
	လေး အလိုက	lei: alou ga.

| anew (over again) | အသစ်တဖန် | athi' da. ban |

for good (adv)	အမြဲတမ်း	amje: dan:
never (adv)	ဘယ်တော့မှ	be do hma.
again (adv)	တဖန်	tahpan
now (at present)	အခုတော့	akhu dau.
often (adv)	ခဏခဏ	khana. khana.
then (adv)	ထိုသို့ဖြစ်လျှင်	htou dhou. bji' shin
urgently (quickly)	အမြန်	aman
usually (adv)	ပုံမှန်	poun hman
by the way, ...	စကားမစပ်	zaga: ma. za'
possibly	ဖြင်နိုင်သည်	hpjin nain de
probably (adv)	ဖြစ်နိုင်သည်	hpji' nein de
maybe (adv)	ဖြစ်နိုင်သည်	hpji' nein de
besides ...	ဒါ့အပြင်	da. apjin
that's why ...	ဒါကြောင့်	da gjaun.
in spite of ...	သော်လည်း	tho lei:
thanks to ...	ကြောင့်	kjaun.
what (pron.)	ဘာ	ba
that (conj.)	ဟု	hu
something	တစ်ခုခု	ti' khu. gu.
anything (something)	တစ်ခုခု	ti' khu. gu.
nothing	ဘာမှ	ba hma.
who (pron.)	ဘယ်သူ	be dhu.
someone	တစ်ယောက်ယောက်	ti' jau' jau'
somebody	တစ်ယောက်ယောက်	ti' jau' jau'
nobody	ဘယ်သူမှ	be dhu hma.
nowhere (a voyage to ~)	ဘယ်ကိုမှ	be gou hma.
nobody's	ဘယ်သူမှမပိုင်သော	be dhu hma ma. bain de.
somebody's	တစ်ယောက်ယောက်ရဲ့	ti' jau' jau' je.
so (I'm ~ glad)	ဒီလို	di lou
also (as well)	ထို့ပြင်လည်း	htou. bjin le:
too (as well)	လည်းဘဲ	le: be:

18. Function words. Adverbs. Part 2

Why?	ဘာကြောင့်လဲ	ba gjaun. le:
for some reason	တစ်ခုခုကြောင့်	ti' khu. gu. gjaun.
because ...	အဘယ်ကြောင့်ဆိုသော်	abe gjo:n. zou dho
for some purpose	တစ်ခုခုအတွက်	ti' khu. gu. atwe'
and	နှင့်	hnin.
or	သို့မဟုတ်	thou. ma. hou'
but	ဒါပေမဲ့	da bei me.
for (e.g., ~ me)	အတွက်	atwe'
too (~ many people)	အလွန်	alun
only (exclusively)	သာ	tha

| exactly (adv) | အတိအကျ | ati. akja. |
| about (more or less) | ခန့် | khan. |

approximately (adv)	ခန့်မှန်းခြေအားဖြင့်	khan hman: gjei a: bjin.
approximate (adj)	ခန့်မှန်းခြေဖြစ်သော	khan hman: gjei bji' te.
almost (adv)	နီးပါး	ni: ba:
the rest	ကျန်သော	kjan de.

the other (second)	တခြားသော	tacha: de.
other (different)	အခြားသော	apja: de.
each (adj)	တိုင်း	tain:
any (no matter which)	မဆို	ma. zou
many (adj)	အမြောက်အများ	amjau' amja:
much (adv)	အများကြီး	amja: gji:
many, much (a lot of)	အမြောက်အများ	amjau' amja:
many people	များစွာသော	mja: zwa de.
all (everyone)	အားလုံး	a: loun:

in return for ...	အစား	asa:
in exchange (adv)	အစား	asa:
by hand (made)	လက်ဖြင့်	le' hpjin.
hardly (negative opinion)	ဖြစ်နိုင်ခြေ နည်းသည်	hpji' nain gjei ni: de

probably (adv)	ဖြစ်နိုင်သည်	hpji' nein de
on purpose (intentionally)	တမင်	tamin
by accident (adv)	အမှတ်တမဲ့	ahma' ta. me.

very (adv)	သိပ်	thei'
for example (adv)	ဥပမာအားဖြင့်	upama a: bjin.
between	ကြား	kja:
among	ကြားထဲတွင်	ka: de: dwin:
so much (such a lot)	ဒီလောက်	di lau'
especially (adv)	အထူးသဖြင့်	a htu: dha. hjin.

Basic concepts. Part 2

19. Opposites

rich (adj)	ချမ်းသာသော	chan: dha de.
poor (adj)	ဆင်းရဲသော	hsin: je: de.
ill, sick (adj)	နေမကောင်းသော	nei ma. kaun: de.
well (not sick)	ကျန်းမာသော	kjan: ma de.
big (adj)	ကြီးသော	kji: de.
small (adj)	သေးသော	thei: de.
quickly (adv)	မြန်မြန်	mjan mjan
slowly (adv)	ဖြည်းဖြည်း	hpjei: bjei:
fast (adj)	မြန်သော	mjan de.
slow (adj)	ဖြည်းသော	hpjei: de.
glad (adj)	ပျော်ရွှင်သော	pjo shwin de.
sad (adj)	ဝမ်းနည်းသော	wan: ne: de.
together (adv)	အတူတကွ	atu da. kwa.
separately (adv)	သီးခြင်းစီ	thi: gjin: zi
aloud (to read)	ကျယ်လောင်စွာ	kje laun zwa
silently (to oneself)	တိတ်ဆိတ်စွာ	tei' hsei' swa
tall (adj)	မြင့်သော	mjin. de.
low (adj)	ပုသော	pu dho:
deep (adj)	နက်သော	ne' te.
shallow (adj)	တိမ်သော	tein de
yes	ဟုတ်တယ်	hou' te
no	မဟုတ်ဘူး	ma hou' bu:
distant (in space)	ဝေးသော	wei: de.
nearby (adj)	နီးသော	ni: de.
far (adv)	အဝေးမှာ	awei: hma
nearby (adv)	အနီးမှာ	ani: hma
long (adj)	ရှည်သော	shei lja: zu: sha. zwa ode
short (adj)	တိုသော	tou de.
good (kindhearted)	သဘောကောင်းသော	thabo: kaun: de.

evil (adj)	ယုတ်မာသော	jou' ma de.
married (adj)	မိန်းမရှိသော	mein: ma. shi. de.
single (adj)	တစ်ဦးတည်းဖြစ်သော	ti' u: te: hpi' te.

| to forbid (vt) | တားမြစ်သည် | ta: mji' te |
| to permit (vt) | ခွင့်ပြုသည် | khwin bju. de |

| end | အဆုံး | ahsoun: |
| beginning | အစ | asa. |

| left (adj) | ဘယ် | be |
| right (adj) | ညာဘက် | nja be' |

| first (adj) | ပထမ | pahtama. |
| last (adj) | နောက်ဆုံးဖြစ်သော | nau' hsoun: bji' te. |

| crime | ရာဇဝတ်မှု | raza. wu' hma. |
| punishment | အပြစ်ပေးခြင်း | apja' pei: gjin: |

| to order (vt) | အမိန့်ချသည် | amin. gja. de |
| to obey (vi, vt) | နာခံသည် | na gan de |

| straight (adj) | ဖြောင့်တန်းသော | hpjaun. dan: de. |
| curved (adj) | ကောက်ကွေ့သော | kau' kwe. de. |

| paradise | ကောင်းကင်ဘုံ | kaun: gin boun |
| hell | ငရဲ | nga. je: |

| to be born | မွေးဖွားသည် | mwei: bwa: de |
| to die (vi) | ကွယ်လွန်သည် | kwe lun de |

| strong (adj) | သန်မာသော | than ma de. |
| weak (adj) | အားပျော့သော | a: bjo. de. |

| old (adj) | အိုမင်းသော | ou min de. |
| young (adj) | ငယ်ရွယ်သော | ngwe jwe de. |

| old (adj) | အိုဟောင်းသော | ou haun: de. |
| new (adj) | သစ်သော | thi' te. |

| hard (adj) | မာသော | ma de. |
| soft (adj) | နူးညံ့သော | nu: njan. de. |

| warm (tepid) | နွေးသော | nwei: de. |
| cold (adj) | အေးသော | ei: de. |

| fat (adj) | ဝသော | wa. de. |
| thin (adj) | ပိန်သော | pein de. |

narrow (adj)	ကျဉ်းသော	kjin de.
wide (adj)	ကျယ်သော	kje de.
good (adj)	ကောင်းသော	kaun: de.

29

bad (adj)	လိုးသော	hsou: de.
brave (adj)	ရဲရင့်သော	je: jin. de.
cowardly (adj)	ကြောက်တတ်သော	kjau' ta' te.

20. Weekdays

Monday	တနင်္လာ	tanin: la
Tuesday	အင်္ဂါ	in ga
Wednesday	ဗုဒ္ဓဟူး	bou' da. hu:
Thursday	ကြာသာပတေး	kja dha ba. dei:
Friday	သောကြာ	thau' kja
Saturday	စနေ	sanei
Sunday	တနင်္ဂနွေ	tanin: ganwei

today (adv)	ယနေ့	ja. nei.
tomorrow (adv)	မနက်ဖြန်	mane' bjan
the day after tomorrow	သဘက်ခါ	dhabe' kha
yesterday (adv)	မနေ့က	ma. nei. ka.
the day before yesterday	တနေ့က	ta. nei. ga.

day	နေ့	nei.
working day	ရုံးဖွင့်ရက်	joun: hpwin je'
public holiday	ပွဲတော်ရက်	pwe: do je'
day off	ရုံးပိတ်ရက်	joun: bei' je'
weekend	ရုံးပိတ်ရက်များ	joun: hpwin je' mja:

all day long	တနေ့လုံး	ta. nei. loun:
the next day (adv)	နောက်နေ့	nau' nei.
two days ago	လွန်ခဲ့သော နှစ်ရက်က	lun ge: de. hni' ja' ka.
the day before	အကျိုနေ့မှာ	akjou nei. hma
daily (adj)	နေ့စဉ်	nei. zin
every day (adv)	နေ့တိုင်း	nei dain:

week	ရက်သတ္တပတ်	je' tha' daba'
last week (adv)	ပြီးခဲ့တဲ့အပတ်က	pji: ge. de. apa' ka.
next week (adv)	လာမယ့်အပတ်မှာ	la. me. apa' hma
weekly (adj)	အပတ်စဉ်	apa' sin
every week (adv)	အပတ်စဉ်	apa' sin
twice a week	တစ်ပတ် နှစ်ကြိမ်	ti' pa' hni' kjein
every Tuesday	အင်္ဂါနေ့တိုင်း	in ga nei. dain:

21. Hours. Day and night

morning	နံနက်ခင်း	nan ne' gin:
in the morning	နံနက်ခင်းမှာ	nan ne' gin: hma
noon, midday	မွန်းတည့်	mun: de.
in the afternoon	နေ့လယ်စာစားဆိုင်းပြီးနောက်	nei. le za za: gjein bji: nau'
evening	ညနေခင်း	nja. nei gin:

in the evening	ညနေခင်းမှာ	nja. nei gin: hma
night	ည	nja
at night	ညမှာ	nja hma
midnight	သန်းခေါင်ယံ	than: gaun jan
second	စက္ကန့်	se' kan.
minute	မိနစ်	mi. ni'
hour	နာရီ	na ji
half an hour	နာရီဝက်	na ji we'
a quarter-hour	ဆယ့်ငါးမိနစ်	hse. nga: mi. ni'
fifteen minutes	၁၅ မိနစ်	ta' hse. nga: mi ni'
24 hours	နှစ်ဆယ်လေးနာရီ	hni' hse lei: na ji
sunrise	နေထွက်ချိန်	nei dwe' gjein
dawn	အာရုဏ်ဦး	a joun u:
early morning	နံနက်စောစော	nan ne' so: zo:
sunset	နေဝင်ချိန်	nei win gjein
early in the morning	နံနက်အစောပိုင်း	nan ne' aso: bain:
this morning	ယနေ့နံနက်	ja. nei. nan ne'
tomorrow morning	မနက်ဖြန်နံနက်	mane' bjan nan ne'
this afternoon	ယနေ့နေ့လယ်	ja. nei. nei. le
in the afternoon	နေ့လယ်စာစားရှိန်ပြီးနောက်	nei. le za za: gjein bji: nau'
tomorrow afternoon	မနက်ဖြန်မွန်းလွဲပိုင်း	mane' bjan mun: lwe: bain:
tonight (this evening)	ယနေ့ညနေ	ja. nei. nja. nei
tomorrow night	မနက်ဖြန်ညနေ	mane' bjan nja. nei
at 3 o'clock sharp	၃ နာရီတွင်	thoun: na ji dwin
about 4 o'clock	၄ နာရီခန့်တွင်	lei: na ji khan dwin
by 12 o'clock	၁၂ နာရီအရောက်	hse. hni' na ji ajau'
in 20 minutes	နောက် မိနစ် ၂၀ မှာ	nau' mi. ni' hni' se hma
in an hour	နောက်တစ်နာရီမှာ	nau' ti' na ji hma
on time (adv)	အချိန်ကိုက်	achein kai'
a quarter to ...	မတ်တင်း	ma' tin:
within an hour	တစ်နာရီအတွင်း	ti' na ji atwin:
every 15 minutes	၁၅ မိနစ်တိုင်း	ta' hse. nga: mi ni' htain:
round the clock	၂၄ နာရီလုံး	hna' hse. lei: na ji

22. Months. Seasons

January	ဇန်နဝါရီလ	zan na. wa ji la
February	ဖေဖော်ဝါရီလ	hpei bo wa ji la
March	မတ်လ	ma' la.
April	ဧပြီလ	ei bji la.
May	မေလ	mei la.
June	ဇွန်လ	zun la.

July	ဇူလိုင်လ	zu lain la.
August	ဩဂုတ်လ	o: gou' la.
September	စက်တင်ဘာလ	sa' htin ba la.
October	အောက်တိုဘာလ	au' tou ba la
November	နိုဝင်ဘာလ	nou win ba la.
December	ဒီဇင်ဘာလ	di zin ba la.
spring	နွေဦးရာသီ	nwei: u: ja dhi
in spring	နွေဦးရာသီမှာ	nwei: u: ja dhi hma
spring (as adj)	နွေဦးရာသီနှင့်ဆိုင်သော	nwei: u: ja dhi hnin. zain de.
summer	နွေရာသီ	nwei: ja dhi
in summer	နွေရာသီမှာ	nwei: ja dhi hma
summer (as adj)	နွေရာသီနှင့်ဆိုင်သော	nwei: ja dhi hnin. zain de.
fall	ဆောင်းဦးရာသီ	hsaun: u: ja dhi
in fall	ဆောင်းဦးရာသီမှာ	hsaun: u: ja dhi hma
fall (as adj)	ဆောင်းဦးရာသီနှင့်ဆိုင်သော	hsaun: u: ja dhi hnin. zain de.
winter	ဆောင်းရာသီ	hsaun: ja dhi
in winter	ဆောင်းရာသီမှာ	hsaun: ja dhi hma
winter (as adj)	ဆောင်းရာသီနှင့်ဆိုင်သော	hsaun: ja dhi hnin. zain de.
month	လ	la.
this month	ဒီလ	di la.
next month	နောက်လ	nau' la
last month	ယခင်လ	jakhin la.
a month ago	ပြီးခဲ့တဲ့တစ်လကျော်	pji: ge. de. di' la. gjo
in a month (a month later)	နောက်တစ်လကျော်	nau' ti' la. gjo
in 2 months (2 months later)	နောက်နှစ်လကျော်	nau' hni' la. gjo
the whole month	တစ်လလုံး	ti' la. loun:
all month long	တစ်လလုံး	ti' la. loun:
monthly (~ magazine)	လစဉ်	la. zin
monthly (adv)	လစဉ်	la. zin
every month	လတိုင်း	la. dain:
twice a month	တစ်လနှစ်ကြိမ်	ti' la. hni' kjein:
year	နှစ်	hni'
this year	ဒီနှစ်မှာ	di hna' hma
next year	နောက်နှစ်မှာ	nau' hni' hnma
last year	ယခင်နှစ်မှာ	jakhin hni' hma
a year ago	ပြီးခဲ့တဲ့တစ်နှစ်ကျော်က	pji: ge. de. di' hni' kjo ga.
in a year	နောက်တစ်နှစ်ကျော်	nau' ti' hni' gjo
in two years	နောက်နှစ်နှစ်ကျော်	nau' hni' hni' gjo
the whole year	တစ်နှစ်လုံး	ti' hni' loun:
all year long	တစ်နှစ်လုံး	ti' hni' loun:

every year	နှစ်တိုင်း	hni' tain:
annual (adj)	နှစ်စဉ်ဖြစ်သော	hni' san bji' te.
annually (adv)	နှစ်စဉ်	hni' san
4 times a year	တစ်နှစ်လေးကြိမ်	ti' hni' lei: gjein

date (e.g., today's ~)	နေ့စွဲ	nei. zwe:
date (e.g., ~ of birth)	ရက်စွဲ	je' swe:
calendar	ပြက္ခဒိန်	pje' gadein

half a year	နှစ်ဝက်	hni' we'
six months	နှစ်ဝက်	hni' we'
season (summer, etc.)	ရာသီ	ja dhi
century	ရာစု	jazu.

23. Time. Miscellaneous

time	အချိန်	achein
moment	အခိုက်အတန့်	akhai' atan.
instant (n)	ခဏ	khana.
instant (adj)	ချက်ချင်း	che' chin:
lapse (of time)	ကာလအပိုင်းအခြား	ka la apain: acha:
life	ဘဝ	ba. wa.
eternity	ထာဝရ	hta wa. ja.

epoch	ခေတ်	khi'
era	ခေတ်	khi'
cycle	စက်ဝန်း	se' wun:
period	အချိန်ပိုင်း	achein bain:
term (short-~)	သက်တမ်း	the' tan

the future	အနာဂတ်	ana ga'
future (as adj)	အနာဂတ်	ana ga'
next time	နောက်တစ်ကြိမ်	nau' ti' kjein
the past	အတိတ်	ati'
past (recent)	လွန်ခဲ့သော	lun ge. de.
last time	ပြီးခဲ့သောတစ်ခေါက်	pji: ge. dho di' gau'

later (adv)	နောက်မှ	nau' hma.
after (prep.)	ပြီးနောက်	pji: nau'
nowadays (adv)	ယခုအချိန်	jakhu. achein
now (at this moment)	အခု	akhu.
immediately (adv)	ချက်ချင်း	che' chin:
soon (adv)	မကြာခင်	ma. gja gin
in advance (beforehand)	ကြိုတင်	kjou tin

a long time ago	တော်တော်ကြာကြာက	to do gja gja
recently (adv)	သိပ်မကြာခင်က	thei' ma. gja gjin ga.
destiny	ကံတရား	kan daja:
memories (childhood ~)	အမှတ်တရ	ahma' ta ra
archives	မော်ကွန်း	mo gun:

during ...	အချိန်အတွင်း	achein atwin
long, a long time (adv)	ကြာကြာ	kja gja
not long (adv)	ခဏ.	khana.
early (in the morning)	စောစော	so: zo:
late (not early)	နောက်ကျမှ	nau' kja. hma.

forever (for good)	အမြဲတမ်း	amje: dan:
to start (begin)	စတင်သည်	sa. tin de
to postpone (vt)	ရွှေ့ဆိုင်းသည်	shwei. zain: de

at the same time	တချိန်တည်းမှာ	takhein de: hma
permanently (adv)	အမြဲတမ်း	amje: dan:
constant (noise, pain)	ဆက်တိုက်ဖြစ်သော	hse' dain bja' de.
temporary (adj)	ယာယီဖြစ်သော	ja ji bji' te.

sometimes (adv)	တခါတလေ	takha talei
rarely (adv)	ရှားရှားပါးပါး	sha: sha: ba: ba:
often (adv)	ခဏခဏ	khana. khana.

24. Lines and shapes

square	စတုရန်း	satu. jan:
square (as adj)	စတုရန်းပုံဖြစ်သော	satu. jan: boun bji' te.
circle	အဝိုင်း	awain:
round (adj)	ဝိုင်းသော	wain: de.
triangle	တြိဂံ	tri. gan
triangular (adj)	တြိဂံပုံဖြစ်သော	tri. gan bou hpi' te

oval	ဘဲဥပုံ	be: u. boun
oval (as adj)	ဘဲဥပုံဖြစ်သော	be: u. boun pja' de.
rectangle	ထောင့်မှန်စတုဂံ	htaun. hman zatu. gan
rectangular (adj)	ထောင့်မှန်ဖြစ်သော	htaun. hman hpji' te.

pyramid	ဟူးချွန်းပုံ	htu. gjwan: boun
rhombus	ရမ်ဘ	ran bu
trapezoid	ထရာပီးဇီးယမ်း	htaja bi: zi: jan:
cube	ကုဗတုံး	ku ba. toun:
prism	ပရစ်ဇမ်	pa. ji' zan

circumference	အဝန်း	awun:
sphere	ထုလုံး	htu. loun:
ball (solid sphere)	စိုးမောင်းလုံးဝန်းသော	mou maun loun: wun: de.
diameter	အချင်း	achin:
radius	အချင်းဝက်	achin: we'
perimeter (circle's ~)	ပတ်လည်အနား	pa' le ana:
center	ဗဟို	ba hou

horizontal (adj)	အလျားလိုက်	alja: lai'
vertical (adj)	ဒေါင်လိုက်	daun lou'
parallel (n)	အပြိုင်	apjain

parallel (as adj)	အပြိုင်ဖြစ်သော	apjain bja' te.
line	မျဉ်း	mjin:
stroke	ချက်	che'
straight line	မျဉ်းဖြောင့်	mjin: baun.
curve (curved line)	မျဉ်းကွေး	mjin: gwei:
thin (line, etc.)	ပါးသော	pa: de.
contour (outline)	ကွန်တိုမျဉ်း	kun tou mjin:
intersection	ဖြတ်မှတ်	hpja' hma'
right angle	ထောင့်မှန်	htaun. hman
segment	အပိုင်း	apain:
sector (circular ~)	စက်ဝိုင်းစိတ်	se' wain: zei'
side (of triangle)	အနား	ana:
angle	ထောင့်	htaun.

25. Units of measurement

weight	အလေးချိန်	alei: gjein
length	အရှည်	ashei
width	အကျယ်	akje
height	အမြင့်	amjin.
depth	အနက်	ane'
volume	ထုထည်	du. de
area	အကျယ်အဝန်း	akje awun:
gram	ဂရမ်	ga ran
milligram	မိလီဂရမ်	mi li ga. jan
kilogram	ကီလိုဂရမ်	ki lou ga jan
ton	တန်	tan
pound	ပေါင်	paun
ounce	အောင်စ	aun sa.
meter	မီတာ	mi ta
millimeter	မိလီမီတာ	mi li mi ta
centimeter	စင်တီမီတာ	sin ti mi ta
kilometer	ကီလိုမီတာ	ki lou mi ta
mile	မိုင်	main
inch	လက်မ	le' ma
foot	ပေ	pei
yard	ကိုက်	kou'
square meter	စတုရန်းမီတာ	satu. jan: mi ta
hectare	ဟက်တာ	he' ta
liter	လီတာ	li ta
degree	ဒီဂရီ	di ga ji
volt	ဗို့	boi.
ampere	အမ်ပီယာ	an bi ja
horsepower	မြင်းကောင်ရေအား	mjin: gaun jei a:

quantity	အရေအတွက်	ajei adwe'
a little bit of ...	နည်းနည်း	ne: ne:
half	တစ်ဝက်	ti' we'
dozen	ဒါဇင်	da zin
piece (item)	ခု	khu.

| size | အတိုင်းအတာ | atain: ata |
| scale (map ~) | စကေး | sakei: |

minimal (adj)	အနည်းဆုံး	ane: zoun
the smallest (adj)	အသေးဆုံး	athei: zoun:
medium (adj)	အလယ်အလတ်	ale ala'
maximal (adj)	အများဆုံး	amja: zoun:
the largest (adj)	အကြီးဆုံး	akji: zoun:

26. Containers

canning jar (glass ~)	ဖန်ဘူး	hpan bu:
can	သံဘူး	than bu:
bucket	ရေပုံး	jei boun:
barrel	စည်ပိုင်း	si bain:

wash basin (e.g., plastic ~)	ဇလုံ	za loun
tank (100L water ~)	သံစည်	than zi
hip flask	အရက်ပုလင်းပြား	aje' pu lin: pja:
jerrycan	ဒါဆီပုံး	da' hsi boun:
tank (e.g., tank car)	တိုင်ကီ	tain ki

mug	မတ်ခွက်	ma' khwe'
cup (of coffee, etc.)	ခွက်	khwe'
saucer	အောက်ခံပန်းကန်ပြား	au' khan ban: kan pja:
glass (tumbler)	ဖန်ခွက်	hpan gwe'
wine glass	ဝိုင်ခွက်	wain gwe'
stock pot (soup pot)	ပေါင်းအိုး	paun: ou:

| bottle (~ of wine) | ပုလင်း | palin: |
| neck (of the bottle, etc.) | ပုလင်းလည်ပင်း | palin: le bin: |

carafe (decanter)	ဖန်ရှိုင့်	hpan gjain.
pitcher	ကရား	kaja:
vessel (container)	အိုးခွက်	ou: khwe'
pot (crock, stoneware ~)	မြေအိုး	mjei ou:
vase	ပန်းအိုး	pan: ou:

flacon, bottle (perfume ~)	ပုလင်း	palin:
vial, small bottle	ပုလင်းကလေး	palin: galei:
tube (of toothpaste)	ဘူး	bu:

| sack (bag) | ဂုံနီအိတ် | goun ni ei' |
| bag (paper ~, plastic ~) | အိတ် | ei' |

pack (of cigarettes, etc.)	ဘူး	bu:
box (e.g., shoebox)	စက္ကူဘူး	se' ku bu:
crate	သေတ္တာ	thi' ta
basket	တောင်း	taun:

27. Materials

material	အထည်	a hte
wood (n)	သစ်သား	thi' tha:
wood-, wooden (adj)	သစ်သားနှင့်လုပ်သော	thi' tha: hnin. lou' te,
glass (n)	ဖန်	hpan
glass (as adj)	ဖန်နှင့်လုပ်သော	hpan hnin. lou' te
stone (n)	ကျောက်	kjau'
stone (as adj)	ကျောက်ဖြင့်လုပ်ထားသော	kjau' hpjin. lou' hta: de.
plastic (n)	ပလတ်စတစ်	pa. la' sa. ti'
plastic (as adj)	ပလတ်စတစ်နှင့်လုပ်သော	pa. la' sa. ti' hnin. zain de
rubber (n)	ရော်ဘာ	jo ba
rubber (as adj)	ရော်ဘာနှင့်လုပ်သော	jo ba hnin. lou' te.
cloth, fabric (n)	အထည်	a hte
fabric (as adj)	အထည်နှင့်လုပ်သော	a hte hnin. lou' te.
paper (n)	စက္ကူ	se' ku
paper (as adj)	စက္ကူနှင့်လုပ်သော	se' ku hnin. lou' te.
cardboard (n)	စက္ကူထူ	se' ku htu
cardboard (as adj)	စက္ကူထူနှင့်လုပ်သော	se' ku htu hnin. lou' te.
polyethylene	ပေါ်လီသင်း	po li thin:
cellophane	မှန်ကြည်စက္ကူ	hman gji se' ku
linoleum	ကျမ်းခင်း	kjan: khin:
	ဖိယောင်းပုဆိုး	hpa jaun: pou hsou:
plywood	အထပ်သား	a hta' tha:
porcelain (n)	ကြွေ	kjwei
porcelain (as adj)	ကြွေနှင့်လုပ်သော	kjwei hnin. lou' te
clay (n)	မြေစေး	mjei zei:
clay (as adj)	မြေထည်	mjei de
ceramic (n)	ကြွေထည်မြေထည်	kjwei de mjei de
ceramic (as adj)	ကြွေထည်မြေထည်နှင့်လုပ်သော	kjwei de mjei de hnin. lou' te.

28. Metals

metal (n)	သတ္တု	tha' tu.
metal (as adj)	သတ္တုနှင့်လုပ်သော	tha' tu. hnin. lou' te.

alloy (n)	သတ္တုစပ်	tha' tu. za'
gold (n)	ရွှေ	shwei
gold, golden (adj)	ရွှေနှင့်လုပ်သော	shwei hnin. lou' te
silver (n)	ငွေ	ngwei
silver (as adj)	ငွေနှင့်လုပ်သော	ngwei hnin. lou' de.
iron (n)	သံ	than
iron-, made of iron (adj)	သံနှင့်လုပ်သော	than hnin. lou' te.
steel (n)	သံမဏိ	than mani.
steel (as adj)	သံမဏိနှင့်လုပ်သော	than mani. hnin. lou' te.
copper (n)	ကြေးနီ	kjei: ni
copper (as adj)	ကြေးနီနှင့်လုပ်သော	kjei: ni hnin. lou. de.
aluminum (n)	အလူမီနီယံ	alu mi ni jan
aluminum (as adj)	အလူမီနီယံနှင့်လုပ်သော	alu mi ni jan hnin. lou' te.
bronze (n)	ကြေးညို	kjei: njou
bronze (as adj)	ကြေးညိုနှင့်လုပ်သော	kjei: njou hnin. lou' de.
brass	ကြေးဝါ	kjei: wa
nickel	နီကယ်	ni ke
platinum	ရွှေဖြူ	shwei bju
mercury	ပြဒါး	bada:
tin	သံဖြူ	than bju
lead	ခဲ	khe:
zinc	သွပ်	thu'

HUMAN BEING

Human being. The body

human being	လူ	lu
man (adult male)	အမျိုးသား	amjou: dha:
woman	အမျိုးသမီး	amjou: dhami:
child	ကလေး	kalei:
girl	ကောင်မလေး	kaun ma. lei:
boy	ကောင်လေး	kaun lei:
teenager	ဆယ်ကျော်သက်	hse gjo dhe'
old man	လူကြီး	lu gji:
old woman	အမျိုးသမီးကြီး	amjou: dhami: gji:

organism (body)	ဇီဝရုပ်	zi wa ju'
heart	နှလုံး	hnaloun:
blood	သွေး	thwei:
artery	သွေးလွတ်ကြော	thwei hlwa' kjo:
vein	သွေးပြန်ကြော	thwei bjan gjo:
brain	ဦးနှောက်	oun: hnau'
nerve	အာရုံကြော	a joun gjo:
nerves	အာရုံကြောများ	a joun gjo: mja:
vertebra	ကျောရိုးအဆစ်	kjo: jou: ahsi'
spine (backbone)	ကျောရိုး	kjo: jou:
stomach (organ)	အစာအိမ်	asa: ein
intestines, bowels	အူ	au
intestine (e.g., large ~)	အူ	au
liver	အသည်း	athe:
kidney	ကျောက်ကပ်	kjau' ka'
bone	အရိုး	ajou:
skeleton	အရိုးစု	ajou: zu
rib	နံရိုး	nan jou:
skull	ဦးခေါင်းခွံ	u: gaun: gwan
muscle	ကြွက်သား	kjwe' tha:
biceps	လက်ရိုးကြွက်သား	le' jou: gjwe' tha:

triceps	လက်မောင်းနောက်သား	le' maun: nau' tha:
tendon	အရွတ်	ajwa'
joint	အဆစ်	ahsi'
lungs	အဆုတ်	ahsou'
genitals	အင်္ဂါဇာတ်	in ga za'
skin	အရေပြား	ajei bja:

31. Head

head	ခေါင်း	gaun:
face	မျက်နှာ	mje' hna
nose	နှာခေါင်း	hna gaun:
mouth	ပါးစပ်	pa: zi'

eye	မျက်စိ	mje' si.
eyes	မျက်စိများ	mje' si. mja:
pupil	သူငယ်အိမ်	thu nge ein
eyebrow	မျက်ခုံး	mje' khoun:
eyelash	မျက်တောင်	mje' taun
eyelid	မျက်ခွံ	mje' khwan

tongue	လျှာ	sha
tooth	သွား	thwa:
lips	နှုတ်ခမ်း	hna' khan:
cheekbones	ပါးရိုး	pa: jou:
gum	သွားဖုံး	thwahpoun:
palate	အာခေါင်	a gaun

nostrils	နှာခေါင်းပေါက်	hna gaun: bau'
chin	မေးစေ့	mei: zei.
jaw	မေးရိုး	mei: jou:
cheek	ပါး	pa:

forehead	နဖူး	na. hpu:
temple	နားထင်	na: din
ear	နားရွက်	na: jwe'
back of the head	နောက်စေ့	nau' sei
neck	လည်ပင်း	le bin:
throat	လည်ချောင်း	le gjaun:

hair	ဆံပင်	zabin
hairstyle	ဆံပင်ပုံစံ	zabin boun zan
haircut	ဆံပင်ညှပ်သည့်ပုံစံ	zabin hnja' thi. boun zan
wig	ဆံပင်တု	zabin du.

mustache	နှုတ်ခမ်းမွေး	hnou' khan: hmwei:
beard	မုတ်ဆိတ်မွေး	mou' hsei' hmwei:
to have (a beard, etc.)	အရှည်ထားသည်	ashei hta: de
braid	ကျစ်ဆံမြီး	kji' zan mji:
sideburns	ပါးသိုင်းမွေး	pa: dhain: hmwei:

red-haired (adj)	ဆံပင်အနီရောင်ရှိသော	zabin ani jaun shi. de
gray (hair)	အရောင်ဖျော့သော	ajaun bjo. de.
bald (adj)	ထိပ်ပြောင်သော	htei' pjaun de.
bald patch	ဆံပင်ကျွတ်နေသောနေရာ	zabin kju' nei dho nei ja
ponytail	မြင်းမြီးပုံစံဆံပင်	mjin: mji: boun zan zan bin
bangs	ဆံရစ်	hsaji'

32. Human body

hand	လက်	le'
arm	လက်မောင်း	le' maun:
finger	လက်ချောင်း	le' chaun:
toe	ခြေချောင်း	chei gjaun:
thumb	လက်မ	le' ma
little finger	လက်သန်း	le' than:
nail	လက်သည်းခွံ	le' the: dou' tan zin:
fist	လက်သီး	le' thi:
palm	လက်ဝါး	le' wa:
wrist	လက်ကောက်ဝတ်	le' kau' wa'
forearm	လက်ဖျံ	le' hpjan
elbow	တံတောင်ဆစ်	daduan zi'
shoulder	ပခုံး	pakhoun:
leg	ခြေထောက်	chei htau'
foot	ခြေထောက်	chei htau'
knee	ဒူး	du:
calf (part of leg)	ခြေသလုံးကြွက်သား	chei dha. loun: gjwe' dha:
hip	တင်ပါး	tin ba:
heel	ခြေဖနောင့်	chei ba. naun.
body	ခန္ဓာကိုယ်	khan da kou
stomach	ဗိုက်	bai'
chest	ရင်ဘတ်	jin ba'
breast	နို့	nou.
flank	နံပါး	nan ba:
back	ကျော	kjo:
lower back	ခါးအောက်ပိုင်း	kha: au' pain:
waist	ခါး	kha:
navel (belly button)	ချက်	che'
buttocks	တင်ပါး	tin ba:
bottom	နောက်ပိုင်း	nau' pain:
beauty mark	မဲ့	hme.
birthmark (café au lait spot)	မွေးရာပါအမှတ်	mwei: ja ba ahma'
tattoo	တက်တူး	te' tu:
scar	အမာရွတ်	ama ju'

Clothing & Accessories

33. Outerwear. Coats

clothes	အဝတ်အစား	awu' aza:
outerwear	အပေါ်ဝတ်အင်္ကျီ	apo we' in: gji
winter clothing	ဆောင်းတွင်းဝတ်အဝတ်အစား	hsaun: dwin: wu' awu' asa:
coat (overcoat)	ကုတ်အင်္ကျီရှည်	kou' akji shi
fur coat	သားမွေးအနွေးထည်	tha: mwei: anwei: de
fur jacket	အမွေးပွအပေါ်အင်္ကျီ	ahmwei pwa po akji.
down coat	ငှက်မွေးကုတ်အင်္ကျီ	hnge' hmwei: kou' akji.
jacket (e.g., leather ~)	အပေါ်အင်္ကျီ	apo akji.
raincoat (trenchcoat, etc.)	မိုးကာအင်္ကျီ	mou: ga akji
waterproof (adj)	ရေလုံသော	jei loun de.

34. Men's & women's clothing

shirt (button shirt)	ရှပ်အင်္ကျီ	sha' in gji
pants	ဘောင်းဘီ	baun: bi
jeans	ဂျင်းဘောင်းဘီ	gjin: bain: bi
suit jacket	အပေါ်အင်္ကျီ	apo akji.
suit	အနောက်တိုင်းဝတ်စုံ	anau' tain: wu' saun
dress (frock)	ဂါဝန်	ga wun
skirt	စကတ်	saka'
blouse	ဘလောက်စ်အင်္ကျီ	ba. lau' s in: gji
knitted jacket (cardigan, etc.)	ကြယ်သီးပါသော အနွေးထည်	kje dhi: ba de. anwei: dhe
jacket (of woman's suit)	အပေါ်ဖုံးအင်္ကျီ	apo hpoun akji.
T-shirt	တီရှပ်	ti shi'
shorts (short trousers)	ဘောင်းဘီတို	baun: bi dou
tracksuit	အားကစားဝတ်စုံ	a: gaza: wu' soun
bathrobe	ရေချိုးခန်းဝတ်စုံ	jei gjou: gan: wu' soun
pajamas	ညအိပ်ဝတ်စုံ	nja a' wu' soun
sweater	ဆွယ်တာ	hswe da
pullover	ဆွယ်တာ	hswe da
vest	ဝစ်ကုတ်	wi' kou'
tailcoat	တေးလ်ကုတ်အင်္ကျီ	tei: l kou' in: gji
tuxedo	ညစာစားပွဲဝတ်စုံ	nja. za za: bwe: wu' soun

uniform	တူညီဝတ်စုံ	tu nji wa' soun
workwear	အလုပ်ဝင် ဝတ်စုံ	alou' win wu' zoun
overalls	စက်ရုံဝတ်စုံ	se' joun wu' soun
coat (e.g., doctor's smock)	ဂျူတိကုတ်	gju di gou'

35. Clothing. Underwear

underwear	အတွင်းခံ	atwin: gan
boxers, briefs	ယောက်ျားဝတ်အတွင်းခံ	jau' kja: wu' atwin: gan
panties	မိန်းကလေးဝတ်အတွင်းခံ	mein: galei: wa' atwin: gan
undershirt (A-shirt)	စွပ်ကျယ်	su' kje
socks	ခြေအိတ်များ	chei ei' mja:

nightdress	ညအိပ်ဂါဝန်ရှည်	nja a' ga wun she
bra	ဘရာစီယာ	ba ra si ja
knee highs (knee-high socks)	ခြေအိတ်ရှည်	chei ei' shi
pantyhose	အသားကပ်-ဘောင်းဘီရှည်	atha: ka' baun: bi shei
stockings (thigh highs)	စတော့ကင်	sato. kin
bathing suit	ရေကူးဝတ်စုံ	jei ku: wa' zoun

36. Headwear

hat	ဦးထုပ်	u: htou'
fedora	ဦးထုပ်ပျော	u: htou' pjo.
baseball cap	ရှာဒိုးဦးထုပ်	sha dou: u: dou'
flatcap	လူကြီးဆောင်းဦးထုပ်ပြား	lu gji: zaun: u: dou' pja:

beret	ဘယ်ရီဦးထုပ်	be ji u: htu'
hood	အကျိတွင်ပါသော ခေါင်းစွပ်	akji. twin pa dho: gaun: zu'
panama hat	ဦးထုပ်အဝိုင်း	u: htou' awain:
knit cap (knitted hat)	သိုးမွေးခေါင်းစွပ်	thou: mwei: gaun: zu'
headscarf	ခေါင်းစည်းပုဝါ	gaun: zi: bu. wa
women's hat	အမျိုးသမီးဆောင်း ဦးထုပ်	amjou: dhami: zaun: u: htou'

hard hat	ဦးထုပ်အမာ	u: htou' ama
garrison cap	တပ်မတော်သုံးဦးထုပ်	ta' mado dhoun: u: dou'
helmet	အမာစားဦးထုပ်	ama za: u: htou'
derby	ဦးထုပ်လုံး	u: htou' loun:
top hat	ဦးထုပ်မြင့်	u: htou' mjin.

37. Footwear

| footwear | ဖိနပ် | hpana' |
| shoes (men's shoes) | ရှူးဖိနပ် | shu: hpi. na' |

shoes (women's shoes)	မိန်းကလေးစီးရှူးဖိနပ်	mein: galei: zi: shu: bi. na'
boots (e.g., cowboy ~)	လည်ရှည်ဖိနပ်	le she bi. na'
slippers	အိမ်တွင်းစီးကွင်းထိုးဖိနပ်	ein dwin:
tennis shoes (e.g., Nike ~)	အားကစားဖိနပ်	a: gaza: bana'
sneakers (e.g., Converse ~)	ပတ္တူဖိနပ်	pa' tu bi. na'
sandals	ကြိုးသိုင်းဖိနပ်	kjou: dhain: bi. na'
cobbler (shoe repairer)	ဖိနပ်ချုပ်သမား	hpana' chou' tha ma:
heel	ဒေါက်	dau'
pair (of shoes)	အစုံ	asoun.
shoestring	ဖိနပ်ကြိုး	hpana' kjou:
to lace (vt)	ဖိနပ်ကြိုးချည်သည်	hpana' kjou: gjin de
shoehorn	ဖိနပ်စီးရာသွင်းသုံး	hpana' si: ja dhwin dhoun:
	သည့် ဖိနပ်ကော်	dhin. hpana' ko
shoe polish	ဖိနပ်တိုက်ဆေး	hpana' tou' hsei:

38. Textile. Fabrics

cotton (n)	ဝါချည်	wa gji
cotton (as adj)	ဝါချည်မှ	wa gji hma.
flax (n)	ချည်ကြမ်း	che kjan:
flax (as adj)	ချည်ကြမ်းမှ	che kjan: hma.
silk (n)	ပိုးချည်	pou: gje
silk (as adj)	ပိုးသားဖြင့်ပြု	pou: dha: bjin. bju
	လုပ်ထားသော	lou' hta: de.
wool (n)	သိုးမွေးချည်	thou: mwei: gji
wool (as adj)	သိုးမွေးဖြင့်ပြု	thou: mwei: bjin. bju
	လုပ်ထားသော	lou' hta: de.
velvet	ကတ္တီပါ	gadi ba
suede	မျက်နှာပြင်ကြမ်း	mje' hna bin gjain:
	သော်သားရေ	dho dha: jei
corduroy	ချည်ကတ္တီပါ	che gadi ba
nylon (n)	နိုင်လွန်	nain lun
nylon (as adj)	နိုင်လွန်မှ	nain lun hma
polyester (n)	ပေါ်လီအက်စတာ	po li e' sa. ta
polyester (as adj)	ပေါ်လီအက်စတာ	po li e' sa. ta
leather (n)	သားရေ	tha: ei
leather (as adj)	သားရေမှ	tha: jei hma.
fur (n)	သားမွေး	tha: mwei:
fur (e.g., ~ coat)	သားမွေးဖြင့်ပြု	tha: mwei: bjin. bju.
	လုပ်ထားသော	lou' hta: de.

39. Personal accessories

gloves	လက်အိတ်	lei' ei'
mittens	နှစ်ကန့်လက်အိတ်	hni' kan. le' ei'
scarf (muffler)	မာဖလာ	ma ba. la
glasses (eyeglasses)	မျက်မှန်	mje' hman
frame (eyeglass ~)	မျက်မှန်ကိုင်း	mje' hman gain:
umbrella	ထီး	hti:
walking stick	တုတ်ကောက်	tou' kau'
hairbrush	ခေါင်းဘီး	gaun: bi:
fan	ပန်ကန်	pan gan
tie (necktie)	လည်စည်း	le zi:
bow tie	ဖဲပြားပုံလည်စည်း	hpe: bja: boun le zi:
suspenders	ဘောင်းဘီသိုင်းကြိုး	baun: bi dhain: gjou:
handkerchief	လက်ကိုင်ပုဝါ	le' kain bu. wa
comb	ဘီး	bi:
barrette	ဆံညှပ်	hsan hnja'
hairpin	ကလစ်	kali'
buckle	ခါးပတ်ခေါင်း	kha: ba' khaun:
belt	ခါးပတ်	kha: ba'
shoulder strap	ပုခုံးသိုင်းကြိုး	pu. goun: dhain: gjou:
bag (handbag)	လက်ကိုင်အိတ်	le' kain ei'
purse	မိန်းကလေးပုခုံး လွယ်အိတ်	mein: galei: bou goun: lwe ei'
backpack	ကျောပိုးအိတ်	kjo: bou: ei'

40. Clothing. Miscellaneous

fashion	ဖက်ရှင်	hpe' shin
in vogue (adj)	ခေတ်မီသော	khi' mi de.
fashion designer	ဖက်ရှင်ဒီဇိုင်နာ	hpe' shin di zain na
collar	အင်္ကျီကော်လာ	akji. ko la
pocket	အိတ်ကပ်	ei' ka'
pocket (as adj)	အိတ်ဆောင်	ei' hsaun
sleeve	အင်္ကျီလက်	akji. le'
hanging loop	အင်္ကျီချိတ်ကွင်း	akji. gjei' kwin:
fly (on trousers)	ဘောင်းဘီလျှာဆက်	baun: bi ja ze'
zipper (fastener)	ဇစ်	zi'
fastener	ချိတ်စရာ	che' zaja
button	ကြယ်သီး	kje dhi:
buttonhole	ကြယ်သီးပေါက်	kje dhi: bau'
to come off (ab. button)	ပြုတ်ထွက်သည်	pjou' htwe' te

to sew (vi, vt)	စက်ချုပ်သည်	se' khjou' te
to embroider (vi, vt)	ပန်းထိုးသည်	pan: dou: de
embroidery	ပန်းထိုးခြင်း	pan: dou: gjin:
sewing needle	အပ်	a'
thread	အပ်ချည်	a' chi
seam	ချုပ်ရိုး	chou' jou:
to get dirty (vi)	ညစ်ပေသွားသည်	nji' pei dhwa: de
stain (mark, spot)	အစွန်းအထင်း	aswan: ahtin:
to crease, crumple (vi)	တွန့်ကြေစေသည်	tun. gjei zei de
to tear, to rip (vt)	ပေါက်ပြဲသွားသည်	pau' pje: dhwa: de
clothes moth	အဝတ်ပိုးဖလံ	awu' pou: hpa. lan

41. Personal care. Cosmetics

toothpaste	သွားတိုက်ဆေး	thwa: tai' hsei:
toothbrush	သွားတိုက်တံ	thwa: tai' tan
to brush one's teeth	သွားတိုက်သည်	thwa: tai' te
razor	သင်တုန်းဓား	thin toun: da:
shaving cream	မုတ်ဆိတ်ရိတ် ဆပ်ပြာ	mou' zei' jei' hsa' pja
to shave (vi)	ရိတ်သည်	jei' te
soap	ဆပ်ပြာ	hsa' pja
shampoo	ခေါင်းလျှော်ရည်	gaun: sho je
scissors	ကတ်ကြေး	ka' kjei:
nail file	လက်သည်းတိုက်တံစဉ်း	le' the:
nail clippers	လက်သည်းညှပ်	le' the: hnja'
tweezers	ဇာဂနာ	za ga. na
cosmetics	အလှကုန်ပစ္စည်း	ahla. koun pji' si:
face mask	မျက်နှာပေါင်းတင်ခြင်း	mje' hna baun: din gjin:
manicure	လက်သည်းအလှပြင်ခြင်း	le' the: ahla bjin gjin
to have a manicure	လက်သည်းအလှပြင်သည်	le' the: ahla bjin de
pedicure	ခြေသည်းအလှပြင်သည်	chei dhi: ahla. pjin de
make-up bag	မိတ်ကပ်အိတ်	mi' ka' ei'
face powder	ပေါင်ဒါ	paun da
powder compact	ပေါင်ဒါဘူး	paun da bu:
blusher	ပါးနီ	pa: ni
perfume (bottled)	ရေမွှေး	jei mwei:
toilet water (lotion)	ရေမွှေး	jei mwei:
lotion	လိုးရှင်း	lou shin:
cologne	အော်ဒီကလုန်းရေမွှေး	o di ka lun: jei mwei:
eyeshadow	မျက်ခွံဆိုးဆေး	mje' khwan zou: zei:
eyeliner	အိုင်းလိုင်နာတောင့်	ain: lain: na daun.
mascara	မျက်တောင်ခြယ်ဆေး	mje' taun gje zei:

lipstick	နှုတ်ခမ်းနီ	hna' khan: ni
nail polish, enamel	လက်သည်းဆိုးဆေး	le' the: azou: zei:
hair spray	ဆံပင်သုံး စပရေး	zabin dhoun za. ba. jei:
deodorant	ချွေးနံ့ပျောက်ဆေး	chwei: nan. bjau' hsei:

cream	ခရင်မ်	khajin m
face cream	မျက်နှာခရင်မ်	mje' hna ga. jin m
hand cream	ဟန်ခရင်မ်	han kha. rin m
anti-wrinkle cream	အသားရှုံ့ကြောက်ကာကွယ်ဆေး	atha: gjau' ka gwe zei:
day cream	နေ့လိမ်းခရင်မ်	nei. lein: ga jin'm
night cream	ညလိမ်းခရင်မ်	nja lein: khajinm
day (as adj)	နေ့လယ်ဘက်သုံးသော	nei. le be' thoun: de.
night (as adj)	ညဘက်သုံးသော	nja. be' thoun: de.

tampon	အတောင့်	ataun.
toilet paper (toilet roll)	အိမ်သာသုံးစက္ကူ	ein dha dhoun: se' ku
hair dryer	ဆံပင်အခြောက်ခံစက်	zabin achou' hsan za'

42. Jewelry

jewelry, jewels	လက်ဝတ်ရတနာ	le' wa' ja. da. na
precious (e.g., ~ stone)	အဖိုးတန်	ahpou: dan
hallmark stamp	ရွှေ့ကဲ့ငွေကဲ့မှတ်	shwei ge: ngwei ge: hma'

ring	လက်စွပ်	le' swa'
wedding ring	လက်ထပ်လက်စွပ်	le' hta' le' swa'
bracelet	လက်ကောက်	le' kau'

earrings	နားကပ်	na: ka'
necklace (~ of pearls)	လည်ဆွဲ	le zwe:
crown	သရဖူ	tharahpu:
bead necklace	လည်ဆွဲပုတီး	le zwe: bu. di:

diamond	စိန်	sein
emerald	မြ	mja.
ruby	ပတ္တမြား	pa' ta. mja:
sapphire	နီလာ	ni la
pearl	ပုလဲ	pale:
amber	ပယင်း	pajin:

43. Watches. Clocks

watch (wristwatch)	နာရီ	na ji
dial	နာရီဒိုက်ခွက်	na ji dai' hpwe'
hand (of clock, watch)	နာရီလက်တံ	na ji le' tan
metal watch band	နာရီကြိုး	na ji gjou:
watch strap	နာရီကြိုး	na ji gjou:
battery	ဓာတ်ခဲ	da' khe:

to be dead (battery)	အားကုန်သည်	a: kun de
to change a battery	ဘတ်ထရီလဲသည်	ba' hta ji le: de
to run fast	မြန်သည်	mjan de
to run slow	နောက်ကျသည်	nau' kja. de
wall clock	တိုင်ကင်နာရီ	tain ka' na ji
hourglass	သဲနာရီ	the: naji
sundial	နေနာရီ	nei na ji
alarm clock	နှီးစက်	hnou: ze'
watchmaker	နာရီပြင်ဆရာ	ma ji bjin zaja
to repair (vt)	ပြင်သည်	pjin de

Food. Nutricion

44. Food

meat	အသား	atha:
chicken	ကြက်သား	kje' tha:
Rock Cornish hen (poussin)	ကြက်ကလေး	kje' ka. lei:
duck	ဘဲသား	be: dha:
goose	ဘဲငန်းသား	be: ngan: dha:
game	တောကောင်သား	to: gaun dha:
turkey	ကြက်ဆင်သား	kje' hsin dha:
pork	ဝက်သား	we' tha:
veal	နွားကလေးသား	nwa: ga. lei: dha:
lamb	သိုးသား	thou: tha:
beef	အမဲသား	ame: dha:
rabbit	ယုန်သား	joun dha:
sausage (bologna, etc.)	ဝက်အူချောင်း	we' u gjaun:
vienna sausage (frankfurter)	အသားချောင်း	atha: gjaun:
bacon	ဝက်ဆားနယ်ခြောက်	we' has: ne gjau'
ham	ဝက်ပေါင်ခြောက်	we' paun gjau'
gammon	ဝက်ပေါင်ကြက်တိုက်	we' paun gje' tai'
pâté	အနှစ်အခဲပျော့	ahni' akhe pjo.
liver	အသည်း	athe:
hamburger (ground beef)	ကြိတ်သား	kjei' tha:
tongue	လျှာ	sha
egg	ဥ	u.
eggs	ဥများ	u. mja:
egg white	အကာ	aka
egg yolk	အနှစ်	ahni'
fish	ငါး	nga:
seafood	ပင်လယ်အစားအစာ	pin le asa: asa
crustaceans	အခွံမာရေနေသတ္တဝါ	akhun ma jei nei dha' ta. wa
caviar	ငါးဥ	nga: u.
crab	ကဏန်း	kanan:
shrimp	ပုစွန်	bazun
oyster	ကမာကောင်	kama kaun
spiny lobster	ကျောက်ပုစွန်	kjau' pu. zun

octopus	ရေဘဝဲသား	jei ba. we: dha:
squid	ပြည်ကြီးငါး	pjei gji: nga:
sturgeon	စတာဂျင်ငါး	sata gjin nga:
salmon	ဆော်လမွန်ငါး	hso: la. mun nga:
halibut	ပင်လယ်ငါးကြီးသား	pin le nga: gji: dha:
cod	ငါးကြီးဆီထုတ်သောငါး	nga: gji: zi dou' de. nga:
mackerel	မက်ကရယ်ငါး	me' ka. je nga:
tuna	တူနာငါး	tu na nga:
eel	ငါးရှဉ့်	nga: shin.
trout	ထရောက်ငါး	hta. jau' nga:
sardine	ငါးသေတ္တာငါး	nga: dhei ta' nga:
pike	ပိုက်ငါး	pai' nga
herring	ငါးသလောက်	nga: dha. lau'
bread	ပေါင်မုန့်	paun moun.
cheese	ဒိန်ခဲ	dain ge:
sugar	သကြား	dhagja:
salt	ဆား	hsa:
rice	ဆန်စပါး	hsan zaba
pasta (macaroni)	အီတာလီခေါက်ဆွဲ	ita. li khau' hswe:
noodles	ခေါက်ဆွဲ	gau' hswe:
butter	ထောပတ်	hto: ba'
vegetable oil	ဆီ	hsi
sunflower oil	နေကြာပန်းဆီ	nei gja ban: zi
margarine	ဟင်းရွက်အဆီခဲ	hin: jwe' ahsi khe:
olives	သံလွင်သီး	than lun dhi:
olive oil	သံလွင်ဆီ	than lun zi
milk	နွားနို့	nwa: nou.
condensed milk	နို့ဆီ	ni. zi
yogurt	ဒိန်ချဉ်	dain gjin
sour cream	နို့ချဉ်	nou. gjin
cream (of milk)	မလိုင်	ma. lain
mayonnaise	ခါပျစ်ပျစ်စားပြိန်ရည်	kha' pji' pji' sa: mjein jei
buttercream	ထောပတ်မလိုင်	hto: ba' ma. lein
groats (barley ~, etc.)	နံစားဆေ့	nhnan za: zei.
flour	ဂျုံမုန့်	gjoun hmoun.
canned food	စည်သွပ်ပုံးများ	si dhwa' bu: mja:
cornflakes	ပြောင်းဖူးမုန့်ဆန်း	pjaun: bu: moun. zan:
honey	ပျားရည်	pja: je
jam	ယို	jou
chewing gum	ပီကေ	pi gei

45. Drinks

water	ရေ	jei
drinking water	သောက်ရေ	thau' jei
mineral water	ဓာတ်ဆားရည်	da' hsa: ji
still (adj)	ဂက်စ်မပါသော	ga' s ma. ba de.
carbonated (adj)	ဂက်စ်ပါသော	ga' s ba de.
sparkling (adj)	ဗုပါကလင်	saba ga. lin
ice	ရေခဲ	jei ge:
with ice	ရေခဲနှင့်	jei ge: hnin.
non-alcoholic (adj)	အယ်လ်ကိုဟောမပါသော	e kou ho: ma. ba de.
soft drink	အယ်လ်ကိုဟောဟုတ်သော သောက်စရာ	e kou ho: ma. hou' te. dhau' sa. ja
refreshing drink	အအေး	aei:
lemonade	လီမွန်ဖျော်ရည်	li mun hpjo ji
liquors	အယ်လ်ကိုဟောပါဝင်သော သောက်စရာ	e kou ho: ba win de. dhau' sa. ja
wine	ဝိုင်	wain
white wine	ဝိုင်ဖြူ	wain gju
red wine	ဝိုင်နီ	wain ni
liqueur	အရက်ချိုပြင်း	aje' gjou pjin
champagne	ရှန်ပိန်	shan pein
vermouth	ရန့်သင်းရသော ဇေးဇိန်ဝိုင်	jan dhin: dho: zei: zein wain
whiskey	ဝီစကီ	wi sa. gi
vodka	ဗော့ကာ	bo ga
gin	ဂျင်	gjin
cognac	ကော့ညက်	ko. nja'
rum	ရန်	ran
coffee	ကော်ဖီ	ko hpi
black coffee	ဘလက်ကော်ဖီ	ba. le' ko: phi
coffee with milk	ကော်ဖီနှင့်ရော	ko hpi ni. jo:
cappuccino	ကပူချီနီ	ka. pu chi ni.
instant coffee	ကော်ဖီမစ်	ko hpi mi'
milk	နွားနို့	nwa: nou.
cocktail	ကော့တေး	ko. dei:
milkshake	မစ်ရှိတ်	mi' shei'
juice	အချိုရည်	achou ji
tomato juice	ခရမ်းချဉ်သီးအချိုရည်	khajan: chan dhi: achou jei
orange juice	လိမ္မော်ရည်	limmo ji
freshly squeezed juice	အသီးဖျော်ရည်	athi: hpjo je
beer	ဘီယာ	bi ja
light beer	အရောင်ဖျော့သောဘီယာ	ajaun bjau. de. bi ja

dark beer	အရောင်ရင့်သောဘီယာ	ajaun jin. de. bi ja
tea	လက်ဖက်ရည်	le' hpe' ji
black tea	လက်ဖက်နက်	le' hpe' ne'
green tea	လက်ဖက်စိမ်း	le' hpe' sein:

46. Vegetables

vegetables	ဟင်းသီးဟင်းရွက်	hin: dhi: hin: jwe'
greens	ဟင်းခတ်အမွေးရွက်	hin: ga' ahmwei: jwe'
tomato	ခရမ်းချဉ်သီး	khajan: chan dhi:
cucumber	သခွါးသီး	thakhwa: dhi:
carrot	မုန်လာဥနီ	moun la u. ni
potato	အာလူး	a lu:
onion	ကြက်သွန်နီ	kje' thwan ni
garlic	ကြက်သွန်ဖြူ	kje' thwan bju
cabbage	ဂေါ်ဖီ	go bi
cauliflower	ပန်းဂေါ်ဖီ	pan: gozi
Brussels sprouts	ဂေါ်ဖီထုပ်အသေးစား	go bi dou' athei: za:
broccoli	ပန်းဂေါ်ဖီအစိမ်း	pan: gozi asein:
beet	မုန်လာဥနီလုံး	moun la u. ni loun:
eggplant	ခရမ်းသီး	khajan: dhi:
zucchini	ဘူးသီး	bu: dhi:
pumpkin	ဖရုံသီး	hpa joun dhi:
turnip	တရုတ်မုန်လာဥ	tajou' moun la u.
parsley	တရုတ်နံနံပင်	tajou' nan nan bin
dill	စမြိတ်ပင်	samjei' pin
lettuce	ဆလပ်ရွက်	hsa. la' jwe'
celery	တရုတ်နံနံကြီး	tajou' nan nan gji:
asparagus	ကညွတ်မာပင်	ka. nju' ma bin
spinach	ဒေါက်ခွ	dau' khwa.
pea	ပဲစေ့	pe: zei.
beans	ပဲအမျိုးမျိုး	pe: amjou: mjou:
corn (maize)	ပြောင်းဖူး	pjaun: bu:
kidney bean	ပိုလ်စားပဲ	bou za: be:
bell pepper	ငရုတ်သီး	nga jou' thi:
radish	မုန်လာဥသေး	moun la u. dhei:
artichoke	အာတီချော	a ti cho.

47. Fruits. Nuts

fruit	အသီး	athi:
apple	ပန်းသီး	pan: dhi:

pear	သစ်တော်သီး	thi' to dhi:
lemon	သံပုယိုသီး	than bu. jou dhi:
orange	လိမ္မော်သီး	limmo dhi:
strawberry (garden ~)	စတော်ဘယ်ရီသီး	sato be ri dhi:

mandarin	ပျားလိမ္မော်သီး	pja: lein mo dhi:
plum	ဆီးသီး	hsi: dhi:
peach	မက်မွန်သီး	me' mwan dhi:
apricot	တရုတ်ဆီးသီး	jau' hsi: dhi:
raspberry	ရက်စဘယ်ရီ	re' sa be ji
pineapple	နာနတ်သီး	na na' dhi:

banana	ငှက်ပျောသီး	hnge' pjo: dhi:
watermelon	ဖရဲသီး	hpa. je: dhi:
grape	စပျစ်သီး	zabji' thi:
cherry	ချယ်ရီသီး	che ji dhi:
sour cherry	ချယ်ရီချဉ်သီး	che ji gjin dhi:
sweet cherry	ချယ်ရီချိုသီး	che ji gjou dhi:
melon	သခွားမွှေးသီး	thakhwa: hmwei: dhi:

grapefruit	ဂရိတ်ဖရုသီး	ga. ri' hpa. ju dhi:
avocado	ထောပတ်သီး	hto: ba' thi:
papaya	သင်္ဘောသီး	thin: bo: dhi:
mango	သရက်သီး	thaje' thi:
pomegranate	တလည်းသီး	tale: dhi:

redcurrant	အနီရောင်ဘယ်ရီသီး	ani jaun be ji dhi:
blackcurrant	ဘလက်ကားရန့်	ba. le' ka: jan.
gooseberry	ကလားဆီးဖျူ	ka. la: his: hpju
bilberry	ဘီဘယ်ရီအသီး	bi: be ji athi:
blackberry	ရှမ်းဆီးသီး	shan: zi: di:

raisin	စပျစ်သီးခြောက်	zabji' thi: gjau'
fig	သဖန်းသီး	thahpjan: dhi:
date	စွန်ပလွံသီး	sun palun dhi:

peanut	မြေပဲ	mjei be:
almond	ဗာဒံသီး	ba dan di:
walnut	သစ်ကြားသီး	thi' kja: dhi:
hazelnut	ဟောဇယ်သီး	ho: ze dhi:
coconut	အုန်းသီး	aun: dhi:
pistachios	ပွမာသီး	khwan ma dhi:

48. Bread. Candy

bakers' confectionery (pastry)	မုန့်ရှို	moun. gjou
bread	ပေါင်မုန့်	paun moun.
cookies	ဘီစကစ်	bi za. ki'
chocolate (n)	ချောကလက်	cho: ka. le'

chocolate (as adj)	ရှောကလက်အရ သာရှိသော	cho: ka. le' aja. dha shi. de.
candy (wrapped)	သကြားလုံး	dhagja: loun:
cake (e.g., cupcake)	ကိတ်	kei'
cake (e.g., birthday ~)	ကိတ်မုန့်	kei' moun.
pie (e.g., apple ~)	ပိုင်မုန့်	pain hmoun.
filling (for cake, pie)	သွပ်ထားသောအစာ	thu' hta: dho: asa
jam (whole fruit jam)	ယို	jou
marmalade	အထူးပြုလုပ်ထားသော ယို	a htu: bju. lou' hta: de. jou
wafers	ဝေဖာ	wei hpa
ice-cream	ရေခဲမုန့်	jei ge: moun.
pudding	ပူတင်း	pu tin:

49. Cooked dishes

course, dish	ဟင်းပွဲ	hin: bwe:
cuisine	အစားအသောက်	asa: athau'
recipe	ဟင်းချက်နည်း	hin: gji' ne:
portion	တစ်ယောက်စာဟင်းပွဲ	ti' jau' sa hin: bwe:
salad	အသုပ်	athou'
soup	စွပ်ပြုတ်	su' pjou'
clear soup (broth)	ဟင်းရည်	hin: ji
sandwich (bread)	အသားညှပ်ပေါင်မုန့်	atha: hnja' paun moun.
fried eggs	ကြက်ဥကြော်	kje' u. kjo
hamburger (beefburger)	ဟန်ဘာဂါ	han ba ga
beefsteak	အမဲသားတုံး	ame: dha: doun:
side dish	အရံဟင်း	ajan hin:
spaghetti	အီတာလီခေါက်ဆွဲ	ita. li khau' hswe:
mashed potatoes	အာလူးနွားနှံ့ဖျော်	a luu: nwa: nou. bjo
pizza	ပီဇာ	pi za
porridge (oatmeal, etc.)	အုတ်ချိုယာဂု	ou' gjoun ja gu.
omelet	ကြက်ဥခေါက်ကြော်	kje' u. khau' kjo
boiled (e.g., ~ beef)	ပြုတ်ထားသော	pjou' hta: de.
smoked (adj)	ကြပ်တင်ထားသော	kja' tin da: de.
fried (adj)	ကြော်ထားသော	kjo da de.
dried (adj)	ခြောက်နေသော	chau' nei de.
frozen (adj)	အေးခဲနေသော	ei: khe: nei de.
pickled (adj)	သားရည်စိမ်ထားသော	hsa:
sweet (sugary)	ချိုသော	chou de.
salty (adj)	ငန်သော	ngan de.
cold (adj)	အေးသော	ei: de.
hot (adj)	ပူသော	pu dho:

bitter (adj)	ခါးသော	kha: de.
tasty (adj)	အရသာရှိသော	aja. dha shi. de.
to cook in boiling water	ပြုတ်သည်	pjou' te
to cook (dinner)	ချက်သည်	che' de
to fry (vt)	ကြော်သည်	kjo de
to heat up (food)	အပူပေးသည်	apu bei: de
to salt (vt)	ဆားထည့်သည်	hsa: hte. de
to pepper (vt)	အစပ်ထည့်သည်	asin hte. dhe
to grate (vt)	ခြစ်သည်	chi' te
peel (n)	အခွံ	akhun
to peel (vt)	အခွံနွှာသည်	akhun hnwa de

50. Spices

salt	ဆား	hsa:
salty (adj)	ငန်သော	ngan de.
to salt (vt)	ဆားထည့်သည်	hsa: hte. de
black pepper	ငရုတ်ကောင်း	nga jou' kaun:
red pepper (milled ~)	ငရုတ်သီး	nga jou' thi:
mustard	မုန်ညင်း	moun njin:
horseradish	သင်္ဘောဒန့်သလွန်	thin: bo: dan. dha lun
condiment	ဟင်းခတ်အမှုန့် အမျိုးမျိုး	hin: ga' ahnun. amjou: mjou:
spice	ဟင်းခတ်အမွှေးအကြိုင်	hin: ga' ahmwei: akjain
sauce	ဆော့	hso.
vinegar	ရှာလကာရည်	sha la. ga je
anise	စမုန်စပါးပင်	samoun zaba: bin
basil	ပင်စိမ်း	pin zein:
cloves	လေးညှင်း	lei: hnjin:
ginger	ဂျင်း	gjin:
coriander	နံနံပင်	nan nan bin
cinnamon	သစ်ကြံပိုးခေါက်	thi' kjan bou: gau'
sesame	နှမ်း	hnan:
bay leaf	ကရဝေးရွက်	ka ja wei: jwe'
paprika	ပန်းငရုတ်မှုန့်	pan: nga. jou' hnoun.
caraway	ကရဝေး	ka. ja. wei:
saffron	ကုံကုမံ	koun kou man

51. Meals

food	အစားအစာ	asa; asa
to eat (vi, vt)	စားသည်	sa: de

breakfast	နံနက်စာ	nan ne' za
to have breakfast	နံနက်စာစားသည်	nan ne' za za: de
lunch	နေ့လယ်စာ	nei. le za
to have lunch	နေ့လယ်စာစားသည်	nei. le za za de
dinner	ညစာ	nja. za
to have dinner	ညစာစားသည်	nja. za za: de
appetite	စားချင်စိတ်	sa: gjin zei'
Enjoy your meal!	စားကောင်းပါစေ	sa: gaun: ba zei
to open (~ a bottle)	ဖွင့်သည်	hpwin. de
to spill (liquid)	ဖိတ်ကျသည်	hpi' kja de
to spill out (vi)	မှောက်သည်	hmau' de
to boil (vi)	ဆူပွက်သည်	hsu. bwe' te
to boil (vt)	ဆူပွက်သည်	hsu. bwe' te
boiled (~ water)	ဆူပွက်ထားသော	hsu. bwe' hta: de.
to chill, cool down (vt)	အအေးခံသည်	aei: gan de
to chill (vi)	အေးသွားသည်	ei: dhwa: de
taste, flavor	အရသာ	aja. dha
aftertaste	ပအာခြင်း	pa. achin:
to slim down (lose weight)	ဝိတ်ချသည်	wei' cha. de
diet	ဓာတ်စာ	da' sa
vitamin	ဗီတာမင်	bi ta min
calorie	ကယ်လိုရီ	ke lou ji
vegetarian (n)	သက်သက်လွတ်စားသူ	the' the' lu' za: dhu
vegetarian (adj)	သက်သက်လွတ်စားသော	the' the' lu' za: de.
fats (nutrient)	အဆီ	ahsi
proteins	အသားဓာတ်	atha: da'
carbohydrates	ကစီဓာတ်	ka. zi da'
slice (of lemon, ham)	အရှပ်	acha'
piece (of cake, pie)	အတုံး	atoun:
crumb (of bread, cake, etc.)	အစအန	asa an

52. Table setting

spoon	ဇွန်း	zun:
knife	ဓား	da:
fork	ခက်ရင်း	khajin:
cup (e.g., coffee ~)	ခွက်	khwe'
plate (dinner ~)	ပန်းကန်ပြား	bagan: bja:
saucer	အောက်ခံပန်းကန်ပြား	au' khan ban: kan pja:
napkin (on table)	လက်သုတ်ပုဝါ	le' thou' pu. wa
toothpick	သွားကြားထိုးတံ	thwa: kja: dou: dan

53. Restaurant

restaurant	စားသောက်ဆိုင်	sa: thau' hsain
coffee house	ကော်ဖီဆိုင်	ko hpi zain
pub, bar	ဘား	ba:
tearoom	လက်ဖက်ရည်ဆိုင်	le' hpe' ji zain
waiter	စားပွဲထိုး	sa: bwe: dou:
waitress	စားပွဲထိုးမိန်းကလေး	sa: bwe: dou: mein: ga. lei:
bartender	အရက်ဘားဝန်ထမ်း	aje' ba: wun dan:
menu	စားသောက်ဖွယ်စာရင်း	sa: thau' hpwe za jin:
wine list	ဝိုင်စာရင်း	wain za jin:
to book a table	စားပွဲကြိုတင်	sa: bwe: gjou din
	မှာယူသည်	hma ju de
course, dish	ဟင်းပွဲ	hin: bwe:
to order (meal)	မှာသည်	hma de
to make an order	မှာသည်	hma de
aperitif	နှတ်မြိန်ဆေး	hna' mjein zei:
appetizer	နှတ်မြိန်စာ	hna' mjein za
dessert	အချိုပွဲ	achou bwe:
check	ကျသင့်ငွေ	kja. thin. ngwei
to pay the check	ကုန်ကျငွေရှင်းသည်	koun gja ngwei shin: de
to give change	ပြန်အမ်းသည်	pjan an: de
tip	မုန့်ဖိုး	moun. bou:

Family, relatives and friends

54. Personal information. Forms

name (first name)	အမည်	amji
surname (last name)	မိသားစုအမည်	mi. dha: zu. amji
date of birth	မွေးနေ့	mwei: nei.
place of birth	မွေးရပ်	mwer: ja'
nationality	လူမျိုး	lu mjou:
place of residence	နေရပ်ဒေသ	nei ja' da. dha.
country	နိုင်ငံ	nain ngan
profession (occupation)	အလုပ်အကိုင်	alou' akain
gender, sex	လိင်	lin
height	အရပ်	aja'
weight	ကိုယ်အလေးချိန်	kou alei: chain

55. Family members. Relatives

mother	အမေ	amei
father	အဖေ	ahpei
son	သား	tha;
daughter	သမီး	thami:
younger daughter	သမီးအငယ်	thami: ange
younger son	သားအငယ်	tha: ange
eldest daughter	သမီးအကြီး	thami: akji:
eldest son	သားအကြီး	tha: akji:
brother	ညီအစ်ကို	nji a' kou
elder brother	အစ်ကို	akou
younger brother	ညီ	nji
sister	ညီအစ်မ	nji a' ma
elder sister	အစ်မ	ama.
younger sister	ညီမ	nji ma.
cousin (masc.)	ဝမ်းကွဲအစ်ကို	wan: kwe: i' kou
cousin (fem.)	ဝမ်းကွဲညီမ	wan: kwe: nji ma.
mom, mommy	မေမေ	mei mei
dad, daddy	ဖေဖေ	hpei hpei
parents	မိဘတွေ	mi. ba. dwei
child	ကလေး	kalei:

children	ကလေးများ	kalei: mja:
grandmother	အဘွား	ahpwa
grandfather	အဘိုး	ahpou:
grandson	မြေး	mjei:
granddaughter	မြေးမ	mjei: ma.
grandchildren	မြေးများ	mjei: mja:
uncle	ဦးလေး	u: lei:
aunt	အဒေါ်	ado
nephew	တူ	tu
niece	တူမ	tu ma.
mother-in-law (wife's mother)	ယောက္ခမ	jau' khama.
father-in-law (husband's father)	ယောက္ခထီး	jau' khadi:
son-in-law (daughter's husband)	သားမက်	tha: me'
stepmother	မိထွေး	mi. dwei:
stepfather	ပထွေး	pahtwei:
infant	နို့စို့ကလေး	nou. zou. galei:
baby (infant)	ကလေးငယ်	kalei: nge
little boy, kid	ကလေး	kalei:
wife	မိန်းမ	mein: ma.
husband	ယောက်ျား	jau' kja:
spouse (husband)	ခင်ပွန်း	khin bun:
spouse (wife)	ဇနီး	zani:
married (masc.)	မိန်းမရှိသော	mein: ma. shi. de.
married (fem.)	ယောက်ျားရှိသော	jau' kja: shi de
single (unmarried)	လူလွတ်ဖြစ်သော	lu lu' hpji te.
bachelor	လူပျို	lu bjou
divorced (masc.)	တစ်ခုလပ်ဖြစ်သော	ti' khu. la' hpji' te.
widow	မုဆိုးမ	mu. zou: ma.
widower	မုဆိုးဖို	mu. zou: bou
relative	ဆွေမျိုး	hswe mjou:
close relative	ဆွေမျိုးရင်းချာ	hswe mjou: jin: gja
distant relative	ဆွေမျိုးနီးစပ်	hswe mjou: ni: za'
relatives	မွေးချင်းများ	mwei: chin: mja:
orphan (boy or girl)	မိဘမဲ့	mi. ba me.
orphan (boy)	မိဘမဲ့ကလေး	mi. ba me. ga lei:
orphan (girl)	မိဘမဲ့ကလေးမ	mi. ba me. ga lei: ma
guardian (of a minor)	အုပ်ထိန်းသူ	ou' htin: dhu
to adopt (a boy)	သားအဖြစ်မွေးစားသည်	tha: ahpji' mwei: za: de
to adopt (a girl)	သမီးအဖြစ်မွေးစားသည်	thami: ahpji' mwei: za: de

56. Friends. Coworkers

friend (masc.)	သူငယ်ချင်း	thu nge gjin:
friend (fem.)	မိန်းကလေးသူငယ်ချင်း	mein: galei: dhu nge gjin:
friendship	ခင်မင်ရင်းနှီးမှု	khin min jin: ni: hmu.
to be friends	ခင်မင်သည်	khin min de
buddy (masc.)	အပေါင်းအသင်း	apaun: athin:
buddy (fem.)	အပေါင်းအသင်း	apaun: athin:
partner	လုပ်ဖော်ကိုင်ဖက်	lou' hpo kain be'
chief (boss)	အကြီးအကဲ	akji: ake:
superior (n)	အထက်လူကြီး	a hte' lu gji:
owner, proprietor	ပိုင်ရှင်	pain shin
subordinate (n)	လက်အောက်ခံအမှုထမ်း	le' au' khan ahmu. htan:
colleague	လုပ်ဖော်ကိုင်ဖက်	lou' hpo kain be'
acquaintance (person)	အကျွမ်းဝင်မှု	akjwan: win hmu.
fellow traveler	ခရီးဖော်	khaji: bo
classmate	တစ်တန်းတည်းသား	ti' tan: de: dha:
neighbor (masc.)	အိမ်နီးနားချင်း	ein ni: na: gjin:
neighbor (fem.)	မိန်းကလေးအိမ်နီး နားချင်း	mein: galei: ein ni: na: gjin:
neighbors	အိမ်နီးနားချင်းများ	ein ni: na: gjin: mja:

57. Man. Woman

woman	အမျိုးသမီး	amjou: dhami:
girl (young woman)	မိန်းကလေး	mein: ga. lei:
bride	သတို့သမီး	dhadou. thami:
beautiful (adj)	လှပသော	hla. ba. de.
tall (adj)	အရပ်မြင့်သော	aja' mjin. de.
slender (adj)	သွယ်လျှသော	thwe lja de.
short (adj)	အရပ်ပုသော	aja' pu. de.
blonde (n)	ဆံပင်ရွှေရောင် ဖျော့မိန်းကလေး	zabin shwei jaun bjo. min: ga lei:
brunette (n)	ဆံပင်နက်သောမိန်းကလေး	zabin ne' de.min: ga lei:
ladies' (adj)	အမျိုးသမီးနှင့် လိုင်သော	amjou: dhami: hnin. zain dho:
virgin (girl)	အပျိုစင်	apjou zin
pregnant (adj)	ကိုယ်ဝန်ဆောင်ထားသော	kou wun hsaun da: de.
man (adult male)	အမျိုးသား	amjou: dha:
blond (n)	ဆံပင်ရွှေရောင် ဖျော့ယောက်ျားလေး	zabin shwei jaun bjo. jau' gja: lei:

brunet (n)	သံပင်နက်သော ယောက်ျားလေး	zabin ne' de. jau' gja: lei:
tall (adj)	အရပ်မြင့်သော	aja' mjin. de.
short (adj)	အရပ်ပုသော	aja' pu. de.
rude (rough)	ရိုင်းစိုင်းသော	jain: zain: de.
stocky (adj)	တုတ်ခိုင်သော	tou' khain de.
robust (adj)	တောင့်တင်းသော	taun. din: de
strong (adj)	သန်မာသော	than ma de.
strength	ခွန်အား	khwan a:
stout, fat (adj)	ဝသော	wa. de.
swarthy (adj)	ညိုသော	njou de.
slender (well-built)	သွယ်လျသော	thwe lja de.
elegant (adj)	ကျော့ရှင်းသော	kjo. shin: de

58. Age

age	အသက်အရွယ်	athe' ajwe'
youth (young age)	ပျိုရွယ်ရိန်	pjou jwe gjein
young (adj)	ငယ်ရွယ်သော	ngwe jwe de.
younger (adj)	ပိုငယ်သော	pou nge de.
older (adj)	အသက်ပိုကြီးသော	athe' pou kji: de.
young man	လူငယ်	lu nge
teenager	ဆယ်ကျော်သက်	hse gjo dhe'
guy, fellow	လူငယ်	lu nge
old man	လူကြီး	lu gji:
old woman	အမျိုးသမီးကြီး	amjou: dhami: gji:
adult (adj)	အရွယ်ရောက်သော	ajwe' jau' te.
middle-aged (adj)	သက်လတ်ပိုင်း	the' la' pain:
elderly (adj)	အိုမင်းသော	ou min de.
old (adj)	အသက်ကြီးသော	athe' kji: de.
retirement	အငြိမ်းစားလစာ	anjein: za: la. za
to retire (from job)	အငြိမ်းစားယူသည်	anjein: za: ju dhe
retiree	အငြိမ်းစား	anjein: za:

59. Children

child	ကလေး	kalei:
children	ကလေးများ	kalei: mja:
twins	အမွှာ	ahmwa
cradle	ကလေးပုခက်	kalei: pou khe'
rattle	ဂျောက်ဂျက်	gjo' gja'

diaper	ခဲးတောင်းကျွက်အထည်	kha: daun: gjai' ahte
pacifier	ချိုလိမ်	chou lein
baby carriage	ကလေးလက်တွန်းလှည်း	kalei: le' twan: hle:
kindergarten	ကလေးထိန်းကျောင်း	kalei: din: kjaun:
babysitter	ကလေးထိန်း	kalei: din:

childhood	ကလေးဘဝ	kalei: ba. wa.
doll	အရုပ်မ	ajou' ma
toy	ကစားစရာအရုပ်	gaza: zaja ajou'
construction set (toy)	ပြန်ဆက်ရသော ကလေး ကစားစရာ	pjan za' ja de. galei: gaza: zaja

well-bred (adj)	လိမ္မာသော	limmo: de
ill-bred (adj)	ဆိုးသွမ်းသော	hsou: dhwan: de.
spoiled (adj)	အလိုလိုက်ခံရသော	alou lou' khan ja de.

to be naughty	ဆိုးသည်	hsou:de
mischievous (adj)	ကျီစယ်တတ်သော	kji ze da' de.
mischievousness	ကျီစယ်သည်	kji ze de
mischievous child	အဆော့မက်သောကလေး	ahsau me' dho: ga. lei:

| obedient (adj) | နာခံတတ်သော | na gan da' te. |
| disobedient (adj) | မနာခံသော | ma. na gan de. |

docile (adj)	လိမ္မာသော	limmo: de
clever (smart)	တော်သော	to de.
child prodigy	ပါရမီရှင်ကလေး	pa rami shin galei:

60. Married couples. Family life

to kiss (vt)	နမ်းသည်	nan: de
to kiss (vi)	အနမ်းပေးသည်	anan: pei: de
family (n)	မိသားစု	mi. dha: zu.
family (as adj)	မျိုးရိုး	mjou: jou:
couple	စုံတွဲ	soun dwe:
marriage (state)	အိမ်ထောင်သည်	ein daun de
hearth (home)	အိမ်	ein
dynasty	မင်းဆက်	min: ze'

| date | ချိန်းတွေ့ခြင်း | chein: dwei chin: |
| kiss | အနမ်း | anan: |

love (for sb)	အချစ်	akja'
to love (sb)	ချစ်သည်	chi' te
beloved	ချစ်လှစွာသော	chi' hla. zwa de.

tenderness	ကြင်နာမှု	kjin na hmu.
tender (affectionate)	ကြင်နာသော	kjin na hmu. de.
faithfulness	သစ္စာ	thi' sa
faithful (adj)	သစ္စာရှိသော	thi' sa shi. de.

| care (attention) | ဂရုစိုက်ခြင်း | ga ju. sai' chin: |
| caring (~ father) | ဂရုစိုက်သော | ga ju. sai' te. |

newlyweds	လက်ထပ်ကာစဖြစ်သော	le' hta' ka za. bji' de.
honeymoon	ပျားရည်စမ်းကာလ	pja: je zan: ga la.
to get married (ab. woman)	ယောက်ျားယူသည်	jau' kja: ju de

| to get married (ab. man) | မိန်းမယူသည် | mein: ma. ju de |

wedding	မင်္ဂလာဆောင်ပွဲ	min ga. la zaun bwe:
golden wedding	ရွှေရတု	shwei jadu.
anniversary	နှစ်ပတ်လည်	hni' ba' le

| lover (masc.) | လင်ငယ် | lin nge |
| mistress (lover) | မယားငယ် | ma. ja: nge |

| adultery | ဖောက်ပြန်ခြင်း | hpau' pjan gjin |
| to cheat on ... (commit adultery) | ဖောက်ပြန်သည် | hpau' pjan de |

jealous (adj)	သဝန်တိုသော	thawun dou de.
to be jealous	သဝန်တိုသည်	thawun dou de
divorce	ကွာရှင်းခြင်း	kwa shin gjin:
to divorce (vi)	ကွာရှင်းသည်	kwa shin: de

to quarrel (vi)	ငြင်းခုံသည်	njin: goun de
to be reconciled (after an argument)	ပြန်လည်သင့်မြတ်သည်	pjan le dhin. mja' te
together (adv)	အတူတကွ	atu da. kwa.
sex	လိင်ကိစ္စ	lein gei' sa.

happiness	ပျော်ရွှင်မှု	pjo shwin hmu
happy (adj)	ပျော်ရွှင်သော	pjo shwin de.
misfortune (accident)	ကံဆိုးခြင်း	kan hsou: chin:
unhappy (adj)	ကံဆိုးသော	kan hsoun de.

Character. Feelings. Emotions

61. Feelings. Emotions

feeling (emotion)	ခံစားချက်	khan za: che'
feelings	ခံစားချက်များ	khan za: che' mja:
to feel (vt)	ခံစားရသည်	khan za ja, de
hunger	ဆာခြင်း	hsa gjin:
to be hungry	ဗိုက်ဆာသည်	bai' hsa de
thirst	ရေဆာခြင်း	jei za gjin:
to be thirsty	ရေဆာသည်	jei za de
sleepiness	အိပ်ချင်ခြင်း	ei' chin gjin:
to feel sleepy	အိပ်ချင်သည်	ei' chin de
tiredness	ပင်ပန်းခြင်း	pin ban: chin:
tired (adj)	ပင်ပန်းသော	pin ban: de.
to get tired	ပင်ပန်းသည်	pin ban: de
mood (humor)	စိတ်ခံစားမှု	sei' khan za: hmu.
boredom	ပြီးငွေ့ခြင်း	ngji: ngwei. chin:
to be bored	ပျင်းသည်	pjin: de
seclusion	မမြင်ကွယ်ရာ	ma. mjin gwe ja
to seclude oneself	မျက်ကွယ်ပြုသည်	mje' kwe' pju. de
to worry (make anxious)	စိတ်ပူအောင်လုပ်သည်	sei' pu aun lou' te
to be worried	စိတ်ပူသည်	sei' pu de
worrying (n)	စိုးရမ်မှု	sou: jein hmu.
anxiety	စိုးရိမ်ပူပန်မှု	sou: jein bu ban hmu.
preoccupied (adj)	ကိုယ့်တာစိရပ်ရပ်တွင် နှစ်မြှုပ်နေသော	kei. sa ti' ja' ja' twin ni' mju' nei de.
to be nervous	စိတ်လှုပ်ရှားသည်	sei' hlou' sha: de
to panic (vi)	တုန်လှုပ်ချောက်ချားသည်	toun hlou' chau' cha: de
hope	မျှော်လင့်ချက်	hmjo. lin. gje'
to hope (vi, vt)	မျှော်လင့်သည်	hmjo. lin. de
certainty	ကျိန်းသေ	kjein: dhei
certain, sure (adj)	ကျိန်းသေသော	kjein: dhei de.
uncertainty	မရေရာခြင်း	ma. jei ja gjin:
uncertain (adj)	မရေရာသော	ma. jei ja de.
drunk (adj)	အရက်မူးသော	aje' mu: de.
sober (adj)	အရက်မမူးသော	aje' ma mu: de.
weak (adj)	အားပျော့သော	a: bjo. de.
happy (adj)	ပျော်ရွှင်သော	pjo shwin de.

to scare (vt)	လန့်သည်	lan. de
fury (madness)	ရူးသွပ်ခြင်း	ju: dhu' chin
rage (fury)	ဒေါသ	do: dha.

depression	စိတ်ဓာတ်ကျခြင်း	sei' da' cha. gjin:
discomfort (unease)	စိတ်ကသိကအောက်ဖြစ်ခြင်း	sei' ka thi ga au' hpji' chin:
comfort	စိတ်ချမ်းသာခြင်း	sei' chan: dha gjin:
to regret (be sorry)	နောင်တရသည်	naun da. ja. de
regret	နောင်တရခြင်း	naun da. ja. gjin:
bad luck	ကံဆိုးခြင်း	kan hsou: chin:
sadness	ဝမ်းနည်းခြင်း	wan: ne: gjin:

shame (remorse)	အရှက်	ashe'
gladness	ဝမ်းသာမှု	wan: dha hmu.
enthusiasm, zeal	စိတ်အားထက်သန်မှု	sei' a: de' than hmu
enthusiast	စိတ်အားထက်သန်သူ	sei' a: de' than hmu
to show enthusiasm	စိတ်အွားထက်သန်မှု ပြသည်	sei' a: de' than hmu. bja. de

62. Character. Personality

character	စရိုက်	zajai'
character flaw	အားနည်းချက်	a: ne: gje'
mind	ဦးနောက်	oun: hnau'
reason	ဆင်ခြင်တုံတရား	hsin gjin doun da. ja:

conscience	အသိတရား	athi. taja:
habit (custom)	အကျင့်	akjin.
ability (talent)	စွမ်းရည်	swan: ji
can (e.g., ~ swim)	လုပ်နိုင်သည်	lou' nain de

patient (adj)	သည်းခံတတ်သော	thi: khan da' te
impatient (adj)	သည်းမခံတတ်သော	thi: ma. gan da' te
curious (inquisitive)	စပ်စုသော	sa' su. de.
curiosity	စပ်စုခြင်း	sa' su. gjin:

modesty	ကုန်းရှေ့	ein darei
modest (adj)	ကုန်းရှေ့ရှိသော	ein darei shi. de
immodest (adj)	ကုန်းရှေ့မရှိသော	ein darei ma. shi. de

laziness	ပျင်းရိခြင်း	pjin: ji. gjin:
lazy (adj)	ပျင်းရိသော	pjin: ji. de.
lazy person (masc.)	ငပျင်း	nga. bjin:

cunning (n)	ကလိမ်ကျစ်လုပ်ခြင်း	kalein kji' lou' chin
cunning (as adj)	ကလိမ်ကကျစ်ကျသော	kalein ka. kji' kja de.
distrust	သံသယဝင်ခြင်း	than thaja.
distrustful (adj)	သံသယဝင်သော	than thaja. win de.
generosity	ရက်ရောမှု	je' jo: hmu.
generous (adj)	ရက်ရောသော	je' jo: de.

talented (adj)	ပါရမီရှိသော	pa rami shi. de
talent	ပါရမီ	pa rami

courageous (adj)	သတ္တိရှိသော	tha' ti. shi. de.
courage	သတ္တိ	tha' ti.
honest (adj)	ရိုးသားသော	jou: dha: de.
honesty	ရိုးသားမှု	jou: dha: hmu.

careful (cautious)	ဂရုစိုက်သော	ga ju. sai' te.
brave (courageous)	ရဲရင့်သော	je: jin. de.
serious (adj)	လေးနက်သော	lei: ne' de.
strict (severe, stern)	တင်းကျပ်သော	tin: gja' te

decisive (adj)	တိကျပြတ်သားသော	ti. gja. bja' tha: de.
indecisive (adj)	မတိကျမ ပြတ်သားသော	ma. di. gja. ma. bja' tha: de.

shy, timid (adj)	ရှက်တတ်သော	she' ta' te.
shyness, timidity	ရှက်ရွံ့မှု	she' jwan. hmu.

confidence (trust)	မိမိကိုယ်မိမိယုံကြည်မှု	mi. mi. kou mi. mi. gji hmu.
to believe (trust)	ယုံကြည်သည်	joun kji de
trusting (credulous)	အယုံလွယ်သော	ajoun lwe de.

sincerely (adv)	ဟန်မဆောင်ဘဲ	han ma. zaun be:
sincere (adj)	ဟန်မဆောင်တတ်သော	han ma. zaun da' te
sincerity	ရိုးသားမှု	jou: dha: hmu.
open (person)	ပွင့်လင်းသော	pwin: lin: de.

calm (adj)	တိတ်ဆိတ်သော	tei' hsei' te
frank (sincere)	ပွင့်လင်းသော	pwin: lin: de.
naïve (adj)	အယုံလွယ်သော	ajoun lwe de.
absent-minded (adj)	စဉ်းစားဉာဏ်မရှိသော	sin: za: njan ma. shi. de.
funny (odd)	ရယ်စရာကောင်းသော	je zaja gaun: de.

greed, stinginess	လောဘကြီးခြင်း	lau ba. gji: gjin:
greedy, stingy (adj)	လောဘကြီးသော	lau ba. gji: de.
stingy (adj)	တွန့်တိုသော	tun. dou de.
evil (adj)	ယုတ်မာသော	jou' ma de.
stubborn (adj)	ခေါင်းမာသော	gaun: ma de.
unpleasant (adj)	မဖွယ်မရာဖြစ်သော	ma. bwe ma. ja bji' te.

selfish person (masc.)	တစ်ကိုယ်ကောင်းဆန်သူ	ti' kai gaun: zan dhu
selfish (adj)	တစ်ကိုယ်ကောင်းဆန်သော	ti' kai gaun: zan de.
coward	ငကြောက်	nga. gjau'
cowardly (adj)	ကြောက်တတ်သော	kjau' ta' te.

63. Sleep. Dreams

to sleep (vi)	အိပ်သည်	ei' ja de
sleep, sleeping	အိပ်ခြင်း	ei' chin:

dream	အိပ်မက်	ei' me'
to dream (in sleep)	အိပ်မက်မက်သည်	ei' me' me' te
sleepy (adj)	အိပ်ချင်သော	ei' chin de.
bed	ခုတင်	khu. din
mattress	မွေ့ယာ	mwei. ja
blanket (comforter)	စောင်	saun
pillow	ခေါင်းအုံး	gaun: oun:
sheet	အိပ်ရာခင်း	ei' ja khin:
insomnia	အိပ်မပျော်နိုင်ခြင်း	ei' ma. bjo nain gjin:
sleepless (adj)	အိပ်မပျော်သော	ei' ma. bjo de.
sleeping pill	အိပ်ဆေး	ei' hsei:
to take a sleeping pill	အိပ်ဆေးသောက်သည်	ei' hsei: thau' te
to feel sleepy	အိပ်ချင်သည်	ei' chin de
to yawn (vi)	သမ်းသည်	than: de
to go to bed	အိပ်ရာဝင်သည်	ei' ja win de
to make up the bed	အိပ်ရာခင်းသည်	ei' ja khin: de
to fall asleep	အိပ်ပျော်သွားသည်	ei' pjo dhwa: de
nightmare	အိပ်မက်ဆိုး	ei' me' hsou:
snore, snoring	ဟောက်သံ	hau' than
to snore (vi)	ဟောက်သည်	hau' te
alarm clock	နှိုးစက်	hnou: ze'
to wake (vt)	နှိုးသည်	hnou: de
to wake up	နိုးသည်	nou: de
to get up (vi)	အိပ်ရာထသည်	ei' ja hta. de
to wash up (wash face)	မျက်နှာသစ်သည်	mje' hna dhi' te

64. Humour. Laughter. Gladness

humor (wit, fun)	ဟာသ	ha dha.
sense of humor	ဟာသအမြင်	ha dha. amjin
to enjoy oneself	ပျော်ရွှင်သည်	pjo shwin de
cheerful (merry)	ပျော်ရွှင်သော	pjo shwin de.
merriment (gaiety)	ပျော်ရွှင်မှု	pjo shwin hmu
smile	အပြုံး	apjoun:
to smile (vi)	ပြုံးသည်	pjoun: de
to start laughing	ရယ်လိုက်သည်	je lai' te
to laugh (vi)	ရယ်သည်	je de
laugh, laughter	ရယ်သံ	je dhan
anecdote	ဟာသဇာတ်လမ်း	ha dha. za' lan
funny (anecdote, etc.)	ရယ်စရာကောင်းသော	je zaja gaun: de.
funny (odd)	ရယ်စရာကောင်းသောသူ	je zaja gaun: de. dhu
to joke (vi)	စနောက်သည်	sanau' te
joke (verbal)	ရယ်စရာ	je zaja

joy (emotion)	ဝမ်းသာမှု	wan: dha hmu.
to rejoice (vi)	ဝမ်းသာသည်	wan: dha de
joyful (adj)	ဝမ်းသာသော	wan dha de.

65. Discussion, conversation. Part 1

| communication | ဆက်သံပြောဆိုခြင်း | hse' hsan bjou: zou gjin |
| to communicate | ဆက်သံပြောဆိုသည် | hse' hsan bjou: zou de |

conversation	စကားဝမြည်	zaga: zamji
dialog	အပြန်အလှန်ပြောခြင်း	apjan a hlan bau gjin:
discussion (discourse)	ဆွေးနွေးခြင်း	hswe: nwe: gjin:
dispute (debate)	အငြင်းပွားမှု	anjin: bwa: hmu.
to dispute, debate	ငြင်းခုံသည်	njin: goun de

interlocutor	ပါဝင်ဆွေးနွေးသူ	pa win zwei: nwei: dhu
topic (theme)	ခေါင်းစဉ်	gaun: zin
point of view	ရှုထောင့်	shu. daun.
opinion (point of view)	အမြင်	amjin
speech (talk)	စကား	zaga:

discussion (of report, etc.)	ဆွေးနွေးခြင်း	hswe: nwe: gjin:
to discuss (vt)	ဆွေးနွေးသည်	hswe: nwe: de
talk (conversation)	စကားပြောပုံ	zaga: bjo: boun
to talk (to chat)	စကားပြောသည်	zaga: bjo: de
meeting (encounter)	တွေ့ဆုံမှု	twei: hsoun hmu
to meet (vi, vt)	တွေ့ဆုံသည်	twei: hsoun de

proverb	စကားပုံ	zaga: boun
saying	စကားပုံ	zaga: boun
riddle (poser)	စကားထာ	zaga: da
to pose a riddle	စကားထာဖွက်သည်	zaga: da bwe' te
password	စကားဝှက်	zaga: hwe'
secret	လျှို့ဝှက်ချက်	shou. hwe' che'

oath (vow)	ကျမ်းသစ္စာ	kjan: thi' sa
to swear (an oath)	ကျမ်းသစ္စာဆိုသည်	kjan: thi' sa hsou de
promise	ကတိ	ka ti
to promise (vt)	ကတိပေးသည်	gadi pei: de

advice (counsel)	အကြံဉာဏ်	akjan njan
to advise (vt)	အကြံပေးသည်	akjan bei: de
to follow one's advice	အကြံကိုလက်ခံသည်	akjan kou le' khan de
to listen to ... (obey)	နားထောင်သည်	na: daun de

news	သတင်း	dhadin:
sensation (news)	သတင်းထူး	dhadin: du:
information (report)	သတင်းအချက်အလက်	dhadin: akje' ale'
conclusion (decision)	သုံးသပ်ချက်	thoun: dha' che'
voice	အသံ	athan

compliment	ချီးမွမ်းစကား	chi: mun: zaga:
kind (nice)	ကြင်နာသော	kjin na hmu. de.
word	စကားလုံး	zaga: loun:
phrase	စကားစု	zaga: zu.
answer	အဖြေ	ahpei
truth	အမှန်တရား	ahman da ja:
lie	မုသား	mu. dha:
thought	အတွေး	atwei:
idea (inspiration)	အကြံ	akjan
fantasy	စိတ်ကူးယဉ်အိပ်မက်	sei' ku: jin ei' me'

66. Discussion, conversation. Part 2

respected (adj)	လေးစားရသော	lei: za: ja. de.
to respect (vt)	လေးစားသည်	lei: za: de
respect	လေးစားမှု	lei: za: hmu.
Dear … (letter)	လေးစားရပါသော	lei: za: ja. ba. de.
to introduce (sb to sb)	မိတ်ဆက်ပေးသည်	mi' hse' pei: de
to make acquaintance	မိတ်ဆက်သည်	mi' hse' te
intention	ရည်ရွယ်ချက်	ji jwe gje'
to intend (have in mind)	ရည်ရွယ်သည်	ji jwe de
wish	ဆန္ဒ	hsan da.
to wish (~ good luck)	ဆန္ဒပြုသည်	hsan da. bju de
surprise (astonishment)	အံ့သြခြင်း	an. o: chin:
to surprise (amaze)	အံ့သြစေသည်	an. o: sei: de
to be surprised	အံ့သြသည်	an. o. de
to give (vt)	ပေးသည်	pei: de
to take (get hold of)	ယူသည်	ju de
to give back	ပြန်ပေးသည်	pjan bei: de
to return (give back)	ပြန်ပေးသည်	pjan bei: de
to apologize (vi)	တောင်းပန်သည်	thaun: ban de
apology	တောင်းပန်ခြင်း	thaun: ban gjin:
to forgive (vt)	ခွင့်လွှတ်သည်	khwin. hlu' te
to talk (speak)	အပြန်အလှန်ပြောသည်	apjan a hlan bau de
to listen (vi)	နားထောင်သည်	na: daun de
to hear out	နားထောင်သည်	na: daun de
to understand (vt)	နားလည်သည်	na: le de
to show (to display)	ပြသည်	pja. de
to look at …	ကြည့်သည်	kji. de
to call (yell for sb)	ခေါ်သည်	kho de

to distract (disturb)	နှောင့်ယှက်သည်	hnaun. hje' te
to disturb (vt)	နှောင့်ယှက်သည်	hnaun. hje' te
to pass (to hand sth)	တဆင့်ပေးသည်	tahsin. bei: de
demand (request)	တောင်းဆိုချက်	taun: hsou che'
to request (ask)	တောင်းဆိုသည်	taun: hsou: de
demand (firm request)	တောင်းဆိုခြင်း	taun: hsou: chin:
to demand (request firmly)	တိုက်တွန်းသည်	tai' tun: de
to tease (call names)	ကျီစယ်သည်	kji ze de
to mock (make fun of)	သရော်သည်	thajo: de
mockery, derision	သရော်ခြင်း	thajo: gjin:
nickname	ချစ်စနိုးပေး	chi' sa. nou: bei:
	ထားသောနာမည်	da: dho: na me
insinuation	စောင်းပြောမှု	saun: bjo: hmu.
to insinuate (imply)	စောင်းပြောသည်	saun: bjo: de
to mean (vt)	ဆိုလိုသည်	hsou lou de
description	ဖော်ပြချက်	hpjo bja. gje'
to describe (vt)	ဖော်ပြသည်	hpjo bja. de
praise (compliments)	ချီးမွမ်းခြင်း	chi: mun: gjin:
to praise (vt)	ချီးမွမ်းသည်	chi: mun: de
disappointment	စိတ်ပျက်ခြင်း	sei' pje' chin
to disappoint (vt)	စိတ်ပျက်စေသည်	sei' pje' sei de
to be disappointed	စိတ်ပျက်သည်	sei' pje' te
supposition	ယူဆခြင်း	ju za. chin:
to suppose (assume)	ယူဆသည်	ju za. de
warning (caution)	သတိပေးခြင်း	dhadi. pei: gjin:
to warn (vt)	သတိပေးသည်	dhadi. pei: de

67. Discussion, conversation. Part 3

to talk into (convince)	စည်းရုံးသည်	si: joun: de
to calm down (vt)	ဖျောင်းဖျသည်	hpjaun: bja de
silence (~ is golden)	နှုတ်ဆိတ်ခြင်း	hnou' hsei' chin:
to be silent (not speaking)	နှုတ်ဆိတ်သည်	hnou' hsei' te
to whisper (vi, vt)	တီးတိုးပြောသည်	ti: dou: bjo de
whisper	တီးတိုးပြောသံ	ti: dou: bjo dhan
frankly, sincerely (adv)	ရှင်းရှင်းပြောရရင်	shin: shin: bjo: ja. jin
in my opinion …	မိမိအမြင်အားဖြင့်	mi. mi. amjin a: bjin.
detail (of the story)	အသေးစိတ်မှု	athei: zi' hmu.
detailed (adj)	အသေးစိတ်သော	athei: zi' te.
in detail (adv)	အသေးစိတ်	athei: zi'
hint, clue	အရိပ်အမြွက်	aji' ajmwe'

to give a hint	အရိပ်အမြွက်ပေးသည်	aji' ajmwe: pei: de
look (glance)	အသွင်	athwin
to have a look	ကြည့်သည်	kji. de
fixed (look)	မလှုပ်မရှားသော	ma. hlou' sha: de
to blink (vi)	မျက်တောင်ခတ်သည်	mje' taun ga' te
to wink (vi)	မျက်စိတစ်ဖက်မှိတ်သည်	mje' zi. di' hpe' hmei' te
to nod (in assent)	ခေါင်းညိတ်သည်	gaun: njei' te
sigh	သက်ပြင်းချခြင်း	the' pjin: gja. gjin:
to sigh (vi)	သက်ပြင်းချသည်	the' pjin: gja. de
to shudder (vi)	သိမ့်သိမ့်တုန်သည်	thein. dhein. doun de
gesture	လက်ဟန်ခြေဟန်	le' han hpjei han
to touch (one's arm, etc.)	ထိသည်	hti. de
to seize (e.g., ~ by the arm)	ဖမ်းကိုင်သည်	hpan: gain de
to tap (on the shoulder)	ပုတ်သည်	pou' te
Look out!	ဂရုစိုက်ပါ	ga ju. sai' pa
Really?	တကယ်လား	dage la:
Are you sure?	သေချာလား	thei gja la:
Good luck!	အောင်မြင်ပါစေ	aun mjin ba zei
I see!	ရှင်းပါတယ်	shin: ba de
What a pity!	စိတ်မကောင်းပါဘူး	sei' ma. kaun: ba bu:

68. Agreement. Refusal

consent	သဘောတူညီချက်	dhabo: tu nji gje'
to consent (vi)	သဘောတူသည်	dhabo: tu de
approval	လက်ခံခြင်း	le' khan gjin:
to approve (vt)	လက်ခံသည်	le' khan de
refusal	ငြင်းဆန်ခြင်း	njin: zan gjin:
to refuse (vi, vt)	ငြင်းဆန်သည်	njin: zan de
Great!	အရမ်းကောင်း	ajan: gaun:
All right!	ကောင်းတယ်	kaun: de
Okay! (I agree)	ကောင်းပြီ	kaun: bji
forbidden (adj)	တားမြစ်ထားသော	ta: mji' hta: te.
it's forbidden	မလုပ်ရ	ma. lou' ja.
it's impossible	မဖြစ်နိုင်	ma. bji' nain
incorrect (adj)	မှားသော	hma: de.
to reject (~ a demand)	ပယ်ချသည်	pe gja. de
to support (cause, idea)	ထောက်ခံသည်	htau' khan de
to accept (~ an apology)	လက်ခံသည်	le' khan de
to confirm (vt)	အတည်ပြုသည်	ati pju. de
confirmation	အတည်ပြုချက်	ati pju. gje'
permission	ခွင့်ပြုချက်	khwin bju. che'
to permit (vt)	ခွင့်ပြုသည်	khwin bju. de

| decision | လုံးဖြတ်ချက် | hsoun: hpja' cha' |
| to say nothing (hold one's tongue) | နှုတ်ဆိတ်သည် | hnou' hsei' te |

condition (term)	အခြေအနေ	achei anei
excuse (pretext)	ဆင်ခြေ	hsin gjei
praise (compliments)	ချီးမွမ်းခြင်း	chi: mun: gjin:
to praise (vt)	ချီးမွမ်းသည်	chi: mun: de

69. Success. Good luck. Failure

success	အောင်မြင်မှု	aun mjin hmu.
successfully (adv)	အောင်မြင်စွာ	aun mjin zwa
successful (adj)	အောင်မြင်သော	aun mjin dho:

luck (good luck)	ကံကောင်းခြင်း	kan gaun: gjin:
Good luck!	အောင်မြင်ပါစေ	aun mjin ba zei
lucky (e.g., ~ day)	ကံကောင်းစွာရှိသော	kan gaun zwa ja. shi. de.
lucky (fortunate)	ကံကောင်းသော	kan kaun: de.

failure	မအောင်မြင်ခြင်း	ma. aun mjin gjin:.
misfortune	ကံဆိုးခြင်း	kan hsou: chin:
bad luck	ကံဆိုးခြင်း	kan hsou: chin:
unsuccessful (adj)	မအောင်မြင်သော	ma. aun mjin de.
catastrophe	ကပ်ဘေး	ka' bei:

pride	ဂုဏ်	goun
proud (adj)	ဂုဏ်ယူသော	goun dhu de.
to be proud	ဂုဏ်ယူသည်	goun dhu de

winner	အနိုင်ရသူ	anain ja. dhu
to win (vi)	အနိုင်ရသည်	anain ja de
to lose (not win)	ရှုံးသည်	shoun: de
try	ကြိုးစားမှု	kjou: za: hmu.
to try (vi)	ကြိုးစားသည်	kjou: za: de
chance (opportunity)	အခွင့်အရေး	akhwin. ajei:

70. Quarrels. Negative emotions

shout (scream)	အော်သံ	o dhan
to shout (vi)	အော်သည်	o de
to start to cry out	စတင်အော်သည်	sa. tin o de

quarrel	ငြင်းခုံခြင်း	njin: goun gjin:
to quarrel (vi)	ငြင်းခုံသည်	njin: goun de
fight (squabble)	ခိုက်ရန်ဖြစ်ခြင်း	khai' jan bji' chin:
to make a scene	ခိုက်ရန်ဖြစ်သည်	khai' jan bji' te
conflict	အငြင်းပွားမှု	anjin: bwa: hmu.

misunderstanding	နားလည်မှုလွဲခြင်း	na: le hmu. lwe: gjin:
insult	စော်ကားမှု	so ga: hmu
to insult (vt)	စော်ကားသည်	so ga: de
insulted (adj)	အစော်ကားခံရသော	aso ka: gan ja de.
resentment	စိတ်နာမှု	sei' na hmu.
to offend (vt)	စိတ်နာအောင်လုပ်သည်	sei' na aun lou' te
to take offense	စိတ်နာသည်	sei' na de

indignation	မခံမရပ်နိုင် ဖြစ်ခြင်း	ma. gan ma. ja' nain bji' chin
to be indignant	မခံမရပ်နိုင်ဖြစ်သည်	ma. gan ma. ja' nain bji' te
complaint	တိုင်ပြောခြင်း	tain bjo: gjin:
to complain (vi, vt)	တိုင်ပြောသည်	tain bjo: de

apology	တောင်းပန်ခြင်း	thaun: ban gjin:
to apologize (vi)	တောင်းပန်သည်	thaun: ban de
to beg pardon	တောင်းပန်သည်	thaun: ban de

criticism	ဝေဖန်မှု	wei ban hmu.
to criticize (vt)	ဝေဖန်သည်	wei ban de
accusation (charge)	စွပ်စွဲခြင်း	su' swe: chin:
to accuse (vt)	စွပ်စွဲသည်	su' swe: de

revenge	လက်စားချေခြင်း	le' sa: gjei gjin:
to avenge (get revenge)	လက်စားချေသည်	le' sa: gjei de
to pay back	ပြန်ဆပ်သည်	pjan za' te

disdain	အထင်သေးခြင်း	a htin dhei: gjin:
to despise (vt)	အထင်သေးသည်	a htin dhei: de
hatred, hate	အမုန်း	amun:
to hate (vt)	မုန်းသည်	moun: de

nervous (adj)	စိတ်လှုပ်ရှားသော	sei' hlou' sha: de.
to be nervous	စိတ်လှုပ်ရှားသည်	sei' hlou' sha: de
angry (mad)	စိတ်ဆိုးသော	sei' hsou: de.
to make angry	ဒေါသထွက်စေသည်	do: dha. dwe' sei de

humiliation	မျက်နှာပျက်ရခြင်း	mje' hna bje' ja gjin:
to humiliate (vt)	မျက်နှာပျက်စေသည်	mje' hna bje' sei de
to humiliate oneself	အရှက်ရသည်	ashe' ja. de

| shock | တုန်လှုပ်ချောက်ချားခြင်း | toun hlou' chau' cha: gjin: |
| to shock (vt) | တုန်လှုပ်ချောက်ချားသည် | toun hlou' chau' cha: de |

| trouble (e.g., serious ~) | ဒုက္ခ | dou' kha. |
| unpleasant (adj) | မဖွယ်မရာဖြစ်သော | ma. bwe ma. ja bji' te. |

fear (dread)	ကြောက်ရွံ့ခြင်း	kjau' jun. gjin:
terrible (storm, heat)	အလွန်	alun
scary (e.g., ~ story)	ထိတ်လန့်သော	htei' lan. de
horror	ကြောက်မက်ဖွယ်ရာ	kjau' ma' hpwe ja
awful (crime, news)	ကြောက်မက်ဖွယ်ဖြစ်သော	kjau' ma' hpwe bja' te.

to begin to tremble	တုန်သည်	toun de
to cry (weep)	ငိုသည်	ngou de
to start crying	မျက်ရည်ဝဲသည်	mje' je we: de
tear	မျက်ရည်	mje' je
fault	အပြစ်	apja'
guilt (feeling)	စိတ်မသန့်ခြင်း	sei' ma. dhan. gjin:
dishonor (disgrace)	အရှက်	ashe'
protest	ကန့်ကွက်ချက်	kan gwe' che'
stress	စိတ်ဖိစီးမှု	sei' hpi zi: hmu.
to disturb (vt)	နှောင့်ယှက်သည်	hnaun. hje' te
to be furious	ဒေါသထွက်သည်	do: dha. dwe' de
mad, angry (adj)	ဒေါသကြီးသော	do: dha. gji: de.
to end (~ a relationship)	အဆုံးသတ်သည်	ahsoun: tha' te
to swear (at sb)	ဆူပူကြိမ်းမောင်းသည်	hsu. bu gjein: maun: de
to scare (become afraid)	လန့်သွားသည်	lan. dhwa: de
to hit (strike with hand)	ရိုက်သည်	jai' te
to fight (street fight, etc.)	ခိုက်ရန်ဖြစ်သည်	khai' jan bji' te
to settle (a conflict)	ဖျန်ဖြေပေးသည်	hpan bjei bjei: de
discontented (adj)	မကျေနပ်သော	ma. gjei na' te.
furious (adj)	ပြင်းထန်သော	pjin: dan dho:
It's not good!	ဒါ မကောင်းဘူး	da ma. gaun: dhu:
It's bad!	ဒါတော့ဆိုးတယ်	da do. zou: de

Medicine

sickness	ရောဂါ	jo: ga
to be sick	ဖျားနာသည်	hpa: na de
health	ကျန်းမာရေး	kjan: ma jei:

runny nose (coryza)	နာစေးခြင်း	hna zei: gjin:
tonsillitis	အာသီးရောင်ခြင်း	a sha. jaun gjin:
cold (illness)	အအေးမိခြင်း	aei: mi. gjin:
to catch a cold	အအေးမိသည်	aei: mi. de

bronchitis	ရောင်းဆိုးရင်ကျပ်နာ	gaun: ou: jin gja' na
pneumonia	အဆုတ်ရောင်ရောဂါ	ahsou' jaun jo: ga
flu, influenza	တုပ်ကွေး	tou' kwei:

nearsighted (adj)	အဝေးမှုန်သော	awei: hmun de.
farsighted (adj)	အနီးမှုန်	ani: hmoun
strabismus (crossed eyes)	မျက်စိဝွဲခြင်း	mje' zi. zwei gjin:
cross-eyed (adj)	မျက်စိဝွဲသော	mje' zi. zwei de.
cataract	နာမကျန်းဖြစ်ခြင်း	na. ma. gjan: bji' chin:
glaucoma	ရေတိမ်	jei dein

stroke	လေသင်တုန်းဖြစ်ခြင်း	lei dhin doun: bja' chin:
heart attack	နလုံးဖောက်ပြန်မှု	hnaloun: bau' bjan hmu.
myocardial infarction	နလုံးကြွက်သား ပုပ်ခြင်း	hnaloun: gjwe' tha: bou' chin:

paralysis	သွက်ချာပါဒ	thwe' cha ba da.
to paralyze (vt)	ဆိုင်းတွဲသွားသည်	hsain: dwa dhwa: de

allergy	မတည့်ခြင်း	ma. de. gjin:
asthma	ပန်းနာ	pan: na
diabetes	ဆီးချိုရောဂါ	hsi: gjou jau ba

toothache	သွားကိုက်ခြင်း	thwa: kai' chin:
caries	သွားပိုးစားခြင်း	thwa: pou: za: gjin:

diarrhea	ဝမ်းလျှောခြင်း	wan: sho: gjin:
constipation	ဝမ်းချုပ်ခြင်း	wan: gjou' chin:
stomach upset	ဗိုက်နာခြင်း	bai' na gjin:
food poisoning	အစာအဆိပ်သင့်ခြင်း	asa: ahsei' thin. gjin:
to get food poisoning	အစားမှားခြင်း	asa: hma: gjin:

arthritis	အဆစ်ရောင်နာ	ahsi' jaun na
rickets	အရိုးပျော့နာ	ajou: bjau. na

rheumatism	ဒူလာ	du la
atherosclerosis	နှလုံးသွေးကြော အဆီပိတ်ခြင်း	hna. loun: twei: kjau ahsi pei' khin:
gastritis	အစာအိမ်ရောင်ရမ်းနာ	asa: ein jaun jan: na
appendicitis	အူအတက်ရောင်ခြင်း	au hte' jaun gjin:
cholecystitis	သည်းခြေပြွန်ရောင်ခြင်း	thi: gjei bjun jaun gjin:
ulcer	ဖက်ခွက်နာ	hpe' khwe' na
measles	ဝက်သက်	we' the'
rubella (German measles)	ဂျုက်သိုး	gjou' thou:
jaundice	အသားဝါရောဂါ	atha: wa jo: ga
hepatitis	အသည်းရောင်ရောဂါ	athe: jaun jau ba
schizophrenia	စိတ်ကစဉ့်ကလျားရောဂါ	sei' ga. zin. ga. lja: jo: ga
rabies (hydrophobia)	ခွေးရူးပြန်ရောဂါ	khwei: ju: bjan jo: ba
neurosis	စိတ်မှမမှန်ခြင်း	sei' mu ma. hman gjin:
concussion	ဦးနှောက်ထိခိုက်ခြင်း	oun: hnau' hti. gai' chin:
cancer	ကင်ဆာ	kin hsa
sclerosis	အသားမှျင်ခက် မာသွားခြင်း	atha: hmjin kha' ma dwa: gjin:
multiple sclerosis	အာရုံကြောပျက်စီး ရောင်ရမ်းသည့်ရောဂါ	a joun gjo: bje' si: jaun jan: dhi. jo: ga
alcoholism	အရက်နာစွဲခြင်း	aje' na zwe: gjin:
alcoholic (n)	အရက်သမား	aje' dha. ma:
syphilis	ဆစ်ဖလစ်ကာလ သားနာရောဂါ	his' hpa. li' ka la. dha: jo: ba
AIDS	ကိုယ်ခံအားကျကုန်း စက်ရောဂါ	kou khan a: kja ku: za' jau ba
tumor	အသားပို	atha: pou
malignant (adj)	ကင်ဆာဖြစ်နေသော	kin hsa bji' nei de.
benign (adj)	ပြန့်ပွားခြင်း မရှိသော	pjan. bwa: gjin: ma. shi. de.
fever	အဖျားတက်ရောဂါ	ahpja: de' jo: ga
malaria	ငှက်ဖျားရောဂါ	hnge' hpja: jo: ba
gangrene	ဂန်ဂရိန်းနာရောဂါ	gan ga. ji na jo: ba
seasickness	လှိုင်းမူးခြင်း	hlain: mu: gjin:
epilepsy	ဝက်ရူးပြန်ရောဂါ	we' ju: bjan jo: ga
epidemic	ကပ်ရောဂါ	ka' jo ba
typhus	တိုက်ဖိုက်ရောဂါ	tai' hpai' jo: ba
tuberculosis	တီဘီရောဂါ	ti bi jo: ba
cholera	ကာလဝမ်းရောဂါ	ka la. wan: jau ga
plague (bubonic ~)	ကပ်ဆိုး	ka' hsou:

72. Symptoms. Treatments. Part 1

symptom	လက္ခဏာ	le' khana
temperature	အပူရှိန်	apu gjein
high temperature (fever)	ကိုယ်အပူရှိန်တက်	kou apu chain de'
pulse (heartbeat)	သွေးခုန်နှန်း	thwei: khoun hnan:
dizziness (vertigo)	မူးနောက်ခြင်း	mu: nau' chin:
hot (adj)	ပူသော	pu dho:
shivering	တုန်ခြင်း	toun gjin:
pale (e.g., ~ face)	ဖြူရော်သော	hpju jo de.
cough	ချောင်းဆိုးခြင်း	gaun: zou: gjin:
to cough (vi)	ချောင်းဆိုးသည်	gaun: zou: de
to sneeze (vi)	နှာချေသည်	hna gjei de
faint	အားနည်းခြင်း	a: ne: gjin:
to faint (vi)	သတိလစ်သည်	dhadi. li' te
bruise (hématome)	ပွန်းပဲ့ဒက်ရာ	pun: be. dan ja
bump (lump)	ဆောင့်မိခြင်း	hsaun. mi. gjin:
to bang (bump)	ဆောင့်မိသည်	hsaun. mi. de.
contusion (bruise)	ပွန်းပဲ့ဒက်ရာ	pun: be. dan ja
to get a bruise	ပွန်းပဲ့ဒက်ရာရသည်	pun: be. dan ja ja. de
to limp (vi)	ထော့နဲ့ထော့နဲ့လျှောက်သည်	hto. ne. hto. ne. shau' te
dislocation	အဆစ်လွဲခြင်း	ahsi' lwe: gjin:
to dislocate (vt)	အဆစ်လွဲသည်	ahsi' lwe: de
fracture	ကျိုးအက်ခြင်း	kjou: e' chin:
to have a fracture	ကျိုးအက်သည်	kjou: e' te
cut (e.g., paper ~)	ရှသည်	sha. de
to cut oneself	ရှမိသည်	sha. mi. de
bleeding	သွေးထွက်ခြင်း	thwei: htwe' chin:
burn (injury)	မီးလောင်သည့်ဒက်ရာ	mi: laun de. dan ja
to get burned	မီးလောင်ဒက်ရာရသည်	mi: laun dan ja ja. de
to prick (vt)	ဖောက်သည်	hpau' te
to prick oneself	ကိုယ်တိုင်ဖောက်သည်	kou tain hpau' te
to injure (vt)	ထိခိုက်ဒက်ရာရသည်	hti. gai' dan ja ja. de
injury	ထိခိုက်ဒက်ရာ	hti. gai' dan ja
wound	ဒက်ရာ	dan ja
trauma	စိတ်ဒက်ရာ	sei' dan ja
to be delirious	ကယောင်ကတမ်းဖြစ်သည်	kajaun ka dan: bi' te
to stutter (vi)	တုံ့နှေးတုံ့	toun. hnei: toun.
	နှေးဖြစ်သံည်	hnei: bji' te
sunstroke	အပူလျပ်ခြင်း	apu hlja' chin

73. Symptoms. Treatments. Part 2

pain, ache	နာကျင်မှု	na gjin hmu.
splinter (in foot, etc.)	ပို့ထွက်သောအစ	pe. dwe' tho: asa.
sweat (perspiration)	ချွေး	chwei:
to sweat (perspire)	ချွေးထွက်သည်	chwei: htwe' te
vomiting	အန်ခြင်း	an gjin:
convulsions	အကြောလိုက်ခြင်း	akjo: lai' chin:
pregnant (adj)	ကိုယ်ဝန်ဆောင်ထားသော	kou wun hsaun da: de.
to be born	မွေးဖွားသည်	mwei: bwa: de
delivery, labor	မီးဖွားခြင်း	mi: bwa: gjin:
to deliver (~ a baby)	မီးဖွားသည်	mi: bwa: de
abortion	ကိုယ်ဝန်ဖျက်ချခြင်း	kou wun hpje' cha chin:
breathing, respiration	အသက်ရှုခြင်း	athe' shu gjin:
in-breath (inhalation)	ဝင်လေ	win lei
out-breath (exhalation)	ထွက်လေ	htwe' lei
to exhale (breathe out)	အသက်ရှုထုတ်သည်	athe' shu dou' te
to inhale (vi)	အသက်ရှုသွင်းသည်	athe' shu dhwin: de
disabled person	ကိုယ်အင်္ဂါမသန် စွမ်းသူ	kou an ga ma. dhan swan: dhu
cripple	မသန်မစွမ်းသူ	ma. dhan ma. zwan dhu
drug addict	ဆေးစွဲသူ	hsei: zwe: dhu
deaf (adj)	နားမကြားသော	na: ma. gja: de.
mute (adj)	ဆွံ့အသော	hsun. ade.
deaf mute (adj)	ဆွံ့အ နားမကြားသူ	hsun. ana: ma. gja: dhu
mad, insane (adj)	စိတ်မနှံ့သော	sei' ma. hnan. de.
madman (demented person)	စိတ်မနှံ့သူ	sei' ma. hnan. dhu
madwoman	စိတ်ဝေဒနာရှင် မိန်းကလေး	sei' wei da. na shin mein: ga. lei:
to go insane	ရူးသွပ်သည်	ju: dhu' de
gene	မျိုးရိုးဗီဇ	mjou: jou: bi za.
immunity	ကိုယ်ခံအား	kou gan a:
hereditary (adj)	မျိုးရိုးလိုက်သော	mjou: jou: lou' te.
congenital (adj)	မွေးရာပါဖြစ်သော	mwei: ja ba bji' te.
virus	ဗိုင်းရပ်ပိုးမွှား	bain: ja' pou: hmwa:
microbe	အဏုဇီဝရုပ်	anu zi wa. jou'
bacterium	ဘက်တီးရီးယားပိုး	be' ti: ji: ja: bou:
infection	ရောဂါကူးစက်မှု	jo ga gu: ze' hmu.

74. Symptoms. Treatments. Part 3

hospital	ဆေးရုံ	hsei: joun
patient	လူနာ	lu na
diagnosis	ရောဂါစစ်ဆေးခြင်း	jo ga zi' hsei: gjin:
cure	ဆေးကုထုံး	hsei: ku. doun:
medical treatment	ဆေးဝါးကုသမှု	hsei: wa: gu. dha. hmu.
to get treatment	ဆေးကုသမှုခံယူသည်	hsei: ku. dha. hmu. dha de
to treat (~ a patient)	ပြုစုသည်	pju. zu. de
to nurse (look after)	ပြုစုစောင့်ရှောက်သည်	pju. zu. zaun. shau' te
care (nursing ~)	ပြုစုစောင့်ရှောက်ခြင်း	pju. zu. zaun. shau' chin:
operation, surgery	ခွဲစိတ်ကုသခြင်း	khwe: zei' ku. dha. hin:
to bandage (head, limb)	ပတ်တီးစည်းသည်	pa' ti: ze: de
bandaging	ပတ်တီးစည်းခြင်း	pa' ti: ze: gjin:
vaccination	ကာကွယ်ဆေးထိုးခြင်း	ka gwe hsei: dou: gjin:
to vaccinate (vt)	ကာကွယ်ဆေးထိုးသည်	ka gwe hsei: dou: de
injection, shot	ဆေးထိုးခြင်း	hsei: dou: gjin:
to give an injection	ဆေးထိုးသည်	hsei: dou: de
attack	ရောဂါ ရုတ်တရက်	jo ga jou' ta. je'
	ကျရောက်ခြင်း	kja. jau' chin:
amputation	ဖြတ်တောက်ကုသခြင်း	hpja' tau' ku. dha gjin:
to amputate (vt)	ဖြတ်တောက်ကုသသည်	hpja' tau' ku. dha de
coma	မေ့မြောခြင်း	mei. mjo: gjin:
to be in a coma	မေ့မြောသည်	mei. mjo: de
intensive care	အစွမ်းကုန်ပြုစုခြင်း	aswan: boun bju. zu. bjin:
to recover (~ from flu)	ရောဂါသက်သာလာသည်	jo ga dhe' tha la de
condition (patient's ~)	ကျန်းမာရေးအခြေအနေ	kjan: ma jei: achei a nei
consciousness	ပြန်လည်သတိရလာခြင်း	pjan le dhadi. ja. la. gjin:
memory (faculty)	မှတ်ဉာဏ်	hma' njan
to pull out (tooth)	နှုတ်သည်	hna' te
filling	သွားပေါက်ဖာထေးမှု	thwa: bau' hpa dei: hmu.
to fill (a tooth)	ဖာသည်	hpa de
hypnosis	အိပ်မွေ့ရှုခြင်း	ei' mwei. gja. gjin:
to hypnotize (vt)	အိပ်မွေ့ရှသည်	ei' mwei. gja. de

75. Doctors

doctor	ဆရာဝန်	hsa ja wun
nurse	သူနာပြု	thu na bju.
personal doctor	ကိုယ်ရေး ဆရာဝန်	kou jei; hsaja wun
dentist	သွားဆရာဝန်	thwa: hsaja wun
eye doctor	မျက်စိဆရာဝန်	mje' si. za. ja wun

internist	ရောဂါရှာဖွေရေး ဆရာဝန်	jo ga sha bwei jei: hsaja wun
surgeon	ခွဲစိတ်ကုဆရာဝန်	khwe: hsei' ku hsaja wun
psychiatrist	စိတ်ရောဂါအထူးကု ဆရာဝန်	sei' jo: ga ahtu: gu. zaja wun
pediatrician	ကလေးအထူးကုဆရာဝန်	kalei: ahtu: ku. hsaja wun
psychologist	စိတ်ပညာရှင်	sei' pjin nja shin
gynecologist	မီးယပ်ရောဂါအထူး ကုဆရာဝန်	mi: ja' jo: ga ahtu: gu za. ja wun
cardiologist	နှလုံးရောဂါအထူး ကုဆရာဝန်	hnaloun: jo: ga ahtu: gu. zaja wun

76. Medicine. Drugs. Accessories

medicine, drug	ဆေးဝါး	hsei: wa:
remedy	ကုသခြင်း	ku. dha. gjin:
to prescribe (vt)	ဆေးအညွှန်းပေးသည်	hsa: ahnjun: bwe: de
prescription	ဆေးညွှန်း	hsei: hnjun:
tablet, pill	ဆေးပြား	hsei: bja:
ointment	လိမ်းဆေး	lein: zei:
ampule	လေလုံဖန်ပုလင်းငယ်	lei loun ban bu. lin: nge
mixture, solution	စပ်ဆေးရည်	sa' ei: je
syrup	ဖျော်ရည်ဆီ	hpjo jei zi
capsule	ဆေးတောင့်	hsei: daun.
powder	အမှုန့်	ahmoun.
gauze bandage	ပတ်တီး	pa' ti:
cotton wool	ဝွမ်းလိပ်	gwan: lei'
iodine	တင်ဂျာအိုင်ဒင်း	tin gja ein din:
Band-Aid	ပလာစတာ	pa. la sata
eyedropper	မျက်စဉ်းခတ်ကိရိယာ	mje' zin: ba' ki. ji. ja
thermometer	အပူရှိန်တိုင်းကိရိယာ	apu gjein dain: gi. ji. ja
syringe	ဆေးထိုးပြွတ်	hsei: dou: bju'
wheelchair	ဘီးတပ်ကုလားထိုင်	bi: da' ku. la: dain
crutches	ချိုင်းထောက်	chain: dau'
painkiller	အကိုက်အခဲပျောက်ဆေး	akai' akhe: pjau' hsei:
laxative	ဝမ်းနုတ်ဆေး	wan: hnou' hsei:
spirits (ethanol)	အရက်ပြံ	aje' pjan
medicinal herbs	ဆေးဖက်ဝင်အပင်များ	hsei: hpa' win apin mja:
herbal (~ tea)	ဆေးဖက်ဝင်အပင် နှင့်ဆိုင်သော	hsei: hpa' win apin hnin. zain de.

77. Smoking. Tobacco products

tobacco	ဆေးရွက်ကြီး	hsei: jwe' kji:
cigarette	စီးကရက်	si: ga. ja'
cigar	ဆေးပြင်းလိပ်	hsei: bjin: li'
pipe	ဆေးတံ	hsei: dan
pack (of cigarettes)	ဘူး	bu:
matches	မီးခြစ်ဆံများ	mi: gji' zain mja:
matchbox	မီးခြစ်ဆံဘူး	mi: gji' zain bu:
lighter	မီးခြစ်	mi: gji'
ashtray	ဆေးလိပ်ပြာခွက်	hsei: lei' pja gwe'
cigarette case	စီးကရက်အလှဘူး	si: ga. ja' ahla. bu:
cigarette holder	စီး့ကရက်ထည့်သောက်သည့် ပြွန်တံငယ်	si: ga. ja' hti. dau' thi. bjwan dan nge
filter (cigarette tip)	ဖင်ဇီခံ	hpin zi gan
to smoke (vi, vt)	ဆေးလိပ်သောက်သည်	hsei: lei' ma. dhau' te
to light a cigarette	ဆေးလိပ်မီးညှိသည်	hsei: lei' mi: hni. de
smoking	ဆေးလိပ်သောက်ခြင်း	hsei: lei' ma. dhau' chin:
smoker	ဆေးလိပ်သောက်သူ	hsei: lei' ma. dhau' thu
stub, butt (of cigarette)	ဆေးလိပ်တို	hsei: lei' tou
smoke, fumes	မီးခိုး	mi: gou:
ash	ပြာ	pja

HUMAN HABITAT

City

city, town	မြို့	mjou.
capital city	မြို့တော်	mjou. do
village	ရွာ	jwa
city map	မြို့လမ်းညွှန်မြေပုံ	mjou. lan hnjun mjei boun
downtown	မြို့လယ်ခေါင်	mjou. le gaun
suburb	ဆင်ခြေဖုံးအရပ်	hsin gjei aja'
suburban (adj)	ဆင်ခြေဖုံး အရပ်ဖြစ်သော	hsin gjei hpoun aja' hpa' te.
outskirts	မြို့စွန်	mjou. zun
environs (suburbs)	ပတ်ဝန်းကျင်	pa' wun: gjin:
city block	စည်ကားရာမြို့လယ်နေရာ	si: ga: ja mjou. le nei ja
residential block (area)	လူနေရပ်ကွက်	lu nei ja' kwe'
traffic	ယာဉ်အသွားအလာ	jin athwa: ala
traffic lights	မီးပွိုင့်	mi: bwain.
public transportation	ပြည်သူပိုင်ရထီးသွား ပို့ဆောင်ရေး	pji dhu bain gaji: dhwa: bou. zaun jei:
intersection	လမ်းဆုံ	lan: zoun
crosswalk	လူကူးမျဉ်းကြား	lu gu: mji: gja:
pedestrian underpass	မြေအောက်လမ်းကူး	mjei au' lan: gu:
to cross (~ the street)	လမ်းကူးသည်	lan: gu: de
pedestrian	လမ်းသွားလမ်းလာ	lan: dhwa: lan: la
sidewalk	လူသွားလမ်း	lu dhwa: lan:
bridge	တံတား	dada:
embankment (river walk)	ကမ်းနားတာမံ	kan: na: da. man
fountain	ရေပန်း	jei ban:
allée (garden walkway)	ရိုင်သာလမ်း	jei' tha lan:
park	ပန်းခြံ	pan: gjan
boulevard	လမ်းဝယ်	lan: ge
square	ရင်ပြင်	jin bjin
avenue (wide street)	လမ်းမကြီး	lan: mi. gji:
street	လမ်း	lan:
side street	လမ်းသွယ်	lan: dhwe
dead end	လမ်းဆုံး	lan: zoun:

house	အိမ်	ein
building	အဆောက်အဦ	ahsau' au
skyscraper	မိုးမျှော်တိုက်	mou: hmjo tou'
facade	အိမ်ရှေ့နံရံ	ein shei. nan jan
roof	အမိုး	amou:
window	ပြတင်းပေါက်	badin: pau'
arch	မုခ်ဝ	mou' wa.
column	တိုင်	tain
corner	ထောင့်	htaun.
store window	ဆိုင်ရှေ့ပစ္စည်း	hseun shei. bji' si:
	အခင်းအကျင်း	akhin: akjin:
signboard (store sign, etc.)	ဆိုင်းဘုတ်	hsain: bou'
poster (e.g., playbill)	ပိုစတာ	pou sata
advertising poster	ကြော်ငြာပိုစတာ	kjo nja bou sata
billboard	ကြော်ငြာဆိုင်းဘုတ်	kjo nja zain: bou'
garbage, trash	အမှိုက်	ahmai'
trash can (public ~)	အမှိုက်ပုံး	ahmai' poun:
to litter (vi)	လွှင့်ပစ်သည်	hlwin. bi' te
garbage dump	အမှိုက်ပုံ	ahmai' poun
phone booth	တယ်လီဖုန်းဆက်ရန်နေရာ	te li hpoun: ze' jan nei ja
lamppost	လမ်းမီး	lan: mi:
bench (park ~)	ခုံတန်းရှည်	khoun dan: shei
police officer	ရဲ	je:
police	ရဲ	je:
beggar	သူတောင်းစား	thu daun: za:
homeless (n)	အိမ်ယာမဲ့	ein ja me.

79. Urban institutions

store	ဆိုင်	hsain
drugstore, pharmacy	ဆေးဆိုင်	hsei: zain
eyeglass store	မျက်မှန်ဆိုင်	mje' hman zain
shopping mall	ဈေးဝင်ဝင်တာ	zei: wun zin da
supermarket	ကုန်တိုက်ကြီး	koun dou' kji:
bakery	မုန့်တိုက်	moun. dai'
baker	ပေါင်မုန့်ဖုတ်သူ	paun moun. bou' dhu
pastry shop	မုန့်ဆိုင်	moun. zain
grocery store	ကုန်စုံဆိုင်	koun zoun zain
butcher shop	အသားဆိုင်	atha: ain
produce store	ဟင်းသီးဟင်းရွက်ဆိုင်	hin: dhi: hin: jwe' hsain
market	ဈေး	zei:
coffee house	ကော်ဖီဆိုင်	ko hpi zain
restaurant	စားသောက်ဆိုင်	sa: thau' hsain

pub, bar	ဘီယာဆိုင်	bi ja zain:
pizzeria	ပီဇာမုန့်ဆိုင်	pi za moun. zain
hair salon	ဆံပင်ညှပ်ဆိုင်	zain hnja' hsain
post office	စာတိုက်	sa dai'
dry cleaners	အဝတ်အခြောက်လျှော် လုပ်ငန်း	awu' achou' hlo: lou' ngan:
photo studio	ဓာတ်ပုံရိုက်ခန်း	da' poun jai' khan:
shoe store	ဖိနပ်ဆိုင်	hpana' sain
bookstore	စာအုပ်ဆိုင်	sa ou' hsain
sporting goods store	အားကစားပစ္စည်းဆိုင်	a: gaza: pji' si: zain
clothes repair shop	စက်ပြင်ဆိုင်	se' pjin zain
formal wear rental	ဝတ်စုံအငှားဆိုင်	wa' zoun ahnga: zain
video rental store	အခွေငှားဆိုင်	akhwei hnga: zain:
circus	ဆပ်ကပ်	hsa' ka'
zoo	တိရစ္ဆာန်ဥယျာဉ်	tharei' hsan u. jin
movie theater	ရုပ်ရှင်ရုံ	jou' shin joun
museum	ပြတိုက်	pja. dai'
library	စာကြည့်တိုက်	sa gji. dai'
theater	ကဇာတ်ရုံ	ka. za' joun
opera (opera house)	အော်ပရာဇာတ်ရုံ	o pa ra za' joun
nightclub	နိုက်ကလပ်	nai' ka. la'
casino	လောင်းကစားရုံ	laun: gaza: joun
mosque	ဗလီ	bali
synagogue	ရှူဟူဒီဘုရား ရှိုးဂေါ့ကျောင်း	ja. hu di bu. ja: shi. gou: gjaun:
cathedral	ဘုရားရှိခိုးကျောင်းတော်	hpaja: gjaun: do:
temple	ဘုရားကျောင်း	hpaja: gjaun:
church	ဘုရားကျောင်း	hpaja: gjaun:
college	တက္ကသိုလ်	te' kathou
university	တက္ကသိုလ်	te' kathou
school	စာသင်ကျောင်း	sa dhin gjaun:
prefecture	စီရင်စုနယ်	si jin zu. ne
city hall	မြို့တော်ခန်းမ	mjou. do gan: ma.
hotel	ဟိုတယ်	hou te
bank	ဘဏ်	ban
embassy	သံရုံး	than joun:
travel agency	ခရီးသွားလုပ်ငန်း	khaji: thwa: lou' ngan:
information office	သတင်းအချက်အလက်ဌာန	dhadin: akje' ale' hta. na.
currency exchange	ငွေလဲရန်နေရာ	ngwei le: jan nei ja
subway	မြေအောက်ဉမင်လမ်း	mjei au' u. min lan:
hospital	ဆေးရုံ	hsei: joun
gas station	ဆီဆိုင်	hsi: zain
parking lot	ကားပါကင်	ka: pa kin

80. Signs

signboard (store sign, etc.)	ဆိုင်းဘုတ်	hsain: bou'
notice (door sign, etc.)	သတိပေးစာ	dhadi. pei: za
poster	ပိုစတာ	pou sata
direction sign	လမ်းညွှန်	lan: hnjun
arrow (sign)	လမ်းညွှန်မြား	lan: hnjun hmja:
caution	သတိပေးခြင်း	dhadi. pei: gjin:
warning sign	သတိပေးချက်	dhadi. pei: gje'
to warn (vt)	သတိပေးသည်	dhadi. pei: de
rest day (weekly ~)	ရုံးပိတ်ရက်	joun: bei' je'
timetable (schedule)	အချိန်ဇယား	achein zaja:
opening hours	ဖွင့်ချိန်	hpwin. gjin
WELCOME!	ကြိုဆိုပါသည်	kjou hsou ba de
ENTRANCE	ဝင်ပေါက်	win bau'
EXIT	ထွက်ပေါက်	htwe' pau'
PUSH	တွန်းသည်	tun: de
PULL	ဆွဲသည်	hswe: de
OPEN	ဖွင့်သည်	hpwin. de
CLOSED	ပိတ်သည်	pei' te
WOMEN	အမျိုးသမီးသုံး	amjou: dhami: dhoun:
MEN	အမျိုးသားသုံး	amjou: dha: dhoun:
DISCOUNTS	လျှော့ဈေး	sho. zei:
SALE	လျှော့ဈေး	sho. zei:
NEW!	အသစ်	athi'
FREE	အခမဲ့	akha me.
ATTENTION!	သတိ	thadi.
NO VACANCIES	အလွတ်မရှိ	alu' ma shi.
RESERVED	ကြိုတင်မှာယူထားပြီး	kjou tin hma ju da: bji:
ADMINISTRATION	စီမံအုပ်ချုပ်ခြင်း	si man ou' chou' chin:
STAFF ONLY	အမှုထမ်းအတွက်အသာ	ahmu. htan: atwe' atha
BEWARE OF THE DOG!	ခွေးကိုက်တတ်သည်	khwei: kai' ta' te
NO SMOKING	ဆေးလိပ်မသောက်ရ	hsei: lei' ma. dhau' ja.
DO NOT TOUCH!	မထိရ	ma. di. ja.
DANGEROUS	အန္တရာယ်ရှိသည်	an dare shi. de.
DANGER	အန္တရာယ်	an dare
HIGH VOLTAGE	ဗို့အားပြင်း	bou. a: bjin:
NO SWIMMING!	ရေမကူးရ	jei ma. gu: ja.
OUT OF ORDER	ပျက်နေသည်	pje' nei de
FLAMMABLE	မီးလောင်တတ်သည်	mi: laun da' te
FORBIDDEN	တားမြစ်သည်	ta: mji' te

| NO TRESPASSING! | မကျူးကျော်ရ | ma. gju: gjo ja |
| WET PAINT | ဆေးမခြောက်သေး | hsei: ma. gjau' dhei: |

81. Urban transportation

bus	ဘတ်စ်ကား	ba's ka:
streetcar	ဓာတ်ရထား	da' ja hta:
trolley bus	ဓာတ်ကား	da' ka:
route (of bus, etc.)	လမ်းကြောင်း	lan: gjaun:
number (e.g., bus ~)	ကားနံပါတ်	ka: nan ba'

to go by ...	ယဉ်စီးသည်	jin zi: de
to get on (~ the bus)	ထိုင်သည်	htain de
to get off ...	ကားပေါ်မှဆင်းသည်	ka: bo hma. zin: de

stop (e.g., bus ~)	မှတ်တိုင်	hma' tain
next stop	နောက်မှတ်တိုင်	nau' hma' tain
terminus	အဆုံးမှတ်တိုင်	ahsoun: hma' tain
schedule	အချိန်ဇယား	achein zaja:
to wait (vt)	စောင့်သည်	saun. de

| ticket | လက်မှတ် | le' hma' |
| fare | ယဉ်စီးခ | jin zi: ga. |

cashier (ticket seller)	ငွေကိုင်	ngwei gain
ticket inspection	လက်မှတ်စစ်ဆေးခြင်း	le' hma' ti' hsei: chin
ticket inspector	လက်မှတ်စစ်ဆေးသူ	le' hma' ti' hsei: dhu:

to be late (for ...)	နောက်ကျသည်	nau' kja. de
to miss (~ the train, etc.)	ကားနောက်ကျသည်	ka: nau' kja de
to be in a hurry	အမြန်လုပ်သည်	aman lou' de

taxi, cab	တက္ကစီ	te' kasi
taxi driver	တက္ကစီမောင်းသူ	te' kasi maun: dhu:
by taxi	တက္ကစီဖြင့်	te' kasi hpjin.
taxi stand	တက္ကစီစုရပ်	te' kasi zu. ja'
to call a taxi	တက္ကစီခေါ်သည်	te' kasi go de
to take a taxi	တက္ကစီငှားသည်	te' kasi hnga: de

traffic	ယဉ်အသွားအလာ	jin athwa: ala
traffic jam	ယဉ်ကြောပိတ်ဆို့မှု	jin gjo: bei' hsou. hmu.
rush hour	အလုပ်ဆင်းရှိန်	alou' hsin: gjain
to park (vi)	ယဉ်ရပ်နားရန်နေရာယူသည်	jin ja' na: jan nei ja ju de
to park (vt)	ကားအားပါကင်ထိုးသည်	ka: a: pa kin dou: de
parking lot	ပါကင်	pa gin

subway	မြေအောက်ဥမင်လမ်း	mjei au' u. min lan:
station	ဘူတာရုံ	bu da joun
to take the subway	ဥမြေအောက်ရထား ဖြင့်သွားသည်	mjei au' ja. da: bjin. dhwa: de

| train | ရထား | jatha: |
| train station | ရထားဘူတာရုံ | jatha: buda joun |

82. Sightseeing

monument	ရုပ်တု	jou' tu.
fortress	ခံတပ်ကြီး	khwan da' kji:
palace	နန်းတော်	nan do
castle	ရဲတိုက်	je: dai'
tower	မျှော်စင်	hmjo zin
mausoleum	ဂူဗိမာန်	gu bi. man

architecture	ဗိသုကာပညာ	bi. thu. ka pjin nja
medieval (adj)	အလယ်ခေတ်နှင့်ဆိုင်သော	ale khei' hnin. zain de.
ancient (adj)	ရှေးကျသော	shei: gja. de
national (adj)	အမျိုးသားနှင့်ဆိုင်သော	amjou: dha: hnin. zain de.
famous (monument, etc.)	နာမည်ကြီးသော	na me gji: de.

tourist	ကမ္ဘာလှည့်ခရီးသည်	ga ba hli. kha. ji: de
guide (person)	လမ်းညွှန်	lan: hnjun
excursion, sightseeing tour	လေ့လာရေးခရီး	lei. la jei: gaji:
to show (vt)	ပြသည်	pja. de
to tell (vt)	ပြောပြသည်	pjo: bja. de

to find (vt)	ရှာတွေ့သည်	sha dwei. de
to get lost (lose one's way)	ပျောက်သည်	pjau' te
map (e.g., subway ~)	မြေပုံ	mjei boun
map (e.g., city ~)	မြေပုံ	mjei boun

souvenir, gift	အမှတ်တရလက်ဆောင်ပစ္စည်း	ahma' ta ra le' hsaun pji' si:
gift shop	လက်ဆောင်ပစ္စည်းဆိုင်	le' hsaun pji' si: zain
to take pictures	ဓာတ်ပုံရိုက်သည်	da' poun jai' te
to have one's picture taken	ဓာတ်ပုံရိုက်သည်	da' poun jai' te

83. Shopping

to buy (purchase)	ဝယ်သည်	we de
purchase	ဝယ်စရာ	we zaja
to go shopping	ဈေးဝယ်ထွက်ခြင်း	zei: we htwe' chin:
shopping	ရှော့ပင်း	sho. bin:

| to be open (ab. store) | ဆိုင်ဖွင့်သည် | hsain bwin. de |
| to be closed | ဆိုင်ပိတ်သည် | hseun bi' te |

footwear, shoes	ဖိနပ်	hpana'
clothes, clothing	အဝတ်အစား	awu' aza:
cosmetics	အလှကုန်ပစ္စည်း	ahla. koun pji' si:
food products	စားသောက်ကုန်	sa: thau' koun

gift, present	လက်ဆောင်	le' hsaun
salesman	ရောင်းသူ	jaun: dhu
saleswoman	ရောင်းသူ	jaun: dhu

check out, cash desk	ငွေရှင်းရန်နေရာ	ngwei shin: jan nei ja
mirror	မှန်	hman
counter (store ~)	ကောင်တာ	kaun da
fitting room	အဝတ်လဲခန်း	awu' le: gan:

to try on	တိုင်းကြည့်သည်	tain: dhi. de
to fit (ab. dress, etc.)	သင့်တော်သည်	thin. do de
to like (I like …)	ကြိုက်သည်	kjai' de

price	ဈေးနှုန်း	zei: hnan:
price tag	ဈေးနှုန်းကပ်ပြား	zei: hnan: ka' pja:
to cost (vt)	ကုန်ကျသည်	koun mja. de
How much?	ဘယ်လောက်လဲ	be lau' le:
discount	လျှော့ဈေး	sho. zei:

inexpensive (adj)	ဈေးမကြီးသော	zei: ma. kji: de.
cheap (adj)	ဈေးပေါသော	zei: po: de.
expensive (adj)	ဈေးကြီးသော	zei: kji: de.
It's expensive	ဒါဈေးကြီးတယ်	da zei: gji: de

rental (n)	ငှားရမ်းခြင်း	hna: jan: chin:
to rent (~ a tuxedo)	ငှားရမ်းသည်	hna: jan: de
credit (trade credit)	အကြွေးစနစ်	akjwei: sani'
on credit (adv)	အကြွေးစနစ်ဖြင့်	akjwei: sa ni' hpjin.

84. Money

money	ပိုက်ဆံ	pai' hsan
currency exchange	လဲလှယ်ခြင်း	le: hle gjin:
exchange rate	ငွေလဲနှုန်း	ngwei le: hnan:
ATM	အလိုအလျောက်ငွေထုတ်စက်	alou aljau' ngwei htou' se'
coin	အကြွေစေ့	akjwei zei.

| dollar | ဒေါ်လာ | do la |
| euro | ယူရို | ju rou |

lira	အီတလီ လိုင်ရာငွေ	ita. li lain ja ngwei
Deutschmark	ဂျာမန်မတ်ငွေ	gja man ma' ngwei
franc	ဖရန့်	hpa. jan.
pound sterling	စတာလင်ပေါင်	sata lin baun
yen	ယန်း	jan:

debt	အကြွေး	akjwei:
debtor	မြီစား	mji za:
to lend (money)	ရေးသည်	chei: de
to borrow (vi, vt)	အကြွေးယူသည်	akjwei: ju de

bank	ဘဏ်	ban
account	ငွေစာရင်း	ngwei za jin:
to deposit (vt)	ထည့်သည်	hte de.
to deposit into the account	ငွေသွင်းသည်	ngwei dhwin: de
to withdraw (vt)	ငွေထုတ်သည်	ngwei dou' te

credit card	အကြွေးဝယ်ကဒ်ပြား	akjwei: we ka' pja
cash	လက်ငင်း	le' ngin:
check	ချက်	che'
to write a check	ချက်ရေးသည်	che' jei: de
checkbook	ချက်စာအုပ်	che' sa ou'

wallet	ပိုက်ဆံအိတ်	pai' hsan ei'
change purse	ပိုက်ဆံအိတ်	pai' hsan ei'
safe	မီးခံသေတ္တာ	mi: gan dhi' ta

heir	အမွေစားအမွေခံ	amwei za: amwei gan
inheritance	အမွေဆက်ခံခဲ့ခြင်း	amwei ze' khan gjin:
fortune (wealth)	အခွင့်အလမ်း	akhwin. alan:

lease	အိမ်ငှား	ein hnga:
rent (money)	အခန်းငှားခ	akhan: hnga: ga
to rent (sth from sb)	ငှားသည်	hnga: de

price	ဈေးနှုန်း	zei: hnan:
cost	ကုန်ကျစရိတ်	koun gja. za. ji'
sum	ပေါင်းလဒ်	paun: la'

to spend (vt)	သုံးစွဲသည်	thoun: zwe: de
expenses	စရိတ်စက	zaei' zaga.
to economize (vi, vt)	ချွေတာသည်	chwei da de
economical	တွက်ခြေကိုက်သော	twe' chei kai' te.

to pay (vi, vt)	ပေးချေသည်	pei: gjei de
payment	ပေးချေသည့်ငွေ	pei: gjei de. ngwei
change (give the ~)	ပြန်အမ်းငွေ	pjan an: ngwe

tax	အခွန်	akhun
fine	ဒဏ်ငွေ	dan ngwei
to fine (vt)	ဒဏ်ရိုက်သည်	dan jai' de

85. Post. Postal service

post office	စာတိုက်	sa dai'
mail (letters, etc.)	မေးလ်	mei: l
mailman	စာပို့သမား	sa bou. dhama:
opening hours	ဖွင့်ချိန်	hpwin. gjin

| letter | စာ | sa |
| registered letter | မှတ်ပုံတင်ပြီးသောစာ | hma' poun din bji: dho: za: |

postcard	ပို့စ်ကတ်	pou. sa. ka'
telegram	ကြေးနန်း	kjei: nan:
package (parcel)	ပါဆယ်	pa ze
money transfer	ငွေလွှဲခြင်း	ngwei hlwe: gjin:
to receive (vt)	လက်ခံရရှိသည်	le' khan ja. shi. de
to send (vt)	ပို့သည်	pou. de
sending	ပို့ခြင်း	pou. gjin:
address	လိပ်စာ	lei' sa
ZIP code	စာပို့သင်္ကေတ	sa bou dhin kei ta.
sender	ပို့သူ	pou. dhu
receiver	လက်ခံသူ	le' khan dhu
name (first name)	အမည်	amji
surname (last name)	မိဘသားစု မျိုး၊ ရိုးနာမည်	mi. dha: zu. mjou: jou: na mji
postage rate	စာပို့ခ နှုန်းထား	sa bou. kha. hnan: da:
standard (adj)	စံနှုန်းသတ်မှတ် ထားသော	san hnoun: dha' hma' hta: de.
economical (adj)	ကုန်ကျငွေသက် သာသော	koun gja ngwe dhe' dha de.
weight	အလေးချိန်	alei: gjein
to weigh (~ letters)	ချိန်သည်	chein de
envelope	စာအိတ်	sa ei'
postage stamp	တံဆိပ်ခေါင်း	da zei' khaun:
to stamp an envelope	တံဆိပ်ခေါင်းကပ်သည်	da zei' khaun: ka' te

Dwelling. House. Home

86. House. Dwelling

house	အိမ်	ein
at home (adv)	အိမ်မှာ	ein hma
yard	ခြံမြေကွက်လပ်	chan mjei gwe' la'
fence (iron ~)	ခြံစည်းရိုး	chan zi: jou:
brick (n)	အုတ်	ou'
brick (as adj)	အုတ်ဖြင့်လုပ်ထားသော	ou' hpjin. lou' hta: de.
stone (n)	ကျောက်	kjau'
stone (as adj)	ကျောက်ဖြင့်လုပ်ထားသော	kjau' hpjin. lou' hta: de.
concrete (n)	ကွန်ကရစ်	kun ka. ji'
concrete (as adj)	ကွန်ကရစ်လောင်းထားသော	kun ka. ji' laun: da: de.
new (new-built)	သစ်သော	thi' te.
old (adj)	ဟောင်းသော	haun: de.
ramshackle	အိုဟောင်းပျက်စီးနေသော	ou haun: pje' si: nei dho:
modern (adj)	ခေတ်မီသော	khi' mi de.
multistory (adj)	အထပ်များစွာပါသော	a hta' mja: swa ba de.
tall (~ building)	မြင့်သော	mjin. de.
floor, story	အထပ်	a hta'
single-story (adj)	အထပ်တစ်ထပ်တည်း ဖြစ်သော	a hta' ta' hta' te: hpja' tho:
1st floor	မြေညီထပ်	mjei nji da'
top floor	အပေါ်ဆုံးထပ်	apo zoun: da'
roof	အမိုး	amou:
chimney	မီးရိုးခေါင်းတိုင်	mi: gou: gaun: dain
roof tiles	အုတ်ကြွပ်ပြား	ou' gju' pja:
tiled (adj)	အုတ်ကြွပ်ဖြင့်မိုးထားသော	ou' gju' hpjin: mou' hta: de.
attic (storage place)	ထပ်ခိုး	hta' khou:
window	ပြတင်းပေါက်	badin: pau'
glass	ဖန်	hpan
window ledge	ပြတင်းအောက်ခြေဘောင်	badin: au' chei dhaun
shutters	ပြတင်းကာ	badin: ga
wall	နံရံ	nan jou:
balcony	ဝရန်တာ	wa jan da
downspout	ရေဆင်းပိုက်	jei zin: bai'
upstairs (to be ~)	အပေါ်မှာ	apo hma
to go upstairs	တက်သည်	te' te

| to come down (the stairs) | ဆင်းသည် | hsin: de |
| to move (to new premises) | အိမ်ပြောင်းသည် | ein bjaun: de |

87. House. Entrance. Lift

entrance	ဝင်ပေါက်	win bau'
stairs (stairway)	လှေကား	hlei ga:
steps	လှေကားထစ်	hlei ga: di'
banister	လှေကားလက်ရန်း	hlei ga: le' jan:
lobby (hotel ~)	ဧည့်ခန်းမ	e. gan: ma.

mailbox	စာတိုက်ပုံး	sa dai' poun:
garbage can	အမှိုက်ပုံး	ahmai' poun:
trash chute	အမှိုက်ဆင်းပိုက်	ahmai' hsin: bai'

elevator	ဓာတ်လှေကား	da' hlei ga:
freight elevator	ဝန်တင်ဓာတ်လှေကား	wun din da' hlei ga:
elevator cage	ကုန်တင်ဓာတ်လှေကား	koun din ga' hlei ga:
to take the elevator	ဓာတ်လှေကားစီးသည်	da' hlei ga: zi: de

apartment	တိုက်ခန်း	tai' khan:
residents (~ of a building)	နေထိုင်သူများ	nei dain dhu mja:
neighbor (masc.)	အိမ်နီးနားချင်း	ein ni: na: gjin:
neighbor (fem.)	မိန်းကလေးအိမ်နီးနားချင်း	mein: galei: ein: ni: na: gjin:
neighbors	အိမ်နီးနားချင်းများ	ein ni: na: gjin: mja:

88. House. Electricity

electricity	လျှပ်စစ်ဓာတ်အား	hlja' si' da' a:
light bulb	မီးသီး	mi: dhi:
switch	ခလုတ်	khalou'
fuse (plug fuse)	ဖျူးစ်	hpju: s

cable, wire (electric ~)	ဝိုင်ယာကြိုး	wain ja gjou:
wiring	လျှပ်စစ်ကြိုးသွယ်တန်းမှု	hlja' si' kjou: dhwe dan: hmu
electricity meter	လျှပ်စစ်မီတာ	hlja' si' si da
readings	ပြသောပမာဏ	pja. dho: ba ma na.

89. House. Doors. Locks

door	တံခါး	daga:
gate (vehicle ~)	ဂိတ်	gei'
handle, doorknob	တံခါးလက်ကိုင်	daga: le' kain
to unlock (unbolt)	သော့ဖွင့်သည်	tho. bwin. de

to open (vt)	ဖွင့်သည်	hpwin. de
to close (vt)	ပိတ်သည်	pei' te
key	သော့	tho.
bunch (of keys)	အတွဲ	atwe:
to creak (door, etc.)	တကျီကျီမြည်သည်	ta kjwi. kjwi. mji de
creak	တကျီကျီမြည်သံ	ta kjwi. kjwi. mji dhan
hinge (door ~)	ပတ္တာ	pa' ta
doormat	ခြေသုတ်ခုံ	chei dhou' goun
door lock	တံခါးဂျက်	daga: gje'
keyhole	သော့ပေါက်	tho. bau'
crossbar (sliding bar)	မင်းတုံး	min: doun:
door latch	တံခါးချက်	daga: che'
padlock	သော့ခလောက်	tho. ga. lau'
to ring (~ the door bell)	ခေါင်းလောင်းမြည်သည်	gaun: laun: mje de
ringing (sound)	ခေါင်းလောင်းမြည်သံ	gaun: laun: mje dhan
doorbell	လူခေါ် ခေါင်းလောင်း	lu go gaun: laun:
doorbell button	လူခေါ် ခေါင်းလောင်းခလုတ်	lu go gaun: laun: khalou'
knock (at the door)	တံခါးခေါက်သံ	daga: khau' than
to knock (vi)	တံခါးခေါက်သည်	daga: khau' te
code	သင်္ကေတဂဏန်း	thin gei ta. hwe'
combination lock	ကုဒ်သော့	kou' tho.
intercom	အိမ်တွင်းဆက်သွယ်	ein dwin: ze' dhwe
	မှုစနစ်	hmu. zani'
number (on the door)	နံပါတ်	nan ba'
doorplate	အိမ်တံခါးရှေ့	ein da ga: shei.
	ဆိုင်းဘုတ်	hsain: bou'
peephole	ချောင်းကြည့်ပေါက်	chaun: gje. bau'

<h2>90. Country house</h2>

village	ရွာ	jwa
vegetable garden	အသီးအရွက်စိုက်ခင်း	athi: ajwe' sai' khin:
fence	ခြံစည်းရိုး	chan zi: jou:
picket fence	ခြံစည်းရိုးတိုင်	chan zi: jou: dain
wicket gate	မလွယ်ပေါက်	ma. lwe bau'
granary	ကျီ	kji
root cellar	မြေအောက် အစာသိုလှောင်ခန်း	mjei au' asa dhou hlaun gan:
shed (garden ~)	ဂိုဒေါင်	gou daun
water well	ရေတွင်း	jei dwin:
stove (wood-fired ~)	မီးဖို	mi: bou
to stoke the stove	မီးပြင်းအောင်ထိုးသည်	mi: bjin: aun dou: de
firewood	ထင်း	htin:
log (firewood)	ထင်းတုံး	tin: doun:

veranda	ဝရန်တာ	wa jan da
deck (terrace)	စကြ	sin gja.
stoop (front steps)	အိမ်ရှေ့လှေကား	ein shei. hlei ga:
swing (hanging seat)	ဒန်း	dan:

91. Villa. Mansion

country house	တောအိမ်	to: ein
villa (seaside ~)	ကမ်းခြေအပန်းဖြေအိမ်	kan: gjei apan: hpjei ein
wing (~ of a building)	တံစက်မြိတ်	toun ze' mei'

garden	ဥယျာဉ်	u. jin
park	ပန်းရံ	pan: gjan
conservatory (greenhouse)	ဖန်လုံအိမ်	hpan ain
to look after (garden, etc.)	ပြုစုစောင့်ရှောက်သည်	pju. zu. zaun. shau' te

swimming pool	ရေကူးကန်	jei ku: gan
gym (home gym)	အိမ်တွင်း ကျွန်းမာ ရေးလေ့ကျင့်ရုံ	ein dwin: gjan: ma jei: lei. gjin. joun
tennis court	တင်းနစ်ကွင်း	tin: ni' kwin:
home theater (room)	အိမ်တွင်း ရုပ်ရှင်ရုံ	ein dwin: jou' shin joun
garage	ဂိုဒေါင်	gou daun

| private property | တသီးပုဂ္ဂလိက ပိုင်ဆိုင်မြေ၊ပစ္စည်း | tadhi: pou' ga li ka. bain: zain mjei pji' si: |
| private land | တသီးပုဂ္ဂလိက ပိုင်နယ်မြေ | tadhi: pou' ga li ka. bain: mjei |

| warning (caution) | သတိပေးချက် | dhadi. pei gje' |
| warning sign | သတိပေးဆိုင်းပုဒ် | dhadi. pei zain: bou' |

security	လုံခြုံရေး	loun gjoun jei:
security guard	လုံခြုံရေးအစောင့်	loun gjoun jei: asaun.
burglar alarm	သူခိုးလှန် ခေါင်းလောင်း	thu khou: hlan. khaun: laun:

92. Castle. Palace

castle	ရဲတိုက်	je: dai'
palace	နန်းတော်	nan do
fortress	ခံတပ်ကြီး	khwan da' kji:

wall (round castle)	ရဲတိုက်နံရံဝိုင်း	je: dai' nan jan wain:
tower	မျှော်စင်	hmjo zin
keep, donjon	ရဲတိုက်ဗဟို မျှော်စင်ခံတပ်ကြီး	je: dai' ba. hou hmjo zin gan ta' kji:
portcullis	ဆိုင်းကြီးသုံးသပ် ကွန်ရက်တံခါးကြီး	hsain: kjou: dhoun: dhan kwan ja' dan ga: kji:

underground passage	မြေအောက်လမ်း	mjei au' lan:
moat	ကျုံး	kjun:
chain	ကြိုး	kjou:
arrow loop	မြှားတံလွှတ်ပေါက်	hmja: dan hlwa' pau'

magnificent (adj)	ခမ်းနားသော	khan: na: de.
majestic (adj)	ခုံညားထည်ဝါသော	khan nja: hte wa de.
impregnable (adj)	မထိုးဖောက်နိုင်သော	ma. dou: bau' nein de.
medieval (adj)	အလယ်ခေတ်နှင့်ဆိုင်သော	ale khei' hnin. zain de.

93. Apartment

apartment	တိုက်ခန်း	tai' khan:
room	အခန်း	akhan:
bedroom	အိပ်ခန်း	ei' khan:
dining room	ထမင်းစားခန်း	htamin: za: gan:
living room	ဧည့်ခန်း	e. gan:
study (home office)	အိမ်တွင်းရုံးခန်းလေး	ein dwin: joun: gan: lei:

| entry room | ဝင်ပေါက် | win bau' |
| bathroom (room with a bath or shower) | ရေချိုးခန်း | jei gjou gan: |

| half bath | အိမ်သာ | ein dha |

ceiling	မျက်နှာကြက်	mje' hna gje'
floor	ကြမ်းပြင်	kan: pjin
corner	ထောင့်	htaun.

94. Apartment. Cleaning

| to clean (vi, vt) | သန့်ရှင်းရေးလုပ်သည် | than. shin: jei' lou' te |
| to put away (to stow) | သန့်ရှင်းရေးလုပ်သည် | than. shin: jei' lou' te |

dust	ဖုန်	hpoun
dusty (adj)	ဖုန်ထူသော	hpoun du de.
to dust (vt)	ဖုန်သုတ်သည်	hpoun dou' te
vacuum cleaner	ဖုန်စုပ်စက်	hpoun zou' se'
to vacuum (vt)	ဖုန်စုပ်စက်ဖြင့် စုပ်သည်	hpoun zou' se' chin. zou' te
to sweep (vi, vt)	တံမြက်စည်းလှည်းသည်	tan mje' si: hle: de
sweepings	အမှိုက်များ	ahmai' mja:
order	စနစ်တကျ	sani' ta. gja.
disorder, mess	ရှုပ်ပွေခြင်း	shou' pwei gjin:

| mop | လက်ကိုင်ရှည်ကြမ်းသုတ်ဖဝါ | le' kain she gjan: dhou' hpa' |

dust cloth	ဖုန်သုတ်အဝတ်	hpoun dou' awu'
short broom	တံမြက်စည်း	tan mje' si:
dustpan	အမှိုက်ကော	ahmai' go

95

95. Furniture. Interior

furniture	ပရိဘောဂ	pa ri. bo: ga.
table	စားပွဲ	sa: bwe:
chair	ကုလားထိုင်	kala: dain
bed	ကုတင်	ku din
couch, sofa	ဆိုဖာ	hsou hpa
armchair	လက်တင်ပါသောကုလားထိုင်	le' tin ba dho: ku. la: dain
bookcase	စာအုပ်စင်	sa ou' sin
shelf	စင်	sin
wardrobe	ဗီရို	bi jou
coat rack (wall-mounted ~)	နံရံကပ်အဝတ်ချိတ်စင်	nan jan ga' awu' gei' zin
coat stand	အဝတ်ချိတ်စင်	awu' gjei' sin
bureau, dresser	အံဆွဲပါ မှန်တင်ခုံ	an. zwe: pa hman din khoun
coffee table	စားပွဲပု	sa: bwe: bu.
mirror	မှန်	hman
carpet	ကော်ဇော	ko zo:
rug, small carpet	ကော်ဇော	ko zo:
fireplace	မီးလင်းဗို	mi: lin: bou
candle	ဖယောင်းတိုင်	hpa. jaun dain
candlestick	ဖယောင်းတိုင်စိုက်သောတိုင်	hpa. jaun dain zou' tho dain
drapes	ခန်းဆီးရည်	khan: zi: shei
wallpaper	နံရံကပ်စက္ကူ	nan jan ga' se' ku
blinds (jalousie)	ယင်းလိပ်	jin: lei'
table lamp	စားပွဲတင်မီးအိမ်	sa: bwe: din mi: ein
wall lamp (sconce)	နံရံကပ်မီး	nan jan ga' mi:
floor lamp	မတ်တတ်မီးစဆလောင်း	ma' ta' mi: za. laun:
chandelier	မီးပန်းဆိုင်း	mi: ban: zain:
leg (of chair, table)	ခြေထောက်	chei htau'
armrest	လက်တန်း	le' tan:
back (backrest)	နောက်မီ	nau' mi
drawer	အံဆွဲ	an. zwe:

96. Bedding

bedclothes	အိပ်ရာခင်းများ	ei' ja khin: mja:
pillow	ခေါင်းအုံး	gaun: oun:
pillowcase	ခေါင်းအုပ်	gaun: zu'
duvet, comforter	စောင်	saun

| sheet | အိပ်ရာခင်း | ei' ja khin: |
| bedspread | အိပ်ရာဖုံး | ei' ja hpoun: |

97. Kitchen

kitchen	မီးဖိုခန်း	mi: bou gan:
gas	ဓာတ်ငွေ့	da' ngwei.
gas stove (range)	ဂတ်စ်မီးဖို	ga' s mi; bou
electric stove	လျှပ်စစ်မီးဖို	hlja' si' si: bou
oven	မုန့် ဖုတ်ရန်ဖို	moun. bou' jan bou
microwave oven	မိုက်ခရိုဝေ့ဗ်	mou' kha. jou wei. b

refrigerator	ရေခဲသေတ္တာ	je ge: dhi' ta
freezer	ရေခဲခန်း	jei ge: gan:
dishwasher	ပန်းကန်ဆေးစက်	bagan: zei ze'

meat grinder	အသားကြိတ်စက်	atha: kjei' za'
juicer	အသီးဖျော်စက်	athi: hpjo ze'
toaster	ပေါင်မုန့်ကင်စက်	paun moun. gin ze'
mixer	မွှေစက်	hmwei ze'

coffee machine	ကော်ဖီဖျော်စက်	ko hpi hpjo ze'
coffee pot	ကော်ဖီအိုး	ko hpi ou:
coffee grinder	ကော်ဖီကြိတ်စက်	ko hpi kjei ze'

kettle	ရေနွေးကရားအိုး	jei nwei: gaja: ou:
teapot	လက်ဘက်ရည်အိုး	le' be' ji ou:
lid	အိုးအဖုံး	ou: ahpoun:
tea strainer	လက်ဖက်ရည်စစ်	le' hpe' ji zi'

spoon	ဇွန်း	zun:
teaspoon	လက်ဖက်ရည်ဇွန်း	le' hpe' ji zwan:
soup spoon	အရည်သောက်ဇွန်း	aja: dhau' zun:
fork	ခက်ရင်း	khajin:
knife	ဓား	da:

tableware (dishes)	အိုးခွက်ပန်းကန်	ou: kwe' pan: gan
plate (dinner ~)	ပန်းကန်ပြား	bagan: bja:
saucer	အောက်ခံပန်းကန်ပြား	au' khan ban: kan pja:

shot glass	ဖန်ခွက်	hpan gwe'
glass (tumbler)	ဖန်ခွက်	hpan gwe'
cup	ခွက်	khwe'

sugar bowl	သကြားခွက်	dhagja: khwe'
salt shaker	ဆားဘူး	hsa: bu:
pepper shaker	ငြုတ်ကောင်းဘူး	njou' kaun: bu:
butter dish	ထောပတ်ခွက်	hto: ba' khwe'
stock pot (soup pot)	ပေါင်းအိုး	paun: ou:
frying pan (skillet)	ဟင်းကြော်အိုး	hin: gjo ou:

ladle	ဟင်းခပ်ဇွန်း	hin: ga' zun
colander	ဆန့်ခါ	zaga
tray (serving ~)	လင်ပန်း	lin ban:
bottle	ပုလင်း	palin:
jar (glass)	ဖန်ဘူး	hpan bu:
can	သံဘူး	than bu:
bottle opener	ပုလင်းဖောက်တံ	pu. lin: bau' tan
can opener	သံဘူးဖောက်တံ	than bu: bau' tan
corkscrew	ဝက်အူဖောက်တံ	we' u bau' dan
filter	ရေစစ်	jei zi'
to filter (vt)	စစ်သည်	si' te
trash, garbage (food waste, etc.)	အမှိုက်	ahmai'
trash can (kitchen ~)	အမှိုက်ပုံး	ahmai' poun:

98. Bathroom

bathroom	ရေချိုးခန်း	jei gjou gan:
water	ရေ	jei
faucet	ရေပိုက်ခေါင်း	jei bai' khaun:
hot water	ရေပူ	jei bu
cold water	ရေအေး	jei ei:
toothpaste	သွားတိုက်ဆေး	thwa: tai' hsei:
to brush one's teeth	သွားတိုက်သည်	thwa: tai' te
toothbrush	သွားတိုက်တံ	thwa: tai' tan
to shave (vi)	ရိတ်သည်	jei' te
shaving foam	မုတ်ဆိတ်ညှို့ရိတ်သုံး	mou' hsei' jei' thoun:
	ဆပ်ပြာမြှုပ်	za' pja hmjou'
razor	သင်တုန်းဓား	thin toun: da:
to wash (one's hands, etc.)	ဆေးသည်	hsei: de
to take a bath	ရေချိုးသည်	jei gjou: de
shower	ရေပန်း	jei ban:
to take a shower	ရေချိုးသည်	jei gjou: de
bathtub	ရေချိုးကန်	jei gjou: gan
toilet (toilet bowl)	အိမ်သာ	ein dha
sink (washbasin)	လက်ဆေးကန်	le' hsei: kan
soap	ဆပ်ပြာ	hsa' pja
soap dish	ဆပ်ပြာခွက်	hsa' pja gwe'
sponge	ရေမြှုပ်	jei hmjou'
shampoo	ခေါင်းလျှော်ရည်	gaun: sho je
towel	တဘက်	tabe'

bathrobe	ရေချိုးခန်းဝတ်စုံ	jei gjou: gan: wu' soun
laundry (laundering)	အဝတ်လျှော်ခြင်း	awu' sho gjin
washing machine	အဝတ်လျှော်စက်	awu' sho ze'
to do the laundry	ဒီဘီလျှော်သည်	dou bi jo de
laundry detergent	အဝတ်လျှော်ဆပ်ပြာမှုန့်	awu' sho hsa' pja hmun.

99. Household appliances

TV set	ရုပ်မြင်သံကြားစက်	jou' mjin dhan gja: ze'
tape recorder	အသံသွင်းစက်	athan dhwin: za'
VCR (video recorder)	ဗီဒီယိုပြစက်	bi di jou bja. ze'
radio	ရေဒီယို	rei di jou
player (CD, MP3, etc.)	ပလေယာစက်	pa. lei ja ze'

video projector	ဗီဒီယိုပရိုဂျက်တာ	bi di jou pa. jou gje' da
home movie theater	အိမ်တွင်းရုပ်ရှင်ခန်း	ein dwin: jou' shin gan:
DVD player	ဒီဗီဒီပလေယာ	di bi di ba lei ja
amplifier	အသံချဲ့စက်	athan che. zek
video game console	ဂိမ်းခလုတ်	gein: kha lou'

video camera	ဗွီဒီယိုကင်မရာ	bwi di jou kin ma. ja
camera (photo)	ကင်မရာ	kin ma. ja
digital camera	ဒီဂျစ်တယ်ကင်မရာ	digji' te gin ma. ja

vacuum cleaner	ဖုန်စုပ်စက်	hpoun zou' se'
iron (e.g., steam ~)	မီးပူ	mi: bu
ironing board	မီးပူပွတ်တိုက်ရန်စင်	mi: bu tai' jan zin

telephone	တယ်လီဖုန်း	te li hpoun:
cell phone	မိုဘိုင်းဖုန်း	mou bain: hpoun:
typewriter	လက်နှိပ်စက်	le' hnei' se'
sewing machine	အပ်ချုပ်စက်	a' chou' se'

microphone	စကားပြောခွက်	zaga: bjo: gwe'
headphones	နားကြပ်	na: kja'
remote control (TV)	အဝေးထိန်းကိရိယာ	awei: htin: ki. ja. ja

CD, compact disc	စီဒီပြား	si di bja:
cassette, tape	တိပ်ခွေ	tei' khwei
vinyl record	ရှေးခေတ်သုံးဓာတ်ပြား	shei: gi' thoun da' pja:

100. Repairs. Renovation

renovations	အသစ်ပြုပြင်ဆောက်လုပ်ခြင်း	athi' pju. bin zau' lou' chin:
to renovate (vt)	အသစ်ပြုပြင်ဆောက်လုပ်သည်	athi' pju. bin zau' lou' te
to repair, to fix (vt)	ပြန်လည်ပြင်ဆင်သည်	pjan le bjin zin de
to put in order	အစီအစဉ်တကျထားသည်	asi asin da. gja. da: de

to redo (do again)	ပြန်လည်ပြုပြင်သည်	pjan le bju. bjin de
paint	သုတ်ဆေး	thou' hsei:
to paint (~ a wall)	ဆေးသုတ်သည်	hsei: dhou' te
house painter	အိမ်ဆေးသုတ်သူ	ein zei: dhou' thu
paintbrush	ဆေးသုတ်တံ	hsei: dhou' tan

| whitewash | ထုံး | htoun: |
| to whitewash (vt) | ထုံးသုတ်သည် | htoun: dhou' te |

wallpaper	နံရံကပ်စက္ကူ	nan jan ga' se' ku
to wallpaper (vt)	နံရံစက္ကူကပ်သည်	nan ja' se' ku ga' te
varnish	အရောင်တင်ဆီ	ajaun din zi
to varnish (vt)	အရောင်တင်သည်	ajaun din de

101. Plumbing

water	ရေ	jei
hot water	ရေပူ	jei bu
cold water	ရေအေး	jei ei;
faucet	ရေပိုက်ခေါင်း	jei bai' khaun:

drop (of water)	ရေစက်	jei ze'
to drip (vi)	ရေစက်ကျသည်	jei ze' kja. de
to leak (ab. pipe)	ယိုစိမ့်သည်	jou zein. de
leak (pipe ~)	ယိုပေါက်	jou bau'
puddle	ရေအိုင်	jei ain

pipe	ရေပိုက်	jei bai'
valve (e.g., ball ~)	အဖွင့်အပိတ်လေဗာတ်	ahpwin apei' khalou'
to be clogged up	အပေါက်ဆို့သည်	apau' zou. de

tools	ကိရိယာများ	ki. ji. ja mja:
adjustable wrench	ရှရင်	khwa shin
to unscrew (lid, filter, etc.)	ဖြုတ်သည်	hpjei: de
to screw (tighten)	ဝက်အူကျပ်သည်	we' u gja' te

to unclog (vt)	ဆို့နေသည့်ကို	hsou. nei de gou
	ပြန်ဖွင့်သည်	bjan bwin. de
plumber	ပိုက်ပြင်သူ	pai' bjin dhu
basement	မြေအောက်ခန်း	mjei au' khan:
sewerage (system)	မိလ္လာစနစ်	mein la zani'

102. Fire. Conflagration

fire (accident)	မီး	mi:
flame	မီးတောက်	mi: tau'
spark	မီးပွါး	mi: bwa;
smoke (from fire)	မီးခိုး	mi: gou:

torch (flaming stick)	မီးတုတ်	mi: dou'
campfire	မီးပုံ	mi: boun
gas, gasoline	လောင်စာ	laun za
kerosene (type of fuel)	ရေနံဆီ	jei nan zi
flammable (adj)	မီးလောင်လွယ်သော	mi: laun lwe de.
explosive (adj)	ပေါက်ကွဲစေသော	pau' kwe: zei de.
NO SMOKING	ဆေးလိပ်မသောက်ရ	hsei: lei' ma. dhau' ja.
safety	ဘေးကင်းမှု	bei: gin: hmu
danger	အန္တရာယ်	an dare
dangerous (adj)	အန္တရာယ်ရှိသော	an dare shi. de.
to catch fire	မတော်တဆမီးစွဲသည်	ma. do da. za. mi: zwe: de
explosion	ပေါက်ကွဲမှု	pau' kwe: hmu.
to set fire	မီးရှို့သည်	mi: shou' de
arsonist	မီးရှို့မှုကျူး လွန်သူ	mi: shou' hmu. gju: lun dhu
arson	မီးရှို့မှု	mi: shou' hmu.
to blaze (vi)	မီးတောက်ကြီး	mi: tau' kji:
to burn (be on fire)	မီးလောင်သည်	mi: laun de
to burn down	မီးကျွမ်းသည်	mi: kjwan: de
to call the fire department	မီးသတ်ဌာနသို့ အကြောင်းကြားသည်	mi: dha' hta. na. dhou akjaun: gja: de
firefighter, fireman	မီးသတ်သမား	mi: tha' dhama:
fire truck	မီးသတ်ကား	mi: tha' ka:
fire department	မီးသတ်ဦးစီးဌာန	mi: dha' i: zi: hta. na.
fire truck ladder	မီးသတ်လှေကား	mi: tha' hlei ga:
fire hose	မီးသတ်ပိုက်	mi: tha' bai'
fire extinguisher	မီးသတ်ဘူး	mi: tha' bu:
helmet	ဟဲလ်မက်ဦးထုပ်	he: l me u: htou'
siren	အရှက်ပေးညံသံ	ache' pei: ou' o: dhan
to cry (for help)	အကူအညီအော်ဟစ်တောင်း ခံသည်	aku anji o hi' taun: gan de.
to call for help	အကူအညီတောင်းသည်	aku anji daun: de
rescuer	ကယ်ဆယ်သူ	ke ze dhu
to rescue (vt)	ကယ်ဆယ်သည်	ke ze de
to arrive (vi)	ရောက်ရှိသည်	jau' shi. de
to extinguish (vt)	မီးသတ်သည်	mi: tha' de
water	ရေ	jei
sand	သဲ	the:
ruins (destruction)	အပျက်အစီး	apje' asi:
to collapse (building, etc.)	ယိုယွင်းသည်	jou jwin: de
to fall down (vi)	ပြိုကျသည်	pjou gja. de
to cave in (ceiling, floor)	ပြိုကျသည်	pjou gja de
piece of debris	အကျိုးအပဲ့	akjou: ape.

ash	မြာ	pja
to suffocate (die)	အသက်ရှူကျပ်သည်	athe' shu gja' te
to be killed (perish)	အသတ်ခံရသည်	atha' khan ja. de

HUMAN ACTIVITIES

Job. Business. Part 1

office (company ~)	ရုံး	joun:
office (of director, etc.)	ရုံးခန်း	joun: gan:
reception desk	ကြိုဆိုလက်ခံရာနေရာ	kjou hsou le' khan ja nei ja
secretary	အတွင်းရေးမှူး	atwin: jei: hmu:
secretary (fem.)	အတွင်းရေးမှူးမ	atwin: jei: hmu: ma
director	ဒါရိုက်တာ	da je' ta
manager	မန်နေဂျာ	man nei gji
accountant	စာရင်းကိုင်	sajin: gain
employee	ဝန်ထမ်း	wun dan:
furniture	ပရိဘောဂ	pa ri. bo: ga.
desk	စားပွဲ	sa: bwe:
desk chair	အလုပ်ထိုင်ခုံ	alou' htain goun
drawer unit	အံဆွဲပါသောပ	an. zwe: dho: pa.
	ရိဘောဂအစုံ	ji. bo: ga. soun
coat stand	ကုတ်အင်္ကျီချိတ်စင်	kou' akji gji' sin
computer	ကွန်ပျူတာ	kun pju ta
printer	ပုံနှိပ်စက်	poun nei' se'
fax machine	ဖက်စ်ကူးစက်	hpe's ku: ze'
photocopier	ဓာတ်ပုံကူးစက်	da' poun gu: ze'
paper	စက္ကူ	se' ku
office supplies	ရုံးသုံးကိရိယာများ	joun: dhoun: gi. ji. ja mja:
mouse pad	မောက်စ်အောက်ခံပြား	mau's au' gan bja:
sheet (of paper)	အရွက်	ajwa'
binder	ဖိုင်	hpain
catalog	စာရင်း	sajin:
phone directory	ဖုန်းလမ်းညွှန်	hpoun: lan: hnjun
documentation	မှတ်တမ်းတင်ခြင်း	hma' tan: din gjin:
brochure	ကြော်ငြာစာစောင်	kjo nja za zaun
(e.g., 12 pages ~)		
leaflet (promotional ~)	လက်ကမ်းစာစောင်	le' kan: za zaun:
sample	နမူနာ	na. mu na
training meeting	လေ့ကျင့်ရေးအစည်းအဝေး	lei. kjin. jei: asi: awei:
meeting (of managers)	အစည်းအဝေး	asi: awei:

lunch time	နေ့လည်စာစားချိန်	nei. le za za: gjein
to make a copy	မိတ္တူကူးသည်	mi' tu gu: de
to make multiple copies	မိတ္တူကူးသည်	mi' tu gu: de
to receive a fax	ဖက်စ်လက်ခံရရှိသည်	hpe's le' khan ja. shi. de
to send a fax	ဖက်စ်ပို့သည်	hpe's pou. de
to call (by phone)	ဖုန်းဆက်သည်	hpoun: ze' te
to answer (vt)	ဖြေသည်	hpjei de
to put through	ဆက်သွယ်သည်	hse' thwe de
to arrange, to set up	စီစဉ်သည်	si zin de
to demonstrate (vt)	သရုပ်ပြသည်	thajou' pja. de
to be absent	ပျက်ကွက်သည်	pje' kwe' te
absence	ပျက်ကွက်ခြင်း	pje' kwe' chin

104. Business processes. Part 1

business	လုပ်ငန်း	lou' ngan:
occupation	လုပ်ဆောင်မှု	lou' hsaun hmu.
firm	စီးပွားရေးလုပ်ငန်း	si: bwa: jei: lou' ngan:
company	ကုမ္ပဏီ	koun pani
corporation	ကော်ပိုရေးရှင်း	ko bou jei: shin:
enterprise	စီးပွားရေးလုပ်ငန်း	si: bwa: jei: lou' ngan:
agency	ကိုယ်စားလှယ်လုပ်ငန်း	kou za: hle lou' ngan:
agreement (contract)	သဘောတူညီမှုစာချုပ်	dhabo: tu nji hmu. za gjou'
contract	ကန်ထထရိုက်	kan ta jou'
deal	အပေးအယူ	apei: aju
order (to place an ~)	ကြိုတင်မှာယူခြင်း	kjou din hma ju chin:
terms (of the contract)	စည်းကမ်းချက်	si: kan: gje'
wholesale (adv)	လက်ကား	le' ka:
wholesale (adj)	လက်ကားဖြစ်သော	le' ka: bji' te.
wholesale (n)	လက်ကားရောင်းချမှု	le' ka: jaun: gja. hmu.
retail (adj)	လက်လီစနစ်	le' li za. ni'
retail (n)	လက်လီရောင်းချမှု	le' li jaun: gja. hmu.
competitor	ပြိုင်ဘက်	pjain be'
competition	ပြိုင်ဆိုင်မှု	pjain zain hmu
to compete (vi)	ပြိုင်ဆိုင်သည်	pjain zain de
partner (associate)	စီးပွားဖက်	si: bwa: be'
partnership	စီးပွားဖက်ဖြစ်ခြင်း	si: bwa: be' bji' chin:
crisis	အခက်အခဲကာလ	akhe' akhe: ga la.
bankruptcy	ဒေဝါလီခံရခြင်း	dei wa li gan ja gjin
to go bankrupt	ဒေဝါလီခံသည်	dei wa li gan de
difficulty	အခက်အခဲ	akhe' akhe:
problem	ပြဿနာ	pjadhana

catastrophe	ကပ်ဘေး	ka' bei:
economy	စီးပွားရေး	si: bwa: jei:
economic (~ growth)	စီးပွားရေးနှင့်ဆိုင်သော	si: bwa: jei: hnin zain de.
economic recession	စီးပွားရေးကျဆင်းမှု	si: bwa: jei: gja zin: hmu.

| goal (aim) | ပန်းတိုင် | pan: dain |
| task | လုပ်ငန်းတာဝန် | lou' ngan: da wan |

to trade (vi)	ကုန်သွယ်သည်	koun dhwe de
network (distribution ~)	ကွန်ရက်	kun je'
inventory (stock)	ပစ္စည်းစာရင်း	pji' si: za jin:
range (assortment)	အပိုင်းအခြား	apain: acha:

leader (leading company)	ခေါင်းဆောင်	gaun: zaun
large (~ company)	ကြီးမားသော	kji: ma: de.
monopoly	တစ်ဦးတည်းချုပ်ကိုင်ထား	ti' u: te: gjou' kain da:

theory	သီအိုရီ	thi ou ji
practice	လက်တွေ့	le' twei.
experience (in my ~)	အတွေ့အကြုံ	atwei. akjoun
trend (tendency)	ဦးတည်ရာ	u: ti ja
development	ဖွံ့ဖြိုးတိုးတက်မှု	hpjun. bjou: dou: de' hmu.

105. Business processes. Part 2

| profit (foregone ~) | အကျိုးအမြတ် | akjou: amja' |
| profitable (~ deal) | အကျိုးအမြတ်ရှိသော | akjou: amja' shi. de. |

delegation (group)	ကိုယ်စားလှယ်အဖွဲ့	kou za: hle ahpwe.
salary	လစာ	la. za
to correct (an error)	အမှားပြင်သည်	ahma: pjin de
business trip	စီးပွားရေးခရီးစဉ်	si: bwa: jei: khaji: zin
commission	ကော်မရှင်	ko ma. shin

to control (vt)	ထိန်းချုပ်သည်	htein: gjou' te
conference	ဆွေးနွေးပွဲ	hswe: nwe: bwe:
license	လိုင်စင်	lain zin
reliable (~ partner)	ယုံကြည်စိတ်ချရသော	joun kji zei' cha. ja. de.

initiative (undertaking)	စတင်ခြင်း	sa. tin gjin:
norm (standard)	စံနှုန်း	san hnoun:
circumstance	အခြေအနေ	achei anei
duty (of employee)	တာဝန်	ta wun

organization (company)	အဖွဲ့အစည်း	ahpwe. asi:
organization (process)	စီစဉ်ခြင်း	si zin gjin:
organized (adj)	စီစဉ်ထားသော	si zin dha de.
cancellation	ပယ်ဖျက်ခြင်း	pe hpje' chin:
to cancel (call off)	ပယ်ဖျက်သည်	pe hpje' te
report (official ~)	အစီရင်ခံစာ	asi jin gan za

patent	မူပိုင်ခွင့်	mu bain gwin.
to patent (obtain patent)	မူပိုင်ခွင့်မှတ်ပုံတင်သည်	mu bain gwin. hma' poun din de
to plan (vt)	စီစဉ်သည်	si zin de

bonus (money)	အပိုဆုကြေး	apou zu. gjei:
professional (adj)	ပညာရှင်အဆင့်တတ်ကျွမ်းသော	pjin nja ahsin da' kjwan: de.
procedure	လုပ်ထုံးလုပ်နည်း	lou' htoun: lou' ne:

to examine (contract, etc.)	စစ်စားသည်	sin: za: de
calculation	တွက်ချက်ခြင်း	twe' che' chin:
reputation	ဂုဏ်သတင်း	goun dha din:
risk	စွန့်စားခြင်း	sun. za: gjin:

to manage, to run	ညွှန်ကြားသည်	hnjun gja: de
information (report)	သတင်းအချက်အလက်	dhadin: akje' ale'
property	ပိုင်ဆိုင်မှု	pain zain hmu
union	အသင်း	athin:

life insurance	အသက်အာမခံ	athe' ama. khan
to insure (vt)	အာမခံသည်	a ma. gan de
insurance	အာမခံ	a ma. khan

auction (~ sale)	လေလံပွဲ	lei lan bwe:
to notify (inform)	အကြောင်းကြားသည်	akjaun: kja: de
management (process)	အုပ်ချုပ်မှု	ou' chou' hmu.
service (~ industry)	ဝန်ဆောင်မှု	wun: zaun hmu.

forum	ဖိုရမ်	hpou jan
to function (vi)	လည်ပတ်သည်	le ba' te
stage (phase)	အဆင့်	ahsin.
legal (~ services)	ဥပဒေဆိုင်ရာ	u. ba. dei zain ja
lawyer (legal advisor)	ရှေ့နေ	shei. nei

106. Production. Works

plant	စက်ရုံ	se' joun
factory	အလုပ်ရုံ	alou' joun
workshop	ဝပ်ရှော့	wu' sho,
works, production site	ထုတ်လုပ်ရာလုပ်ငန်းခွင်	htou' lou' ja lou' ngan: gwin

industry (manufacturing)	စက်မှုလုပ်ငန်း	se' hmu. lou' ngan:
industrial (adj)	စက်မှုလုပ်ငန်းနှင့်ဆိုင်သော	se' hmu. lou' ngan: hnin. zain de.
heavy industry	အကြီးစားစက်မှုလုပ်ငန်း	akji: za: ze' hmu. lou' ngan:
light industry	အသေးစားစက်မှုလုပ်ငန်း	athei: za: za' hmu. lou' ngan:
products	ထုတ်ကုန်	htou' koun

to produce (vt)	ထုတ်လုပ်သည်	tou' lou' te
raw materials	ကုန်ကြမ်း	koun gjan:
foreman (construction ~)	အလုပ်သမားခေါင်း	alou' dha ma: gaun:
workers team (crew)	အလုပ်သမားအဖွဲ့	alou' dha ma: ahpwe.
worker	အလုပ်သမား	alou' dha ma:
working day	ရုံးဖွင့်ရက်	joun: hpwin je'
pause (rest break)	ရပ်နားခြင်း	ja' na: gjin:
meeting	အစည်းအဝေး	asi: awei:
to discuss (vt)	ဆွေးနွေးသည်	hswe: nwe: de
plan	အစီအစဉ်	asi asin
to fulfill the plan	အကောင်အထည်ဖော်သည်	akaun ahte bo de
rate of output	ကုန်ထုတ်နှုန်း	koun dou' hnan:
quality	အရည်အသွေး	aji athwei:
control (checking)	စစ်ဆေးခြင်း	si' hsei: gjin:
quality control	အရည်အသွေးစစ်ဆေး	aji athwei: za' hsei:
	သုံးသပ်မှု	thon dha' hma
workplace safety	လုပ်ငန်းခွင်လုံ	lou' ngan: gwin loun
	ခြုံမှု	gjun hmu.
discipline	စည်းကမ်း	si: kan:
violation	ချိုးဖောက်ခြင်း	chou: hpau' chin:
(of safety rules, etc.)		
to violate (rules)	ချိုးဖောက်သည်	chou: hpau' te
strike	သပိတ်မှောက်ခြင်း	thabei' hmau' chin:
striker	သပိတ်မှောက်သူ	thabei' hmau' thu
to be on strike	သပိတ်မှောက်သည်	thabei' hmau' te
labor union	အလုပ်သမားသမဂ္ဂ	alou' dha ma: dha. me' ga
to invent (machine, etc.)	တီထွင်သည်	ti htwin de
invention	တီထွင်မှု	ti htwin hmu.
research	သုတေသန	thu. tei thana
to improve (make better)	တိုးတက်ကောင်းမွန်စေသည်	tou: te' kaun: mun zei de
technology	နည်းပညာ	ne: bi nja
technical drawing	နည်းပညာဆိုင်ရာပုံကြမ်း	ne bi nja zain ja boun gjan:
load, cargo	ဝန်	wun
loader (person)	ကုန်ထမ်းသမား	koun din dhama:
to load (vehicle, etc.)	ကုန်တင်သည်	koun din de
loading (process)	ကုန်တင်ခြင်း	koun din gjin
to unload (vi, vt)	ကုန်ချသည်	koun gja de
unloading	ကုန်ချခြင်း	koun gja gjin:
transportation	သယ်ယူပို့ဆောင်ရေး	the ju bou. zaun jei:
transportation company	သယ်ယူပို့ဆောင်ရေး	the ju bou. zaun jei:
	ကုမ္ပဏီ	koun pa. ni
to transport (vt)	ပို့ဆောင်သည်	pou. zaun de
freight car	တွဲ	twe:
tank (e.g., oil ~)	တိုင်ကီ	tain ki

107

truck	ကုန်တင်ကား	koun din ka:
machine tool	ဖြတ်စက်	hpja' se'
mechanism	စက်ကိရိယာ	se' kari. ja

industrial waste	စက်ရှုံနဲ့ပစ်ပစ္စည်း	se' joun zun bi' pji' si:
packing (process)	ထုတ်ပိုးမှု	htou' pou: hmu.
to pack (vt)	ထုတ်ပိုးသည်	htou' pou: de

107. Contract. Agreement

contract	ကန်ထရိုက်	kan ta jou'
agreement	သဘောတူညီမှု	dhabo: tu nji hmu.
addendum	ပူးတွဲ	pu: twe:

to sign a contract	သဘောတူစာချုပ်ချုပ်သည်	dhabo: tu za gjou' gjou' te
signature	လက်မှတ်	le' hma'
to sign (vt)	လက်မှတ်ထိုးသည်	le' hma' htou: de
seal (stamp)	တံဆိပ်	da zei'

subject of the contract	သဘောတူညီမှု- အကြောင်းအရာ	dhabo: tu nji hmu. akjaun: aja
clause	အပိုဒ်ငယ်	apai' nge
parties (in contract)	စာချုပ်ပါအဖွဲ့များ	sa gjou' pa ahpwe. mja:
legal address	တရားဝင်နေရပ်လိပ်စာ	taja: win nei ja' lei' sa

to violate the contract	သဘောတူညီမှု ချိုးဖောက်သည်	dhabo: tu nji hmu. gjou: bau' te
commitment (obligation)	အထူးသဖြင့်	a htu: dha. hjin.
responsibility	တာဝန်ဝတ္တရား	ta wun wu' taja:
force majeure	မလွန်ဆန်နိုင်သောအဖြစ်	ma. lun zan nain de. ahpji'
dispute	အငြင်းအခုံ	anjin: akhoun
penalties	ပြစ်ဒဏ်များ	pji' dan mja:

108. Import & Export

import	သွင်းကုန်	thwin: goun
importer	သွင်းကုန်လုပ်ငန်းရှင်	thwin: goun lou' ngan: shin
to import (vt)	တင်သွင်းသည်	tin dhwin: de
import (as adj.)	သွင်းကုန်နှင့်ဆိုင်သော	thwin: goun hnin. zain de.

export (exportation)	ပို့ကုန်	pou. goun
exporter	ပို့ကုန်လုပ်ငန်းရှင်	pou. goun lou' ngan: shin
to export (vi, vt)	ကုန်တင်ပို့သည်	koun tin pou. de
export (as adj.)	တင်ပို့သော	tin bou. de.

goods (merchandise)	ကုန်ပစ္စည်း	koun pji' si:
consignment, lot	ပို့ကုန်	pou. goun
weight	အလေးချိန်	alei: gjein

volume	ပမာဏ	pa. ma na.
cubic meter	ကုဗမီတာ	ku. ba mi ta
manufacturer	ထုတ်လုပ်သူ	tou' lou' thu
transportation company	သယ်ယူပို့ဆောင်ရေး ကုမ္ပဏီ	the ju bou. zaun jei: koun pa. ni
container	ကွန်တိန်နာ	kun tein na
border	နယ်နိမိတ်	ne ni. mei'
customs	အကောက်ခွန်	akau' khun
customs duty	အကောက်ခွန်နှုန်း	akau' khun hnoun:
customs officer	အကောက်ခွန်အရာရှိ	akau' khun aja shi.
smuggling	မှောင်ခို	hmaun gou
contraband (smuggled goods)	မှောင်ခိုပစ္စည်း	hmaun gou pji' si:

109. Finances

stock (share)	စတော့ရှယ်ယာ	sato, shera
bond (certificate)	ငွေချေးစာချုပ်	ngwei gjei: za gju'
promissory note	ငွေပေးချေရန် ကတိစာချုပ်	ngwei bei: gjei jan ga. di. za gju'
stock exchange	စတော့ရှယ်ယာဈိုင်	sato. shera dain
stock price	စတော့ဈေးနှုန်း	sato. zei: hnoun:
to go down (become cheaper)	ဈေးနှုန်းကျဆင်းသည်	zei: hnan: gja. zin: de
to go up (become more expensive)	ဈေးနှုန်းတက်သည်	zei: hnan: de' de
share	ရှယ်ယာ	she ja
controlling interest	ရှယ်ပုဒ္ဒအများစုကို ပိုင်ဆိုင်ခြင်း	she ja amja: zu. gou bain zain gjin:
investment	ရင်းနှီးမြှုပ်နှံမှု	jin: hni: hmjou' hnan hmu.
to invest (vt)	ရင်းနှီးမြှုပ်နှံသည်	jin: hni: hmjou' hnan de
percent	ရာခိုင်နှုန်း	ja gain hnan:
interest (on investment)	အတိုး	atou:
profit	အမြတ်	amja'
profitable (adj)	အမြတ်ရသော	amja' ja de.
tax	အခွန်	akhun
currency (foreign ~)	ငွေကြေး	ngwei kjei:
national (adj)	အမျိုးသားနှင့်ဆိုင်သော	amjou: dha: hnin. zain de.
exchange (currency ~)	လဲလှယ်ခြင်း	le: hle gjin:
accountant	စာရင်းကိုင်	sajin: gain
accounting	စာရင်းကိုင်လုပ်ငန်း	sajin: gain lou' ngan:

bankruptcy	ဒေဝါလီခံရခြင်း	dei wa li gan ja gjin
collapse, crash	ရုတ်တရက်ပြိုးပွဲးရေး ထိုးကျခြင်း	jou' ta ja' si: bwa: jei: dou: gja. gjin:
ruin	ကြီးစွာသောအပျက်အစီး	kji: zwa dho apje' asi:
to be ruined (financially)	ပျက်စီးဆုံးရှုံးသည်	pje' si: zoun: shoun: de
inflation	ငွေကြေးဖောင်းပွခြင်း	ngwei kjei: baun: bwa. gjin:
devaluation	ငွေကြေးတန် ဖိုးရှခြင်း	ngwei kjei: dan bou: gja gjin:
capital	အရင်းအနှီးငွေ	ajin: ani: ngwei
income	ဝင်ငွေ	win ngwei
turnover	အနှတ်အသိမ်း	anou' athin:
resources	အရင်းအမြစ်များ	ajin: amja' mja:
monetary resources	ငွေကြေးအရင်းအမြစ်များ	ngwei kjei: ajin: amji' mja:
overhead	အထွေထွေ အသုံးစရိတ်	a htwei htwei athoun: za. jei'
to reduce (expenses)	လျှော့ချသည်	sho. cha. de

110. Marketing

marketing	ဈေးကွက်ရှာဖွေရေး	zei: gwe' sha bwei jei:
market	ဈေးကွက်	zei: gwe'
market segment	ဈေးကွက်အစိတ်အပိုင်း	zei: gwe' asei' apain:
product	ထုတ်ကုန်	htou' koun
goods (merchandise)	ကုန်ပစ္စည်း	koun pji' si:
brand	အမှတ်တံဆိပ်	ahma' tan zin
trademark	ကုန်အမှတ်တံဆိပ်	koun ahma' tan hsi'
logotype	မူပိုင်အမှတ်တံဆိပ်	mu bain ahma' dan zei'
logo	တံဆိပ်	da zei'
demand	တောင်းဆိုချက်	taun: hsou che'
supply	ထောက်ပံ့ခြင်း	htau' pan. gjin:
need	လိုအပ်မှု	lou a' hmu.
consumer	သုံးစွဲသူ	thoun: zwe: dhu
analysis	ခွဲခြမ်းစိတ်ဖြာခြင်း	khwe: gjan: zei' hpa gjin:
to analyze (vt)	ခွဲခြမ်းစိတ်ဖြာသည်	khwe: gjan: zei' hpa de
positioning	နေရာရှာခြင်း	nei ja hja gjin:
to position (vt)	နေရာရှာသည်	nei ja sha de
price	ဈေးနှုန်း	zei: hnan:
pricing policy	ဈေးနှုန်းမူဝါဒ	zei: hnan: m wada.
price formation	ဈေးနှုန်းဖြစ်တည်ခြင်း	zei: hnan: bji' te gjin:

111. Advertising

advertising	ကြော်ငြာ	kjo nja
to advertise (vt)	ကြော်ငြာသည်	kjo nja de

budget	ဘတ်ဂျက်	ba' gje'
ad, advertisement	ခန့်မှန်းခြေရ သုံးငွေစာရင်း	khan hman: gjei ja. dhu: ngwei za jin:
TV advertising	တီဗီကြော်ငြာ	ti bi gjo nja
radio advertising	ရေဒီယိုကြော်ငြာ	rei di jou gjo nja
outdoor advertising	ပြင်ပကြော်ငြာ	pjin ba. gjo nja
mass media	လူထုဆက်သွယ်ရေး	lu du. ze' thwe jei:
periodical (n)	ပုံမှန်ထုတ် မဂ္ဂဇင်း	poun hmein dou' ma' ga. zin:
image (public appearance)	ပုံရိပ်	poun jei'
slogan	ကြွေးကြော်သံ	kjwei: kjo dhan
motto (maxim)	ဆောင်ပုဒ်	hsaun bou'
campaign	အစီအစဉ်	asi asin
advertising campaign	ကြော်ငြာအစီအစဉ်	kjo nja a si asin
target group	ပစ်မှတ်အုပ်စု	pi' hma' ou'zu.
business card	လုပ်ငန်းသုံးလိပ် စာကဒ်ပြား	lou' ngan: loun: lei' sa ka' pja:
leaflet (promotional ~)	လက်ကမ်းစာစောင်	le' kan: za zaun:
brochure (e.g., 12 pages ~)	ကြော်ငြာစာအုပ်ငယ်	kjo nja za ou' nge
pamphlet	လက်ကမ်းစာစောင်	le' kan: za zaun:
newsletter	သတင်းလွှာ	dhadin: hlwa
signboard (store sign, etc.)	ဆိုင်းဘုတ်	hsain: bou'
poster	ပိုစတာ	pou sata
billboard	ကြော်ငြာဆိုင်းဘုတ်	kjo nja zain: bou'

112. Banking

bank	ဘဏ်	ban
branch (of bank, etc.)	ဘဏ်ခွဲ	ban gwe:
bank clerk, consultant	အတိုင်ပင်ခံပုဂ္ဂိုလ်	atain bin gan bou' gou
manager (director)	မန်နေဂျာ	man nei gji
bank account	ဘဏ်ငွေစာရင်း	ban ngwei za jin
account number	ဘဏ်စာရင်းနံပါတ်	ban zajin: nan. ba'
checking account	ဘဏ်စာရင်းရှင်	ban zajin: shin
savings account	ဘဏ်ငွေစုစာရင်း	ban ngwei zu. za jin
to open an account	ဘဏ်စာရင်းဖွင့်သည်	ban zajin: hpwin de
to close the account	ဘဏ်စာရင်းပိတ်သည်	ban zajin: bi' te
to deposit into the account	ငွေသွင်းသည်	ngwei dhwin: de
to withdraw (vt)	ငွေထုတ်သည်	ngwei dou' te
deposit	အပ်ငွေ	a' ngwei
to make a deposit	ငွေအပ်သည်	ngwei a' te

wire transfer	ကြေးနန်းဖြင့်ငွေလွှဲခြင်း	kjei: nan: bjin. ngwe hlwe: gjin
to wire, to transfer	ကြေးနန်းဖြင့် ငွေလွှဲသည်	kjei: nan: bjin. ngwe hlwe: de
sum	ပေါင်းလဒ်	paun: la'
How much?	ဘယ်လောက်လဲ	be lau' le:
signature	လက်မှတ်	le' hma'
to sign (vt)	လက်မှတ်ထိုးသည်	le' hma' htou: de
credit card	အကြွေးဝယ်ကဒ်- ရေက်ဒစ်ကဒ်	achwei: we ka' - ka' je' da' ka'
code (PIN code)	ကုဒ်နံပါတ်	kou' nan ba'
credit card number	ရေက်ဒစ်ကဒ်နံပါတ်	kha. je' di' ka' nan ba'
ATM	အလိုအလျောက်ငွေထုတ်စက်	alou aljau' ngwei htou' se'
check	ချက်လက်မှတ်	che' le' hma'
to write a check	ချက်ရေးသည်	che' jei: de
checkbook	ချက်စာအုပ်	che' sa ou'
loan (bank ~)	ရေးငွေ	chei: ngwei
to apply for a loan	ရေးငွေလျှောက် လွှာတင်သည်	chei: ngwei shau' hlwa din de
to get a loan	ရေးငွေရယူသည်	chei: ngwei ja. ju de
to give a loan	ရေးငွေထုတ်ပေးသည်	chei: ngwei htou' pei: de
guarantee	အာမခံပစ္စည်း	a ma. gan bji' si:

113. Telephone. Phone conversation

telephone	တယ်လီဖုန်း	te li hpoun:
cell phone	မိုဘိုင်းဖုန်း	mou bain: hpoun:
answering machine	ဖုန်းဘွေးစက်	hpoun: du: ze'
to call (by phone)	ဖုန်းဆက်သည်	hpoun: ze' te
phone call	အဝင်ဖုန်း	awin hpun:
to dial a number	နံပါတ် နှိပ်သည်	nan ba' hnei' te
Hello!	ဟာလို	ha. lou
to ask (vt)	မေးသည်	mei: de
to answer (vi, vt)	ဖြေသည်	hpjei de
to hear (vt)	ကြားသည်	ka: de
well (adv)	ကောင်းကောင်း	kaun: gaun:
not well (adv)	အရမ်းမကောင်း	ajan: ma. gaun:
noises (interference)	ဖြတ်ဝင်သည့်ရှုည်သံ	hpja' win dhi. zu njan dhan
receiver	တယ်လီဖုန်းနားကြပ်ပိုင်း	te li hpoun: na: gja' pain:
to pick up (~ the phone)	ဖုန်းကောက်ကိုင်သည်	hpoun: gau' gain de
to hang up (~ the phone)	ဖုန်းချသည်	hpoun: gja de

busy (engaged)	လိုင်းမအားသော	lain: ma. a: de.
to ring (ab. phone)	မြည်သည်	mji de
telephone book	တယ်လီဖုန်းလမ်း ညွှန်စာအုပ်	te li hpoun: lan: hnjun za ou'
local (adj)	ပြည်တွင်း:ဒေသ တွင်:ဖြစ်သော	pji dwin: dei. dha dwin: bji' te.
local call	ပြည်တွင်းခေါ် ဆိုမှု	pji dwin: go zou hmu.
long distance (~ call)	အဝေးခေါ် ဆိုနိုင်သော	awei: go zou nain de.
long-distance call	အဝေးခေါ် ဆိုမှု	awei: go zou hmu.
international (adj)	အပြည်ပြည်ဆိုင်ရာဖြစ်သော	apji pji zain ja bja' de.
international call	အပြည်ပြည်ဆိုင်ရာခေါ် ဆိုမှု	apji pji zain ja go: zou hmu

114. Cell phone

cell phone	မိုဘိုင်းဖုန်း	mou bain: hpoun:
display	ပြသခြင်း	pja. dha. gjin:
button	ခလုတ်	khalou'
SIM card	ဆင်းကဒ်	hsin: ka'
battery	ဘတ်ထရီ	ba' hta ji
to be dead (battery)	ဖုန်းအားကုန်သည်	hpoun: a: goun: de
charger	အားသွင်းကြိုး	a: dhwin: gjou:
menu	အစားအသောက်စာရင်း	asa: athau' sa jin:
settings	ချိန်ညှိခြင်း	chein hnji. chin:
tune (melody)	တီးလုံး	ti: loun:
to select (vt)	ရွေးချယ်သည်	jwei: che de
calculator	ဂဏန်းပေါင်းစက်	ganan: baun: za'
voice mail	အသံမေးလ်	athan mei:l
alarm clock	နှိုးစက်	hnou: ze'
contacts	ဖုန်းအဆက်အသွယ်များ	hpoun: ase' athwe mja:
SMS (text message)	မက်ဆေ့ရှ်	me' zei. gja
subscriber	အသုံးပြုသူ	athoun: bju. dhu

115. Stationery

ballpoint pen	ဘောပင်	bo pin
fountain pen	ဖောင်တိန်	hpaun din
pencil	ခဲတံ	khe: dan
highlighter	အရောင်တောက်မင်တံ	ajaun dau' min dan
felt-tip pen	ရေးဆေးစုတ်တံ	jei zei: zou' tan
notepad	မှတ်စုစာအုပ်	hma' su. za ou'
agenda (diary)	နေ့စဉ်မှတ်တမ်းစာအုပ်	nei. zin hma' tan: za ou'

ruler	ပေတံ	pei dan
calculator	ဂဏန်းပေါင်းစက်	ganan: baun: za'
eraser	ခဲဖျက်	khe: bje'
thumbtack	ထိပ်ပြားကြီးသံမှို	htei' pja: gji: dhan hmou
paper clip	တွယ်ချိတ်	twe gjei'
glue	ကော်	ko
stapler	စတက်ပလာ	sate' pa. la
hole punch	အပေါက်ဖောက်စက်	apau' hpau' se'
pencil sharpener	ခဲချွန်စက်	khe: chun ze'

116. Various kinds of documents

account (report)	အစီရင်ခံစာ	asi jin gan za
agreement	သဘောတူညီမှု	dhabo: tu nji hmu.
application form	လျှောက်လွှာပုံစံ	shau' hlwa ban zan
authentic (adj)	စစ်မှန်သော	si' hman de.
badge (identity tag)	တံဆိပ်	da zei'
business card	လုပ်ငန်းသုံးလိပ်	lou' ngan: loun: lei'
	စာကဒ်ပြား	sa ka' pja:
certificate (~ of quality)	အသိအမှတ်ပြုလက်မှတ်	athi ahma' pju la' hma'
check (e.g., draw a ~)	ချက်စာချွက်	che' sa jwe'
check (in restaurant)	ကျသင့်ငွေ	kja. thin. ngwei
constitution	ဖွဲ့စည်းပုံအခြေ	hpwe. zi: boun akhei
	ခံဥပဒေ	gan u. ba. dei
contract (agreement)	စာချုပ်	sa gjou'
copy	မိတ္တူ	mi' tu
copy (of contract, etc.)	မိတ္တူ	mi' tu
customs declaration	အကောက်ခွန်ကြေညာချက်	akau' khun gjei nja gje'
document	စာရွက်စာတမ်း	sajwe' zatan:
driver's license	ကားမောင်းလိုင်စင်	ka: maun: lain zin
addendum	ပူးတွဲ	pu: twe:
form	ပုံစံ	poun zan
ID card (e.g., FBI ~)	သက်သေခံကဒ်ပြား	the' thei gan ga' pja:
inquiry (request)	စုံစမ်းမေးမြန်းခြင်း	soun zan: mei: mjan: gjin:
invitation card	ဖိတ်စာကဒ်	hpi' sa ka'
invoice	ငွေတောင်းခံလွှာ	ngwei daun: gan hlwa
law	ဥပဒေ	u. ba. dei
letter (mail)	စာ	sa
letterhead	ကုမ္ပဏီစာတမ်း	koun pani za dan:
	ပါ စာရွက်	ba za jwe'
list (of names, etc.)	စာရင်း	sajin:
manuscript	လက်ရေးစာမူ	le' jei: za mu
newsletter	သတင်းလွှာ	dhadin: hlwa
note (short letter)	မှတ်စု	hma' su.

pass (for worker, visitor)	ဝင်ခွင့်ကဒ်ပြား	win gwin. ga' pja
passport	နိုင်ငံကူးလက်မှတ်	nain ngan gu: le' hma'
permit	ပါမစ်	pa mi'
résumé	ကိုယ်ရေးမှတ်တမ်းအကျဉ်း	kou jei: hma' tan: akjun:
debt note, IOU	ကြွေးမြီဝန်ခံချက်	kjwei: mji wun gan gje'
receipt (for purchase)	လက်ခံရရှိကြောင်းပြေစာ	le' khan ja shi kjaun: bjei za
sales slip, receipt	ငွေရပြေစာ	ngwei ja. bei za
report (mil.)	အစီရင်ခံစာ	asi jin gan za
to show (ID, etc.)	ပြသည်	pja. de
to sign (vt)	လက်မှတ်ထိုးသည်	le' hma' htou: de
signature	လက်မှတ်	le' hma'
seal (stamp)	တံဆိပ်	da zei'
text	စာသား	sa dha:
ticket (for entry)	လက်မှတ်	le' hma'
to cross out	ခြစ်ပစ်သည်	chi' pi' te
to fill out (~ a form)	ဖြည့်သည်	hpjei. de
waybill (shipping invoice)	ကုန်ပို့လွှာ	koun pou. hlwa
will (testament)	သေတမ်းစာ	thei dan: za

117. Kinds of business

accounting services	စာရင်းကိုင်ဝန်ဆောင်မှု	sajin: gain wun zaun hmu.
advertising	ကြော်ငြာ	kjo nja
advertising agency	ကြော်ငြာလုပ်ငန်း	kjo nja lou' ngan:
air-conditioners	လေအေးစက်	lei ei: ze'
airline	လေကြောင်း	lei gjaun:
alcoholic beverages	အရက်သေစာ	aje' dhei za
antiques (antique dealers)	ရှေးဟောင်းပစ္စည်း	shei: haun: bji' si:
art gallery (contemporary ~)	အနုပညာပြခန်း	anu. pjin ja pja. gan:
audit services	စာရင်းစစ်ဆေးခြင်း	sajin: zi' hsei: gjin:
banking industry	ဘဏ်လုပ်ငန်း	ban lou' ngan:
bar	ဘား	ba:
beauty parlor	အလှပြင်ဆိုင်	ahla. bjin zain:
bookstore	စာအုပ်ဆိုင်	sa ou' hsain
brewery	ဘီယာချက်စက်ရုံ	bi ja gje' se' joun
business center	စီးပွားရေးလုပ်ငန်းစင်တာ	si: bwa: jei: lou' ngan: zin da
business school	စီးပွားရေးကျောင်း	si: bwa: jei: gjaun:
casino	လောင်းကစားရုံ	laun: gaza: joun
construction	ဆောက်လုပ်ရေးလုပ်ငန်း	hsau' lou' jei: lou' ngan:
consulting	လူနာစမ်းသပ်ဝန်	lu na zan: dha' khan:
dental clinic	သွားဆေးခန်း	thwa: hsei: gan:

design	ဒီဇိုင်း	di zain:
drugstore, pharmacy	ဆေးဆိုင်	hsei: zain
dry cleaners	အဝတ်အခြောက်လျှော် လုပ်ငန်း	awu' achou' hlo: lou' ngan:
employment agency	အလုပ်အကိုင်ရှာဖွေ ရေးလုပ်ငန်း	alou' akain sha hpwei jei: lou' ngan:
financial services	ငွေကြေးဝန်ဆောင် မှုလုပ်ငန်း	ngwei kjei: wun zaun hmu lou' ngan:
food products	စားသုံးကုန်များ	sa: dhoun: goun mja:
funeral home	အသုဘဝန်ဆောင် မှုလုပ်ငန်း	athu. ba. wun zaun hmu. lou' ngan:
furniture (e.g., house ~)	ပရိဘောဂ	pa ri. bo: ga.
clothing, garment	အဝတ်အစား	awu' aza:
hotel	ဟိုတယ်	hou te
ice-cream	ရေခဲမုန့်	jei ge: moun.
industry (manufacturing)	စက်မှုလုပ်ငန်း	se' hmu. lou' ngan:
insurance	အာမခံလုပ်ငန်း	a ma. khan lou' ngan:
Internet	အင်တာနက်	in ta na'
investments (finance)	ရင်းနှီးမြှုပ်နှံမှု	jin: hni: hmjou' hnan hmu.
jeweler	လက်ဝတ်ရတနာကုန်သည်	le' wa' ja. da. na goun de
jewelry	လက်ဝတ်ရတနာ	le' wa' ja. da. na
laundry (shop)	ဒိုဘီလုပ်ငန်း	dou bi lou' ngan:
legal advisor	ဥပဒေအကြံပေး	u. ba. dei akjan bei:
light industry	အရွေးစားစက်မှု လုပ်ငန်း	athei: za: za' hmu. lou' ngan:
magazine	မဂ္ဂဇင်းစာစောင်	ma' ga. zin: za zaun
mail order selling	အော်ဒါကိုစာတိုက်မှ ပို့ဆောင်ခြင်း	o da ko sa dai' hma. bou. hsaun gjin:
medicine	ဆေးပညာ	hsei: pjin nja
movie theater	ရုပ်ရှင်ရုံ	jou' shin joun
museum	ပြတိုက်	pja. dai'
news agency	သတင်းဌာန	dhadin: hta. na.
newspaper	သတင်းစာ	dhadin: za
nightclub	နိုက်ကလပ်	nai' ka. la'
oil (petroleum)	ရေနံ	jei nan
courier services	ပစ္စည်းပို့ဆောင်ရေး လုပ်ငန်း	pji' si: bou. zain jei: lou' ngan:
pharmaceutics	လူသုံးဆေးဝါး လုပ်ငန်း	lu dhoun: zei: wa: lou' ngan:
printing (industry)	ပုံနှိပ်ခြင်း	poun nei' chin:
publishing house	ပုံနှိပ်ထုတ်ဝေ သည့်ကုမ္ပဏီ	poun nei' htou' wei dhi. koun pani
radio (~ station)	ရေဒီယို	rei di jou
real estate	အိမ်ခြံမြေလုပ်ငန်း	ein gjan mjei lu' ngan:
restaurant	စားသောက်ဆိုင်	sa: thau' hsain

security company	လုံခြုံရေးအကျိုး ဆောင်ကုမ္ပဏီ	loun gjoun jei: akjou: zaun koun pa. ni
sports	အားကစား	a: gaza:
stock exchange	စတော့ရောင်းဝယ်ရေးဌာန	sato. jaun: we jei: hta. na.
store	ဆိုင်	hsain
supermarket	ကုန်တိုက်ကြီး	koun dou' kji:
swimming pool (public ~)	ရေကူးကန်	jei ku: gan
tailor shop	အင်္ကျီချုပ်လုပ်ငန်း	a' chou' lu' ngan:
television	ရုပ်မြင်သံကြား	jou' mjin dhan gja:
theater	ကဇာတ်ရုံ	ka. za' joun
trade (commerce)	ကုန်သွယ်ရေး	koun dhwe jei:
transportation	သယ်ယူပို့ဆောင်ရေး လုပ်ငန်း	the ju bou. zaun jei: lou' ngan:
travel	ခရီးသွားလုပ်ငန်း	khaji: thwa: lou' ngan:
veterinarian	တိရစ္ဆာန်ကုဆရာဝန်	tharei' hsan gu. zaja wun
warehouse	ကုန်လှောင်ရုံ	koun hlaun joun
waste collection	စွန့်ပစ်ပစ္စည်းစုဆောင်း ခြင်း	sun. bi' pji' si: zu zaun: ghin:

Job. Business. Part 2

118. Show. Exhibition

exhibition, show	ပြပွဲ	pja. bwe:
trade show	ကုန်စည်ပြပွဲ	koun zi pja pwe
participation	ပါဝင်ဆင်နွှဲမှု	pa win zhin hnwe: hmu.
to participate (vi)	ပါဝင်ဆင်နွှဲသည်	pa win zin hnwe: de
participant (exhibitor)	ပါဝင်ဆင်နွှဲသူ	pa win zhin hnwe: dhu
director	ဒါရိုက်တာ	da je' ta
organizers' office	ဦးစီးဦးဆောင်သူအဖွဲ့	u: zi: u: zaun dhu ahpwe:
organizer	စီစဉ်သူ	si zin dhu
to organize (vt)	စီစဉ်သည်	si zin de
participation form	ပါဝင်ရန်ဖြည့်စွက်ရသောပုံစံ	pa win jan bje zwe' ja. dho: boun zan
to fill out (vt)	ဖြည့်သည်	hpjei. de
details	အသေးစိတ်အချက်အလက်များ	athei zi' ache' ala' mja:
information	သတင်းအချက်အလက်	dhadin: akje' ale'
price (cost, rate)	ဈေးနှုန်း	zei: hnan:
including	အပါအဝင်	apa awin
to include (vt)	ပါဝင်သည်	pa win de
to pay (vi, vt)	ပေးချေသည်	pei: gjei de
registration fee	မှတ်ပုံတင်ခ	hma' poun din ga.
entrance	ဝင်ပေါက်	win bau'
pavilion, hall	ပြခန်းယာယီအဆောက်အအုံ	pja. gan: ja ji ahsau' aoun
to register (vt)	စာရင်းသွင်းသည်	sajin: dhwin: de
badge (identity tag)	တံဆိပ်	da zei'
booth, stand	ပြပွဲစင်	pja. bwe: zin
to reserve, to book	ကြိုတင်မှာသည်	kjou tin hma de
display case	ပစ္စည်းပြရန်မှန်ဘောင်	pji' si: bja. jan hman baun
spotlight	မီးမောင်း	mi: maun:
design	ဒီဇိုင်း	di zain:
to place (put, set)	နေရာချသည်	nei ja gja de
to be placed	တည်ရှိသည်	ti shi. de
distributor	ဖြန့်ဝေသူ	hpjan. wei dhu
supplier	ပေးသွင်းသူ	pei: dhwin: dhu
to supply (vt)	ပေးသွင်းသည်	pei: dhwin: de

country	နိုင်ငံ	nain ngan
foreign (adj)	နိုင်ငံခြားနှင့် ဆိုင်သော	nain ngan gja: hnin. zain de.
product	ထုတ်ကုန်	htou' koun

association	အဖွဲ့အစည်း	ahpwe. asi:
conference hall	ဆွေးနွေးပွဲခန်းမ	hswe: nwe: bwe: gan: ma.
congress	ညီလာခံ	nji la gan
contest (competition)	ပြိုင်ပွဲ	pjain bwe:

visitor (attendee)	ဧည့်သည်	e. dhe
to visit (attend)	လာရောက်လေ့လာသည်	la jau' lei. la de
customer	ဖောက်သည်	hpau' te

119. Mass Media

newspaper	သတင်းစာ	dhadin: za
magazine	မဂ္ဂဇင်းစာစောင်	ma' ga. zin: za zaun
press (printed media)	စာနယ်ဇင်း	sa ne zin:
radio	ရေဒီယို	rei di jou
radio station	ရေဒီယိုဌာန	rei di jou hta. na.
television	ရုပ်မြင်သံကြား	jou' mjin dhan gja:

presenter, host	အစီအစဉ်တင်ဆက်သူ	asi asin din ze' thu
newscaster	သတင်းကြေညာသူ	dhadin: gjei nja dhu
commentator	အစီရင်ခံသူ	asi jin gan dhu

journalist	သတင်းစာဆရာ	dhadin: za zaja
correspondent (reporter)	သတင်းထောက်	dhadin: dau'
press photographer	သတင်းဓာတ်ပုံ ရိုက်ကူးသူ	dhadin: da' poun jai' ku: dhu
reporter	သတင်းထောက်	dhadin: dau'

| editor | အယ်ဒီတာ | e di ta |
| editor-in-chief | အယ်ဒီတာချုပ် | e di ta chu' |

to subscribe (to …)	ပေးသွင်းသည်	pei: dhwin: de
subscription	လစဉ်ကြေး	la. zin gjei:
subscriber	လစဉ်ကြေးပေးသွင်းသူ	la. zin gjei: bei: dhwin: dhu
to read (vi, vt)	ဖတ်သည်	hpa' te
reader	စာဖတ်သူ	sa hpa' thu

circulation (of newspaper)	စောင်ရေ	saun jei
monthly (adj)	လစဉ်	la. zin
weekly (adj)	အပတ်စဉ်	apa' sin
issue (edition)	အကြိမ်	akjein
new (~ issue)	အသစ်ဖြစ်သော	athi' hpji' te.

| headline | ခေါင်းစဉ် | gaun: zin |
| short article | ဆောင်းပါးငယ် | hsaun: ba: nge |

column (regular article)	ပင်တိုင်ဆောင်းပါး	pin dain zaun: ba:
	ရှင်ကဏ္ဍ	shin gan da.
article	ဆောင်းပါး	hsaun: ba:
page	စာမျက်နှာ	sa mje' hna

reportage, report	သတင်းပေးပို့ချက်	dhadin: bei: bou. gje'
event (happening)	အဖြစ်အပျက်	a hpji' apje'
sensation (news)	သတင်းထူး	dhadin: du:
scandal	မကောင်းသတင်း	ma. gaun dhadin:
scandalous (adj)	ကျော်မကောင်းကြား	kjo ma. kaun: pja:
	မကောင်းသော	ma. kaun de
great (~ scandal)	ကြီးကျယ်ခမ်းနားသော	kji: kje khin: na: de.

show (e.g., cooking ~)	အစီအစဉ်	asi asin
interview	အင်တာဗျူး	in ta bju:
live broadcast	တိုက်ရိုက်ထုတ်လွှင့်မှု	tai' jai' htou' hlwin. hmu.
channel	လိုင်း	lain:

120. Agriculture

agriculture	စိုက်ပျိုးရေး	sai' pjou: jei:
peasant (masc.)	တောင်သူလယ်သမား	taun dhu le dhama:
peasant (fem.)	တောင်သူအမျိုးသမီး	taun dhu amjou: dhami:
farmer	လယ်သမား	le dhama:

tractor (farm ~)	ထွန်စက်	htun ze'
combine, harvester	ရိတ်သိမ်းသီး	jei' thein:/ thi:
	နင်ရွေစက်	hnan gjwei ze'

plow	ထယ်	hte
to plow (vi, vt)	ထယ်ထိုးသည်	hte dou: de
plowland	ထယ်ထိုးစက်	hte dou: ze'
furrow (in field)	ထယ်ကြောင်း	hte gjaun:

to sow (vi, vt)	မျိုးကြဲသည်	mjou: gje de
seeder	မျိုးကြဲစက်	mjou: gje ze'
sowing (process)	မျိုးကြဲခြင်း	mjou: gje gjin:

| scythe | မြက်ယှဉ်းဓား | mje' jan: da: |
| to mow, to scythe | မြက်ရိတ်သည် | mje' jei' te |

| spade (tool) | ဆော်ပြား | ko pja: |
| to till (vt) | ထွန်ယက်သည် | htun je' te |

hoe	ပေါက်ပြား	pja' bja:
to hoe, to weed	ပေါင်းသင်သည်	paun: dhin de
weed (plant)	ပေါင်းပင်	paun: bin

| watering can | အပင်ရေလောင်းပုံး | apin jei laun: boun: |
| to water (plants) | ရေလောင်းသည် | jei laun: de |

watering (act)	ရေလောင်းခြင်း	jei laun: gjin:
pitchfork	ကောက်ဆွ	kau' hswa
rake	ထွန်ခြစ်	htun gji'

fertilizer	မြေသြဇာ	mjei o: za
to fertilize (vt)	မြေသြဇာကျွေးသည်	mjei o: za gjwei: de
manure (fertilizer)	မြေသြဇာ	mjei o: za

field	လယ်ကွင်း	le gwin:
meadow	မြင်ခင်းပြင်	mjin gin: bjin
vegetable garden	အသီးအရွက်စိုက်ခင်း	athi: ajwe' sai' khin:
orchard (e.g., apple ~)	သစ်သီးခြံ	thi' thi: gjan

to graze (vt)	စားကျက်တွင်လွှတ်ထားသည်	sa: gja' twin hlu' hta' de
herder (herdsman)	သိုးနွားထိန်းကျောင်းသူ	thou: nwa: ou' kjaun: dhu
pasture	စားကျက်	sa: gja'

| cattle breeding | ဥသိရိစ္တားမွေး မြူရေးလုပ်ငန်း | tharei' hsan mwei: mju jei: lou' ngan: |
| sheep farming | သိုးမွေးမြူရေး လုပ်ငန်း | thou: mwei: mju je: lou' ngan: |

plantation	ခြံ	chan
row (garden bed ~s)	ဘောင်	baun
hothouse	မှန်လုံအိမ်	hman loun ein

| drought (lack of rain) | မိုးခေါင်ခြင်း | mou: gaun gjin |
| dry (~ summer) | ခြောက်သွေ့သော | chau' thwei. de. |

grain	နှံစားပင်တို့၏အစေ့	hnan za: bin dou. i. asei.
cereal crops	မှယောစပါး	mu. jo za. ba:
to harvest, to gather	ရိတ်သိမ်းသည်	jei' thein: de

miller (person)	ဂျုံစက်ပိုင်ရှင်	gjoun ze' pain shin
mill (e.g., gristmill)	သီးနှံကြိတ်ခွဲစက်	thi: hnan gji' khwei: ze'
to grind (grain)	ကြိတ်သည်	kjei' te
flour	ဂျုံမှုန့်	gjoun hmoun.
straw	ကောက်ရိုး	kau' jou:

121. Building. Building process

construction site	ဆောက်လုပ်ရေးလုပ် ငန်းခွင်	hsau' lou' jei: lou' ngan: gwin
to build (vt)	ဆောက်လုပ်သည်	hsau' lou' te
construction worker	ဆောက်လုပ် ရေးအလုပ်သမား	hsau' lou' jei: alou' dha. ma:

project	ပရောဂျက် စီမံကိန်း	pa jo: gje' si man gein:
architect	ဗိသုကာပညာရှင်	bi. thu. ka pjin nja shin
worker	အလုပ်သမား	alou' dha ma:

foundation (of a building)	အုတ်မြစ်	ou' mja'
roof	အမိုး	amou:
foundation pile	မြေစိုက်တိုင်	mjei zai' tain
wall	နံရံ	nan jou:

| reinforcing bars | ခြင်းဆင် | njan: zin |
| scaffolding | ခြင်း | njan: |

concrete	ကွန်ကရစ်	kun ka. ji'
granite	နမ်းဖတ်ကျောက်	hnan: ba' kjau'
stone	ကျောက်	kjau'
brick	အုတ်	ou'

sand	သဲ	the:
cement	ဘိလပ်မြေ	bi la' mjei
plaster (for walls)	သရွတ်	thaju'
to plaster (vt)	သရွတ်ကိုင်သည်	thaju' kain de

paint	သုတ်ဆေး	thou' hsei:
to paint (~ a wall)	ဆေးသုတ်သည်	hsei: dhou' te
barrel	စည်ပိုင်း	si bain:

crane	ကရိန်းစက်	karein: ze'
to lift, to hoist (vt)	မသည်	ma. de
to lower (vt)	ချသည်	cha. de

bulldozer	လမ်းကြိတ်စက်	lan: gji' se'
excavator	မြေတူးစက်	mjei du: ze'
scoop, bucket	ကော်ခွက်	ko khwe'
to dig (excavate)	တူးသည်	tu: de
hard hat	ဒက်ခံဦးထုပ်	dan gan u: dou'

122. Science. Research. Scientists

science	သိပ္ပံပညာ	thei' pan pin nja
scientific (adj)	သိပ္ပံပညာဆိုင်ရာ	thei' pan pin nja zein ja
scientist	သိပ္ပံပညာရှင်	thei' pan pin nja shin
theory	သီအိုရီ	thi ou ji

axiom	နဂိုမှန်အဆို	na. gou hman ahsou
analysis	ခွဲခြမ်းစိတ်ဖြာခြင်း	khwe: gjan: zei' hpa gjin:
to analyze (vt)	ခွဲခြမ်းစိတ်ဖြာသည်	khwe: gjan: zei' hpa de
argument (strong ~)	အကြောင်းပြချက်	akjaun: pja. gje'
substance (matter)	အတည်	a hte
hypothesis	အခြေခံသဘောတာ ရားအယူအဆ	achei khan dha. bo da. ja: aju ahsa.

dilemma	အကျပ်ရိုက်ခြင်း	akja' shi' chin:
dissertation	သုတေသနစာတမ်း	thu. tei thana za dan:
dogma	တရားသေလက်ခံ ထားသောဝါဒ	taja: dhei le' khan da: dho: wa da

doctrine	ဩဝါဒ	thja. wa da.
research	သုတေသန	thu. tei thana
to research (vt)	သုတေသနပြုသည်	thu. tei thana bjou de
tests (laboratory ~)	စမ်းသပ်ခြင်း	san: dha' chin:
laboratory	လက်တွေ့ခန်း	le' twei. gan:
method	နည်းလမ်း	ne: lan:
molecule	မော်လီကျူး	mo li gju:
monitoring	စောင့်ကြည့်စစ်ဆေးခြင်း	saun. gji. zi' hsei: gjin:
discovery (act, event)	ရှာဖွေတွေ့ရှိမှု	sha hpwei dwei. shi. hmu.
postulate	လက်ခံထားသည့်အဆို	le' khan da: dhe. ahsou
principle	အခြေခံသဘောတရား	achei khan dha. bo da. ja:
forecast	ကြိုတင်ခန့်မှန်းချက်	kjou din khan hman: gje'
to forecast (vt)	ကြိုတင်ခန့်မှန်းသည်	kjou din khan hman: de
synthesis	သမ္မာရ	than ba ra.
trend (tendency)	ဦးတည်ရာ	u: ti ja
theorem	သီအိုရမ်	thi ou jan
teachings	သင်ကြားချက်	thin kja: gje'
fact	အချက်အလက်	ache' ale'
expedition	ငူးစမ်းလေ့လာရေးခရီး	su: zan: lei. la nei: khaji:
experiment	စမ်းသပ်လုပ်ဆောင်ချက်	san: dha' lou' hsaun gje'
academician	အ္ကကယ်ဒမီသိပ္ပပညာ ရှင်	ake da ni dhan pa' pjin shin
bachelor (e.g., ~ of Arts)	တက္ကသိုလ် ပထမဘွဲ့	te' kathou pahtama. bwe:
doctor (PhD)	ပါရဂူဘွဲ့	pa ja gu bwe.
Associate Professor	လက်ထောက်ပါမောက္ခ	le' htau' pa mau' kha.
Master (e.g., ~ of Arts)	မဟာဘွဲ့	maha bwe.
professor	ပါမောက္ခ	pamau' kha

Professions and occupations

123. Job search. Dismissal

job	အလုပ်	alou'
staff (work force)	ဝန်ထမ်းအင်အား	wun dan: in a:
personnel	အမှုထမ်း	ahmṵ. htan:
career	သက်မွေးမှုလုပ်ငန်း	the' hmei: hmu. lou' ngan:
prospects (chances)	တက်လမ်း	te' lan:
skills (mastery)	ကျွမ်းကျင်မှု	kjwan: gjin hmu.
selection (screening)	လက်ရွေးစင်	le' jwei: zin
employment agency	အလုပ်အကိုင်ရှာဖွေရေး-အကျိုးဆောင်လုပ်ငန်း	alou' akain sha hpei jei: akjou: zaun lou' ngan:
résumé	ပညာရည်မှတ်တမ်းအကျဉ်း	pjin nja je hma' tan: akjin:
job interview	အလုပ်အင်တာဗျူး	alou' in da bju:
vacancy, opening	အလုပ်လစ်လပ်နေရာ	alou' li' la' nei ja
salary, pay	လစာ	la. za
fixed salary	ပုံသေလစာ	poun dhei la. za
pay, compensation	ပေးရေသည့်ငွေ	pei: gjei de. ngwei
position (job)	ရာထူး	ja du:
duty (of employee)	တာဝန်	ta wun
range of duties	တာဝန်များ	ta wun mja:
busy (I'm ~)	အလုပ်များသော	alou' mja: de.
to fire (dismiss)	အလုပ်ထုတ်သည်	alou' htou' de
dismissal	ထုတ်ပယ်ခြင်း	htou' pe gjin:
unemployment	အလုပ်လက်မဲ့ဦးရေ	alou' le' me. u: jei
unemployed (n)	အလုပ်လက်မဲ့	alou' le' me.
retirement	အငြိမ်းစားလစာ	anjein: za: la. za
to retire (from job)	အငြိမ်းစားယူသည်	anjein: za: ju dhe

124. Business people

director	ညွှန်ကြားရေးမှူး	hnjun gja: jei: hmu:
manager (director)	မန်နေဂျာ	man nei gji
boss	အကြီးအကဲ	akji: ake:
superior	အထက်လူကြီး	a hte' lu gji:
superiors	အထက်လူကြီးများ	a hte' lu gji: mja:

| president | ဥက္ကဋ္ဌ | ou' kahta. |
| chairman | ဥက္ကဋ္ဌ | ou' kahta. |

deputy (substitute)	ဒုတိယ	du. di. ja.
assistant	လက်ထောက်	le' htau'
secretary	အတွင်းရေးမှူး	atwin: jei: hmu:
personal assistant	ကိုယ်ရေးအရာရှိ	kou jei: aja shi.

businessman	စီးပွားရေးလုပ်ငန်းရှင်	si: bwa: jei: lou' ngan: shin
entrepreneur	စီးပွားရေးလုပ်ငန်းရှင်	si: bwa: jei: lou' ngan: shin
founder	တည်ထောင်သူ	ti daun dhu
to found (vt)	တည်ထောင်သည်	ti daun de

incorporator	ဖွဲ့စည်းသူ	hpwe. zi: dhu
partner	အကျိုးတူလုပ်ဖော်ကိုင်ဘက်	akjou: du lou' hpo kain be'
stockholder	အစုရှင်	asu. shin

millionaire	သန်းကြွယ်သူဌေး	than: gjwe dhu dei:
billionaire	ဘီလျံနာသူဌေး	bi ljan na dhu dei:
owner, proprietor	ပိုင်ရှင်	pain shin
landowner	မြေပိုင်ရှင်	mjei bain shin

client	ဖောက်သည်	hpau' te
regular client	အမြဲတမ်းဖောက်သည်	amje: dan: zau' te
buyer (customer)	ဝယ်သူ	we dhu
visitor	ဧည့်သည်	e. dhe

professional (n)	ကျွမ်းကျင်သူ	kjwan: gjin dhu
expert	ကျွမ်းကျင်ပညာရှင်	kjwan: gjin bi nja shin
specialist	အထူးကျွမ်းကျင်သူ	a htu: kjwan: gjin dhu

| banker | ဘဏ်လုပ်ငန်းရှင် | ban lou' ngan: shin |
| broker | စီးပွါးရေးအကျိုးဆောင် | si: bwa: jei: akjou: zaun |

cashier, teller	ငွေကိုင်	ngwei gain
accountant	စာရင်းကိုင်	sajin: gain
security guard	အစောင့်	asaun.

investor	ရင်းနှီးမြှုပ်နှံသူ	jin: hni: hmjou' hnan dhu
debtor	မြီစား	mji za:
creditor	ကြွေးရှင်	kjwei: shin
borrower	ချေးသူ	chei: dhu

| importer | သွင်းကုန်လုပ်ငန်းရှင် | thwin: goun lou' ngan: shin |
| exporter | ပို့ကုန်လုပ်ငန်းရှင် | pou. goun lou' ngan: shin |

manufacturer	ထုတ်လုပ်သူ	tou' lou' thu
distributor	ဖြန့်ဝေသူ	hpjan. wei dhu
middleman	တစ်ဆင့်ခံရောင်းသူ	ti' hsin. gan jaun: dhu

| consultant | အတိုင်ပင်ခံပုဂ္ဂိုလ် | atain bin gan bou' gou |
| sales representative | ကိုယ်စားလှယ် | kou za: hle |

agent	ကိုယ်စားလှယ်	kou za: hle
insurance agent	အာမခံကိုယ်စားလှယ်	a ma. khan gou za: hle

125. Service professions

cook	စားဖိုမှူး	sa: hpou hmu:
chef (kitchen chef)	စားဖိုမှူးကြီး	sa: hpou hmu: gji:
baker	ပေါင်မုန့်ဖုတ်သူ	paun moun. bou' dhu
bartender	အရက်ဘားဝန်ထမ်း	aje' ba: wun dan:
waiter	စားပွဲထိုး	sa: bwe: dou:
waitress	စားပွဲထိုးမိန်းကလေး	sa: bwe: dou: mein: ga. lei:
lawyer, attorney	ရှေ့နေ	shei. nei
lawyer (legal expert)	ရှေ့နေ	shei. nei
notary public	ရှေ့နေ	shei. nei
electrician	လျပ်စစ်ပညာရှင်	hlja si' pa. nja shin
plumber	ပိုက်ပြင်သူ	pai' bjin dhu
carpenter	လက်သမား	le' tha ma:
masseur	အနှိပ်သမား	anei' thama:
masseuse	အနှိပ်သမ	anei' thama.
doctor	ဆရာဝန်	hsa ja wun
taxi driver	တက္ကစီမောင်းသူ	te' kasi maun: dhu
driver	ယာဉ်မောင်း	jin maun:
delivery man	ပစ္စည်းပို့သူ	pji' si: bou. dhu
chambermaid	ဟိုတယ်သန့်ရှင်းရေး ဝန်ထမ်း	hou te than. shin wun dam:
security guard	အစောင့်	asaun.
flight attendant (fem.)	လေယာဉ်မယ်	lei jan me
schoolteacher	ဆရာ	hsa ja
librarian	စာကြည့်တိုက်ဝန်ထမ်း	sa gji. dai' wun dan:
translator	ဘာသာပြန်	ba dha bjan
interpreter	စကားပြန်	zaga: bjan
guide	လမ်းညွှန်	lan: hnjun
hairdresser	ဆံသဆရာ	hsan dha. zaja
mailman	စာပို့သမား	sa bou. dhama:
salesman (store staff)	ဆိုင်အရောင်းဝန်ထမ်း	hsain ajaun: wun dan:
gardener	ဥယျာဉ်မှူး	u. jin hmu:
domestic servant	အိမ်စေအမှုထမ်း	ein zei ahmu. dan:
maid (female servant)	အိမ်စေအမျိုးသမီး	ein zei amjou: dhami:
cleaner (cleaning lady)	သန့်ရှင်းရေးသမ	than. shin: jei: dhama.

126. Military professions and ranks

private	တပ်သား	ta' tha:
sergeant	တပ်ကြပ်ကြီး	ta' kja' kji:
lieutenant	ဗိုလ်	bou
captain	ဗိုလ်ကြီး	bou gjl
major	ဗိုလ်မှူး	bou hmu:
colonel	ဗိုလ်မှူးကြီး	bou hmu: gji:
general	ဗိုလ်ချုပ်	bou gjou'
marshal	ထိပ်တန်းအရာရှိ	htei' tan: aja shi.
admiral	ရေတပ်ဗိုလ်ချုပ်ကြီး	jei da' bou chou' kji:
military (n)	တပ်မတော်နှင့်ဆိုင်သော	ta' mado hnin. zain de.
soldier	စစ်သား	si' tha:
officer	အရာရှိ	aja shi.
commander	ခေါင်းဆောင်	gaun: zaun
border guard	နယ်ခြားစောင့်	ne gja: zaun.
radio operator	ဆက်သွယ်ရေးတပ်သား	hse' thwe jei: da' tha:
scout (searcher)	ကင်းထောက်	kin: dau'
pioneer (sapper)	မိုင်းရှင်းသူ	main: shin: dhu
marksman	လက်ဖြောင့်တပ်သား	le' hpaun. da' tha:
navigator	လေကြောင်းပြ	lei gjaun: bja.

127. Officials. Priests

king	ဘုရင်	ba. jin
queen	ဘုရင်မ	ba jin ma.
prince	အိမ်ရှေ့မင်းသား	ein shei. min: dha:
princess	မင်းသမီး	min: dhami:
czar	ဇာဘုရင်	za bou jin
czarina	ဇာဘုရင်မ	za bou jin ma
president	သမ္မတ	thamada.
Secretary (minister)	ဝန်ကြီး	wun: gji:
prime minister	ဝန်ကြီးချုပ်	wun: gji: gjou'
senator	ဆီနိတ်လွှတ်တော်အမတ်	hsi nei' hlwa' do: ama'
diplomat	သံတမန်	than taman.
consul	ကောင်စစ်ဝန်	kaun si' wun
ambassador	သံအမတ်	than ama'
counselor (diplomatic officer)	ကောင်စီဝင်	kaun si wun
official, functionary (civil servant)	အမှုဆောင်အရာရှိ	ahmu. zaun aja shi.

| prefect | သီးသန့်နယ်မြေ
အုပ်ချုပ်ပိုရေးမှူး | thi: dhan. ne mjei
ou' chou' ei: hmu: |
| mayor | မြို့တော်ဝန် | mjou. do wun |

| judge | တရားသူကြီး | taja: dhu gji: |
| prosecutor
(e.g., district attorney) | အစိုးရာရှေ့ နေ | asou' ja shei. nei |

missionary	သာသနာပြုသူ	tha dha. na bju. dhu
monk	ဘုန်းကြီး	hpoun: gji:
abbot	ကျောင်းထိုင်ဆရာတော်	kjaun: dain zaja do
rabbi	ဂျူးဘာသာဓမ္မရေး ခေါင်းဆောင်	gju: ba dha jei: gaun: zaun:

vizier	မှတ်ဆလင်အမတ်	mu' hsa. lin ama'
shah	ရှားဘုရင်	sha: bu. shin
sheikh	အာရပ်စော်ဘွား	a ra' so bwa:

128. Agricultural professions

beekeeper	ပျားမွေးသူ	pja: mwei: dhu
herder, shepherd	သိုး၊နွားအုပ်ကျောင်းသူ	thou:/ nwa: ou' kjaun: dhu
agronomist	သီးနှံစိုက်ပျိုး ရေးပညာရှင်	thi: hnan zai' pjou: jei: pin nja shin
cattle breeder	တိရစ္ဆာန်မျိုး ဖောက်သူ	tharei' hsan mjou: hpau' thu
veterinarian	တိရစ္ဆာန်ဆရာဝန်	tharei' hsan zaja wun

farmer	လယ်သမား	le dhama:
winemaker	ဝိုင်ဖောက်သူ	wain bau' thu
zoologist	သတ္တဗေဒပညာရှင်	tha' ta. bei da. pin nja shin
cowboy	နွားကျောင်းသား	nwa: gjaun: dha:

129. Art professions

| actor | သရုပ်ဆောင်မင်းသား | thajou' hsaun min: dha: |
| actress | သရုပ်ဆောင်မင်းသမီး | thajou' hsaun min: dha: |

| singer (masc.) | အဆိုတော် | ahsou do |
| singer (fem.) | အဆိုတော် | ahsou do |

| dancer (masc.) | အကဆရာ | aka. hsa. ja |
| dancer (fem.) | အကဆရာမ | aka. hsa. ja ma |

performer (masc.)	သရုပ်ဆောင်သူ	thajou' hsaun dhu
performer (fem.)	သရုပ်ဆောင်သူ	thajou' hsaun dhu
musician	ဂီတပညာရှင်	gi ta. bjin nja shin
pianist	စန္ဒရားဆရာ	san daja: zaja

guitar player	ဂစ်တာပညာရှင်	gi' ta bjin nja shin
conductor (orchestra ~)	ဂီတမှူး	gi ta. hmu
composer	တေးရေးဆရာ	tei: jei: hsaja
impresario	ဇာတ်ဆရာ	za' hsaja

film director	ရုပ်ရှင်ဒါရိုက်တာ	jou' shin da jai' ta
producer	ထုတ်လုပ်သူ	htou' lou' thu
scriptwriter	ဇာတ်ညွှန်းဆရာ	za' hnjun: za ja
critic	ဝေဖန်သူ	wei ban dhu

writer	စာရေးဆရာ	sajei: zaja
poet	ကဗျာဆရာ	ka. bja zaja
sculptor	ပန်းပုဆရာ	babu hsaja
artist (painter)	ပန်းချီဆရာ	bagji zaja

juggler	လက်လှည့်ဆရာ	le' hli. za. ja.
clown	လူရွှင်တော်	lu shwin do
acrobat	ကျွမ်းဘားပြသူ	kjwan: ba: bja dhu
magician	မျက်လှည့်ဆရာ	mje' hle. zaja

130. Various professions

doctor	ဆရာဝန်	hsa ja wun
nurse	သူနာပြု	thu na bju.
psychiatrist	စိတ်ရောဂါအထူးကု ဆရာဝန်	sei' jo: ga ahtu: gu. zaja wun
dentist	သွားဆရာဝန်	thwa: hsaja wun
surgeon	ခွဲစိတ်ကုဆရာဝန်	khwe: hsei' ku hsaja wun

astronaut	အာကာသယာဉ်မှူး	akatha. jin hmu:
astronomer	နက္ခတ္တဗေဒ ပညာရှင်	ne' kha' ta. bei da. pji nja shin
pilot	လေယာဉ်မှူး	lei jan hmu:

driver (of taxi, etc.)	ယာဉ်မောင်း	jin maun:
engineer (train driver)	ရထားမောင်းသူ	jatha: maun: dhu
mechanic	စက်ပြင်ဆရာ	se' pjin zaja

miner	သတ္တုတွင်း အလုပ်သမား	tha' tu. dwin: alou' thama:
worker	အလုပ်သမား	alou' dha ma:
locksmith	သော့ပြင်ဆရာ	tho. bjin zaja
joiner (carpenter)	ကျည်းပေါင်းခွေလက်သမား	kji: baun: gwei le' dha ma:
turner (lathe operator)	တွင်ခုံအလုပ်သမား	twin goun alou' dhama:
construction worker	ဆောက်လုပ် ရေးအလုပ်သမား	hsau' lou' jei: alou' dha. ma:
welder	ဂဟေဆော်သူ	gahei hso dhu

professor (title)	ပါမောက္ခ	pamau' kha
architect	ဗိသုကာပညာရှင်	bi. thu. ka pjin nja shin
historian	သမိုင်းပညာရှင်	thamain: pin nja shin

scientist	သိပ္ပံပညာရှင်	thei' pan pin nja shin
physicist	ရူပဗေဒပညာရှင်	ju bei da. bin nja shin
chemist (scientist)	ဓာတုဗေဒပညာရှင်	da tu. bei da. bjin nja shin
archeologist	ရှေးဟောင်းသုတေသန နပညာရှင်	shei: haun thu. dei dha. na. bji nja shin
geologist	ဘူမိဗေဒ ပညာရှင်	buu mi. bei da. bjin nja shin
researcher (scientist)	သုတေသနပညာရှင်	thu. tei thana pin nja shin
babysitter	ကလေးထိန်း	kalei: din:
teacher, educator	ဆရာ	hsa ja
editor	အယ်ဒီတာ	e di ta
editor-in-chief	အယ်ဒီတာချုပ်	e di ta chu'
correspondent	သတင်းထောက်	dhadin: dau'
typist (fem.)	လက်နှိပ်စက်ရိုက်သူ	le' ni' se' jou' thu
designer	ဒီဇိုင်နာ	di zain na
computer expert	ကွန်ပျူတာပညာရှင်	kun pju ta ba. nja shin
programmer	ပရိုဂရမ်မာ	pa. jou ga. jan ma
engineer (designer)	အင်ဂျင်နီယာ	in gjin ni ja
sailor	သင်္ဘောသား	thin: bo: dha:
seaman	သင်္ဘောသား	thin: bo: dha:
rescuer	ကယ်ဆယ်သူ	ke ze dhu
fireman	မီးသတ်သမား	mi: tha' dhama:
police officer	ရဲ	je:
watchman	အစောင့်	asaun.
detective	စုံထောက်	soun dau'
customs officer	အကောက်ခွန်အရာရှိ	akau' khun aja shi.
bodyguard	သက်တော်စောင့်	the' to zaun.
prison guard	ထောင်စောင့်	htaun zaun.
inspector	ရဲအုပ်	je: ou'
sportsman	အားကစားသမား	a: gaza: dhama:
trainer, coach	နည်းပြ	ne: bja.
butcher	သားသတ်သမား	tha: dha' thama:
cobbler (shoe repairer)	ဖိနပ်ချုပ်သမား	hpana' chou' tha ma:
merchant	ကုန်သည်	koun de
loader (person)	ကုန်ထမ်းသမား	koun din dhama:
fashion designer	ဖက်ရှင်ဒီဇိုင်နာ	hpe' shin di zain na
model (fem.)	မော်ဒယ်	mo de

131. Occupations. Social status

schoolboy	ကျောင်းသား	kjaun: dha:
student (college ~)	ကျောင်းသား	kjaun: dha:

philosopher	ဒဿနပညာရှင်	da' thana. pjin nja shin
economist	ဘောဂဗေဒပညာရှင်	bo ga bei da ba nja shin
inventor	တီထွင်သူ	ti htwin dhu

unemployed (n)	အလုပ်လက်မဲ့	alou' le' me.
retiree	အငြိမ်းစား	anjein: za:
spy, secret agent	သူလျှို	thu shou

prisoner	ထောင်သား	htaun dha:
striker	သပိတ်မှောက်သူ	thabei' hmau' thu
bureaucrat	ဗျူရိုကရက်အရာရှိ	bju jou ka. je' aja shi.
traveler (globetrotter)	ခရီးသွား	khaji: thwa:

gay, homosexual (n)	လိင်တူချင်းဆက်ဆံသူ	lein du cjin: ze' hsan dhu
hacker	ဟက်ကာ	he' ka
hippie	လူမှုဝေလှများကို သွေဖယ်သူ	lu hmu. da. lei. mja: gou

bandit	ဓားပြ	damja.
hit man, killer	လူသတ်သမား	lu dha' thama:
drug addict	ဆေးစွဲသူ	hsei: zwe: dhu
drug dealer	မူးယစ်ဆေးရောင်းဝယ်သူ	mu: ji' hsei: jaun we dhu
prostitute (fem.)	ပြည့်တန်ဆာ	pjei. dan za
pimp	ဖာခေါင်း	hpa gaun:

sorcerer	မှော်ဆရာ	hmo za. ja
sorceress (evil ~)	မှော်ဆရာမ	hmo za. ja ma.
pirate	ပင်လယ်ဓားပြ	pin le da: bja.
slave	ကျွန်	kjun
samurai	ဆာမူရိုင်း	hsa mu jain:
savage (primitive)	လူရိုင်း	lu jain:

Sports

132. Kinds of sports. Sportspersons

sportsman	အားကစားသမား	a: gaza: dhama:
kind of sports	အားကစားအမျိုးအစား	a: gaza: amjou: asa:
basketball	ဘတ်စကတ်ဘော	ba' sa. ka' bo:
basketball player	ဘတ်စကတ်ဘောက စားသမား	ba' sa. ka' bo ka. za: dha ma:
baseball	ဘေ့စ်ဘောအားကစား	bei'. bo a: gaza
baseball player	ဘေ့စ်ဘောကစားသမား	bei'. bo a: gaza dha ma:
soccer	ဘောလုံးအားကစား	bo loun: a: gaza:
soccer player	ဘောလုံးကစားသမား	bo loun: gaza: dhama:
goalkeeper	ဂိုးသမား	gou: dha ma:
hockey	ဟော်ကီ	hou ki
hockey player	ဟော်ကီကစားသမား	hou ki gaza: dha ma:
volleyball	ဘော်လီဘောအားကစား	bo li bo: a: gaza:
volleyball player	ဘောလီဘောကစားသမား	bo li bo: a: gaza: dhama:
boxing	လက်ဝှေ့	le' hwei.
boxer	လက်ဝှေ့သမား	le' hwei. dhama:
wrestling	နပန်းကစားခြင်း	naban: gaza: gjin:
wrestler	နပန်းသမား	naban: dhama:
karate	ကရာတေးအားကစား	ka. ra tei: a: gaza:
karate fighter	ကရာတေးကစားသမား	ka. ra tei: a: gaza: ma:
judo	ဂျူဒိုအားကစား	gju dou a: gaza:
judo athlete	ဂျူဒိုကစားသမား	gju dou a: gaza: dhama:
tennis	တင်းနစ်	tin: ni'
tennis player	တင်းနစ်ကစားသူ	tin: ni' gaza: dhu
swimming	ရေကူးအားကစား	jei ku: a: gaza:
swimmer	ရေကူးသူ	jei ku: dhu
fencing	ဓားရေးယှဉ်ပြိုင် ကစားခြင်း	da: jei: shin bjain ga. za: gjin
fencer	ဓားရေးယှဉ်ပြိုင် ကစားသူ	da: jei: shin bjain ga. za: dhu

chess	စစ်တုရင်	si' tu. jin
chess player	စစ်တုရင်ကစားသမား	si' tu. jin gaza: dhama:
alpinism	တောင်တက်ခြင်း	taun de' chin:
alpinist	တောင်တက်သမား	taun de' thama:
running	အပြေး	apjei:
runner	အပြေးသမား	apjei: dha. ma:
athletics	ပြေးခုန်ပစ်	pjei: goun bi'
athlete	ပြေးခုန်ပစ်ကစားသူ	pjei: goun bi' gaza: dhu
horseback riding	မြင်းစီးခြင်း	mjin: zi: gjin:
horse rider	မြင်းစီးသူ	mjin: zi: dhu
figure skating	စကိတ်စီးကပြခြင်း	sakei' si: ga. bja. gjin:
figure skater (masc.)	စကိတ်စီးကပြသူ	sakei' si: ga. bja. dhu
figure skater (fem.)	စကိတ်စီးကပြမယ်	sakei' si: ga. bja. me
powerlifting	အလေးမ	a lei: ma
powerlifter	အလေးမသူ	a lei: ma dhu
car racing	ကားမောင်းပြိုင်ခြင်း	ka: maun: bjein gjin:
racer (driver)	ပြိုင်ကားမောင်းသူ	pjain ga: maun: dhu
cycling	စက်ဘီးစီးခြင်း	se' bi: zi: gjin
cyclist	စက်ဘီးစီးသူ	se' bi: zi: dhu
broad jump	အလျားခုန်	alja: khun
pole vault	တုတ်ထောက်ခုန်	tou' htau' khoun
jumper	ခုန်သူ	khoun dhu

133. Kinds of sports. Miscellaneous

football	အမေရိကန်ဘောလုံး	amei ji kan dho: loun:
badminton	ကြက်တောင်	kje' daun
biathlon	သေနတ်ပစ်	thei na' pi'
billiards	ဘိလိယက်	bi li je'
bobsled	ပြိုင်စွတ်ဖား	pjain zwa' hpa:
bodybuilding	ကာယာဗလ	ka ja ba. la.
water polo	ဝါတာပိုလို	wa ta pou lou
handball	လက်ပစ်ဘောလုံးကစားနည်း	le' pi' bo: loun: gaza: ne:
golf	ဂေါက်ရိုက်ခြင်း	gou' jai' chin:
rowing, crew	လှေလှော်ခြင်း	hlei hlo gjin:
scuba diving	ရေငုပ်ခြင်း	jei ngou' chin:
cross-country skiing	နှင်းလျှောစကိတ်စီး	hnin: sho: zakei' si:
	ပြိုင်ပွဲ	bjain bwe:
table tennis (ping-pong)	စားပွဲတင်တင်းနစ်	sa: bwe: din din: ni'

sailing	ရွက်လွင့်ခြင်း	jwe' hlwn. jgin:
rally racing	ကားပြိုင်ခြင်း	ka: bjain gjin:
rugby	ရတ်ဘီဘောလုံးအားကစား	re' bi bo: loun: a: gaza:
snowboarding	နှင်းလျောစကိတ်စီးခြင်း	hnin: sho: zakei' si: gjin:
archery	မြှားပစ်	hmja: bi'

134. Gym

barbell	အလေးတန်း	a lei: din:
dumbbells	ဒမ်ဘယ်အလေးတုန်း	dan be alei: doun:
training machine	လေ့ကျင့်ခန်းပြုလုပ်ရန်စက်	lei. kjin. gan: pju. lou' jan ze'
exercise bicycle	လေ့ကျင့်ခန်းစက်ဘီး	lei. kjin. gan: ze' bi:
treadmill	ပြေးစက်	pjei: ze'
horizontal bar	ဘားတန်း	ba: din:
parallel bars	ပြိုင်တန်း	pjain dan:
vault (vaulting horse)	မြင်းခုံ	mjin: goun
mat (exercise ~)	အားကစားဖျာ	a: gaza: bja
jump rope	ကြိုး	kjou:
aerobics	အေရိုးဘစ်	e jou: bi'
yoga	ယောဂ	jo: ga.

135. Hockey

hockey	ဟော်ကီ	hou ki
hockey player	ဟော်ကီကစားသမား	hou ki gaza: dha ma:
to play hockey	ဟော်ကီကစားသည်	hou ki gaza: de
ice	ရေခဲ	jei ge:
puck	ရော်ဘာဒိုးပြား	jo ba dou: bja:
hockey stick	ဟော်ကီရိုက်တံ	hou ki jai' tan
ice skates	ရေခဲပြင်စကိတ်	jei ge: bjin za. gei'
board (ice hockey rink ~)	အကာပြား	aka pja:
shot	ရိုက်ချက်	jai' che'
goaltender	ဂိုးသမား	gou: dha ma:
goal (score)	ဂိုး	gou:
to score a goal	ဂိုးသွင်းသည်	gou: dhwin: de
period	အပိုင်း	apain:
second period	ဒုတိယပိုင်း	du. di. ja. bain:
substitutes bench	အစားကစားသမားထိုင်ခုံ	ajan ka. za: dha. ma: dain goun

136. Soccer

soccer	ဘောလုံးအားကစား	bo loun: a: gaza:
soccer player	ဘောလုံးကစားသမား	bo loun: gaza: dhama:
to play soccer	ဘောလုံးကန်သည်	bo loun: gan de
major league	မေဂျာလိဂ်	mei gja lei'
soccer club	ဘောလုံးကလပ်	bo loun: kala'
coach	နည်းပြ	ne: bja.
owner, proprietor	ပိုင်ရှင်	pain shin
team	အသင်း	athin:
team captain	အသင်းခေါင်းဆောင်	ahin: gaun: zaun
player	ကစားသမား	gaza: dhama:
substitute	အရံကစားသမား	ajan ka. za: dha. ma:
forward	ရှေ့တန်း	shei. dan:
center forward	ရှေ့တန်းအလယ်	shei. dan: ale
scorer	အမှတ်မှတ်သူ	ahma' hma' thu
defender, back	နောက်တန်းကစားသမား	nau' tan: ka. za: dha. ma:
midfielder, halfback	ကွင်းလယ်လူ	kwin: le dhu
match	ပြိုင်ပွဲ	pjain bwe:
to meet (vi, vt)	တွေ့ဆုံသည်	twei. hsoun de
final	ဗိုလ်လုပွဲ	bou lu. bwe:
semi-final	အကြိုဗိုလ်လုပွဲ	akjou bou lu. pwe:
championship	တံခွန်စိုက်ပြိုင်ပွဲ	dagun zai' pjein bwe:
period, half	အချိန်	achein
first period	ပထမပိုင်း	pahtama. bain:
half-time	နားချိန်	na: gjein
goal	ဂိုးပေါက်	gou: bau'
goalkeeper	ဂိုးသမား	gou: dha ma:
goalpost	ဂိုးတိုင်	gou: dain
crossbar	ဂိုးဘားတန်း	gou: ba: dan
net	ပိုက်	pai'
to concede a goal	ဂိုးလွတ်သွားသည်	gou: lu' thwa: de
ball	ဘောလုံး	bo loun:
pass	ပေးခြင်း	pei: gjin:
kick	ကစ်	ki'
to kick (~ the ball)	ကန်သည်	kan de
free kick (direct ~)	ပြစ်ဒဏ်ဘော	pji' dan de.
corner kick	ဒေါင့်ကန်ဘော	daun. gan bo:
attack	တိုက်စစ်	tai' si'
counterattack	တန်ပြန်တိုက်စစ်	tan bjan dai' si'
combination	ပေါင်းစပ်ခြင်း	paun: za' chin:
referee	ဒိုင်လူကြီး	dain dhu gji:
to blow the whistle	လေခွျန်သည်	lei gjun de

whistle (sound)	ခရာ	khaja
foul, misconduct	ဖောင်းဘော	hpaun: bo:
to commit a foul	ဖောင်းဘောဖြစ်သည်	hpaun: bo: hpji' te
to send off	ထုတ်သည်	htou' te

yellow card	အဝါကဒ်	awa ka'
red card	အနီကဒ်	ani ga'
disqualification	ပိတ်ပင်ခြင်း	pei' pin gjin:
to disqualify (vt)	ပိတ်ပင်သည်	pei' pin de

penalty kick	ပန်နယ်တီ	pan ne ti
wall	ဝေါ်ကာခြင်း	wo: ga gjin:
to score (vi, vt)	သွင်းသည်	thin: de
goal (score)	ဂိုး	gou:
to score a goal	ဂိုးသွင်းသည်	gou: dhwin: de

substitution	လူစားလဲခြင်း	lu za: le: gjin:
to replace (a player)	လူစားလဲသည်	lu za: le: de
rules	စည်းမျဉ်းစည်းကမ်း	si: mjin: si: kan:
tactics	ဗျူဟာ	bju ha

stadium	အားကစားရုံ	a: gaza: joun
stand (bleachers)	ပွဲကြည့်စင်	pwe: gje. zi'
fan, supporter	ပရိတ်သတ်	pa. rei' tha'
to shout (vi)	အော်သည်	o de

| scoreboard | ရလဒ်ပြဆိုင်းဘုတ် | jala' pja. zain: bou' |
| score | ရလဒ် | jala' |

defeat	အရှုံး	ashoun:
to lose (not win)	ရှုံးသည်	shoun: de
tie	သရေ	thajei
to tie (vi)	သရေကျသည်	tha. jei gja. de

victory	အောင်ပွဲ	aun bwe:
to win (vi, vt)	အောင်ပွဲခံသည်	aun bwe: khan de
champion	ချန်ပီယံ	chan pi jan
best (adj)	အကောင်းဆုံး	akaun zoun
to congratulate (vt)	ဂုဏ်ပြုသည်	goun bju de

commentator	အစီရင်ခံသူ	asi jin gan dhu
to commentate (vt)	အစီရင်ခံသည်	asi jin gan de
broadcast	ထုတ်လွှင့်မှု	htou' hlwin. hmu.

137. Alpine skiing

skis	နှင်းလျှောစီးစကိတ်	hnin: sho: zi: zakei'
to ski (vi)	နှင်းလျှောစီးသည်	hnin: sho: zi: de
mountain-ski resort	နှင်းလျှောစီးစခန်း	hnin: sho: zi: za. gan:
ski lift	ရွှေ့လျားစက်ခါးပတ်	jwei. lja: ze' kha: ba'

ski poles	နင်းလျှောစီးထောက်တံ	hnin: sho: zi: dau' dan
slope	တောင်စောင်း	taun zaun:
slalom	နင်းလျှောစီးပြိုင်ပွဲ	hnin: sho: zi: bjein bwe:

138. Tennis. Golf

golf	ဂေါက်ရိုက်ခြင်း	gou' jai' chin:
golf club	ဂေါက်အသင်း	go' athin:
golfer	ဂေါက်ရိုက်သမား	gou' jai' thama:
hole	ဂေါက်ကျင်း	gou' kjin:
club	ဟော်ကီရိုက်တံ	hou ki jai' tan
golf trolley	ဂေါက်ကွင်းကား	gou' kwin: ga:
tennis	တင်းနစ်	tin: ni'
tennis court	တင်းနစ်ကစားကွင်း	tin: ni' gaza: kwin:
serve	ပေးဘော	pei: bo:
to serve (vt)	ပေးသည်	pei: de
racket	ရိုက်တံ	jai' tan
net	ပိုက်	pai'
ball	ဘောလုံး	bo loun:

139. Chess

chess	စစ်တုရင်	si' tu. jin
chessmen	စစ်တုရင်ရုပ်များ	si' tu. jin jou' mja:
chess player	စစ်တုရင်ကစားသမား	si' tu. jin gaza: dhama:
chessboard	စစ်တုရင်ခုံ	si' tu. jin goun
chessman	စစ်တုရင်ရုပ်	si' tu. jin jou'
White (white pieces)	အဖြူ	ahpju
Black (black pieces)	အနက်	ane'
pawn	နယ်ရုပ်	ne jou'
bishop	ဘုန်းကြီးရုပ်	hpoun: gji:
knight	မြင်းရုပ်	mjin: jou'
rook	ရထားရုပ်	jatha: jou'
queen	ဘုရင်မ	ba. jin ma.
king	ဘုရင်	ba. jin
move	အကွက်	akwe'
to move (vi, vt)	အကွက်ရွှေ့သည်	akwe' shwei. de
to sacrifice (vt)	စွန့်သည်	sun. de
castling	ရထားကွက်	jtha: kwe'
check	ချက်ကွက်	che' kwe'
checkmate	အပ်ကွက်	a' kwe'
chess tournament	တံခွန်စိုက်စစ်တု ရင်ပြိုင်ပွဲ	dagun zai' si' tu. jin bjein bwe:

Grand Master	စစ်တုရင်ပဟေ့	si' tu. jin bagei:
combination	ပေါင်းစပ်ခြင်း	paun: za' chin:
game (in chess)	ဂိမ်း	gein:
checkers	ကျားထိုးခြင်း	kja: dou: gjin:

140. Boxing

boxing	လက်ဝှေ့	le' hwei.
fight (bout)	တိုက်ခိုက်ခြင်း	tai' khai' chin:
boxing match	လက်ဝှေ့ပွဲ	le' hwei. bwe:
round (in boxing)	အကြိမ်	akjein

| ring | ကြိုးဝိုင်း | kjou: wain: |
| gong | မောင်း | maun: |

punch	ထိုးချက်	htou: gje'
knockdown	အလဲထိုးချက်	ale: htou: gje'
knockout	အမှောက်ထိုးချက်	ahmau' htou: gje'
to knock out	အလဲထိုးသည်	ale: htou: de

| boxing glove | လက်အိတ် | lei' ei' |
| referee | ဒိုင် | dain |

lightweight	အငယ်တန်း	ange dan:
middleweight	အလယ်တန်း	ale: dan:
heavyweight	အကြီးတန်း	akji: din:

141. Sports. Miscellaneous

Olympic Games	အိုလံပစ်အားကစားပွဲ	ou lan bi' a: gaza: bwe
winner	အနိုင်ရသူ	anain ja. dhu
to be winning	အနိုင်ရသည်	anain ja de
to win (vi)	နိုင်သည်	nain de

| leader | ခေါင်းဆောင် | gaun: zaun |
| to lead (vi) | ဦးဆောင်သည် | u: zaun de |

first place	ပထမဆု	pahtama. zu.
second place	ဒုတိယဆို	du. di. ja. zou
third place	တတိယဆု	tati. ja. zu.

medal	ဆုတံဆိပ်	hsu. dazei'
trophy	နိုင်ဆု	dain: zu.
prize cup (trophy)	ဆုဖလား	hsu. bala:
prize (in game)	ဆု	hsu.
main prize	အဓိကဆု	adi. ka. zu.
record	မှတ်တမ်း	hma' tan:
to set a record	မှတ်တမ်းတင်သည်	hma' tan: din de

final	ဗိုလ်လုပွဲ	bou lu. bwe:
final (adj)	နောက်ဆုံးဖြစ်သော	nau' hsoun: bji' te.
champion	ချန်ပီယံ	chan pi jan
championship	တံခွန်စိုက်ပြိုင်ပွဲ	dagun zai' pjein bwe:
stadium	အားကစားရုံ	a: gaza: joun
stand (bleachers)	ပွဲကြည့်စင်	pwe: gje. zi'
fan, supporter	ပရိတ်သတ်	pa. rei' tha'
opponent, rival	ပြိုင်ဘက်	pjain be'
start (start line)	စမှတ်	sahma'
finish line	ဆုံးမှတ်	hsoun: hma'
defeat	လက်လျော့ခြင်း	le' sho. gjin:
to lose (not win)	ရှုံးသည်	shoun: de
referee	ဒိုင်လူကြီး	dain dhu gji:
jury (judges)	အကဲဖြတ်ဒိုင်လူ ကြီးအဖွဲ့	ake: hpja dain lu gji: ahpwe.
score	ရလဒ်	jala'
tie	သရေ	thajei
to tie (vi)	သရေကျသည်	tha. jei gja. de
point	ရမှတ်	ja. hma'
result (final score)	ရလဒ်	jala'
period	အပိုင်း	apain:
half-time	ပွဲလယ်နားရှိန်	pwe: le na: gjein
doping	ဆေးသုံးခြင်း	hsei: dhoun: gjin:
to penalize (vt)	ပြစ်ဒဏ်ပေးသည်	pji' dan bei: de
to disqualify (vt)	ပိတ်ပင်သည်	pei' pin de
apparatus	တန်ဆာပလာ	tan za ba. la
javelin	လှံ	hlan
shot (metal ball)	သံလုံး	than loun:
ball (snooker, etc.)	ဘောလုံး	bo loun:
aim (target)	ချိန်သီး	chein dhi:
target	ပစ်မှတ်	pi' hma'
to shoot (vi)	ပစ်သည်	pi' te
accurate (~ shot)	တိတိကျကျဖြစ်သော	ti. ti. kja. kja. hpji te.
trainer, coach	နည်းပြ	ne: bja.
to train (sb)	လေ့ကျင့်ပေးသည်	lei. kjin. bei: de
to train (vi)	လေ့ကျင့်သည်	lei. kjin. de
training	လေ့ကျင့်ခြင်း	lei. kjin. gjin
gym	အားကစားခန်းမ	a: gaza: gan: ma.
exercise (physical)	လေ့ကျင့်ခန်း	lei. kjin. gan:
warm-up (athlete ~)	သွေးပူလေ့ကျင့်ခန်း	thwei: bu lei. kjin. gan:

Education

142. School

school	စာသင်ကျောင်း	sa dhin gjaun:
principal (headmaster)	ကျောင်းအုပ်ကြီး	ko: ou' kji:
pupil (boy)	ကျောင်းသား	kjaun: dha:
pupil (girl)	ကျောင်းသူ	kjaun: dhu
schoolboy	ကျောင်းသား	kjaun: dha:
schoolgirl	ကျောင်းသူ	kjaun: dhu
to teach (sb)	သင်ကြားသည်	thin kja: de
to learn (language, etc.)	သင်ယူသည်	thin ju de
to learn by heart	အလွတ်ကျက်သည်	alu' kje' de
to learn (~ to count, etc.)	သင်ယူသည်	thin ju de
to be in school	ကျောင်းတက်သည်	kjaun: de' de
to go to school	ကျောင်းသွားသည်	kjaun: dhwa: de
alphabet	အက္ခရာ	e' kha ja
subject (at school)	ဘာသာရပ်	ba da ja'
classroom	စာသင်ခန်း	sa dhin gan:
lesson	သင်ခန်းစာ	thin gan: za
recess	အနားချိန်	ana: gjain
school bell	ခေါင်းလောင်းသံ	gaun: laun: dhan
school desk	စာရေးခုံ	sajei: khoun
chalkboard	ကျောက်သင်ပုန်း	kjau' thin boun:
grade	အမှတ်	ahma'
good grade	အမှတ်အဆင့်မြင့်	ahma' ahsin. mjin.
bad grade	အမှတ်အဆင့်နိမ့်	ahma' ahsin. nin.
to give a grade	အမှတ်ပေးသည်	ahma' pei: de
mistake, error	အမှား	ahma:
to make mistakes	အမှားလုပ်သည်	ahma: lou' te
to correct (an error)	အမှားပြင်သည်	ahma: pjin de
cheat sheet	ခိုးကူးရန်စာ	khou: gu: jan za
	ရွက်အပိုင်းအစ	jwe' apain: asa.
homework	အိမ်စာ	ein za
exercise (in education)	လေ့ကျင့်ခန်း	lei. kjin. gan:
to be present	ရှိသည်	shi. de
to be absent	ပျက်ကွက်သည်	pje' kwe' te

to miss school	အတန်းပျက်ကွက်သည်	atan: bje' kwe' te
to punish (vt)	အပြစ်ပေးသည်	apja' pei: de
punishment	အပြစ်ပေးခြင်း	apja' pei: gjin:
conduct (behavior)	အပြုအမူ	apju amu
report card	စာမေးပွဲမှတ်တမ်း	sa mei: hma' tan:
pencil	ခဲတံ	khe: dan
eraser	ခဲဖျက်	khe: bje'
chalk	မြေဖြူ	mjei bju
pencil case	ခဲတံပူး	khe: dan bu:
schoolbag	ကျောင်းသုံးလွယ်အိတ်	kjaun: dhoun: lwe ji'
pen	ဘောပင်	bo pin
school notebook	လေ့ကျင့်ခန်းစာအုပ်	lei. kjin. gan: za ou'
textbook	ဖတ်စာအုပ်	hpa' sa au'
drafting compass	ထောက်ဆူး	htau' hsu:
to make technical drawings	ပုံကြမ်းဆွဲသည်	poun: gjam: zwe: de
technical drawing	နည်းပညာဆိုင်ရာပုံကြမ်း	ne bi nja zain ja boun gjan:
poem	ကဗျာ	ka. bja
by heart (adv)	အလွတ်	alu'
to learn by heart	အလွတ်ကျက်သည်	alu' kje' de
school vacation	ကျောင်းပိတ်ရက်	kjaun: bi' je'
to be on vacation	အားလပ်ရက်ရသည်	a: la' je' ja. de
to spend one's vacation	အားလပ်ရက်ဖြတ်သန်းသည်	a: la' je' hpja' than: de
test (written math ~)	အခန်းဆုံးစစ်ဆေးမှု	akhan: zain zi' hsei: hmu
essay (composition)	စာစီစာကုံး	sa zi za koun:
dictation	သတ်ပုံခေါ်ပေးခြင်း	tha' poun go bei: gjin:
exam (examination)	စာမေးပွဲ	sa mei: bwe:
to take an exam	စာမေးပွဲဖြေသည်	sa mei: bwe: bjei de
experiment (e.g., chemistry ~)	လက်တွေ့လုပ်ဆောင်မှု	le' twei: lou' zaun hma.

143. College. University

academy	အထူးပညာသင်ကျောင်း	a htu: bjin nja dhin kjaun:
university	တက္ကသိုလ်	te' kathou
faculty (e.g., ~ of Medicine)	ဌာန	hta. na.
student (masc.)	ကျောင်းသား	kjaun: dha:
student (fem.)	ကျောင်းသူ	kjaun: dhu
lecturer (teacher)	သင်ကြားပို့ချရှသူ	thin kja: bou. gja. dhu
lecture hall, room	စာသင်ခန်း	sa dhin gan:
graduate	ဘွဲ့ရသူ	bwe. ja. dhu

diploma	ဒီပလိုမာ	di' lou ma
dissertation	သုတေသနစာတမ်း	thu. tei thana za dan:
study (report)	သုတေသနစာတမ်း	thu. tei thana za dan
laboratory	လက်တွေ့ခန်း	le' twei. gan:
lecture	သင်ကြားပို့ချမှု	thin kja: bou. gja. hmu.
coursemate	အတန်းဖော်	atan: hpo
scholarship	ပညာသင်ဆု	pjin nja dhin zu.
academic degree	တက္ကသိုလ်ဘွဲ့	te' kathou bwe.

144. Sciences. Disciplines

mathematics	သင်္ချာ	thin cha
algebra	အက္ခရာသင်္ချာ	e' kha ja din gja
geometry	ရျိဩမေတြိ	gji o: mei tri
astronomy	နက္ခတ္တဗေဒ	ne' kha' ta. bei da.
biology	ဇီဝဗေဒ	zi: wa bei da.
geography	ပထဝီဝင်	pahtawi win
geology	ဘူမိဗေဒ	buu mi. bei da.
history	သမိုင်း	thamain:
medicine	ဆေးပညာ	hsei: pjin nja
pedagogy	သင်ကြားနည်းပညာ	thin kja: nei: pin nja
law	ဥပဒေဘာသာရပ်	u. ba. bei ba dha ja'
physics	ရူပဗေဒ	ju bei da.
chemistry	ဓာတုဗေဒ	da tu. bei da.
philosophy	ဒဿနိကဗေဒ	da' tha ni. ga. bei da.
psychology	စိတ်ပညာ	sei' pjin nja

145. Writing system. Orthography

grammar	သဒ္ဒါ	dhada
vocabulary	ဝေါဟာရ	wo: ha ra.
phonetics	သဒ္ဒဗေဒ	dhada. bei da.
noun	နာမ်	nan
adjective	နာမဝိသေသန	nan wi. dhei dha. na.
verb	ကြိယာ	kji ja
adverb	ကြိယာဝိသေသန	kja ja wi. dhei dha. na.
pronoun	နာမ်စား	nan za:
interjection	အာမေဍိတ်	a mei dei'
preposition	ဝိဘတ်	wi ba'
root	ဝေါဟာရရင်းမြစ်	wo: ha ra. jin: mji'
ending	အဆုံးသတ်	ahsoun: tha'

prefix	ရှေ့ဆက်ပုဒ်	shei. hse' pou'
syllable	ဝဏ္ဏ	wun na.
suffix	နောက်ဆက်ပုဒ်	nau' ze' pou'

stress mark	ဖိသံသင်္ကေတ	hpi. dhan dha. gei da.
apostrophe	ပိုင်ဆိုင်ခြင်းပြ	pain zain bjin: bja
	သင်္ကေတ	tin kei ta.

period, dot	ဖူးလ်စတော့ပ်	hpu: l za. po. p
comma	ပုဒ်ထီး သင်္ကေတ	pou' hti: tin kei ta.
semicolon	အဖြတ်အရပ်သင်္ကေတ	a hpja' aja' tha ngei da
colon	ကိုလန်	kou lan
ellipsis	စာချန်ပြအမှတ်အသား	sa gjan bja ahma' atha:

| question mark | မေးခွန်းပြအမှတ်အသား | mei: gun: bja. ahma' adha: |
| exclamation point | အာမေဍိတ်အမှတ်အသား | a mei dei' ahma' atha: |

quotation marks	မျက်တောင်အဖွင့်အပိတ်	mje' taun ahpwin. apei'
in quotation marks	မျက်တောင်အဖွင့်	mje' taun ahpwin.
	အပိတ်-အတွင်း	apei' atwin:

| parenthesis | ကွင်း | kwin: |
| in parenthesis | ကွင်းအတွင်း | kwin: atwin: |

hyphen	တုံးတို	toun: dou
dash	တုံးရှည်	toun: she
space (between words)	ကွက်လပ်	kwe' la'

| letter | စာလုံး | sa loun: |
| capital letter | စာလုံးကြီး | sa loun: gji: |

| vowel (n) | သရ | thara. |
| consonant (n) | ဗျည်း | bjin: |

sentence	ဝါကျ	we' kja.
subject	ကံ	kan
predicate	ဝါစက	wa saka.

line	မျဉ်းကြောင်း	mjin: gjaun:
on a new line	မျဉ်းကြောင်းအသစ်ပေါ်မှာ	mjin: gjaun: athi' bo hma.
paragraph	စာပိုဒ်	sa pai'

word	စကားလုံး	zaga: loun:
group of words	စကားစု	zaga: zu.
expression	ဖော်ပြချက်	hpjo bja. gje'
synonym	အနက်တူ	ane' tu
antonym	ဆန့်ကျင်ဘက်အနက်	hsan. gjin ba' ana'

rule	စည်းမျဉ်းစည်းကမ်း	si: mjin: si: kan:
exception	ခြွင်းချက်	chwin: gje'
correct (adj)	မှန်ကန်သော	hman gan de.
conjugation	ကြိယာပုံစံပြောင်းခြင်း	kji ja boun zan pjaun: chin:
declension	သဒ္ဒါပြောင်းလဲပုံ	dhada bjaun: le: boun

nominal case	နာမ်ပြောင်းပုံစံ	nan bjaun: boun zan
question	မေးခွန်း	mei: gun:
to underline (vt)	အလေးထားဖော်ပြသည်	a lei: da: hpo pja. de
dotted line	အစက်မျဉ်း	ase' mjin:

146. Foreign languages

language	ဘာသာစကား	ba dha zaga:
foreign (adj)	နိုင်ငံခြားနှင့်ဆိုင်သော	nain ngan gja: hnin. zain de.
foreign language	နိုင်ငံခြားဘာသာစကား	nain ngan gja: ba dha za ga:
to study (vt)	သင်ယူလေ့လာသည်	thin ju lei. la de
to learn (language, etc.)	သင်ယူသည်	thin ju de

to read (vi, vt)	ဖတ်သည်	hpa' te
to speak (vi, vt)	ပြောသည်	pjo: de
to understand (vt)	နားလည်သည်	na: le de
to write (vt)	ရေးသည်	jei: de

fast (adv)	မြန်မြန်	mjan mjan
slowly (adv)	ဖြည်းဖြည်း	hpjei: bjei:
fluently (adv)	ကျွမ်းကျင်ကျင်ကျင်	kjwan: gjwan: gjin gjin

rules	စည်းမျဉ်းစည်းကမ်း	si: mjin: si: kan:
grammar	သဒ္ဒါ	dhada
vocabulary	ဝေါဟာရ	wo: ha ra.
phonetics	သဒ္ဒဗေဒ	dhada. bei da.

textbook	ဖတ်စာအုပ်	hpa' sa au'
dictionary	အဘိဓာန်	abi. dan
teach-yourself book	မိမိဘာသာလေ့လာနိုင်သောစာအုပ်	mi. mi. ba dha lei. la nain dho: za ou'
phrasebook	နှစ်ဘာသာစကားပြောစာအုပ်	hni' ba dha zaga: bjo: za ou'

cassette, tape	တိပ်ခွေ	tei' khwei
videotape	ရုပ်ရှင်တိပ်ခွေ	jou' shin dei' hpwei
CD, compact disc	စီဒီခွေ	si di gwei
DVD	ဒီဗီဒီခွေ	di bi di gwei

alphabet	အက္ခရာ	e' kha ja
to spell (vt)	စာလုံးပေါင်းသည်	sa loun: baun: de
pronunciation	အသံထွက်	athan dwe'

accent	ဝဲသံ	we: dhan
with an accent	ဝဲသံနှင့်	we: dhan hnin.
without an accent	ဝဲသံမပါဘဲ	we: dhan ma. ba be:
word	စကားလုံး	zaga: loun:
meaning	အဓိပ္ပါယ်	adei' be

course (e.g., a French ~)	သင်တန်း	thin dan:
to sign up	စာရင်းသွင်းသည်	sajin: dhwin: de
teacher	ဆရာ	hsa ja
translation (process)	ဘာသာပြန်ခြင်း	ba dha bjan gjin:
translation (text, etc.)	ဘာသာပြန်ထားချက်	ba dha bjan da: gje'
translator	ဘာသာပြန်	ba dha bjan
interpreter	စကားပြန်	zaga: bjan
polyglot	ဘာသာစကားအများ ပြောနိုင်သူ	ba dha zaga: amja: bjo: nain dhu
memory	မှတ်ညဏ်	hma' njan

147. Fairy tale characters

Santa Claus	ခရစ္စမတ်ဘိုးဘိုး	khari' sa. ma' bou: bou:
Cinderella	စင်ဒရဲလား	sin da. je: la:
mermaid	ရေသူမ	jei dhu ma.
Neptune	နက်ပကျွန်း	ne' pa. gjun:
magician, wizard	မှော်ဆရာ	hmo za. ja
fairy	မှော်ဆရာမ	hmo za. ja ma.
magic (adj)	မှော်ပညာ	hmo ba. nja
magic wand	မှော်တုတ်တံ	hmjo dou' dan
fairy tale	ကလေးပုံပြင်	ka. lei: boun bjin
miracle	အံ့ဖွယ်	an. hpwe
dwarf	လူပုကလေး	u bu. ga. lei:
to turn into ...	ပြောင်းလဲပေးသည်	pjaun: le: bei: de
ghost	သရဲ	thaje:
phantom	တစ္ဆေ	tahsei
monster	ကြောက်မက်ဖွယ်ဧ ရာမသတ္တဝါ	kjau' ma' hpwe ei ja ma. dha' ta wa
dragon	နဂါး	na. ga:
giant	ဘီလူး	bi lu:

148. Zodiac Signs

Aries	မိဿရာသီ	mi. dha ja dhi
Taurus	ပြိဿရာသီ	pjei tha. jadhi
Gemini	မေထုန်ရာသီ	mei doun ja dhi
Cancer	ကရကဋ်ရာသီ	ka. ja. ka' ja dhi
Leo	သိဟ်ရာသီ	thei' ja dhi
Virgo	ကန်ရာသီ	kan ja dhi
Libra	တူရာသီ	tu ja dhi
Scorpio	ဗြိစ္ဆာရာသီ	bjei' hsa. jadhi

Sagittarius	ဓနုရာသီ	dan ja dhi
Capricorn	မကာရ်ရာသီဖွား	ma. ga. j ja dhi bwa:
Aquarius	ကုံရာသီဖွား	koun ja dhi hpwa:
Pisces	မိန်ရာသီဖွား	mein ja dhi bwa:

character	စရိုက် လက္ခဏာ	zajai' le' khana
character traits	ဥာဉ်	njin
behavior	အပြုအမူ	apju amu
to tell fortunes	အနာဂါတ်ဟောကိန်းထုတ်သည်	ana ga' ha gin: htou' te
fortune-teller	အနာဂါတ်ဟောကိန်းထုတ်သူ	ana ga' ha gin: htou' thu
horoscope	ဇာတာ	za da

Arts

149. Theater

theater	ကဇာတ်ရုံ	ka. za' joun
opera	အော်ပရာဇာတ်ရုံ	o pa ra za' joun
operetta	ပျော်ရွှင်ဖွယ် ကဇာတ်တို	pjo shin bwe: gaza' tou
ballet	ဘဲလေးကဇာတ်	be: lei: ga za'
theater poster	ပြဇာတ်ရုံပိုစတာ	pja. za' joun bou zada
troupe (theatrical company)	ဝိုင်းတော်သား	wain: do dha:
tour	လှည့်လည်ကပြဖျော်ဖြေခြင်း	hle. le ga. bja bjo bjei gjin:
to be on tour	လှည့်လည်ကပြဖျော်ဖြေသည်	hle. le ga. bja bjo bjei de
to rehearse (vi, vt)	ဇာတ်တိုက်သည်	za' tou' te
rehearsal	အစမ်းလေ့ကျင့်မှု	asan: lei. kjin. hmu.
repertoire	တင်ဆက်မှု	tin ze' hmu.
performance	ဖျော်ဖြေတင်ဆက်မှု	hpjo bjei din ze' hmu.
theatrical show	ဖျော်ဖြေမှု	hpjo bjei hmu.
play	ဇာတ်လမ်း	za' lan
ticket	လက်မှတ်	le' hma'
box office (ticket booth)	လက်မှတ်အရောင်းဌာန	le' hma' ajaun: hta. na.
lobby, foyer	ဧည့်သည်ဆောင်	e. dhe zaun
coat check (cloakroom)	ကုတ်နှင့်အိတ်အပ်နံခန်း	kou' hnin. i' a' hnan khan:
coat check tag	နံပါတ်ပြား	nan ba' pja:
binoculars	နှစ်လုံးပျူးမှန်ပြောင်း	hni' loun: bju: hman bjaun:
usher	ဧည့်ကြို	e. gjou
orchestra seats	ဇာတ်စင်ထိုင်ခုံ	za' sin dain guan
balcony	လသာဆောင်	la. dha zaun
dress circle	ပထမထပ်ပွဲ ကြည့်ဆောင်	pahtama. da' bwe: gje. zaun
box	လက်မှတ်ရောင်းသည့်နေရာ	le' hma' jaun: dhi. nei ja
row	အတန်း	atan:
seat	နေရာ	nei ja
audience	ပရိတ်သတ်အစုအဝေး	pa. rei' tha' asu. awei:
spectator	ပရိတ်သတ်	pa. rei' tha'
to clap (vi, vt)	လက်ခုပ်တီးသည်	le' khou' ti: de
applause	လက်ခုပ်သြဘာသံ	le' khou' thja ba dhan
ovation	သြဘာပေးခြင်း	thja dha bei: gjin:
stage	စင်	sin
curtain	လိုက်ကာ	lai' ka

| scenery | နောက်ခံကားချပ် | nau' khan gan ga: gja' |
| backstage | ဇာတ်စင်နောက် | za' sin nau' |

scene (e.g., the last ~)	တကယ့်ဖြစ်ရပ်	dage. bji ja'
act	သရုပ်ဆောင်	thajou' hsaun
intermission	ကြားကာလ	ka: ga la.

150. Cinema

| actor | မင်းသား | min: dha: |
| actress | မင်းသမီး | min: dhami: |

movies (industry)	ရုပ်ရှင်လုပ်ငန်း	jou' shin lou' ngan:
movie	ရုပ်ရှင်ကား	jou' shin ga:
episode	ဇာတ်ခန်းတစ်ခန်း	za' khan: ti' khan:

detective movie	စုံထောက်ဇာတ်လမ်း	soun dau' za' lan:
action movie	အက်ရှင်ဇာတ်လမ်း	e' shin za' lan:
adventure movie	စွန့်စားခန်းဇာတ်လမ်း	sun. za: gan: za' lan:
sci-fi movie	သိပ္ပံပိတ်ကူးယဉ်ဇာတ်လမ်း	thei' pan zei' ku: jin za' lan:
horror movie	ထိတ်လန့်ဖွယ်ရုပ်ရှင်	htei' lan. bwe jou' jou'

comedy movie	ဟာသရုပ်ရှင်	ha dha. jou' jou'
melodrama	အပြင်းစားအရောမာ	apjin: za: da. ja ma
drama	အလွမ်းဇာတ်လမ်း	alwan: za' lan:

fictional movie	စိတ်ကူးယဉ်ဇာတ်လမ်း	sei' ku: jin za' lan:
documentary	မှတ်တမ်းရုပ်ရှင်	hma' tan: jou' shin
cartoon	ကာတွန်းဇာတ်လမ်း	ka tun: za' lan:
silent movies	အသံတိတ်ရုပ်ရှင်	athan dei' jou' shin

role (part)	အခန်းကဏ္ဍ	akhan: gan da.
leading role	အဓိကအခန်းကဏ္ဍ	adi. ka. akhan: kan da
to play (vi, vt)	သရုပ်ဆောင်သည်	thajou' hsaun de

movie star	ရုပ်ရှင်စတား	jou' shin za. da:
well-known (adj)	နာမည်ကြီးသော	na me gji: de.
famous (adj)	ကျော်ကြားသော	kjo kja: de.
popular (adj)	လူကြိုက်များသော	lu gjou' mja: de.

script (screenplay)	ဇာတ်ညွှန်း	za' hnjun:
scriptwriter	ဇာတ်ညွှန်းဆရာ	za' hnjun: za ja
movie director	ရုပ်ရှင်ဒါရိုက်တာ	jou' shin da jai' ta
producer	ထုတ်လုပ်သူ	htou' lou' thu
assistant	လက်ထောက်	le' htau'
cameraman	ကင်မရာမန်း	kin ma. ja man:
stuntman	စတန့်သမား	satan. dhama:
double (stand-in)	ပုံစံတု	poun zan du
to shoot a movie	ရုပ်ရှင်ရိုက်သည်	jou' shin jai' te
audition, screen test	စမ်းသပ်ကြည့်ရှုခြင်း	san: dha' chi. shu. gjin:

shooting	ရိုက်ကွင်း	jai' kwin:
movie crew	ရုပ်ရှင်အဖွဲ့	jou' shin ahpwe.
movie set	ဇာတ်အိမ်	za' ein
camera	ကင်မရာ	kin ma. ja

movie theater	ရုပ်ရှင်ရုံ	jou' shin joun
screen (e.g., big ~)	ပိတ်ကား	pei' ka:
to show a movie	ရုပ်ရှင်ပြသည်	jou' shin bja. de

soundtrack	အသံသွင်းတိပ်ခွေ	athan dhwin: di' khwei
special effects	အထူးပြုလုပ်ချက်များ	a htu: bju. lou' che' mja:
subtitles	စာတန်းထိုး	sa dan: dou:
credits	ပါဝင်သူများအမည်စာရင်း	pa win dhu mja: ame zajin:
translation	ဘာသာပြန်	ba dha bjan

151. Painting

art	အနုပညာ	anu. pjin nja
fine arts	သုခုမအနုပညာ	thu. khu. ma. anu. pin nja
art gallery	အနုပညာပြခန်း	anu. pjin pja. gan:
art exhibition	ပြပွဲ	pja. bwe:

painting (art)	ပန်းချီကား	bagji ga:
graphic art	ပုံဆွဲခြင်း	poun zwe: gjin:
	အနုပညာ	anu pjin nja

| abstract art | 57550 စိတ္တဇပန်း | sei' daza. ban: |
| | ချီဆွဲခြင်း | gji zwe: gjin: |

| impressionism | အာရောင်အလင်း | ajaun alin: bjin. ban: |
| | ဖြင့်ပန်းချီဆွဲခြင်း | gji zwe: gjin: |

picture (painting)	ပန်းချီကား	bagji ga:
drawing	ရုပ်ပုံကားချပ်	jou' poun ga: gja'
poster	ပိုစတာ	pou sata

| illustration (picture) | ရုပ်ပုံထည့်သွင်း | jou' poun di. dwin: |
| | ဖော်ပြခြင်&#4152 | bo bja. gjin: |

miniature	ပုံစံအသေးစား	poun zan athei: za:
copy (of painting, etc.)	မိတ္တူ	mi' tu
reproduction	ပုံတူပန်းချီ	poun du ban: gji

mosaic	မှန်စီရွှေချပန်းချီ	hman zi shwei gja ban: gji
stained glass window	မှန်ရောင်စုံ	hman jaun zoun
	ပြတင်းပေါက်	bja. din: bau'

| fresco | နံရံဆေးရေးပန်းချီ | nan jan zei: jei: ban: gji |
| engraving | ပုံထွင်းပညာ | poun dwin: pjin nja |

bust (sculpture)	ကိုယ်တစ်ပိုင်းပုံရုပ်လုံး	kou ti' pain: boun jou' loun:
sculpture	ကျောက်ဆစ်ရုပ်	kjau' hsi' jou'
statue	ရုပ်တု	jou' tu.
plaster of Paris	အင်္ဂတေ	angga. dei

plaster (as adj)	အင်္ဂတေဖြင့်	angga. dei hpjin.
portrait	ပုံတူ	poun du
self-portrait	ကိုယ်တိုင်ရေးပုံတူ	kou tain jou: boun dhu
landscape painting	ရှုခင်းပုံ	shu. gin: boun
still life	သက်မဲ့ဝတ္ထုပုံ	the' me. wu' htu boun
caricature	ရုပ်ပြောင်	jou' pjaun
sketch	ပုံကြမ်း	poun gjan:

paint	သုတ်ဆေး	thou' hsei:
watercolor paint	ရေဆေးပန်းချီ	jei zei: ban: gji
oil (paint)	ဆီ	hsi
pencil	ခဲတံ	khe: dan
India ink	အိန္ဒိယမင်	indi. ja hmin
charcoal	မီးသွေး	mi: dhwei:

| to draw (vi, vt) | ပုံဆွဲသည် | poun zwe: de |
| to paint (vi, vt) | အဆောင်ချယ်သည် | ajaun gje de |

to pose (vi)	ကိုယ်ဟန်ပြသည်	kou han pja de
artist's model (masc.)	ပန်းချီမော်ဒယ်	bagji mo de
artist's model (fem.)	ပန်းချီမော်ဒယ်မိန်းကလေး	bagji mo de mein: ga. lei:

artist (painter)	ပန်းချီဆရာ	bagji zaja
work of art	အနုပညာလက်ရာ	anu. pjin nja le' ja
masterpiece	အပြောင်မြောက်ဆုံးလက်ရာ	apjaun mjau' hsoun: le' ja
studio (artist's workroom)	အလုပ်ခန်း	alou' khan:

canvas (cloth)	ပန်းချီဆွဲရန်ပတ္တူစ	bagji zwe: jan: ba' tu za.
easel	ဒေါက်တိုင်	dau' tain
palette	ပန်းချီဆေးစပ်သည့်ပြား	bagji hsei: za' thi. bja:

frame (picture ~, etc.)	ဘောင်	baun
restoration	နဂိုအတိုင်းပြန်လည်	na. gou atain: bjan le
	မွမ်းမံခြင်း	mun: man gjin:
to restore (vt)	ပြန်လည်မွမ်းမံသည်	pjan le mwan: man de

152. Literature & Poetry

literature	စာပေ	sa pei
author (writer)	စာရေးသူ	sajei: dhu
pseudonym	ကလောင်အမည်	kalaun amji

book	စာအုပ်	sa ou'
volume	ထုထည်	du. de
table of contents	မာတိကာ	ma di. ga
page	စာမျက်နှာ	sa mje' hna
main character	အဓိကဇာတ်ဆောင်	adi. ka. za' hsaun
autograph	အမှတ်တရလက်မှတ်	ahma' ta ra le' hma'
short story	ပုံပြင်	pjoun bjin
story (novella)	ဝတ္ထုဇာတ်လမ်း	wu' htu. za' lan:

novel	ဝတ္ထု	wu' htu.
work (writing)	လက်ရာ	le' ja
fable	ဒဏ္ဍာရီ	dan da ji
detective novel	စုံထောက်ဇာတ်လမ်း	soun dau' za' lan:
poem (verse)	ကဗျာ	ka. bja
poetry	လင်္ကာ	lin ga
poem (epic, ballad)	ကဗျာ	ka. bja
poet	ကဗျာဆရာ	ka. bja zaja
fiction	စိတ်ကူးယဉ်ဇာတ်လမ်း	sei' ku: jin za' lan: ⁄
science fiction	သိပ္ပံဇာတ်လမ်း	thei' pan za' lan:
adventures	စွန့်စားခန်းဇာတ်လမ်း	sun. za: gan: za' lan:
educational literature	ပညာပေးဇာတ်လမ်း	pjin nja bei: za' lan:
children's literature	ကလေးဆိုင်ရာစာပေ	kalei: hsin ja za bei

153. Circus

circus	ဆပ်ကပ်	hsa' ka'
traveling circus	နယ်လှည့်ဆပ်ကပ်အဖွဲ့	ne hle. za' ka' ahpwe:
program	အစီအစဉ်	asi asin
performance	ဖျော်ဖြေတင်ဆက်မှု	hpjo bjel din ze' hmu.
act (circus ~)	ဖျော်ဖြေတင်ဆက်မှု	hpjo bjel din ze' hmu.
circus ring	အစီအစဉ်တင်ဆက်ရာနေရာ	asi asin din ze' ja nei ja
pantomime (act)	ဇာတ်လမ်းသရုပ်ဖော်	za' lan: dha jou' hpo
clown	လူရွှင်တော်	lu shwin do
acrobat	ကျွမ်းဘားပြသူ	kjwan: ba: bja dhu
acrobatics	ကျွမ်းဘားပြုခြင်း	kjwan: ba: bja gjin:
gymnast	ကျွမ်းဘားသမား	kjwan: ba: dhama:
acrobatic gymnastics	ကျွမ်းဘားအားကစား	kjwan: ba: a: gaza:
somersault	ကျွမ်းပစ်ခြင်း	kjwan: bi' chin:
athlete (strongman)	လူသန်ကြီး	lu dhan gji:
tamer (e.g., lion ~)	ယဉ်လာအောင်လေ့ ကျင့်ပေးသူ	jin la aun lei. gjin. bei: dhu
rider (circus horse ~)	မြင်းစီးသူ	mjin: zi: dhu
assistant	လက်ထောက်	le' htau'
stunt	စတန့်	satan.
magic trick	မှော်ဆန်သောလှည့်ကွက်	hmo zan dho hle. gwe'
conjurer, magician	မျက်လှည့်ဆရာ	mje' hle. zaja
juggler	လက်လှည့်ဆရာ	le' hli. za. ja.
to juggle (vi, vt)	လက်လှည့်ပြုသည်	le' hli. bja. de
animal trainer	တိရစ္ဆာန်သင်ကြား ပေးသူ	tharei' hsan dhin gja: bei: dhu
animal training	တိရစ္ဆာန်များကို လေ့ကျင့်ပေးခြင်း	tharei' hsan mja: gou: lei. gjin. bei: gjin:
to train (animals)	လေ့ကျင့်ပေးသည်	lei. kjin. bei: de

154. Music. Pop music

music	ဂီတ	gi ta.
musician	ဂီတပညာရှင်	gi ta. bjin nja shin
musical instrument	တူရိယာ	tu ji. ja
to play …	တီးသည်	ti: de
guitar	ဂီတာ	gi ta
violin	တယော	ta jo:
cello	စီလိုတယောကြီး	si lou tajo: gji:
double bass	ဘော့စ်တယောကြီး	bei'. ta. jo gji:
harp	စောင်း	saun:
piano	စန္ဒရား	san daja:
grand piano	စန္ဒရားကြီး	san daja: gji:
organ	အော်ဂင်	o gin
wind instruments	လေမှုတ်တူရိယာ	lei hmou' tu ji. ja
oboe	အိုဗိုနီ	ou bou hne:
saxophone	ဆက်ဆိုဖုန်း	hse' hso phoun:
clarinet	ကလယ်ရိနက်-ပလွေ	kale ji ne' - pa lwei
flute	ပလွေ	palwei
trumpet	ထရမ်းပက်ခရောငယ်	htajan: be' khaja nge
accordion	အကော်ဒီယံ	ako di jan
drum	စည်	si
duo	နှစ်ယောက်တွဲ	hni' jau' twe:
trio	သုံးယောက်တွဲ	thoun: jau' twe:
quartet	လေးယောက်တစ်တွဲ	lei: jau' ti' twe:
choir	သံပြိုင်အဖွဲ့	than bjain ahpwe.
orchestra	သံစုံတီးဝိုင်း	than zoun di: wain:
pop music	ပေါ့ပ်ဂီတ	po. p gi da.
rock music	ရော့ခ်ဂီတ	ro. kh gi da.
rock group	ရော့ခ်ဂီတအဖွဲ့	ro. kh gi da. ahpwe.
jazz	ဂျတ်ဇ်ဂီတ	gja' z gi ta.
idol	အသည်းစွဲ	athe: zwe:
admirer, fan	နှစ်သက်သူ	hni' the' dhu
concert	တေးဂီတဖြေဖျော်ပွဲ	tei: gi da. bjei bjo bwe:
symphony	သံစုံဝင်တီးတေးသွား	than zoun za' ti: dei: dwa:
composition	ရေးဖွဲ့သီကုံးခြင်း	jei: bwe dhi goun: gjin:
to compose (write)	ရေးဖွဲ့သီကုံးသည်	jei: bwe dhi goun: de
singing (n)	သီချင်းဆိုခြင်း	thachin: zou gjin:
song	သီချင်း	thachin:
tune (melody)	တီးလုံး	ti: loun:
rhythm	စည်းချက်	si gje'
blues	ဘလူးစ်ဂီတ	ba. lu: s gi'

sheet music	ဂီတာသင်္ကေတာများ	gi ta. dhin gei da. mja:
baton	ဂီတာအချက်ပြတုတ်	gi ta. ache' pja dou'
bow	ဘိုးတံ	bou: dan
string	ကြိုး	kjou:
case (e.g., guitar ~)	အိတ်	ei'

Rest. Entertainment. Travel

155. Trip. Travel

tourism, travel	ခရီးသွားလုပ်ငန်း	khaji: thwa: lou' ngan:
tourist	ကမ္ဘာလှည့်ခရီးသည်	ga ba hli. kha. ji: de
trip, voyage	ခရီးထွက်ခြင်း	khaji; htwe' chin:
adventure	စွန့်စားမှု	sun. za: hmu.
trip, journey	ခရီး	khaji:
vacation	ခွင့်ရက်	khwin. je'
to be on vacation	အခွင့်ယူသည်	akhwin. ju de
rest	အနားယူခြင်း	ana: ju gjin:
train	ရထား	jatha:
by train	ရထားနဲ့	jatha: ne.
airplane	လေယာဉ်	lei jan
by airplane	လေယာဉ်နဲ့	lei jan ne.
by car	ကားနဲ့	ka: ne.
by ship	သင်္ဘောနဲ့	thin: bo: ne.
luggage	ဝန်စည်စလည်	wun zi za. li
suitcase	သားရေသေတ္တာ	tha: jei dhi' ta
luggage cart	ပစ္စည်းတင်ရန်တွန်းလှည်း	pji' si: din jan dun: hle:
passport	နိုင်ငံကူးလက်မှတ်	nain ngan gu: le' hma'
visa	ဗီဇာ	bi za
ticket	လက်မှတ်	le' hma'
air ticket	လေယာဉ်လက်မှတ်	lei jan le' hma'
guidebook	လမ်းညွှန်စာအုပ်	lan: hnjun za ou'
map (tourist ~)	မြေပုံ	mjei boun
area (rural ~)	ဒေသ	dei dha.
place, site	နေရာ	nei ja
exotica (n)	အထူးအဆန်းပစ္စည်း	a htu: a hsan: bji' si:
exotic (adj)	အထူးအဆန်းဖြစ်သော	a htu: a hsan: hpja' te.
amazing (adj)	အံ့သြဖွယ်ကောင်းသော	an. o: sa ja kaun de.
group	အုပ်စု	ou' zu.
excursion, sightseeing tour	လေ့လာရေးခရီး	lei. la jei: gaji:
guide (person)	လမ်းညွှန်	lan: hnjun

156. Hotel

hotel	ဟိုတယ်	hou te
motel	မိုတယ်	mou te
three-star (~ hotel)	ကြယ် ၃ ပွင့်အဆင့်	kje thoun: pwin. ahsin.
five-star	ကြယ် ၅ ပွင့်အဆင့်	kje nga: pwin. ahsin.
to stay (in a hotel, etc.)	တည်းခိုသည်	te: khou de
room	အခန်း	akhan:
single room	တစ်ယောက်ခန်း	ti' jau' khan:
double room	နှစ်ယောက်ခန်း	hni' jau' khan:
to book a room	ကြိုတင်မှာယူသည်	kjou tin hma ju de
half board	ကြိုတင်တွစ်ဝက် ငွေချေခြင်း	kjou tin di' we' ngwe gjei gjin:
full board	ငွေအပြည့်ကြို တင်ပေးချေခြင်း	ngwe apjei. kjou din bei: chei chin:
with bath	ရေချိုးခန်းနှင့်	jei gjou gan: hnin.
with shower	ရေပန်းနှင့်	jei ban: hnin.
satellite television	ဂြိုဟ်တုရုပ်မြင် သိကြား	gjou' htu. jou' mjin dhan gja:
air-conditioner	လေအေးပေးစက်	lei ei: bei: ze'
towel	တဘက်	tabe'
key	သော့	tho.
administrator	အုပ်ချုပ်ရေးမှူး	ou' chu' jei: hmu:
chambermaid	သန့်ရှင်းရေးဝန်ထမ်း	than. shin: jei: wun dan:
porter, bellboy	အထမ်းသမား	a htan: dha. ma:
doorman	တံခါးဝမှ စောင့်ကြို	daga: wa. hma. e. kjou
restaurant	စားသောက်ဆိုင်	sa: thau' hsain
pub, bar	ဘား	ba:
breakfast	နံနက်စာ	nan ne' za
dinner	ညစာ	nja. za
buffet	ဘူဖေး	bu hpei:
lobby	နားနေခင်ခန်း	hna jaun gan:
elevator	ဓာတ်လှေကား	da' hlei ga:
DO NOT DISTURB	မနှောင့်ယှက်ရ	ma. hnaun hje' ja.
NO SMOKING	ဆေးလိပ်မသောက်ရ	hsei: lei' ma. dhau' ja.

157. Books. Reading

book	စာအုပ်	sa ou'
author	စာရေးသူ	sajei: dhu
writer	စာရေးဆရာ	sajei: zaja

to write (~ a book)	စာရေးသည်	sajei: de
reader	စာဖတ်သူ	sa hpa' thu
to read (vi, vt)	ဖတ်သည်	hpa' te
reading (activity)	စာဖတ်ခြင်း	sa hpa' chin:

| silently (to oneself) | တိတ်တဆိတ် | tei' ta. hsei' |
| aloud (adv) | ကျယ်လောင်စွာ | kje laun zwa |

to publish (vt)	ပုံနှိပ်ထုတ်ဝေသည်	poun nei' htou' wei de
publishing (process)	ပုံနှိပ်ထုတ်ဝေခြင်း	poun nei' htou' wei gjin:
publisher	ထုတ်ဝေသူ	htou' wei dhu
publishing house	ပုံနှိပ်ထုတ်ဝေ သည့်ကုမ္ပဏီ	poun nei' htou' wei dhi. koun pani

to come out (be released)	ထွက်သည်	htwe' te
release (of a book)	ဖြန့်ချိခြင်း	hpjan. gji gjin:
print run	စာရေးသူ	sajei: dhu

| bookstore | စာအုပ်ဆိုင် | sa ou' hsain |
| library | စာကြည့်တိုက် | sa gji. dai' |

story (novella)	ဝတ္ထုဇာတ်လမ်း	wu' htu. za' lan:
short story	ဝတ္ထုတို	wu' htu. dou
novel	ဝတ္ထု	wu' htu.
detective novel	စုံထောက်ဇာတ်လမ်း	soun dau' za' lan:

memoirs	ကိုယ်တွေ့မှတ်တမ်း	kou twei. hma' tan:
legend	ဒဏ္ဍာရီ	dan da ji
myth	စိတ်ကူးယဉ်	sei' ku: jin

poetry, poems	ကဗျာများ	ka. bja mja:
autobiography	ကိုယ်တိုင်ရေးအတ္ထုပ္ပတ္တိ	kou tain jei' a' tu. bi' ta.
selected works	လက်ရွေးစင်	le' jwei: zin
science fiction	သိပ္ပံဇာတ်လမ်း	thei' pan za' lan:

title	ခေါင်းစဉ်	gaun: zin
introduction	နိဒါန်း	ni. dan:
title page	ခေါင်းစီးစာမျက်နှာ	gaun: zi: za: mje' hna

chapter	ခေါင်းကြီးပိုင်း	gaun: gji: bain:
extract	ကောက်နှုတ်ချက်	kau' hnou' khje'
episode	အပိုင်း	apain:

plot (storyline)	ဇာတ်ကြောင်း	za' kjaun:
contents	မာတိကာ	ma di. ga
table of contents	မာတိကာ	ma di. ga
main character	အဓိကဇာတ်ဆောင်	adi. ka. za' hsaun

volume	တွဲ	du. de
cover	စာအုပ်အဖုံး	sa ou' ahpoun:
binding	အဖုံး	ahpoun:
bookmark	စာညှပ်	sa hnja'

page	စာမျက်နှာ	sa mje' hna
to page through	စာရွက်လှန်သည်	sajwe' hlan de
margins	နယ်နိမိတ်	ne ni. mei'
annotation	မှတ်စာ	hma' sa
(marginal note, etc.)		
footnote	အောက်ခြေမှတ်ချက်	au' chei hma' che'

text	စာသား	sa dha:
type, font	ပုံစံ	poun zan
misprint, typo	ပုံနှိပ်အမှား	poun nei' ahma:

translation	ဘာသာပြန်	ba dha bjan
to translate (vt)	ဘာသာပြန်သည်	ba dha bjan de
original (n)	မူရင်း	mu jin:

famous (adj)	ကျော်ကြားသော	kjo kja: de.
unknown (not famous)	လူမသိသော	lu ma. thi. de.
interesting (adj)	စိတ်ဝင်စားစရာကောင်းသော	sei' win za: zaja gaun: de.
bestseller	ရောင်းအားအကောင်းဆုံး	jo: a: akaun: zoun:

dictionary	အဘိဓာန်	abi. dan
textbook	ဖတ်စာအုပ်	hpa' sa au'
encyclopedia	စွယ်စုံကျမ်း	swe zoun gjan:

158. Hunting. Fishing

hunting	အမဲလိုက်ခြင်း	ame: lai' chin
to hunt (vi, vt)	အမဲလိုက်သည်	ame: lai' de
hunter	မုဆိုး	mou' hsou:

to shoot (vi)	ပစ်သည်	pi' te
rifle	ရိုင်ဖယ်	jain be
bullet (shell)	ကျည်ဆံ	kji. zan
shot (lead balls)	ကျည်စေ့	kji zei.

steel trap	သံမဏိထောင်ချောက်	than mani. daun gjau'
snare (for birds, etc.)	ကျော့ကွင်း	kjo. kwin:
to fall into the steel trap	ထောင်ချောက်မိသည်	htaun gjau' mi de
to lay a steel trap	ထောင်ချောက်ဆင်သည်	htaun gjau' hsin de

poacher	တရားမဝင်ခိုးပစ်သူ	taja: ma. win gou: bi' thu
game (in hunting)	အမဲလိုက်ခြင်း	ame: lai' chin
hound dog	အမဲလိုက်ခွေး	ame: lai' khwei:
safari	ဆာဖာရီတောရိုင်းဒေသ	hsa hpa ji do joun: dei dha.
mounted animal	ရုပ်လုံးဖော်တိရစ္ဆာန်ရုပ်	jou' loun: bo di ja' zan jou'

fisherman, angler	တံငါသည်	da nga dhi
fishing (angling)	ငါးဖမ်းခြင်း	nga: ban: gjin
to fish (vi)	ငါးဖမ်းသည်	nga: ban: de
fishing rod	ငါးများတံ	nga: mja: dan

fishing line	ငါးမျှားကြိုး	nga: mja: gjou:
hook	ငါးမျှားချိတ်	nga: mja: gji'
float, bobber	ငါးမျှားတံဖော့	nga: mja: dan bo.
bait	ငါးစာ	nga: za
to cast a line	ငါးမျှားကြိုးပစ်သည်	nga: mja: gjou: bji' te
to bite (ab. fish)	ကိုက်သည်	kou' de
catch (of fish)	ငါးထည့်စရာ	nga: de. za. ja
ice-hole	ရေခဲပြင်ပေါ်မှအပေါက်	jei ge: bjin bo hma. a. bau'
fishing net	ပိုက်	pai'
boat	လှေ	hlei
to net (to fish with a net)	ပိုက်ချသည်	pai' cha. de
to cast[throw] the net	ပိုက်ပစ်သည်	pai' pi' te
to haul the net in	ပိုက်ဆယ်သည်	pai' hse de
to fall into the net	ပိုက်တိုးမိသည်	pai' tou: mi. de
whaler (person)	ဝေလငါး	wei la. nga:
whaleboat	ဝေလငါးဖမ်းလှေ	wei la. nga: ban: hlei
harpoon	မှိန်း	hmein:

159. Games. Billiards

billiards	ဘီလီယက်	bi li je'
billiard room, hall	ဘီလီယက်ထိုးခန်း	bi li ja' htou: khana:
ball (snooker, etc.)	ဘီလီယက်ဘောလုံး	bi li ja' bo loun:
to pocket a ball	ကျင်းထည့်သည်	kjin: de. de
cue	ကြူတံ	kju dan
pocket	ကျင်း	kjin:

160. Games. Playing cards

diamonds	ထောင့်	htaun.
spades	စပိတ်	sapei'
hearts	ဟတ်	ha'
clubs	ညှင်း	hnjin:
ace	တစ်ဖဲ	ti' hpe:
king	ကင်း	kin:
queen	ကွင်း	kwin:
jack, knave	ဂျက်	gje'
playing card	ဖဲကစားသည်	hpe: ga. za de
cards	ဖဲချပ်များ	hpe: gje' mja:
trump	ဝှက်ဖဲ	hwe' hpe:
deck of cards	ဖဲထုပ်	hpe: dou'
point	အမှတ်	ahma'

to deal (vi, vt)	ဖဲဝေသည်	hpe: wei de
to shuffle (cards)	ကုလားဖန်ထိုးသည်	kala: ban dou de
lead, turn (n)	ဦးဆုံးအလှည့်	u: zoun: ahle.
cardsharp	ဖဲလိမ်သမား	hpe: lin dha ma:

161. Casino. Roulette

casino	လောင်းကစားရုံ	laun: gaza: joun
roulette (game)	နံပါတ်လှည့်လောင်းကစား	nan ba' hle. laun: ga. za:
bet	အလောင်းအစား	alaun: asa:
to place bets	လောင်းကြေးတင်သည်	laun: gjei: tin de

red	အနီ	ani
black	အနက်	ane'
to bet on red	အနီလောင်းသည်	ani laun: de
to bet on black	အနက်လောင်းသည်	ane' laun: de

croupier (dealer)	လောင်းကစားဒိုင်	laun: gaza: dain
to spin the wheel	အဝိုင်းလှည့်သည်	awain: hle. de
rules (of game)	ကစားနည်းစည်းမျဉ်း	gaza: ne: zin: mjin:
chip	တိုကင်ပြား	tou gin bja:

| to win (vi, vt) | နိုင်သည် | nain de |
| win (winnings) | အနိုင် | anain |

| to lose (~ 100 dollars) | ရှုံးသည် | shoun: de |
| loss (losses) | အရှုံး | ashoun: |

player	ကစားသမား	gaza: dhama:
blackjack (card game)	ဘလက်ဂျက်	ba. le' gje'
craps (dice game)	အန်စာတုံးလောင်း ကစားနည်း	an za doun: laun: ga za: ne:
dice (a pair of ~)	အန်စာတုံး	an za doun:
slot machine	ရေးရောင်းစက်	zei: jaun: ze'

162. Rest. Games. Miscellaneous

to stroll (vi, vt)	အပန်းဖြေလမ်းလျှောက်သည်	apin: hpjei lan: jau' the
stroll (leisurely walk)	လမ်းလျှောက်ခြင်း	lan: shau' chin:
car ride	အပန်းဖြေခရီး	apin: hpjei khaji:
adventure	စွန့်စားမှု	sun. za: hmu.
picnic	ပျော်ပွဲစား	pjo bwe: za:

game (chess, etc.)	ဂိမ်း	gein:
player	ကစားသမား	gaza: dhama:
game (one ~ of chess)	ကစားပွဲ	gaza: pwe:
collector (e.g., philatelist)	စုဆောင်းသူ	su. zaun: dhu
to collect (stamps, etc.)	စုဆောင်းသည်	su. zaun: de

collection	စုဆောင်းခြင်း	su. zaun: gjin:
crossword puzzle	စကားလုံးဆက် ပဟေဠိ	zaga: loun: ze' bahei li.
racetrack	ပြေးလမ်း	pjei: lan:
(horse racing venue)		
disco (discotheque)	ဒစ္စကိုကပွဲ	di' sa kou ga. bwe:
sauna	ပေါင်းခံရွှေးထုတ်ခန်း	paun: gan gjwa: dou' khan:
lottery	ထီ	hti
camping trip	အပျော်စခန်းချရခရီး	apjo za. khan: khja kha ni:
camp	စခန်း	sakhan:
tent (for camping)	တဲ	te:
compass	သံလိုက်အိမ်မြှောင်	than lai' ein hmjaun
camper	စခန်းချသူ	sakhan: gja. dhu
to watch (movie, etc.)	ကြည့်သည်	kji. de
viewer	ကြည့်သူ	kji. thu
TV show (TV program)	ရုပ်မြင်သံကြား	jou' mjin dhan gja:
	အစီအစဉ်	asi asan

camera (photo)	ကင်မရာ	kin ma. ja
photo, picture	ဓာတ်ပုံ	da' poun
photographer	ဓာတ်ပုံဆရာ	da' poun za ja
photo studio	ဓာတ်ပုံရိုက်ရန်အခန်း	da' poun jai' jan akhan:
photo album	ဓာတ်ပုံအယ်လ်ဘမ်	da' poun e la. ban
camera lens	ကင်မရာမှန်ဘီလူး	kin ma. ja hman bi lu:
telephoto lens	အဝေးရိုက်သောမှန်ဘီလူး	awei: shi' tho: hman bi lu:
filter	အရောင်စစ်မှန်ပြား	ajaun za' hman bja:
lens	မှန်ဘီလူး	hman bi lu:
optics (high-quality ~)	အလင်းပညာ	alin: bjin
diaphragm (aperture)	ကင်မရာတွင်	kin ma. ja twin
	အလင်းဝင်ပေါက်	alin: win bau'
exposure time	အလင်းရောင်ဖွင့်ပေးချိန်	alin: jaun hpwin bei: gjein
(shutter speed)		
viewfinder	ရိုက်ကွင်းပြသည့်ကိရိယာ	jou' kwin: bja dhe. gi. ji. ja
digital camera	ဒီဂျစ်တယ်ကင်မရာ	digji' te gin ma. ja
tripod	သုံးချောင်းထောက်	thoun: gjaun: dau'
flash	ကင်မရာသုံး	kin ma. ja dhoun:
	လျှပ်တာပြက်မီး	lja' ta. pje' mi:
to photograph (vt)	ဓာတ်ပုံရိုက်သည်	da' poun jai' te
to take pictures	ရိုက်သည်	jai' te
to have one's picture taken	ဓာတ်ပုံရိုက်သည်	da' poun jai' te
focus	ဆုံချက်	hsoun gje'

to focus	ဆုံချက်ချိန်သည်	hsoun gje' chin de
sharp, in focus (adj)	ထင်ရှားပြတ်သားသော	htin sha: bja' tha: de
sharpness	ထင်ရှားပြတ်သားမှု	htin sha: bja' tha: hmu.
contrast	ခြားနားချက်	hpja: na: gje'
contrast (as adj)	မတူညီသော	ma. du nji de.
picture (photo)	ပုံ	poun
negative (n)	နက်ဂတစ်	ne' ga ti'
film (a roll of ~)	ဖလင်	hpa. lin
frame (still)	ဘောင်	baun
to print (photos)	ပရင့်ထုတ်သည်	pa. jin. dou' te

164. Beach. Swimming

beach	ကမ်းခြေ	kan: gjei
sand	သဲ	the:
deserted (beach)	လူသူကင်းမဲ့သော	lu dhu gin: me. de.
suntan	နေရောင်ခြည်- အသားရောင်ညှိုခြင်း	nei gjaun. - atha: jaun njou gjin:
to get a tan	နေတာလုံသည်	nei za hloun de
tan (adj)	အသားညှိုသော	atha: njou de.
sunscreen	နေပူကာလိမ်းဆေး	nei bu gan lein: zei:
bikini	ဘီကီနီ	bi ki ni
bathing suit	ရေကူးဝတ်စုံ	jei ku: wa' zoun
swim trunks	ယောက်ျားဝတ်ဘောင်းဘီတို	jau' kja: wu' baun: bi dou
swimming pool	ရေကူးကန်	jei ku: gan
to swim (vi)	ရေကူးသည်	jei ku: de
shower	ရေပန်း	jei ban:
to change (one's clothes)	အဝတ်လဲသည်	awu' le: de
towel	တဘက်	tabe'
boat	လှေ	hlei
motorboat	မော်တော်ဘုတ်	mo to bou'
water ski	ရေလျှောလျှောစီးအပြား	jei hlwa sho: apja:
paddle boat	ယက်ဘီးတင်လှေ	je' bi: da' hlei
surfing	ရေလျှောလိုင်း	jei hlwa hlain:
surfer	ရေလျှောလိုင်းစီးသူ	jei hlwa hlain: zi: dhu
scuba set	စကူဘာဆက်	sakuba ze'
flippers (swim fins)	ခြေဘာရေယက်ပြား	jo ba jei je' pja:
mask (diving ~)	မျက်နှာဖုံး	mje' hna boun:
diver	ရေငုပ်သမား	jei ngou' tha ma:
to dive (vi)	ရေငုပ်သည်	jei ngou' te
underwater (adv)	ရေအောက်	jei au'
beach umbrella	ကမ်းခြေထီး	kan: gjei hti:

sunbed (lounger)	ပက်လက်ကုလားထိုင်	pje' le' ku. la: din
sunglasses	နေကာမျက်မှန်	nei ga mje' hman
air mattress	လေထိုးအိပ်ယာ	lei dou: i' ja
to play (amuse oneself)	ကစားသည်	gaza: de
to go for a swim	ရေကူးသည်	jei ku: de
beach ball	ဘောလုံး	bo loun:
to inflate (vt)	လေထိုးသည်	lei dou: de
inflatable, air (adj)	လေထိုးနိုင်သော	lei dou: nain de.
wave	လှိုင်း	hlain:
buoy (line of ~s)	ရေကြောင်းပြဖောက်ယာ	jei gjaun: bja. bo: ja
to drown (ab. person)	ရေနစ်သည်	jei ni' te
to save, to rescue	ကယ်ဆယ်သည်	ke ze de
life vest	အသက်ကယ်အင်္ကျီ	athe' kai in: gji
to observe, to watch	စောင့်ကြည့်သည်	saun. gji. de
lifeguard	ကယ်ဆယ်သူ	ke ze dhu

TECHNICAL EQUIPMENT. TRANSPORTATION

Technical equipment

165. Computer

computer	ကွန်ပျူတာ	kun pju ta
notebook, laptop	လပ်တော့	la' to.
to turn on	ဖွင့်သည်	hpwin. de
to turn off	ပိတ်သည်	pei' te
keyboard	ကီးဘုတ်	kji: bou'
key	ကီး	kji:
mouse	မောက်စ်	mau's
mouse pad	မောက်စ်အောက်ခံပြား	mau's au' gan bja:
button	ခလုတ်	khalou'
cursor	ညွှန်းပြား	hnjun: ma:
monitor	မော်နီတာ	mo ni ta
screen	မှန်သားပြင်	hman dha: bjin
hard disk	ဟတ်ဒစ်-အ္ဘချက်အလက်သိမ်းပစ္စည်း	ha' di' akja' ale' thein: bji' si:
hard disk capacity	ဟတ်ဒစ်သိုလှောင်နိုင်မှု	ha' di' thou laun nain hmu.
memory	မှတ်ဉာဏ်	hma' njan
random access memory	ရမ်	ran
file	ဖိုင်	hpain
folder	စာတွဲဖိုင်	sa dwe: bain
to open (vt)	ဖွင့်သည်	hpwin. de
to close (vt)	ပိတ်သည်	pei' te
to save (vt)	သိမ်းဆည်းသည်	thain: zain: de
to delete (vt)	ဖျက်သည်	hpje' te
to copy (vt)	မိတ္တူကူးသည်	mi' tu gu: de
to sort (vt)	ခွဲသည်	khwe: de
to transfer (copy)	ပြန်ကူးသည်	pjan gu: de
program	ပရိုဂရမ်	pa. jou ga. jan
software	ဆော့ဝဲ	hso. hp we:
programmer	ပရိုဂရမ်မာ	pa. jou ga. jan ma
to program (vt)	ပရိုဂရမ်ရေးသည်	pa. jou ga. jan jei: de
hacker	ဟက်ကာ	he' ka

password	စကားဝှက်	zaga: hwe'
virus	ဗိုင်းရပ်စ်	bain ja's
to find, to detect	ရှာဖွေသည်	sha hpwei de
byte	ဘိုက်	bai'
megabyte	မီဂါဘိုက်	mi ga bai'
data	အချက်အလက်	ache' ale'
database	ဒေတာဘေ့စ်	dei da bei. s
cable (USB, etc.)	ကေဘယ်ကြိုး	kei be kjou:
to disconnect (vt)	ဖြုတ်သည်	hpjei: de
to connect (sth to sth)	တပ်သည်	ta' te

166. Internet. E-mail

Internet	အင်တာနက်	in ta na'
browser	ဘရောက်ဆာ	ba. jau' hsa
search engine	ဆာ့ချ်အင်ဂျင်	hsa. ch in gjin
provider	ပံ့ပိုးသူ	pan. bou: dhu
webmaster	ဝဘ်မာစတာ	we' sai' ma sa. ta
website	ဝဘ်ဆိုက်	we' sai'
webpage	ဝဘ်ဆိုဒ်စာမျက်နှာ	we' sai' sa mje' hna
address (e-mail ~)	လိပ်စာ	lei' sa
address book	လိပ်စာမှတ်စု	lei' sa hmat' su.
mailbox	စာတိုက်ပုံး	sa dai' poun:
mail	စာ	sa
full (adj)	ပြည့်သော	pjei. de.
message	သတင်း	dhadin:
incoming messages	အဝင်သတင်း	awin dha din:
outgoing messages	အထွက်သတင်း	a htwe' tha. din:
sender	ပို့သူ	pou. dhu
to send (vt)	ပို့သည်	pou. de
sending (of mail)	ပို့ခြင်း	pou. gjin:
receiver	လက်ခံသူ	le' khan dhu
to receive (vt)	လက်ခံရရှိသည်	le' khan ja. shi. de
correspondence	စာအဆက်အသွယ်	sa ahse' athwe
to correspond (vi)	စာပေးစာယူလုပ်သည်	sa pei: za ju lou' te
file	ဖိုင်	hpain
to download (vt)	ဒေါင်းလော့ဒ်လုပ်သည်	daun: lo. d lou' de
to create (vt)	ဖန်တီးသည်	hpan di: de
to delete (vt)	ဖျက်သည်	hpje' te

deleted (adj)	ဖျက်ပြီးသော	hpje' pji: de.
connection (ADSL, etc.)	ဆက်သွယ်မှု	hse' thwe hmu.
speed	နှုန်း	hnun:
modem	မိုဒမ်း	mou dan:
access	ဝင်လမ်း	win lan
port (e.g., input ~)	ဝဲဘက်	we: be'
connection (make a ~)	အချိတ်အဆက်	achei' ahse'
to connect to … (vi)	ချိတ်ဆက်သည်	chei' hse' te
to select (vt)	ရွေးချယ်သည်	jwei: che de
to search (for …)	ရှာသည်	sha de

167. Electricity

electricity	လျပ်စစ်ဓာတ်အား	hlja' si' da' a:
electric, electrical (adj)	လျှပ်စစ်နှင့်ဆိုင်သော	hlja' si' hnin. zain de.
electric power plant	လျှပ်စစ်ထုတ်လုပ်သောစက်ရုံ	hlja' si' htou' lou' tho: ze' joun
energy	စွမ်းအင်	swan: in
electric power	လျှပ်စစ်စွမ်းအား	hlja' si' swan: a:
light bulb	မီးသီး	mi: dhi:
flashlight	ဓာတ်မီး	da' mi:
street light	လမ်းမီး	lan: mi:
light	အလင်းရောင်	alin: jaun
to turn on	ဖွင့်သည်	hpwin. de
to turn off	ပိတ်သည်	pei' te
to turn off the light	မီးပိတ်သည်	mi: pi' te
to burn out (vi)	မီးကျွမ်းသည်	mi: kjwan: de
short circuit	လျှပ်စီးပတ်လမ်းပြတ်ခြင်း	hlja' si: ba' lan: bja' chin:
broken wire	ဝိုင်ယာကြိုးအပြတ်	wain ja gjou: apja'
contact (electrical ~)	လျှပ်ကူးပစ္စည်း	hlja' ku: pji' si:
light switch	ခလုတ်	khalou'
wall socket	ပလပ်ပေါက်	pa. la' pau'
plug	ပလပ်	pa. la'
extension cord	ကြားဆက်ကြိုး	ka: ze' kjou:
fuse	ဖျူးစ်	hpju: s
cable, wire	ဝိုင်ယာကြိုး	wain ja gjou:
wiring	လျှပ်စစ်ကြိုးသွယ်တပ်နှမှု	hlja' si' kjou: dhwe dan: hmu
ampere	အမ်ပီယာ	an bi ja
amperage	အသံချဲ့စက်	athan che. zek
volt	ဗို့	boi.
voltage	ဗို့အား	bou. a:

| electrical device | လျှပ်စစ်ပစ္စည်း | hlja' si' pji' si: |
| indicator | အချက်ပြ | ache' pja. |

electrician	လျှပ်စစ်ပညာရှင်	hlja' si' pa. nja shin
to solder (vt)	ဂဟေဆော်သည်	gahei hso de
soldering iron	ဂဟေဆော်တံ	gahei hso dan
electric current	လျှပ်စီးကြောင်း	hlja' si: gjaun:

168. Tools

tool, instrument	ကိရိယာ	ki. ji. ja
tools	ကိရိယာများ	ki. ji. ja mja:
equipment (factory ~)	စက်ကိရိယာပစ္စည်းများ	se' kari. ja pji' si: mja:

hammer	တူ	tu
screwdriver	ဝက်အူလှည့်	we' u hli.
ax	ပုဆိန်	pahsein

saw	လွှ	hlwa.
to saw (vt)	လွှတိုက်သည်	hlwa. dai' de
plane (tool)	ရွေးပေါ	jwei bo
to plane (vt)	ရွေးပေါ်ထိုးသည်	jwei bo dou: de
soldering iron	ဂဟေဆော်တံ	gahei hso dan
to solder (vt)	ဂဟေဆော်သည်	gahei hso de

file (tool)	တံစဉ်း	tan zin:
carpenter pincers	သံနှုတ်	than hnou'
lineman's pliers	ပလာယာ	pa. la ja
chisel	ဆောက်	hsau'

drill bit	လွန်	lun
electric drill	လျှပ်စစ်လွန်	hlja' si' lun
to drill (vi, vt)	လွန်ဖြင့်ဖောက်သည်	lun bjin. bau' de

knife	ဓား	da:
pocket knife	မောင်းဂျက်ဓား	maun: gje' da:
blade	ဓားသွား	da: dhwa

sharp (blade, etc.)	ချွန်ထက်သော	chwan de' te.
dull, blunt (adj)	တုံးသော	toun: dho:
to get blunt (dull)	တုံးသွားသည်	toun: dwa de
to sharpen (vt)	သွေးသည်	thwei: de

bolt	မူလီ	mu li
nut	မူလီခေါင်း	mu li gaun:
thread (of a screw)	ဝက်အူရစ်	we' u ji'
wood screw	ဝက်အူ	we' u

| nail | အိမ်ရိုက်သံ | ein jai' than |
| nailhead | သံခေါင်း | than gaun: |

ruler (for measuring)	ပေတံ	pei dan
tape measure	ပေကြိုး	pei gjou:
spirit level	ရေချိန်	jei gjain
magnifying glass	မှန်ဘီလူး	hman bi lu:
measuring instrument	တိုင်းသည့်ကိရိယာ	tain: dhi. ki. ji. ja
to measure (vt)	တိုင်းသည်	tain: de
scale (of thermometer, etc.)	စကေး	sakei:
readings	ပြသောပမာဏ	pja. dho: ba ma na.
compressor	ဖိသိပ်စက်	hpi. dhi' se'
microscope	အကုကြည့်ကိရိယာ	anu gji. gi. ji. ja
pump (e.g., water ~)	လေထိုးစက်	lei dou: ze'
robot	စက်ရုပ်	se' jou'
laser	လေဆာ	lei za
wrench	ခွ	khwa.
adhesive tape	တိပ်	tei'
glue	ကော်	ko
sandpaper	ကော်ဖတ်စက္ကူ	ko hpa' se' ku
spring	ညွှတ်သံခွေ	hnju' dhan gwei
magnet	သံလိုက်	than lai'
gloves	လက်အိတ်	lei' ei'
rope	ကြိုး	kjou:
cord	ကြိုးလုံး	kjou: loun:
wire (e.g., telephone ~)	ဝိုင်ယာကြိုး	wain ja gjou:
cable	ကေဘယ်ကြိုး	kei be kjou:
sledgehammer	တူကြီး	tou gji:
prybar	တူးရွင်း	tu: jwin:
ladder	လှေကား	hlei ga:
stepladder	ခေါက်လှေကား	khau' hlei ka:
to screw (tighten)	ဝက်အူကျစ်သည်	we' u gji' te
to unscrew (lid, filter, etc.)	ဝက်အူဖြုတ်သည်	we' u bju' te
to tighten (e.g., with a clamp)	ကျပ်သည်	kja' te.
to glue, to stick	ကော်ကပ်သည်	ko ka' de
to cut (vt)	ဖြတ်သည်	hpja' te
malfunction (fault)	ချွတ်ယွင်းချက်	chwe' jwin: che'
repair (mending)	ပြန်လည်ပြုပြင်ဆင်ခြင်း	pjan le: bjin zin gjin:
to repair, to fix (vt)	ပြန်လည်ပြုပြင်ဆင်သည်	pjan le bjin zin de
to adjust (machine, etc.)	ညှိသည်	hnji. de
to check (to examine)	စစ်ဆေးသည်	si' hsei: de
checking	စစ်ဆေးခြင်း	si' hsei: gjin:
readings	ပြသောပမာဏ	pja. dho: ba ma na.

reliable, solid (machine)	စိတ်ချရသော	sei' cha. ja. de.
complex (adj)	ရှုပ်ထွေးသော	sha' htwei: de.
to rust (get rusted)	သံချေးတက်သည်	than gjei: da' te
rusty, rusted (adj)	သံချေးတက်သော	than gjei: da' te.
rust	သံချေး	than gjei:

Transportation

169. Airplane

airplane	လေယာဉ်	lei jan
air ticket	လေယာဉ်လက်မှတ်	lei jan le' hma'
airline	လေကြောင်း	lei gjaun:
airport	လေဆိပ်	lei zi'
supersonic (adj)	အသံထက်မြန်သော	athan de' mjan de.
captain	လေယာဉ်မှူး	lei jan hmu:
crew	လေယာဉ်အမှုထမ်းအဖွဲ့	lei jan ahmu. dan: ahpwe.
pilot	လေယာဉ်မောင်းသူ	lei jan maun dhu
flight attendant (fem.)	လေယာဉ်မယ်	lei jan me
navigator	လေကြောင်းပြ	lei gjaun: bja.
wings	လေယာဉ်တောင်ပံ	lei jan daun ban
tail	လေယာဉ်အမြီး	lei jan amji:
cockpit	လေယာဉ်မောင်းအခန်း	lei jan maun akhan:
engine	အင်ဂျင်	in gjin
undercarriage (landing gear)	အောက်ခံဘောင်	au' khan baun
turbine	တာဘိုင်	ta bain
propeller	ပန်ကာ	pan ga
black box	ဘလက်ဘောက်	ba. le' bo'
yoke (control column)	ပဲ့ကိုင်ဘီး	pe. gain bi:
fuel	လောင်စာ	laun za
safety card	အရေးပေါ် လုံခြုံရေး ညွှန်ကြားစာ	ajei: po' choun loun jei: hnjun gja: za
oxygen mask	အောက်ဆီဂျင်မျက်နှာဖုံး	au' hsi gjin mje' hna hpoun:
uniform	ယူနီဖောင်း	ju ni hpaun:
life vest	အသက်ကယ်အင်္ကျီ	athe' kai in: gji
parachute	လေထီး	lei di:
takeoff	ထွက်ခွာခြင်း	htwe' khwa gjin:
to take off (vi)	ပျံတက်သည်	pjan de' te
runway	လေယာဉ်ပြေးလမ်း	lei jan bei: lan:
visibility	မြင်ကွင်း	mjin gwin:
flight (act of flying)	ပျံသန်းခြင်း	pjan dan: gjin:
altitude	အမြင့်	amjin.
air pocket	လေမငြိမ်အရပ်	lei ma ngjin aja'
seat	ထိုင်ခုံ	htain goun

headphones	နားကြပ်	na: kja'
folding tray (tray table)	ခေါက်စားပွဲ	khau' sa: bwe:
airplane window	လေယာဉ်ပြတင်းပေါက်	lei jan bja. din: bau'
aisle	မင်းလမ်း	min: lan:

170. Train

train	ရထား	jatha:
commuter train	လျပ်စစ်တော်အားသုံးရထား	hlja' si' da' a: dhou: ja da:
express train	အမြန်ရထား	aman ja. hta:
diesel locomotive	ဒီဇယ်ရထား	di ze ja da:
steam locomotive	ရေနွေးငွေ့စက်ခေါင်း	jei nwei: ngwei. ze' khaun:
passenger car	အတွဲ	atwe:
dining car	စားသောက်တွဲ	sa: thau' thwe:
rails	ရထားသံလမ်း	jatha dhan lan:
railroad	ရထားလမ်း	jatha: lan:
railway tie	ဇလီဖားတုံး	zali ba: doun
platform (railway ~)	စကြန်	sin gjan
track (~ 1, 2, etc.)	ရထားစကြန်	jatha zin gjan
semaphore	မီးပွိုင့်	mi: bwain.
station	ဘူတာရုံ	bu da joun
engineer (train driver)	ရထားမောင်းသူ	jatha: maun: dhu
porter (of luggage)	အထမ်းသမား	a htan: dha. ma:
car attendant	အစောင့်	asaun.
passenger	ခရီးသည်	khaji: de
conductor (ticket inspector)	လက်မှတ်စစ်ဆေးသူ	le' hma' ti' hsei: dhu:
corridor (in train)	ကော်ရစ်တာ	ko ji' ta
emergency brake	အရေးပေါ်ဘရိတ်	ajei: po' ba ji'
compartment	အခန်း	akhan:
berth	အိပ်စင်	ei' zin
upper berth	အပေါ်ထပ်အိပ်စင်	apo htap ei' sin
lower berth	အောက်ထပ်အိပ်စင်	au' hta' ei' sin
bed linen, bedding	အိပ်ရာခင်း	ei' ja khin:
ticket	လက်မှတ်	le' hma'
schedule	အချိန်ဇယား	achein zaja:
information display	အချက်အလက်ပြနေရာ	ache' ale' pja. nei ja
to leave, to depart	ထွက်ခွါသည်	htwe' khwa de
departure (of train)	အထွက်	a htwe'
to arrive (ab. train)	ဆိုက်ရောက်သည်	hseu' jau' de
arrival	ဆိုက်ရောက်ရာ	hseu' jau' ja
to arrive by train	မီးရထားဖြင့်ရောက်ရှိသည်	mi: ja. da: bjin. jau' shi. de

to get on the train	မီးရထားစီးသည်	mi: ja. da: zi: de
to get off the train	မီးရထားမှဆင်းသည်	mi: ja. da: hma. zin: de
train wreck	ရထားတိုက်ခြင်း	jatha: dai' chin:
to derail (vi)	ရထားလမ်းချော်သည်	jatha: lan: gjo de
steam locomotive	ရေနွေးငွေ့စက်ခေါင်း	jei nwei: ngwei. ze' khaun:
stoker, fireman	မီးထိုးသမား	mi: dou: dhama:
firebox	မီးဖို	mi: bou
coal	ကျောက်မီးသွေး	kjau' mi dhwei:

171. Ship

ship	သင်္ဘော	thin: bo:
vessel	ရေယာဉ်	jei jan
steamship	မီးသင်္ဘော်	mi: dha. bo:
riverboat	အပျော်စီးမော်တော်ဘုတ်ငယ်	apjo zi: mo do bou' nge
cruise ship	ပင်လယ်အပျော်စီးသင်္ဘော	pin le apjo zi: dhin: bo:
cruiser	လေယာဉ်တင်သင်္ဘော	lei jan din
yacht	အပျော်စီးရွက်လှေ	apjo zi: jwe' hlei
tugboat	ဆွဲသင်္ဘော	hswe: thin: bo:
barge	ဖောင်	hpaun
ferry	ကူးတို့သင်္ဘော	gadou. thin: bo:
sailing ship	ရွက်သင်္ဘော	jwe' thin: bo:
brigantine	ရွက်လှေ	jwe' hlei
ice breaker	ရေခဲပြင်ခွဲသင်္ဘော	jei ge: bjin gwe: dhin: bo:
submarine	ရေငုပ်သင်္ဘော	jei ngou' thin: bo:
boat (flat-bottomed ~)	လှေ	hlei
dinghy (lifeboat)	ရော်ဘာလှေ	jo ba hlei
lifeboat	အသက်ကယ်လှေ	athe' kai hlei
motorboat	မော်တော်ဘုတ်	mo to bou'
captain	ရေယာဉ်မှူး	jei jan hmu:
seaman	သင်္ဘောသား	thin: bo: dha:
sailor	သင်္ဘောသား	thin: bo: dha:
crew	သင်္ဘောအမှုထမ်းအဖွဲ့	thin: bo: ahmu. htan: ahpwe.
boatswain	ရေတပ်အရာရှိငယ်	jei da' aja shi. nge
ship's boy	သင်္ဘောသားကလေး	thin: bo: dha: galei:
cook	ထမင်းချက်	htamin: gje'
ship's doctor	သင်္ဘောဆရာဝန်	thin: bo: zaja wun
deck	သင်္ဘောကုန်းပတ်	thin: bo: koun: ba'
mast	ရွက်တိုင်	jwe' tai'

sail	ရွက်	jwe'
hold	ဝမ်းတွင်း	wan: twin:
bow (prow)	ဦးစွန်း	u: zun:
stern	ပဲ့ပိုင်း	pe. bain:
oar	လှော်တက်	hlo de'
screw propeller	သင်္ဘောပန်ကာ	thin: bo ban ga
cabin	သင်္ဘောပေါ်မှအခန်း	thin: bo bo hma. aksan:
wardroom	အရာရှိများရိပ်သာ	aja shi. mja: jin dha
engine room	စက်ခန်း	se' khan:
bridge	ကွပ်ကဲခန်း	ku' ke: khan:
radio room	ရေဒီယိုခန်း	rei di jou gan:
wave (radio)	လှိုင်း	hlain:
logbook	မှတ်တမ်းစာအုပ်	hma' tan: za ou'
spyglass	အဝေးကြည့်မှန်ပြောင်း	awei: gji. hman bjaun:
bell	ခေါင်းလောင်း	gaun: laun:
flag	အလံ	alan
hawser (mooring ~)	သင်္ဘောသုံးလွန်ကြိုး	thin: bo: dhaun: lun gjou:
knot (bowline, etc.)	ကြိုးထုံး	kjou: htoun:
deckrails	လက်ရန်း	le' jan
gangway	သင်္ဘောကုန်းပေါင်	thin: bo: koun: baun
anchor	ကျောက်ဆူး	kjau' hsu:
to weigh anchor	ကျောက်ဆူးနုတ်သည်	kjau' hsu: nou' te
to drop anchor	ကျောက်ဆူးချသည်	kjau' cha. de
anchor chain	ကျောက်ဆူးကြိုး	kjau' hsu: kjou:
port (harbor)	ဆိပ်ကမ်း	hsi: kan:
quay, wharf	သင်္ဘောဆိပ်	thin: bo: zei'
to berth (moor)	ဆိုက်ကပ်သည်	hseu' ka' de
to cast off	စွန့်ပစ်သည်	sun. bi' de
trip, voyage	ခရီးထွက်ခြင်း	khaji: htwe' chin:
cruise (sea trip)	အပျော်ခရီး	apjo gaji:
course (route)	ဦးတည်ရာ	u: ti ja
route (itinerary)	လမ်းကြောင်း	lan: gjaun:
fairway (safe water channel)	သင်္ဘောရေကြောင်း	thin: bo: jei gjaun:
shallows	ရေတိမ်ပိုင်း	jei dein bain:
to run aground	ကမ်းကပ်သည်	kan ka' te
storm	မုန်တိုင်း	moun dain:
signal	အချက်ပြ	ache' pja.
to sink (vi)	နစ်မြုပ်သည်	ni' mjou' te
Man overboard!	လူရေထဲကျ	lu jei de: gja
SOS (distress signal)	အက်စ်အိုအက်စ်	e's o e's
ring buoy	အသက်ကယ်ဘော	athe' kai bo

172. Airport

airport	လေဆိပ်	lei zi'
airplane	လေယာဉ်	lei jan
airline	လေကြောင်း	lei gjaun:
air traffic controller	လေကြောင်းထိန်း	lei kjaun: din:
departure	ထွက်ခွာရာ	htwe' khwa ja
arrival	ဆိုက်ရောက်ရာ	hseu' jau' ja
to arrive (by plane)	ဆိုက်ရောက်သည်	hsai' jau' te
departure time	ထွက်ခွာချိန်	htwe' khwa gjein
arrival time	ဆိုက်ရောက်ချိန်	hseu' jau' chein
to be delayed	နောက်ကျသည်	nau' kja. de
flight delay	လေယာဉ်နောက်ကျခြင်း	lei jan nau' kja. chin:
information board	လေယာဉ်ခရီးစဉ်ပြဘုတ်	lei jan ga. ji: zi bja. bou'
information	သတင်းအချက်အလက်	dhadin: akje' ale'
to announce (vt)	ကြေငြာသည်	kjei nja de
flight (e.g., next ~)	ပျံသန်းမှု	pjan dan: hmu.
customs	အကောက်ဆိပ်	akau' hsein
customs officer	အကောက်ခွန်အရာရှိ	akau' khun aja shi.
customs declaration	အကောက်ခွန်ကြေငြာချက်	akau' khun gjei nja gje'
to fill out (vt)	လျှောက်လွှာဖြည့်သည်	shau' hlwa bji. de
to fill out the declaration	သွယ်ယူပစ္စည်းစာရင်းကြေညာသိည်	the ju pji' si: zajin: kjei nja de
passport control	ပတ်စ်ပို့ထိန်းချုပ်မှု	pa's pou. htein: gju' hmu.
luggage	ဝန်စည်စလည်	wun zi za. li
hand luggage	လက်ဆွဲပစ္စည်း	le' swe: pji' si:
luggage cart	ပစ္စည်းတင်သည့်လှည်း	pji' si: din dhe. hle:
landing	ဆင်းသက်ခြင်း	hsin: dha' chin:
landing strip	အဆင်းလမ်း	ahsin: lan:
to land (vi)	ဆင်းသက်သည်	hsin: dha' te
airstair (passenger stair)	လေယာဉ်လှေကား	lei jan hlei ka:
check-in	စာရင်းသွင်းခြင်း	sajin: dhwin: gjin:
check-in counter	စာရင်းသွင်းကောင်တာ	sajin: gaun da
to check-in (vi)	စာရင်းသွင်းသည်	sajin: dhwin: de
boarding pass	လေယာဉ်ပေါ် တက်ခွင့်လက်မှတ်	lei jan bo de' khwin. le' hma'
departure gate	လေယာဉ်ထွက်ခွာရာဂိတ်	lei jan dwe' khwa ja gei'
transit	အကူးအပြောင်း	aku: apjaun:
to wait (vt)	စောင့်သည်	saun. de
departure lounge	ထွက်ခွာရာခန်းမ	htwe' kha ja gan: ma.
to see off	လိုက်ပို့သည်	lai' bou. de
to say goodbye	နှုတ်ဆက်သည်	hnou' hsei' te

173. Bicycle. Motorcycle

bicycle	စက်ဘီး	se' bi:
scooter	ဆိုင်ကယ်အပေါ့စား	hsain ge apau. za:
motorcycle, bike	ဆိုင်ကယ်	hsain ge
to go by bicycle	စက်ဘီးစီးသည်	se' bi: zi: de
handlebars	လက်ကိုင်	le' kain
pedal	ခြေနင်း	chei nin:
brakes	ဘရိတ်	ba. rei'
bicycle seat (saddle)	စက်ဘီးထိုင်ခုံ	se' bi: dai' goun
pump	လေထိုးတံ	lei dou: tan
luggage rack	နောက်တွဲထိုင်ခုံ	nau' twe: dain goun
front lamp	ရှေ့မီး	shei. mi:
helmet	ဟဲလ်မက်ဦးထုပ်	he: l me u: htou'
wheel	ဘီး	bi:
fender	ဘီးကာ	bi: ga
rim	ခွေ	khwei
spoke	စပုတ်တံ	sapou' tan

Cars

automobile, car	ကား	ka:
sports car	ပြိုင်ကား	pjain ga:
limousine	အလှစီးဖိမ်ခံကား	ahla. zi: zin khan ka:
off-road vehicle	လမ်းကြမ်းမောင်းကား	lan: kjan: maun: ka:
convertible (n)	အမိုးခေါက်ကား	amou: gau' ka:
minibus	မီနီဘတ်စ်	mi ni ba's
ambulance	လူနာတင်ကား	lu na din ga:
snowplow	နှင်းကောက်ကား	hnin: go: ga:
truck	ကုန်တင်ကား	koun din ka:
tanker truck	ရေတင်ကား	jei din ga:
van (small truck)	ပစ္စည်းတင်ဝင်ကား	pji' si: din bin ga:
road tractor (trailer truck)	နောက်တွဲပါကုန်တင်ယာဉ်	nau' twe: ba goun din jan
trailer	နောက်တွဲယာဉ်	nau' twe: jan
comfortable (adj)	သက်တာင့်သက် သာဖြစ်သော	the' taun. the' tha hpji' te.
used (adj)	တစ်ပတ်ရစ်	ti' pa' ji'

hood	စက်ခေါင်းအဖုံး	se' khaun: ahpoun:
fender	ရွှံ့ကာ	shwan. ga
roof	ကားခေါင်မိုး	ka: gaun mou;
windshield	လေကာမှန်	lei ga hman
rear-view mirror	နောက်ကြည့်မှန်	nau' kje. hman
windshield washer	လေကာမှန်ဝါရှာ	lei ga hman wa sha
windshield wipers	လေကာမှန်ရေသုတ်တံ	lei ga hman jei thou' tan
side window	ဘေးတံခါးမှန်	bei: dan ga: hman
window lift (power window)	တံခါးလေလှတ်	daga: kha lou'
antenna	အင်တန်နာတိုင်	in tan na tain
sunroof	နေကာမှန်	nei ga hman
bumper	ကားဘန်ပါ	ka: ban ba
trunk	ပစ္စည်းခန်း	pji' si: khan:
roof luggage rack	ခေါင်မိုးပစ္စည်းတင်စင်	gaun mou: pji' si: din zin

door	တံခါး	daga:
door handle	တံခါးလက်ကိုင်	daga: le' kain
door lock	တံခါးသော့	daga: dho.

license plate	လိုင်စင်ပြား	lain zin bja:
muffler	အသံတိတ်ကိရိယာ	athan dein: gi. ji. ja
gas tank	ဆီတိုင်ကီ	hsi dain gi
tailpipe	အိတ်ဇော	ei' zo:

gas, accelerator	လီဗာ	li ba
pedal	ခြေနင်း	chei nin:
gas pedal	လီဗာနင်းပြား	li ba nin: bja

brake	ဘရိတ်	ba. rei'
brake pedal	ဘရိတ်နင်ပြား	ba. rei' nin bja:
to brake (use the brake)	ဘရိတ်အုပ်သည်	ba. rei' au' te
parking brake	ပါကင်ဘရိတ်	pa gin ba. jei'

clutch	ကလပ်	kala'
clutch pedal	ခြေနင်းကလပ်	chei nin: gala'
clutch disc	ကလပ်ပြား	kala' pja:
shock absorber	ရှော့ခ်အစ်ဆော်ဗာ	sho.kh a' hso ba

wheel	ဘီး	bi:
spare tire	အပိုတာယာ	apou daja
tire	တာယာ	ta ja
hubcap	ဘီးဖုံး	bi: boun:

| driving wheels | တွန်းအားပေးသောဘီးများ | tun: a: bei: do: bi: mja: |
| front-wheel drive (as adj) | ရှေ့ဘီးအုံ | shei. bi: oun |

| rear-wheel drive (as adj) | ဝင်ရိုးအုံ | win jou: oun |
| all-wheel drive (as adj) | အောဝီးလ်ဒရိုက်ဘီးအုံ | o: wi: l da. shik bi: oun |

| gearbox | ဂီယာဘောက် | gi ja bau' |
| automatic (adj) | အလိုအလျောက်ဖြစ်သော | alou aljau' hpji' te. |

| mechanical (adj) | စက်နှင့်ဆိုင်သော | se' hnin. zain de. |
| gear shift | ဂီယာတံ | gi ja dan |

| headlight | ရှေ့မီး | shei. mi: |
| headlights | ရှေ့မီးများ | shei. mi: mja: |

low beam	အောက်မီး	au' mi:
high beam	အဝေးမီး	awei: mi:
brake light	ဘရိတ်မီး	ba. rei' mi:

parking lights	ပါကင်မီး	pa gin mi:
hazard lights	အရေးပေါ်အချက်ပြမီး	ajei: po' che' pja. mi:
fog lights	မြူနှင်းအလင်းဖေါက်မီး	hmju hnin: alin: bau' mi:
turn signal	အကွေ့အချက်ပြမီး	akwei. ache' pja. mi:
back-up light	နောက်ဘက်အချက်ပြမီး	nau' be' ache' pja. mi:

176. Cars. Passenger compartment

car inside (interior)	အတွင်းပိုင်း	atwin: bain:
leather (as adj)	သားရေနှင့်လုပ်ထားသော	tha: jei hnin. lou' hta: de.
velour (as adj)	ကတ္တီပါအထွေစား	gadi ba ahtu za:
upholstery	ကုရှင်	ku shin
instrument (gage)	စံပမာဏတိုင်းကိရိယာ	san bamana dain: gi ji ja
dashboard	ဒက်ရှ်ဘုတ်	de' sh bou'
speedometer	ကားအရှိန်တိုင်းကိရိယာ	ka: ashein dain: ki. ja. ja
needle (pointer)	လက်တံ	le' tan
odometer	ခရီးမိုင်တိုင်းကိရိယာ	khaji: main dain: ki. ji. ja
indicator (sensor)	နိုင်ခွာ့	dain gwa'
level	ရေချိန်	jei gjain
warning light	သတ်ပေးမီး	dhadi. pei: mi:
steering wheel	လက်ကိုင်ဘီး	le' kain bi:
horn	ဟွန်း	hwun:
button	ခလုတ်	khalou'
switch	ခလုတ်	khalou'
seat	ထိုင်ခုံ	htain goun
backrest	နောက်မှီ	nau' mi
headrest	ခေါင်းမှီ	gaun: hmi
seat belt	ထိုင်ခုံခါးပတ်	htain goun ga: pa'
to fasten the belt	ထိုင်ခုံခါးပတ်ပတ်သည်	htain goun ga: pa' pa' te
adjustment (of seats)	ချိန်ညှိခြင်း	chein hnji. chin:
airbag	လေအိတ်	lei i'
air-conditioner	လေအေးပေးစက်	lei ei: bei: ze'
radio	ရေဒီယို	rei di jou
CD player	စီဒီပလေယာ	si di ba. lei ja
to turn on	ဖွင့်သည်	hpwin. de
antenna	အင်တာနာတိုင်	in tan na tain
glove box	ပစ္စည်းထည့်ရန်အံဆွဲ	pji' si: de. jan an ze:
ashtray	ဆေးလိပ်ပြာခွက်	hsei: lei' pja gwe'

177. Cars. Engine

engine	အင်ဂျင်	in gjin
motor	မော်တာစက်	mo da ze'
diesel (as adj)	ဒီဇယ်	di ze
gasoline (as adj)	ဓါတ်ဆီ	da' hsi
engine volume	အင်ဂျင်ထုထည်	in gjin htu. hte
power	စွမ်းအား	swan: a:
horsepower	မြင်းကောင်ရေအား	mjin: gaun jei a:

piston	ပစ္စတင်	pji' sa. tin
cylinder	ဆလင်ဒါ	hsa. lin da
valve	အဆို့ရှင်	ahsou. shin
injector	ထိုးတံ	htou: dan
generator (alternator)	ဂျင်နရေတာ	gjin na. jei ta
carburetor	ကာဗရက်တာ	ka ba. je' ta
motor oil	စက်ဆီ	se' hsi
radiator	ရေတိုင်ကီ	jei dain gi
coolant	အင်ဂျင်အေးစေ သည့်အရည်-ကူးလန့်	in gjin ei: zei dhi. aji - ku: lan.
cooling fan	အအေးပေးပန်ကာ	aei: bei: ban ga
battery (accumulator)	ဘတ်ထရီ	ba' hta ji
starter	စက်နိူးကိရိယာ	se' hnou: ki. ji. ja
ignition	မီးပေးအပိုင်း	mi: bei: apain:
spark plug	မီးပွားပလတ်	mi: bwa: ba. la'
terminal (of battery)	ဘက်ထရီထိပ်စွန်း	be' hta. ji htei' swan:
positive terminal	ဘက်ထရီအဖိုစွန်း	be' hta. ji ahpou zwan:
negative terminal	ဘက်ထရီအမစွန်း	be' hta. ji ama. zwan:
fuse	ဖျူစ်	hpju: s
air filter	လေစစ်ကိရိယာ	lei zi' ki. ji. ja
oil filter	ဆီစစ်ကိရိယာ	hsi za' ki. ji. ja
fuel filter	လောင်စာဆီစစ်ကိရိယာ	laun za hsi zi' ki. ji. ja

178. Cars. Crash. Repair

car crash	ကားတိုက်ခြင်း	ka: dou' chin:
traffic accident	မတွော်တဆဆယာည့်တိုက်မှု	ma. do da. za. jan dai' hmu.
to crash (into the wall, etc.)	ဝင်တိုက်သည်	win dai' te
to get smashed up	အရှိန်ပြင်းစွာတိုက်မိသည်	ashein bjin: zwa daik mi. de
damage	အပျက်အစီး	apje' asi:
intact (unscathed)	မချွတ်ယွင်းသော	ma gjwe' jwin: de.
breakdown	စက်ချွတ်ယွင်းခြင်း	se' chu' jwin: gjin:
to break down (vi)	စက်ချွတ်ယွင်းသည်	se' chu' jwin: de
towrope	လွန်ကြိုးကြီး	lun gjou: gji:
puncture	ဘီးပေါက်ခြင်း	bi: bau' chin:
to be flat	ပြားကပ်သွားသည်	pja: ga' thwa: de
to pump up	လေထိုးသည်	lei dou: de
pressure	ဖိအား	hpi. a:
to check (to examine)	စစ်ဆေးသည်	si' hsei: de
repair	ပြင်ခြင်း	pjin gjin:

auto repair shop	ကားပြင်ဆိုင်	ka: bjin zain
spare part	စက်အပိုပစ္စည်း	se' apou pji' si:
part	အစိတ်အပိုင်း	asei' apain:
bolt (with nut)	မူလီ	mu li
screw (fastener)	ဝက်အူ	we' u
nut	မူလီခေါင်း	mu li gaun:
washer	ဝါရှာ	wa sha
bearing (e.g., ball ~)	ဘယ်ယာရင်	be ja jin
tube	ပိုက်	pai'
gasket (head ~)	ဆက်ရာဂူဖုံးသည့်ကွင်း	hse' ja gou boun: dhe. gwin:
cable, wire	ဝိုင်ယာကြိုး	wain ja gjou:
jack	ဂျိုက်	gjou'
wrench	စွ	khwa.
hammer	တူ	tu
pump	လေထိုးစက်	lei dou: ze'
screwdriver	ဝက်အူလှည့်	we' u hli.
fire extinguisher	မီးသတ်ဘူး	mi: tha' bu:
warning triangle	ရုပ်သတ္တိပေးသော အမှတ်အသား	ja' thati bei: de. ahma' atha:
to stall (vi)	စက် ရုတ်တရက်သေသည်	se' jou' taja' dhei de
stall (n)	အင်ဂျင်စက် သေသွားခြင်း	in gjin sek thei thwa: gjin:
to be broken	ကျိုးသွားသည်	kjou: dhwa: de
to overheat (vi)	စက်အရမ်းပူသွားသည်	se' ajan: bu dhwa: de
to be clogged up	တစ်ဆို့သည်	ti' hsou. de
to freeze up (pipes, etc.)	အေးအောင်လုပ်သည်	ei: aun lou' te
to burst (vi, ab. tube)	ကျိုးပေါက်သည်	kjou: bau' te
pressure	ဖိအား	hpi. a:
level	ရေရှိန်	jei gjain
slack (~ belt)	လျှော့တိလျှော့ခဲ့ဖြစ်သော	ljau. di. ljau. je: hpji' de
dent	အချိုင့်	achoun.
knocking noise (engine)	ခေါက်သံ	khau' dhan
crack	အက်ကြောင်း	e' kjaun:
scratch	ခြစ်ရာ	chi' ja

179. Cars. Road

road	လမ်း	lan:
highway	အဝေးပြေးလမ်းမကြီး	awei: bjei: lan: ma. gji:
freeway	အမြန်လမ်းမကြီး	aman lan: ma. mji:
direction (way)	ဦးတည်ရာ	u: te ja
distance	အကွာအဝေး	akwa awei:

bridge	တံတား	dada:
parking lot	ကားပါကင်	ka: pa kin
square	ရင်ပြင်	jin bjin
interchange	အ၀ေးပြေးလမ်းမ ကြီးများဆုံရာ	awei: bjei: lan: ma. gji: mja: zoun ja
tunnel	ဥမင်လိုဏ်ခေါင်း	u. min lain gaun:
gas station	ဆီဆိုင်	hsi: zain
parking lot	ကားပါကင်	ka: pa kin
gas pump (fuel dispenser)	ဆီပိုက်	hsi pou'
auto repair shop	ကားပြင်ဆိုင်	ka: bjin zain
to get gas (to fill up)	ဓါတ်ဆီထည့်သည်	da' hsi de. de
fuel	လောင်စာ	laun za
jerrycan	ဓာတ်ဆီပုံး	da' hsi boun:
asphalt	နိုင်လွန်ကတ္တရာ	nain lun ga' taja
road markings	လမ်းအမှတ်အသား	lan: ahma' atha:
curb	ပလက်ဖောင်းဘောင်	pa. je' hpaun: baun:
guardrail	လမ်းဘေးအခံအတား	lan: bei: ajan ata:
ditch	လမ်းဘေးမြောင်း	lan: bei: mjaun:
roadside (shoulder)	လမ်းဘေးမြေသား	lan: bei: mjei dha:
lamppost	တိုင်	tain
to drive (a car)	မောင်းနှင်သည်	maun: hnin de
to turn (e.g., ~ left)	ကွေ့သည်	kwei. de
to make a U-turn	ကွေ့သည်	kwei. de
reverse (~ gear)	နောက်ပြန်	nau' pjan
to honk (vi)	ဟွန်းတီးသည်	hwun: di: de
honk (sound)	ဟွန်း	hwun:
to get stuck (in the mud, etc.)	နစ်သည်	ni' te
to spin the wheels	ဘီးလည်စေသည်	bi: le zei de
to cut, to turn off (vt)	ရပ်သည်	ja' te
speed	နှုန်း	hnun:
to exceed the speed limit	သတ်မှတ်နှုန်းထက် ပိုမောင်းသည်	tha' hma' hnoun: de' pou maun: de
to give a ticket	ဒဏ်ရိုက်သည်	dan jai' de
traffic lights	မီးပွိုင့်	mi: bwain.
driver's license	ကားလိုင်စင်	ka: lain zin
grade crossing	ရထားလမ်းကူး	jatha: lan: gu:
intersection	လမ်းဆုံ	lan: zoun
crosswalk	လူကူးမျဉ်းကြား	lu gu: mji: gja:
bend, curve	လမ်းကွေ့	lan: gjou:
pedestrian zone	လမ်းသွားလမ်းလာနေရာ	lan: dhwa: lan: la nei ja

180. Traffic signs

rules of the road	လမ်းစည်းကမ်း	lan: ze: kan:
road sign (traffic sign)	မီးပွိုင့်ဆိုင်ရာ ဆိုင်းဘုတ်များ	mi: bwain. zain ja zain: bou' mja:

passing (overtaking)	ကျော်တက်ခြင်း	kjo de' chin:
curve	လမ်းအကွေ့	lan: akwei.
U-turn	ပစောက်ကွေ့	pa. zau' kwei.
traffic circle	မီးပွိုင့်အဝိုင်းပတ်	mi: bwain. awain: ba'

No entry	လမ်းထဲ မဝင်ရ	lan: de: ma. win ja.
No vehicles allowed	ယာဉ်မဝင်ရအမှတ်အသား	jin ma. win ja. ahma' atha'
No passing	ကျော်မတက်ရ အမှတ်အသား	kjo ma. de ja. ahma' atha:
No parking	ကားရပ်နားခြင်းမပြုရ	ka: ja' na gjin: ma. pju ja
No stopping	ကားမရပ်ရ	ka: ma. ja' ja

dangerous bend	အန္တရာယ်ကွေ့.	an dare gwei.
steep descent	ဆင်ခြေလျှောမတ်စောက်လမ်း	hsin gjei sho: ma' sau' lan:
one-way traffic	တစ်လမ်းသွား	ti' lan: dhwa:
crosswalk	လူကူးမျဉ်းကြား	lu gu: mji: gja:
slippery road	ချော်နေသောလမ်း	cho nei dho: lan:
YIELD	တဖက်ကားကိုဦး	tahpa' ka: gou u:
	စားပေးပါ	za: bei: ba

181

PEOPLE. LIFE EVENTS

Life events

181. Holidays. Event

celebration, holiday	ပျော်ပွဲရှင်ပွဲ	pjo bwe: shin bwe:
national day	အမျိုးသားနေ့	amjou: dha: nei.
public holiday	ပွဲတော်ရက်	pwe: do je'
to commemorate (vt)	အထိမ်းအမှတ်အဖြစ်ကျင်း ပသည်	a htin: ahma' ahpja' kjin: ba. de
event (happening)	အဖြစ်အပျက်	a hpji' apje'
event (organized activity)	အစီအစဉ်	asi asin
banquet (party)	ဂုဏ်ပြုပွဲ	goun bju za: bwe:
reception (formal party)	ဧည့်ကြိုနေရာ	e. gjou nei ja
feast	စားသောက်ဧည့်ခံပွဲ	sa: thau' e. gan bwe:
anniversary	နှစ်ပတ်လည်	hni' ba' le
jubilee	ရတု	jadu.
to celebrate (vt)	ကျင်းပသည်	kjin: ba. de
New Year	နှစ်သစ်ကူး	hni' thi' ku:
Happy New Year!	ပျော်ရွှင်ဖွယ်နှစ်သစ်ကူး ဖြစ်ပါစေ	pjo shin bwe: hni' ku: hpji' ba zei
Santa Claus	ခရစ္စမတ်ဘိုးဘိုး	khari' sa. ma' bou: bou:
Christmas	ခရစ္စမတ်ပွဲတော်	khari' sa. ma' pwe: do
Merry Christmas!	မယ်ရီခရစ္စမတ်	me ji kha. ji' sa. ma'
Christmas tree	ခရစ္စမတ်သစ်ပင်	khari' sa. ma' thi' pin
fireworks (fireworks show)	မီးရှူးမီးပန်း	mi: shu: mi: ban:
wedding	မင်္ဂလာဆောင်ပွဲ	min ga. la zaun bwe:
groom	သတို့သား	dhadou. tha:
bride	သတို့သမီး	dhadou. thami:
to invite (vt)	ဖိတ်သည်	hpi' de
invitation card	ဖိတ်စာကဒ်	hpi' sa ka'
guest	ဧည့်သည်	e. dhe
to visit	အိမ်လည်သွားသည်	ein le dhwa: de
(~ your parents, etc.)		
to meet the guests	ဧည့်သည်ကြိုဆိုသည်	e. dhe gjou zou de
gift, present	လက်ဆောင်	le' hsaun
to give (sth as present)	ပေးသည်	pei: de

to receive gifts	လက်ဆောင်ရသည်	le' hsaun ja. de
bouquet (of flowers)	ပန်းစည်း	pan: ze:
congratulations	ဂုဏ်ပြုခြင်း	goun bju chin:
to congratulate (vt)	ဂုဏ်ပြုသည်	goun bju de
greeting card	ဂုဏ်ပြုကဒ်	goun bju ka'
to send a postcard	ပို့စ်ကဒ်ပေးသည်	pou. s ka' pei: de
to get a postcard	ပို့ စ်ကဒ်လက်ခံ	pou. s ka' le' khan
	ရရှိသည်	ja. shi. de
toast	ဆုတောင်းဂုဏ်ပြုခြင်း	hsu. daun: goun pju. gjin:
to offer (a drink, etc.)	ကျွေးသည်	kjwei: de
champagne	ရှန်ပိန်	shan pein
to enjoy oneself	ပျော်ရွှင်သည်	pjo shwin de
merriment (gaiety)	ပျော်ရွှင်မှု	pjo shwin hmu
joy (emotion)	ပျော်ရွှင်ခြင်း	pjo shwin gjin:
dance	အက	aka.
to dance (vi, vt)	ကသည်	ka de
waltz	ဝေါ့ဇ်အက	wo. z aka.
tango	တန်ဂိုအက	tan gou aka.

182. Funerals. Burial

cemetery	သင်္ချိုင်း	thin gjain:
grave, tomb	အုတ်ဂူ	ou' gu
cross	လက်ဝါးကပ်တိုင်	le' wa: ka' tain
	အမှတ်အသား	ahma' atha:
gravestone	အုတ်ဂူကျောက်တုံး	ou' gu kjau' toun.
fence	ခြံစည်းရိုး	chan zi: jou:
chapel	ဝတ်ပြုဆုတောင်းရာနေရာ	wa' pju. u. daun: ja nei ja
death	သေခြင်းတရား	thei gjin: daja:
to die (vi)	ကွယ်လွန်သည်	kwe lun de
the deceased	ကွယ်လွန်သူ	kwe lun dhu
mourning	ဝမ်းနည်းကြေကွဲခြင်း	wan: ne: gjei gwe gjin:
to bury (vt)	မြေမြှုပ်သဂြိုဟ်သည်	mjei hmjou' dha. gjoun de
funeral home	အသုဘရှုရန်နေရာ	athu. ba. shu. jan nei ja
funeral	စျာပန	za ba. na.
wreath	ပန်းခွေ	pan gwei
casket, coffin	ခေါင်း	gaun:
hearse	နိဗ္ဗာန်ယာဉ်	nei' ban jan
shroud	လူသေပတ်သည့်အဝတ်စ	lu dhei ba' the. awa' za.
funeral procession	အသုဘယာဉ်တန်း	athu. ba. in dan:
funerary urn	အရိုးပြာအိုး	ajain: bja ou:

crematory	မီးသဂြိုလ်ရုံ	mi: dha. gjoun joun
obituary	နာရေးသတင်း	na jei: dha. din:
to cry (weep)	ငိုသည်	ngou de
to sob (vi)	ရှိုက်ငိုသည်	shai' ngou de

183. War. Soldiers

platoon	တပ်စု	ta' su.
company	တပ်ခွဲ	ta' khwe:
regiment	တပ်ရင်း	ta' jin:
army	တပ်မတော်	ta' mado
division	တိုင်းအဆင့်	tain: ahsin.
section, squad	အထူးစစ်သားအဖွဲ့ငယ်	a htu: za' tha: ahpwe. nge
host (army)	စစ်တပ်ဖွဲ့	si' ta' hpwe.
soldier	စစ်သား	si' tha:
officer	အရာရှိ	aja shi.
private	တပ်သား	ta' tha:
sergeant	တပ်ကြပ်ကြီး	ta' kja' kji:
lieutenant	ဗိုလ်	bou
captain	ဗိုလ်ကြီး	bou gji
major	ဗိုလ်မှူး	bou hmu:
colonel	ဗိုလ်မှူးကြီး	bou hmu: gji:
general	ဗိုလ်ချုပ်	bou gjou'
sailor	ရေတပ်သား	jei da' tha:
captain	ဗိုလ်ကြီး	bou gji
boatswain	သင်္ဘောအရာရှိငယ်	thin: bo: aja shi. nge
artilleryman	အမြောက်တပ်သား	amjau' thin de.
paratrooper	လေထီးခုန်စစ်သား	lei di: goun zi' tha:
pilot	လေယာဉ်မှူး	lei jan hmu:
navigator	လေကြောင်းပြ	lei gjaun: bja.
mechanic	စက်ပြင်ဆရာ	se' pjin zaja
pioneer (sapper)	မိုင်းရှင်းသူ	main: shin: dhu
parachutist	လေထီးခုန်သူ	lei di: goun dhu
reconnaissance scout	ကင်းထောက်	kin: dau'
sniper	လက်ဖြောင့်စစ်သား	le' hpaun. zi' tha:
patrol (group)	လှည့်ကင်း	hle. kin:
to patrol (vt)	ကင်းလှည့်သည်	kin: hle. de
sentry, guard	ကင်းသမား	kin: dhama:
warrior	စစ်သည်	si' te
patriot	မျိုးချစ်သူ	mjou: gji dhu
hero	သူရဲကောင်း	thu je: kaun:
heroine	အမျိုးသမီးလှ	amjou: dhami: lu
	စွမ်းကောင်း	swan: gaun:

| traitor | သစ္စာဖောက် | thi' sabau' |
| to betray (vt) | သစ္စာဖောက်သည် | thi' sabau' te |

| deserter | စစ်ပြေး | si' pjei: |
| to desert (vi) | စစ်တပ်မှထွက်ပြေးသည် | si' ta' hma. dwe' pjei: de |

mercenary	ကြေးစားစစ်သား	kjei: za za' tha:
recruit	တပ်သားသစ်	ta' tha: dhi'
volunteer	မိမိ၏ဆန္ဒ	mi. mi. i zan da.
	အရစစ်ထဲဝင်သူ	aja. zi' hte: win dhu

dead (n)	တိုက်ပွဲကျသူ	tai' pwe: gja dhu
wounded (n)	ဒဏ်ရာရသူ	dan ja ja. dhu
prisoner of war	စစ်သုံ့ပန်း	si' thoun. ban:

184. War. Military actions. Part 1

war	စစ်ပွဲ	si' pwe:
to be at war	စစ်ပွဲပါဝင်ဆင်	si' pwe: ba win zin
	နွှဲသည်	hnwe: de
civil war	ပြည်တွင်းစစ်	pji dwin: zi'

treacherously (adv)	သစ္စာဖောက်သွေဗိလျက်	thi' sabau' thwei bi le'
declaration of war	စစ်ကြေငြာခြင်း	si' kjei nja gjin:
to declare (~ war)	ကြေငြာသည်	kjei nja de
aggression	ကျူးကျော်ရန်စမှု	kju: gjo jan za. hmu.
to attack (invade)	တိုက်ခိုက်သည်	tai' khai' te

to invade (vt)	ကျူးကျော်ဝင်ရောက်သည်	kju: gjo win jau' te
invader	ကျူးကျော်ဝင်ရောက်သူ	kju: gjo win jau' thu
conqueror	အောင်နိုင်သူ	aun nain dhu

defense	ကာကွယ်ရေး	ka gwe ei:
to defend (a country, etc.)	ကာကွယ်သည်	ka gwe de
to defend (against …)	ခုခံကာကွယ်သည်	khu. gan ga gwe de

enemy	ရန်သူ	jan dhu
foe, adversary	ပြိုင်ဘက်	pjain be'
enemy (as adj)	ရန်သူ	jan dhu

strategy	မဟာဗျူဟာ	maha bju ha
tactics	ဗျူဟာ	bju ha
order	အမိန့်	amin.
command (order)	အမိန့်	amin.
to order (vt)	အမိန့်ပေးသည်	amin. bei: de
mission	ရည်မှန်းချက်	ji hman: gje'
secret (adj)	လျှို့ဝှက်သော	shou. hwe' te.
battle	တိုက်ပွဲငယ်	tai' pwe: nge
combat	တိုက်ပွဲ	tai' pwe:

attack	တိုက်စစ်	tai' si'
charge (assault)	တဟုန်ထိုးတိုက်ခိုက်ခြင်း	tahoun
to storm (vt)	တရကျမ်းတိုက်ခိုက်သည်	tara gjan: dai' khai' te
siege (to be under ~)	ဝန်းရံလုပ်ကြံခြင်း	wun: jan lou' chan gjin:
offensive (n)	ထိုးစစ်	htou: zi'
to go on the offensive	ထိုးစစ်ဆင်နွှဲသည်	htou: zi' hsin hnwe: de
retreat	ဆုတ်ခွာခြင်း	hsou' khwa gjin
to retreat (vi)	ဆုတ်ခွာသည်	hsou' khwa de
encirclement	ဝန်းရံဝိုတ်လို့ထားခြင်း	wun: jan bei' zou. da: chin:
to encircle (vt)	ဝန်းရံဝိုတ်လို့ထားသည်	wun: jan bei' zou. da: de
bombing (by aircraft)	ဗုံးကြဲချခြင်း	boun: gje: gja. gjin:
to drop a bomb	ဗုံးကြဲချသည်	boun: gje: gja. de
to bomb (vt)	ဗုံးကြဲတိုက်ခိုက်သည်	boun: gje: dai' khai' te
explosion	ပေါက်ကွဲမှု	pau' kwe: hmu.
shot	ပစ်ချက်	pi' che'
to fire (~ a shot)	ပစ်သည်	pi' te
firing (burst of ~)	ပစ်ခတ်ခြင်း	pi' che' chin:
to aim (to point a weapon)	ပစ်မှတ်ချိန်သည်	pi' hma' chein de
to point (a gun)	ချိန်ရွယ်သည်	chein jwe de
to hit (the target)	ပစ်မှတ်ထိသည်	pi' hma' hti. de
to sink (~ a ship)	နစ်မြှုပ်သည်	ni' mjou' te
hole (in a ship)	အပေါက်	apau'
to founder, to sink (vi)	နစ်မြှုပ်သည်	hni' hmjou' te
front (war ~)	ရှေ့တန်း	shei. dan:
evacuation	စစ်ဘေးရှောင်ခြင်း	si' bei: shaun gjin:
to evacuate (vt)	စစ်ဘေးရှောင်သည်	si' bei: shaun de
trench	ကတုတ်ကျင်း	gadou kjin:
barbwire	သံဆူးကြိုး	than zu: gjou:
barrier (anti tank ~)	အတားအဆီး	ata: ahsi:
watchtower	မျှော်စင်	hmjo zin
military hospital	ရှေ့တန်းစစ်ဆေးရုံ	shei. dan: zi' zei: joun
to wound (vt)	ဒဏ်ရာရသည်	dan ja ja. de
wound	ဒဏ်ရာ	dan ja
wounded (n)	ဒဏ်ရာရသူ	dan ja ja. dhu
to be wounded	ဒဏ်ရာရစေသည်	dan ja ja. zei de
serious (wound)	ပြင်းထန်သော	pjin: dan dho:

185. War. Military actions. Part 2

captivity	သုံ့ပန်း	thoun. ban:
to take captive	သုံ့ပန်းအဖြစ်ဖမ်းသည်	thoun. ban: ahpji' hpan: de

to be held captive	သုံ့ပန်းဖြစ်သွားသည်	thoun. ban: bji' thwa: de
to be taken captive	သုံ့ပန်းအဖြစ် အဖမ်းခံရသည်	thoun. ban: ahpji' ahpan: gan ja. de
concentration camp	ညှင်းပန်းနိုပ်စက် ရာစခန်း	hnjin: ban: nei' ze' ja za. gan:
prisoner of war	စစ်သုံ့ပန်း	si' thoun. ban:
to escape (vi)	လွတ်မြောက်သည်	lu' mjau' te
to betray (vt)	သစ္စာဖောက်သည်	thi' sabau' te
betrayer	သစ္စာဖောက်သူ	thi' sabau' thu
betrayal	သစ္စာဖောက်မှု	thi' sabau' hmu.
to execute (by firing squad)	ပစ်သတ်ကွပ်မျက်ခံရသည်	pi' tha' ku' mje' khan ja. de
execution (by firing squad)	ပစ်သတ်ကွပ်မျက်ခြင်း	pi' tha' ku' mje' chin:
equipment (military gear)	ပစ္စည်းကိရိယာများ	pji' si: gi. ji. ja mja:
shoulder board	ပခုံးဘားတန်း	pakhoun: ba: dan:
gas mask	ဓာတ်ငွေ့ကာ မျက်နှာဖုံး	da' ngwei. ga mje' na boun:
field radio	ရေဒီယိုစက်ကွင်း	rei di jou ze' kwin:
cipher, code	လျှို့ဝှက် ကုဒ်သင်္ကေတ	shou. hwe' kou' dha
secrecy	လျှို့ဝှက်ခြင်း	shou hwe' chin:
password	စကားဝှက်	zaga: hwe'
land mine	မြေမြှုပ်မိုင်း	mjei hmja' main:
to mine (road, etc.)	မိုင်းထောင်သည်	main: daun de
minefield	မိုင်းမြေ	main: mjei
air-raid warning	လေကြောင်းအန္တရာယ်သ တိပေးခြည်သည်	lei kjan: an da. ja dha. di. bei: nja. o. dhan
alarm (alert signal)	သတိပွေးခေါ်င်း လောင်းသံ	dhadi. pei: gaun: laun: dhan
signal	အချက်ပြ	ache' pja.
signal flare	အချက်ပြမီးကျည်	ache' pja. mi: gji
headquarters	ဌာနချုပ်	hta. na. gjou'
reconnaissance	ထောက်လှမ်းခြင်း	htau' hlan: gjin:
situation	အခြေအနေ	achei anei
report	အစီရင်ခံစာ	asi jin gan za
ambush	ချုံဗိုတိုက်ခိုက်ခြင်း	choun gou dai' khai' chin:
reinforcement (of army)	စစ်ကူ	si' ku
target	ပစ်မှတ်	pi' hma'
proving ground	လေ့ကျင့်ရေးကွင်း	lei. kjin. jei: gwin:
military exercise	စစ်ရေးလေ့ကျင့်မှု	si' jei: lei. gjin. hmu.
panic	ထိပ်ထိပ်ပြာပြာဖြစ်ခြင်း	htei' htei' pja bja bji' chin:
devastation	ကြီးစွာသောအပျက်အစီး	kji: zwa dho apje' asi:
destruction, ruins	အပျက်အစီး	apje' asi:

to destroy (vt)	ဖျက်ဆီးသည်	hpje' hsi: de
to survive (vi, vt)	အသက်ရှင်ကျန်ရစ်သည်	athe' shin kjin ja' te
to disarm (vt)	လက်နက်သိမ်းသည်	le' ne' thain de
to handle (~ a gun)	ကိုင်တွယ်သည်	kain dwe de

| Attention! | သတိ | thadi. |
| At ease! | သက်သာ | the' tha |

feat, act of courage	စွန့်စားမှု	sun. za: hmu.
oath (vow)	ကျမ်းသစ္စာ	kjan: thi' sa
to swear (an oath)	ကျမ်းသစ္စာဆိုသည်	kjan: thi' sa hsou de

decoration (medal, etc.)	တန်ဆာဆင်မှု	tan za zin hmu.
to award (give medal to)	ဆုတံဆိပ်ချီးမြှင့်သည်	hsu. dazei' chi: hmjin. de
medal	ဆုတံဆိပ်	hsu. dazei'
order (e.g., ~ of Merit)	ဘွဲ့တံဆိပ်	bwe. dan zi'

victory	အောင်ပွဲ	aun bwe:
defeat	အရှုံး	ashoun:
armistice	စစ်ရပ်ဆိုင်းသဘော	si' ja' hsain: dhabo:
	တူညီမှု	du nji hmu.

standard (battle flag)	စံ	san
glory (honor, fame)	ထင်ပေါ် ကျော်ကြားမှု	htin bo gjo gja: hmu.
parade	စစ်ရေးပြ	si' jei: bja.
to march (on parade)	စစ်ရေးပြသည်	si' jei: bja. de

186. Weapons

weapons	လက်နက်	le' ne'
firearms	မီးပွင့်သေနတ်	mi: bwin. dhei na'
cold weapons (knives, etc.)	ဓါးအမျိုးမျိုး	da: mjou: mjou:

chemical weapons	ဓာတုလက်နက်	da tu. le' ne'
nuclear (adj)	နျူကလီးယား	nju ka. li: ja:
nuclear weapons	နျူကလီးယားလက်နက်	nju ka. li: ja: le' ne'

| bomb | ဗုံး | boun: |
| atomic bomb | အက်တမ်ဗုံး | e' tan boun: |

pistol (gun)	ပစ္စတို	pji' sa. tou
rifle	ရိုင်ဖယ်	jain be
submachine gun	မောင်းပြန်သေနတ်	maun: bjan dhei na'
machine gun	စက်သေနတ်	se' thei na'

muzzle	ပြောင်းဝ	pjaun: wa.
barrel	ပြောင်း	pjaun:
caliber	သေနတ်ပြောင်းအချင်း	thei na' pjan: achin:
trigger	ခလုတ်	khalou'

sight (aiming device)	ချိန်ခွက်	chein kwe'
magazine	ကျည်ကပ်	kji ke'
butt (shoulder stock)	သေနတ်ဒင်	thei na' din

| hand grenade | လက်ပစ်ဗုံး | le' pi' boun: |
| explosive | ပေါက်ကွဲစေသောပစ္စည်း | pau' kwe: zei de. bji' si: |

bullet	ကျည်ဆံ	kji. zan
cartridge	ကျည်ဆံ	kji. zan
charge	ကျည်ထိုးခြင်း	kji dou: gjin:
ammunition	ခဲယမ်းမီးကျောက်	khe: jan: mi: kjau'

bomber (aircraft)	ဗုံးကြဲလေယာဉ်	boun: gje: lei jin
fighter	တိုက်လေယာဉ်	tai' lei jan
helicopter	ရဟတ်ယာဉ်	jaha' jan

anti-aircraft gun	လေယာဉ်ပစ်စက်သေနတ်	lei jan pi' ze' dhei na'
tank	တင့်ကား	tin. ga:
tank gun	တင့်အမြောက်	tin. amjau'

artillery	အမြောက်	amjau'
gun (cannon, howitzer)	ရေးဓေတ်အမြောက်	shei: gi' amjau'
to lay (a gun)	ချိန်ရွယ်သည်	chein jwe de

shell (projectile)	အမြောက်ဆံ	amjau' hsan
mortar bomb	စိန်ပြောင်းကျည်	sein bjaun: gji
mortar	စိန်ပြောင်း	sein bjaun:
splinter (shell fragment)	ဗုံးစ	boun: za

submarine	ရေအောက်နှင့်ဆိုင်သော	jei au' hnin. zain de.
torpedo	တော်ပီဒို	to pi dou
missile	ဒုံး	doun:
to load (gun)	ကျည်ထိုးသည်	kji dou: de
to shoot (vi)	သေနတ်ပစ်သည်	thei na' pi' te
to point at (the cannon)	ချိန်သည်	chein de
bayonet	လှံစွပ်	hlan zu'

rapier	ရာပီယာဓားရှည်	ra pi ja da: shei
saber (e.g., cavalry ~)	စစ်သုံးဓားရှည်	si' thoun: da shi
spear (weapon)	လှံ	hlan
bow	လေး	lei:
arrow	မြား	mja:
musket	ပြောင်းရှောသေနတ်	pjaun: gjo: dhei na'
crossbow	ဒူးလေး	du: lei:

187. Ancient people

primitive (prehistoric)	ရှေးဦးကာလ	shei: u: ga la.
prehistoric (adj)	သမိုင်းမတိုင်	thamain: ma. dain
	မီကာလ	mi ga la.

ancient (~ civilization)	ရှေးကျသော	shei: gja. de
Stone Age	ကျောက်ခေတ်	kjau' khi'
Bronze Age	ကြေးခေတ်	kjei: gei'
Ice Age	ရေခဲခေတ်	jei ge: gei'

tribe	မျိုးနွယ်စု	mjou: nwe zu.
cannibal	လူသားစားလူရိုင်း	lu dha: za: lu jain:
hunter	မုဆိုး	mou' hsou:
to hunt (vi, vt)	အမဲလိုက်သည်	ame: lai' de
mammoth	အမွေးရှည်ဆင်ကြီး တစ်မျိုး	ahmwei shei zin kji: ti' mjou:

cave	ဂူ	gu
fire	မီး	mi:
campfire	မီးပုံ	mi: boun
cave painting	နံရံဆေးရေးပန်းချီ	nan jan zei: jei: ban: gji

tool (e.g., stone ax)	ကိရိယာ	ki. ji. ja
spear	လှံ	hlan
stone ax	ကျောက်ပုဆိန်	kjau' pu. hsain
to be at war	စစ်ပွဲတွင်ပါဝင်ဆင် နွှဲသည်	si' pwe: dwin ba win zin hnwe: de
to domesticate (vt)	ယဉ်ပါးစေသည်	jin ba: zei de

idol	ရုပ်တု	jou' tu
to worship (vt)	ကိုးကွယ်သည်	kou: kwe de
superstition	အယူသီးခြင်း	aju dhi: gjin:
rite	ရိုးရာထုံးတမ်းဓလေ့	jou: ja doun: dan: da lei.

evolution	ဆင့်ကဲဖြစ်စဉ်	hsin. ke: hpja' sin
development	ဖွံ့ဖြိုးတိုးတက်မှု	hpjun. bjou: dou: de' hmu.
disappearance (extinction)	ပျောက်ကွယ်ခြင်း	pjau' kwe gjin:
to adapt oneself	နေသားကျရန်ပြင်ဆင်သည်	nei dha: gja. jan bjin zin de

archeology	ရှေးဟောင်းသုတေသန	shei: haun
archeologist	ရှေးဟောင်းသုတေသ နပညာရှင်	shei: haun thu. dei dha. na. bji nja shin
archeological (adj)	ရှေးဟောင်းသုတေသ နပိုင်ရာ	shei: haun thu. dei dha. na. zain ja

excavation site	တူးဖော်ရာနေရာ	tu: hpo ja nei ja
excavations	တူးဖော်မှုလုပ်ငန်း	tu: hpo hmu. lou' ngan:
find (object)	တွေ့ရှိချက်	twei. shi. gje'
fragment	အပိုင်းအစ	apain: asa.

188. Middle Ages

people (ethnic group)	လူမျိုး	lu mjou:
peoples	လူမျိုး	lu mjou:
tribe	မျိုးနွယ်စု	mjou: nwe zu.

tribes	မျိုးနွယ်စုများ	mjou: nwe zu. mja:
barbarians	အရိုင်းအစိုင်းများ	ajou: asain: mja:
Gauls	ဂေါလ်လူမျိုးများ	go l lu mjou: mja:
Goths	ဂေါ့တ်လူမျိုးများ	go. t lu mjou: mja:
Slavs	စလပ်လူမျိုးများ	sala' lu mjou: mja:
Vikings	ဗိုက်ကင်းလူမျိုး	bai' kin: lu mjou:
Romans	ရောမလူမျိုး	ro: ma. lu mjou:
Roman (adj)	ရောမနှင့်ဆိုင်သော	ro: ma. hnin. zain de
Byzantines	ဘိုင်ဇင်တိုင်လူမျိုးများ	bain zin dain lu mjou: mja:
Byzantium	ဘိုင်ဇင်တိုင်အင်ပါယာ	bain zin dain in ba ja
Byzantine (adj)	ဘိုင်ဇင်တိုင်နှင့်ဆိုင်သော	bain zin dain hnin. zain de.
emperor	ဧကရာဇ်	ei gaja'
leader, chief (tribal ~)	ခေါင်းဆောင်	gaun: zaun
powerful (~ king)	အင်အားကြီးသော	in a: kji: de.
king	ဘုရင်	ba. jin
ruler (sovereign)	အုပ်ချုပ်သူ	ou' chou' thu
knight	ဆာဘွဲ့ရသူရဲကောင်း	hsa bwe. ja. dhu je gaun:
feudal lord	မြေရှင်ပဒေသရာဇ်	mjei shin badei dhaja'
feudal (adj)	မြေရှင်ပဒေသရာဇ် စနစ်နှင့်ဆိုင်သော	mjei shin badei dhaja' sani' hnin. zain de.
vassal	မြေကျွန်	mjei gjun
duke	မြို့စားကြီး	mjou. za: gji:
earl	ဗြိတိသျှမှူး မတ်သူရဲကောင်း	bri ti sha hmu: ma' thu je: gaun:
baron	ဘယ်ရွန် အမတ်	be jwan ama'
bishop	ဘုန်းတော်ကြီး	hpoun do: gji:
armor	ချပ်ဝတ်တန်ဆာ	cha' wu' tan za
shield	ဒိုင်း	dain:
sword	ဓား	da:
visor	စစ်မျက်နှာကာ	si' mje' na ga
chainmail	သံဇကာချပ်ဝတ်တန်ဆာ	than za. ga gja' wu' tan za
Crusade	ခရူဆိတ်ဘာသာ ရေးစစ်ပွဲ	kha ju: zei' ba dha jei: zi' pwe:
crusader	ခရူးဆိတ်တိုက်ပ ွဲဝင်သူ	kha ju: zei' dai' bwe: win dhu
territory	နယ်မြေ	ne mjei
to attack (invade)	တိုက်ခိုက်သည်	tai' khai' te
to conquer (vt)	သိမ်းပိုက်စိုးမိုးသည်	thain: bou' sou: mou: de
to occupy (invade)	သိမ်းပိုက်သည်	thain:
siege (to be under ~)	ဝန်းရံလုပ်ကြံခြင်း	wun: jan lou' chan gjin:
besieged (adj)	ဝန်းရံလုပ်ကြံ ခံရသော	wun: jan lou' chan gan ja. de.
to besiege (vt)	ဝန်းရံလုပ်ကြံသည်	wun: jan lou' chan de

inquisition	ကာသိုလိပ်ဘုရားကျောင်း တရားစီရင်အဖွဲ့	ka tho li' bou ja: gjan: ta. ja: zi jin ahpwe.
inquisitor	စစ်ကြောမေးမြန်းသူ	si' kjo: mei: mjan: dhu
torture	ညှဉ်းပန်းနှိပ်စက်ခြင်း	hnjin: ban: hnei' se' chin:
cruel (adj)	ရက်စက်ကြမ်းကြုတ်သော	je' se' kjan: gjou' te
heretic	ဒိဌိ	di hti
heresy	မိစ္ဆာဒိဌိ	mei' hsa dei' hti.
seafaring	ပင်လယ်ပျော်	pin le bjo
pirate	ပင်လယ်ဓားပြ	pin le da: bja.
piracy	ပင်လယ်ဓားပြတိုက်ခြင်း	pin le da: bja. tai' chin:
boarding (attack)	လှေတွန်းပတ်ပေါ် တိုက်ခိုက်ခြင်း	hlei goun: ba' po dou' hpou' chin:
loot, booty	တိုက်ခိုက်ရရှိသောပစ္စည်း	tai' khai' ja. shi. dho: pji' si:
treasures	ရတနာ	jadana
discovery	ရှးစမ်းရှာဖွေခြင်း	su: zan: sha bwei gjin
to discover (new land, etc.)	ရှးစမ်းရှာဖွေသည်	su: zan: sha bwei de
expedition	ရှးစမ်းလေ့လာရေးခရီး	su: zan: lei. la nei: khaji:
musketeer	ပြောင်းရှေ့သေနတ် ကိုင်စစ်သား	pjaun: gjo: dhei na' kain si' tha:
cardinal	ရေဗျန်းခရစ်ယာန် ဘုန်းတော်ကြီး	jei bjan: khaji' jan boun: do gji:
heraldry	မျိုးရိုးဘွဲ့တံဆိပ် များလေ့လာခြင်းပညာ&#4140	mjou: jou: bwe. dan zai' mja: lei. la gjin: pi nja
heraldic (adj)	မျိုးရိုးပညာလေ့လာခြင်း နှင့်ဆိုင်သော	mjou: pi nja lei. la gjin: hnin. zain de.

189. Leader. Chief. Authorities

king	ဘုရင်	ba jin
queen	ဘုရင်မ	ba jin ma.
royal (adj)	ဘုရင်နှင့်ဆိုင်သော	ba. jin hnin. zain de
kingdom	ဘုရင်အုပ်ချုပ် သောနိုင်ငံ	ba jin au' chou' dho nin gan
prince	အိမ်ရှေ့ မင်းသား	ein shei. min: dha:
princess	မင်းသမီး	min: dhami:
president	သမ္မတ	thamada.
vice-president	ဒုသမ္မတ	du. dhamada.
senator	ဆိနိတ်လွှတ်တော်အမတ်	hsi nei' hlwa' do: ama'
monarch	သက်ဦးဆံပိုင်	the'
ruler (sovereign)	အုပ်ချုပ်သူ	ou' chou' thu
dictator	အာဏာရှင်	a na shin
tyrant	ဖိနှိပ်ချုပ်ချယ်သူ	hpana' chou' che dhu
magnate	လုပ်ငန်းရှင်သူဌေးကြီး	lou' ngan: shin dhu dei: gji:
director	ညွှန်ကြားရေးမှူး	hnjun gja: jei: hmu:

chief	အကြီးအကဲ	akji: ake:
manager (director)	မန်နေဂျာ	man nei gji
boss	အကြီးအကဲ	akji: ake:
owner	ပိုင်ရှင်	pain shin

leader	ခေါင်းဆောင်	gaun: zaun
head (~ of delegation)	အဖွဲ့ခေါင်းဆောင်	ahpwe. gaun: zaun:
authorities	အာဏာပိုင်အဖွဲ့	a na bain ahpwe:
superiors	အထက်လူကြီးများ	a hte' lu gji: mja:

governor	ပြည်နယ်အုပ်ချုပ်ရေးမှူး	pji ne ou' chou' jei: hmu:
consul	ကောင်စစ်ဝန်	kaun si' wun
diplomat	သံတမန်	than taman.
mayor	မြို့တော်ဝန်	mjou. do wun
sheriff	နယ်မြေတ္တာဝန်ခံ ရဲအရာရှိ	ne mjei da wun gan je: aja shi.

emperor	ဧကရာဇ်	ei gaja'
tsar, czar	ဇာဘုရင်	za bou jin
pharaoh	ရှေးအီဂျစ်နိုင်ငံဘုရင်	shei: i gji' nain ngan bu. jin
khan	ခန်	khan

190. Road. Way. Directions

| road | လမ်း | lan: |
| way (direction) | လမ်းကြောင်း | lan: gjaun: |

freeway	အမြန်လမ်းမကြီး	aman lan: ma. mji:
highway	အဝေးပြေးလမ်းမကြီး	awei: bjei: lan: ma. gji:
interstate	ပင်မလမ်းမကြီး	pin lan: ma. gji:

| main road | မိန်းလမ်း | mein: lan: |
| dirt road | မြေလမ်း | mjei lan |

| pathway | လူသွားလမ်း | lu dhwa: lan: |
| footpath (troddenpath) | လူသွားလမ်းကလေး | lu dhwa: lan: ga. lei: |

Where?	ဘယ်မှာလဲ	be hma le:
Where (to)?	ဘယ်ကိုလဲ	be gou le:
From where?	ဘယ်ကလဲ	be ga. le:

| direction (way) | ဦးတည်ရာ | u: te ja |
| to point (~ the way) | ညွှန်ပြသည် | hnjun bja. de |

to the left	ဘယ်ဘက်	be be'
to the right	ညာဘက်	nja be'
straight ahead (adv)	တည့်တည့်	te. de.
back (e.g., to turn ~)	နောက်သို့	nau' dhou.
bend, curve	အကွေ့	akwei.
to turn (e.g., ~ left)	ကွေ့သည်	kwei. de

to make a U-turn	ကွေ့သည်	kwei. de
to be visible (mountains, castle, etc.)	မြင်ရသည်	mjin ja. de
to appear (come into view)	မြင်နေရသည်	mjin nei ja. de
stop, halt (e.g., during a trip)	ရပ်နားခြင်း	ja' na: gjin:
to rest, to pause (vi)	အနားယူသည်	ana: ju de
rest (pause)	အနားယူခြင်း	ana: ju gjin:
to lose one's way	လမ်းပျောက်သည်	lan: bjau' de
to lead to ... (ab. road)	ဦးတည်သည်	u: ti de
to come out (e.g., on the highway)	လမ်းပေါ်ထွက်လာသည်	lan: bo dwe' la de
stretch (of road)	တစ်ကန့်	ti' kan.
asphalt	ကတ္တရာစေး	ka' ta' ja zi:
curb	ပလက်ဖောင်းဘောင်	pa. je' hpaun: baun:
ditch	လမ်းဘေးမြောင်း	lan: bei: mjaun:
manhole	မန်းဟိုး	man: hou:
roadside (shoulder)	လမ်းဘေးမြေသား	lan: bei: mjei dha:
pit, pothole	ချိုင့်	chain.
to go (on foot)	သွားသည်	thwa: de
to pass (overtake)	ကျော်တက်သည်	kjo de' te
step (footstep)	ခြေလှမ်း	chei hlan:
on foot (adv)	ခြေလျင်သွားသည်	chei ljin dhwa: de
to block (road)	ပိတ်ဆို့ထားသည်	pei' hsou. da: de
boom gate	မြို့အဝင်ဂိတ်	mjou. awin gei'
dead end	လမ်းဆုံး	lan: zoun:

191. Breaking the law. Criminals. Part 1

bandit	ဓားပြ	damja.
crime	ရာဇဝတ်မှု	raza. wu' hma.
criminal (person)	ရာဇဝတ်သား	raza. wu' tha:
thief	သူခိုး	thu khou:
to steal (vi, vt)	ခိုးသည်	khou: de
stealing, theft	ခိုးမှု	khou: hmu
stealing (larceny)	ခိုးခြင်း	khou: chin:
theft	သူခိုး	thu khou:
to kidnap (vt)	ပြန်ပေးဆွဲသည်	pjan bei: zwe: de
kidnapping	ပြန်ပေးဆွဲခြင်း	pjan bei: zwe: gjin:
kidnapper	ပြန်ပေးဆွဲသမား	pjan bei: dhama:
ransom	ပြန်ရွှေးငွေ	pjan jwei: ngwei
to demand ransom	ပြန်ပေးဆွဲသည်	pjan bei: zwe: de

to rob (vt)	ဓားပြတိုက်သည်	damja. tai' te
robbery	လုယက်မှု	lu. je' hmu.
robber	လုယက်သူ	lu. je' dhu
to extort (vt)	ခြိမ်းခြောက်ပြီး ငွေညှစ်သည်	chein: gjau' pji: ngwe hnji' te
extortionist	ခြိမ်းခြောက်ငွေညှစ်သူ	chein: gjau' ngwe hnji' thu
extortion	ခြိမ်းခြောက်ပြီး ငွေညှစ်ခြင်း	chein: gjau' pji: ngwe hnji' chin:
to murder, to kill	သတ်သည်	tha' te
murder	လူသတ်မှု	lu dha' hmu.
murderer	လူသတ်သမား	lu dha' thama:
gunshot	ပစ်ချက်	pi' che'
to fire (~ a shot)	ပစ်သည်	pi' te
to shoot to death	ပစ်သတ်သည်	pi' tha' te
to shoot (vi)	ပစ်သည်	pi' te
shooting	ပစ်ချက်	pi' che'
incident (fight, etc.)	ဆူပူမှု	hsu. bu hmu.
fight, brawl	ရန်ပွဲ	jan bwe:
Help!	ကူညီပါ	ku nji ba
victim	ရန်ပြုခံရသူ	jab bju. gan ja. dhu
to damage (vt)	ဖျက်ဆီးသည်	hpje' hsi: de
damage	အပျက်အစီး	apje' asi:
dead body, corpse	အလောင်း	alaun:
grave (~ crime)	စိုးရိမ်ဖွယ်ဖြစ်သော	sou: jein bwe bji' te.
to attack (vt)	တိုက်ခိုက်သည်	tai' khai' te
to beat (to hit)	ရိုက်သည်	jai' te
to beat up	ရိုက်သည်	jai' te
to take (rob of sth)	ယူသည်	ju de
to stab to death	ထိုးသတ်သည်	htou: dha' te
to maim (vt)	သေရာပါဒဏ်ရာရစေသည်	thei ja ba dan ja ja. zei de
to wound (vt)	ဒဏ်ရာရသည်	dan ja ja. de
blackmail	ခြိမ်းခြောက်ငွေ ညှစ်ခြင်း	chein: gjau' ngwe hnji' chin:
to blackmail (vt)	ခြိမ်းခြောက်ငွေညှစ်သည်	chein: gjau' ngwe hnji' te
blackmailer	ခြိမ်းခြောက်ငွေညှစ်သူ	chein: gjau' ngwe hnji' thu
protection racket	ရာဇဝတ်ဂိုက်ဆွာက် ကြေးကောက်ခြင်း	raza. wu' goun: hse' kjei: gau' chin:
racketeer	ဆက်ကြေးတောင်း-ရာ ဇဝတ်ဂိုက်	hse' kjei: daun: ra za. wu' gain:
gangster	လူဆိုးဂိုက်ဝင်	lu zou: gain: win
mafia, Mob	မာဖီးယားဂိုက်	ma bi: ja: gain:
pickpocket	ခါးပိုက်နှိုက်	kha: bai' hnai'
burglar	ဖောက်ထွင်းသူခိုး	hpau' htwin: dhu gou:

| smuggling | မှောင်ခို | hmaun gou |
| smuggler | မှောင်ခိုသမား | hmaun gou dhama: |

forgery	လိမ်လည်အတုပြုမှု	lein le atu. bju hmu.
to forge (counterfeit)	အတုလုပ်သည်	atu. lou' te
fake (forged)	အတု	atu.

192. Breaking the law. Criminals. Part 2

rape	မုဒိမ်းမှု	mu. dein: hmu.
to rape (vt)	မုဒိန်းကျင့်သည်	mu. dein: gjin. de
rapist	မုဒိမ်းကျင့်သူ	mu. dein: gjin. dhu
maniac	အရူး	aju:

prostitute (fem.)	ပြည့်တန်ဆာ	pjei. dan za
prostitution	ပြည့်တန်ဆာမှု	pjei. dan za hmu.
pimp	ဖာခေါင်း	hpa gaun:

| drug addict | ဆေးစွဲသူ | hsei: zwe: dhu |
| drug dealer | မူးယစ်ဆေးရောင်းဝယ်သူ | mu: ji' hsei: jaun we dhu |

to blow up (bomb)	ပေါက်ကွဲသည်	pau' kwe: de
explosion	ပေါက်ကွဲမှု	pau' kwe: hmu.
to set fire	မီးရှို့သည်	mi: shou. de
arsonist	မီးရှို့မှုကျူး	mi: shou. hmu. gju:
	လွန်သူ	lun dhu

terrorism	အကြမ်းဖက်ဝါဒ	akjan: be' wa da.
terrorist	အကြမ်းဖက်သမား	akjan: be' tha. ma:
hostage	ဓားစာခံ	daza gan

to swindle (deceive)	လိမ်လည်သည်	lein le de
swindle, deception	လိမ်လည်မှု	lein le hmu.
swindler	လူလိမ်	lu lein

to bribe (vt)	လာဘ်ထိုးသည်	la' htou: de
bribery	လာဘ်ပေးလာဘ်ယူ	la' pei: la' thu
bribe	လာဘ်	la'

poison	အဆိပ်	ahsei'
to poison (vt)	အဆိပ်ခတ်သည်	ahsei' kha' te
to poison oneself	အဆိပ်သောက်သည်	ahsei' dhau' te

suicide (act)	မိမိကိုယ်မိမိ	mi. mi. kou mi. mi.
	သတ်သေခြင်း	dha' thei gjin:
suicide (person)	မိမိကိုယ်မိမိ	mi. mi. kou mi. mi.
	သတ်သေသူ	dha' thei dhu

| to threaten (vt) | ခြိမ်းခြောက်သည် | chein: gjau' te |
| threat | ခြိမ်းခြောက်မှု | chein: gjau' hmu. |

to make an attempt	လုပ်ကြံသည်	lou' kjan de
attempt (attack)	လုပ်ကြံခြင်း	lou' kjan gjin:
to steal (a car)	ခိုးသည်	khou: de
to hijack (a plane)	လေယာဉ်အပိုင်စီးသည်	lei jan apain zi: de
revenge	လက်စားချေခြင်း	le' sa: gjei gjin:
to avenge (get revenge)	လက်စားချေသည်	le' sa: gjei de
to torture (vt)	ညှဉ်းပန်းနှိပ်စက်သည်	hnjin: ban: hnei' se' te
torture	ညှဉ်းပန်းနှိပ်စက်ခြင်း	hnjin: ban: hnei' se' chin:
to torment (vt)	နှိပ်စက်သည်	hnei' se' te
pirate	ပင်လယ်ဓားပြ	pin le da: bja.
hooligan	လမ်းသရဲ	lan: dhaje:
armed (adj)	လက်နက်ကိုင်ဆောင်သော	le' ne' kain zaun de.
violence	ရက်စက်ကြမ်းကြုတ်မှု	je' se' kjan: gjou' hmu.
illegal (unlawful)	တရားမဝင်သော	taja: ma. win de.
spying (espionage)	သူလျှိုလုပ်ခြင်း	thu shou lou' chin:
to spy (vi)	သူလျှိုလုပ်သည်	thu shou lou' te

193. Police. Law. Part 1

justice	တရားမျှတမှု	taja: hmja. ta. hmu.
court (see you in ~)	တရားရုံး	taja: joun:
judge	တရားသူကြီး	taja: dhu gji:
jurors	ဂျူရီအဖွဲ့ဝင်များ	gju ji ahpwe. win mja:
jury trial	ဂျူရီလူကြီးအဖွဲ့	gju ji lu gji: ahpwe.
to judge, to try (vt)	တရားစီရင်သည်	taja: zi jin de
lawyer, attorney	ရှေ့နေ	shei. nei
defendant	တရားပြိုင်	taja: bjain
dock	တရားရုံးဝက်ခ်ရှ	taja: joun: we' khjan
charge	စွပ်စွဲခြင်း	su' swe: chin:
accused	တရားစွဲခံရသော	taja: zwe: gan ja. de.
sentence	စီရင်ချက်	si jin gje'
to sentence (vt)	စီရင်ချက်ချသည်	si jin gje' cha. de
guilty (culprit)	တရားခံ	tajakhan
to punish (vt)	ပြစ်ဒဏ်ပေးသည်	pji' dan bei: de
punishment	ပြစ်ဒဏ်	pji' dan
fine (penalty)	ဒဏ်ငွေ	dan ngwei
life imprisonment	တစ်သက်တစ်ကျွန်းပြစ်ဒဏ်	ti' te' ti' kjun: bji' dan
death penalty	သေဒဏ်	thei dan
electric chair	လျှပ်စစ်ထိုင်ခုံ	hlja' si' dain boun

gallows	ကြိုးစင်	kjou: zin
to execute (vt)	ကွပ်မျက်သည်	ku' mje' te
execution	ကွပ်မျက်ခြင်း	ku' mje' gjin
prison, jail	ထောင်	htaun
cell	အကျဉ်းခန်း	achou' khan:
escort (convoy)	အစောင့်အကြပ်	asaun. akja'
prison guard	ထောင်စောင့်	htaun zaun.
prisoner	ထောင်သား	htaun dha:
handcuffs	လက်ထိပ်	le' htei'
to handcuff (vt)	လက်ထိပ်ခတ်သည်	le' htei' kha' te
prison break	ထောင်ဖောက်ပြေးခြင်း	htaun bau' pjei: gjin:
to break out (vi)	ထောင်ဖောက်ပြေးသည်	htaun bau' pjei: de
to disappear (vi)	ပျောက်ကွယ်သည်	pjau' kwe de
to release (from prison)	ထောင်မှလွတ်သည်	htaun hma. lu' te
amnesty	လွတ်ငြိမ်းချမ်းသာခွင့်	lu' njein: gjan: dha gwin.
police	ရဲ	je:
police officer	ရဲအရာရှိ	je: aja shi.
police station	ရဲစခန်း	je: za. gan:
billy club	သံတုတ်	than dou'
bullhorn	လက်ကိုင်စပီကာ	le' kain za. bi ka
patrol car	ကင်းလှည့်ကား	kin: hle. ka:
siren	အချက်ပေးဥသြသံ	ache' pei: ou' o: dhan
to turn on the siren	အချက်ပေးဥသြဖွင့်သည်	ache' pei: ou' o: zwe: de
siren call	အချက်ပေးဥသြဖွင့်သံ	ache' pei: ou' o: zwe: dhan
crime scene	အခင်းဖြစ်ပွားရာနေရာ	achin: hpji' pwa: ja nei ja
witness	သက်သေ	the' thei
freedom	လွတ်လပ်မှု	lu' la' hmu.
accomplice	ကြံရာပါ	kjan ja ba
to flee (vi)	ပုန်းသည်	poun: de
trace (to leave a ~)	ခြေရာ	chei ja

194. Police. Law. Part 2

search (investigation)	ဝရမ်းရှာဖွေခြင်း	wajan: sha bwei gjin:
to look for …	ရှာသည်	sha de
suspicion	မသင်္ကာမှု	ma. dhin ga hmu.
suspicious (e.g., ~ vehicle)	သံသယဖြစ်ဖွယ်ကောင်းသော	than thaja. bji' hpwe gaun: de.
to stop (cause to halt)	ရပ်သည်	ja' te
to detain (keep in custody)	ထိန်းသိမ်းထားသည်	htein: dhein: da: de
case (lawsuit)	အမှု	ahmu.
investigation	စုံစမ်းစစ်ဆေးခြင်း	soun zan: zi' hsei: gjin:

detective	စုံထောက်	soun dau'
investigator	အလွတ်စုံထောက်	alu' zoun htau'
hypothesis	အဆိုကြမ်း	ahsou gjan:
motive	စေ့ဆော်မှု	sei. zo hmu.
interrogation	စစ်ကြောမှု	si' kjo: hmu.
to interrogate (vt)	စစ်ကြောသည်	si' kjo: de
to question	မေးမြန်းသည်	mei: mjan: de
(~ neighbors, etc.)		
check (identity ~)	စစ်ဆေးသည်	si' hsei: de
round-up (raid)	ဝိုင်းဝန်းမှု	wain: wan: hmu.
search (~ warrant)	ရှာဖွေခြင်း	sha hpwei gjin:
chase (pursuit)	လိုက်လံဖမ်းဆီးခြင်း	lai' lan ban: zi: gjin:
to pursue, to chase	လိုက်သည်	lai' de
to track (a criminal)	ခြေရာခံသည်	chei ja gan de
arrest	ဖမ်းဆီးခြင်း	hpan: zi: gjin:
to arrest (sb)	ဖမ်းဆီးသည်	hpan: zi: de
to catch (thief, etc.)	ဖမ်းမိသည်	hpan: mi. de
capture	သိမ်းခြင်း	thain: gjin:
document	စာရွက်စာတမ်း	sajwe' zatan:
proof (evidence)	သက်သေပြချက်	the' thei pja. gje'
to prove (vt)	သက်သေပြသည်	the' thei pja. de
footprint	ခြေရာ	chei ja
fingerprints	လက်ဗွေရာများ	lei' bwei ja mja:
piece of evidence	သဲလွန်စ	the: lun za.
alibi	ဆင်ခြေ	hsin gjei
innocent (not guilty)	အပြစ်ကင်းသော	apja' kin: de.
injustice	မတရားမှု	ma. daja: hmu.
unjust, unfair (adj)	မတရားသော	ma. daja: de.
criminal (adj)	ပြုမူကျူးလွန်သော	pju. hmu. gju: lun de.
to confiscate (vt)	သိမ်းယူသည်	thein: ju de
drug (illegal substance)	မူးယစ်ဆေးဝါး	mu: ji' hsei: wa:
weapon, gun	လက်နက်	le' ne'
to disarm (vt)	လက်နက်သိမ်းသည်	le' ne' thain de
to order (command)	အမိန့်ပေးသည်	amin: bei: de
to disappear (vi)	ပျောက်ကွယ်သည်	pjau' kwe de
law	ဥပဒေ	u. ba. dei
legal, lawful (adj)	ဥပဒေနှင့် ညီညွတ်သော	u. ba. dei hnin. nji nju' te.
illegal, illicit (adj)	ဥပဒေနှင့်မ ညီညွတ်သော	u. ba. dei hnin. ma. nji nju' te.
responsibility (blame)	တာဝန်ယူခြင်း	ta wun ju gjin:
responsible (adj)	တာဝန်ရှိသော	ta wun shi. de.

NATURE

The Earth. Part 1

space	အာကာသ	akatha.
space (as adj)	အာကာသနှင့်ဆိုင်သော	akatha. hnin zain dho:
outer space	အာကာသဟင်းလင်းပြင်	akatha. hin: lin: bjin
world	ကမ္ဘာ	ga ba
universe	စကြဝဠာ	sa kja wa. la
galaxy	ကြယ်စုတန်း	kje zu. dan:
star	ကြယ်	kje
constellation	ကြယ်နက္ခတ်စု	kje ne' kha' zu.
planet	ဂြိုဟ်	gjou
satellite	ဂြိုဟ်ငယ်	gjou nge
meteorite	ဥက္ကာခဲ	ou' ka ge:
comet	ကြယ်တံခွန်	kje dagun
asteroid	ဂြိုဟ်သိမ်ဂြိုဟ်မွှား	gjou dhein gjou hmwa:
orbit	ပတ်လမ်း	pa' lan:
to revolve	လည်သည်	le de
(~ around the Earth)		
atmosphere	လေထု	lei du.
the Sun	နေ	nei
solar system	နေစကြဝဠာ	nei ze kja. wala
solar eclipse	နေကြတ်ခြင်း	nei gja' chin:
the Earth	ကမ္ဘာလုံး	ga ba loun:
the Moon	လ	la.
Mars	အင်္ဂါဂြိုဟ်	in ga gjou
Venus	သောကြာဂြိုဟ်	thau' kja gjou'
Jupiter	ကြာသပတေးဂြိုဟ်	kja dha ba. dei: gjou'
Saturn	စနေဂြိုဟ်	sanei gjou'
Mercury	ဗုဒ္ဓဟူးဂြိုဟ်	bou' da. gjou'
Uranus	ယူရေးနက်ဂြိုဟ်	ju rei: na' gjou
Neptune	နက်ပကျွန်းဂြိုဟ်	ne' pa. gjun: gjou
Pluto	ပလူတိုဂြိုဟ်	pa lu tou gjou '
Milky Way	နဂါးငွေ့ကြယ်စုတန်း	na. ga: ngwe. gje zu dan:

Great Bear (Ursa Major)	မြောက်ပိုင်းဂရိတ် ဘဲးရ်ကြယ်စု	mjau' pain: gajei' be:j gje zu.
North Star	ဓူဝံကြယ်	du wan gje
Martian	အင်္ဂါဂြိုဟ်သား	in ga gjou dha:
extraterrestrial (n)	အခြားကမ္ဘာဂြိုဟ်သား	apja: ga ba gjou dha
alien	ဂြိုဟ်သား	gjou dha:
flying saucer	ပန်းကန်ပြားပျံ	bagan: bja: bjan
spaceship	အာကာသယာဉ်	akatha. jin
space station	အာကာသစခန်း	akatha. za khan:
blast-off	လွှတ်တင်ခြင်း	hlu' tin gjin:
engine	အင်ဂျင်	in gjin
nozzle	နော်ဇယ်	no ze
fuel	လောင်စာ	laun za
cockpit, flight deck	လေယာဉ်မောင်းအခန်း	lei jan maun akhan:
antenna	အင်တန်နာတိုင်	in tan na tain
porthole	ပြတင်း	badin:
solar panel	နေရောင်ခြည်သုံး ဘတ်ထရီ	nei jaun gje dhoun: ba' hta ji
spacesuit	အာကာသဝတ်စုံ	akatha. wu' soun
weightlessness	အလေးချိန်ကင်းမဲ့ခြင်း	alei: gjein gin: me. gjin:
oxygen	အောက်ဆီဂျင်	au' hsi gjin
docking (in space)	အာကာသထဲချိတ် ဆက်ခြင်း	akatha. hte: chei' hse' chin:
to dock (vi, vt)	အာကာသထဲချိတ်ဆက်သည်	akatha. hte: chei' hse' te
observatory	နက္ခတ်မျှော်စင်	ne' kha' ta. mjo zin
telescope	အဝေးကြည့်မှန်ပြောင်း	awei: gji. hman bjaun:
to observe (vt)	လေ့လာကြည့်ရှုသည်	lei. la kji. hju. de
to explore (vt)	သုတေသနပြုသည်	thu. tei thana bjou de

196. The Earth

the Earth	ကမ္ဘာမြေကြီး	ga ba mjei kji:
the globe (the Earth)	ကမ္ဘာလုံး	ga ba loun:
planet	ဂြိုဟ်	gjou
atmosphere	လေထု	lei du.
geography	ပထဝီဝင်	pahtawi win
nature	သဘာဝ	tha. bawa
globe (table ~)	ကမ္ဘာလုံး	ga ba loun:
map	မြေပုံ	mjei boun
atlas	မြေပုံစာအုပ်	mjei boun za ou'
Europe	ဥရောပ	u. jo: pa

Asia	အာရှ	a sha.
Africa	အာဖရိက	apha. ri. ka.
Australia	သြစတြေးလျ	thja za djei: lja
America	အမေရိက	amei ji ka
North America	မြောက်အမေရိက	mjau' amei ri. ka.
South America	တောင်အမေရိက	taun amei ri. ka.
Antarctica	အန္တာတိတ်	anta di'
the Arctic	အာတိတ်	a tei'

197. Cardinal directions

north	မြောက်အရပ်	mjau' aja'
to the north	မြောက်ဘက်သို့	mjau' be' thou.
in the north	မြောက်ဘက်မှာ	mjau' be' hma
northern (adj)	မြောက်အရပ်နှင့်ဆိုင်သော	mjau' aja' hnin. zain de.
south	တောင်အရပ်	taun aja'
to the south	တောင်ဘက်သို့	taun be' thou.
in the south	တောင်ဘက်မှာ	taun be' hma
southern (adj)	တောင်အရပ်နှင့်ဆိုင်သော	taun aja' hnin. zain de.
west	အနောက်အရပ်	anau' aja'
to the west	အနောက်ဘက်သို့	anau' be' thou.
in the west	အနောက်ဘက်မှာ	anau' be' hma
western (adj)	အနောက်အရပ်နှင့်ဆိုင်သော	anau' aja' hnin. zain dho:
east	အရှေ့အရပ်	ashei. aja'
to the east	အရှေ့ဘက်သို့	ashei. be' hma
in the east	အရှေ့ဘက်မှာ	ashei. be' hma
eastern (adj)	အရှေ့အရပ်နှင့်ဆိုင်သော	ashei. aja' hnin. zain de.

198. Sea. Ocean

sea	ပင်လယ်	pin le
ocean	သမုဒ္ဒရာ	thamou' daja
gulf (bay)	ပင်လယ်ကွေ့	pin le gwe.
straits	ရေလက်ကြား	jei le' kja:
land (solid ground)	ကုန်းမြေ	koun: mei
continent (mainland)	တိုက်	tai'
island	ကျွန်း	kjun:
peninsula	ကျွန်းဆွယ်	kjun: zwe
archipelago	ကျွန်းစု	kjun: zu.
bay, cove	အော်	o
harbor	သင်္ဘောဆိပ်ကမ်း	thin: bo: zei' kan:

lagoon	ပင်လယ်ထုံးအိုင်	pin le doun: ain
cape	အငူ	angu
atoll	သန္တာကျောက်တန်းကျွန်းငယ်	than da gjau' tan: gjun: nge
reef	ကျောက်တန်း	kjau' tan:
coral	သန္တာကောင်	than da gaun
coral reef	သန္တာကျောက်တန်း	than da gjau' tan:
deep (adj)	နက်သော	ne' te.
depth (deep water)	အနက်	ane'
abyss	ချောက်နက်ကြီး	chau' ne' kji:
trench (e.g., Mariana ~)	မြောင်း	mjaun:
current (Ocean ~)	စီးကြောင်း	si: gaun:
to surround (bathe)	ဝိုင်းသည်	wain: de
shore	ကမ်းစပ်	kan: za'
coast	ကမ်းခြေ	kan: gjei
flow (flood tide)	ရေတက်	jei de'
ebb (ebb tide)	ရေကျ	jei gja.
shoal	သောင်စွယ်	thaun zwe
bottom (~ of the sea)	ကြမ်းပြင်	kan: pjin
wave	လှိုင်း	hlain:
crest (~ of a wave)	လှိုင်းခေါင်းဖြူ	hlain: gaun: bju.
spume (sea foam)	အမြှုပ်	a hmjou'
storm (sea storm)	မုန်တိုင်း	moun dain:
hurricane	ဟာရီကိန်းမုန်တိုင်း	ha ji gain: moun dain:
tsunami	ဆူနာမိ	hsu na mi
calm (dead ~)	ရေသေ	jei dhei
quiet, calm (adj)	ငြိမ်သက်အေးဆေးသော	njein dhe' ei: zei: de.
pole	ဝင်ရိုးစွန်း	win jou: zun
polar (adj)	ဝင်ရိုးစွန်းနှင့်ဆိုင်သော	win jou: zun hnin. zain de.
latitude	လတ္တီတွဒ်	la' ti. tu'
longitude	လောင်ဂျီတွဒ်	laun gji twa'
parallel	လတ္တီတွဒ်မျဉ်း	la' ti. tu' mjin:
equator	အီကွေတာ	i kwei: da
sky	ကောင်းကင်	kaun: gin
horizon	မိုးကုပ်စက်ဝိုင်း	mou kou' se' wain:
air	လေထု	lei du.
lighthouse	မီးပြတိုက်	mi: bja dai'
to dive (vi)	ရေငုပ်သည်	jei ngou' te
to sink (ab. boat)	ရေမြုပ်သည်	jei mjou' te
treasures	ရတနာ	jadana

199. Seas' and Oceans' names

Atlantic Ocean	အတ္တလန္တိတ် သမုဒ္ဒရာ	a' ta. lan ti' thamou' daja
Indian Ocean	အိန္ဒိယ သမုဒ္ဒရာ	indi. ja thamou. daja
Pacific Ocean	ပစိဖိတ် သမုဒ္ဒရာ	pa. si. hpi' thamou' daja
Arctic Ocean	အာတိတ် သမုဒ္ဒရာ	a tei' thamou' daja
Black Sea	ပင်လယ်နက်	pin le ne'
Red Sea	ပင်လယ်နီ	pin le ni
Yellow Sea	ပင်လယ်ဝါ	pin le wa
White Sea	ပင်လယ်ဖြူ	pin le bju
Caspian Sea	ကက်စပီယန် ပင်လယ်	ke' za. pi jan pin le
Dead Sea	ပင်လယ်သေ	pin le dhe:
Mediterranean Sea	မြေထဲပင်လယ်	mjei hte: bin le
Aegean Sea	အေဂီယန်းပင်လယ်	ei gi jan: bin le
Adriatic Sea	အဒရီရာတစ်ပင်လယ်	a da yi ya ti' pin le
Arabian Sea	အာရေဗီးယန်း ပင်လယ်	a ra bi: an: bin le
Sea of Japan	ဂျပန် ပင်လယ်	gja pan pin le
Bering Sea	ဘယ်ရင်း ပင်လယ်	be jin: bin le
South China Sea	တောင်တရုတ်ပင်လယ်	taun dajou' pinle
Coral Sea	ကော်ရယ်လ်ပင်လယ်	ko je l pin le
Tasman Sea	တက်စမန်းပင်လယ်	te' sa. man: bin le
Caribbean Sea	ကာရေးဘီးယန်းပင်လယ်	ka rei: bi: jan: bin le
Barents Sea	ဘာရင့်စ် ပင်လယ်	ba jan's bin le
Kara Sea	ကာရာ ပင်လယ်	kara bin le
North Sea	မြောက်ပင်လယ်	mjau' bin le
Baltic Sea	ဘောလ်တစ်ပင်လယ်	bo' l ti' pin le
Norwegian Sea	နော်ဝေးဂျီယန်း ပင်လယ်	no wei: bin le

200. Mountains

mountain	တောင်	taun
mountain range	တောင်တန်း	taun dan:
mountain ridge	တောင်ကြော	taun gjo:
summit, top	ထိပ်	htei'
peak	တောင်ထွတ်	taun htu'
foot (~ of the mountain)	တောင်ခြေ	taun gjei
slope (mountainside)	တောင်စောင်း	taun zaun:
volcano	မီးတောင်	mi: daun
active volcano	မီးတောင်ရှင်	mi: daun shin
dormant volcano	မီးငြိမ်းတောင်	mi: njein: daun

eruption	မီးတောင်ပေါက်ကွဲခြင်း	mi: daun pau' kwe: gjin:
crater	မီးတောင်ဝ	mi: daun wa.
magma	ကျောက်ရည်ပူ	kjau' ji bu
lava	ချောရည်	cho ji
molten (~ lava)	အရည်းပူသော	ajam: bu de.
canyon	တောင်ကြားချိုင့်ဝှမ်းနက်	taun gja: gjain. hwan: ne'
gorge	တောင်ကြား	taun gja:
crevice	အက်ကွဲကြောင်း	e' kwe: gjaun:
abyss (chasm)	ချောက်ကမ်းပါး	chau' kan: ba:
pass, col	တောင်ကြားလမ်း	taun gja: lan:
plateau	ကုန်းပြင်မြင့်	koun: bjin mjin:
cliff	ကျောက်ဆောင်	kjau' hsain
hill	တောင်ကုန်း	taun goun:
glacier	ရေခဲမြစ်	jei ge: mji'
waterfall	ရေတံခွန်	jei dan khun
geyser	ရေပူစမ်း	jei bu zan:
lake	ရေကန်	jei gan
plain	မြေပြန့်	mjei bjan:
landscape	ရှုခင်း	shu. gin:
echo	ပဲ့တင်သံ	pe. din than
alpinist	တောင်တက်သမား	taun de' thama:
rock climber	ကျောက်တောင်တက်သမား	kjau' taun de dha ma:
to conquer (in climbing)	အောင်နိုင်သူ	aun nain dhu
climb (an easy ~)	တောင်တက်ခြင်း	taun de' chin:

201. Mountains names

The Alps	အဲ့လ်ပ်တောင်	e.lp daun
Mont Blanc	မောင့်ဘလန့်စ်တောင်	maun. ba. lan. s taun
The Pyrenees	ပိရန်းနီးစ်တောင်	pi jan: ni:s taun
The Carpathians	ကာပသီယန်စ်တောင်	ka pa. dhi jan s taun
The Ural Mountains	ယူရယ်တောင်တန်း	ju re daun dan:
The Caucasus Mountains	ကော့ကေးဆပ်တောင်တန်း	ko: kei zi' taun dan:
Mount Elbrus	အယ်ဘရပ်စ်တောင်	e ba. ja's daun
The Altai Mountains	အယ်လတိုင်တောင်	e la. tain daun
The Tian Shan	တိုင်ယန်ရှန်းတောင်	tain jan shin: daun
The Pamir Mountains	ပါမီယာတောင်တန်း	pa mi ja daun dan:
The Himalayas	ဟိမဝန္တာတောင်တန်း	hi. ma. wan da daun dan:
Mount Everest	ဧဝရတ်တောင်	ei wa. ja' taun
The Andes	အန်းဒီတောင်တန်း	an: di daun dan:
Mount Kilimanjaro	ကီလီမန်ဂျာရိုတောင်	ki li man gja gou daun

202. Rivers

river	မြစ်	mji'
spring (natural source)	စမ်း	san:
riverbed (river channel)	ရေကြောင်းစီးကြောင်း	jei gjo: zi: gjaun:
basin (river valley)	မြစ်ချိုင့်ဝှမ်း	mji' chain. hwan:
to flow into …	စီးဝင်သည်	si: win de
tributary	မြစ်လက်တက်	mji' le' te'
bank (of river)	ကမ်း	kan:
current (stream)	စီးကြောင်း	si: gaun:
downstream (adv)	ရေစုန်	jei zoun
upstream (adv)	ရေဆန်	jei zan
inundation	ရေကြီးမှု	jei gji: hmu.
flooding	ရေလျှံခြင်း	jei shan gjin:
to overflow (vi)	လျှံသည်	shan de
to flood (vt)	ရေလွှမ်းသည်	jei hlwan: de
shallow (shoal)	ရေတိမ်ပိုင်း	jei dein bain:
rapids	ရေအောက်ကျောက်ဆောင်	jei au' kjau' hsaun
dam	ဆည်	hse
canal	တူးမြောင်း	tu: mjaun:
reservoir (artificial lake)	ရေလှောင်ကန်	jei hlaun gan
sluice, lock	ရေလွှေပေါက်	jei hlwe: bau'
water body (pond, etc.)	ရေထု	jei du.
swamp (marshland)	ရွှံ့ညွန်	shwan njun
bog, marsh	စိမ့်မြေ	sein. mjei
whirlpool	ရေဝဲ	jei we:
stream (brook)	ချောင်းကလေး	chaun: galei:
drinking (ab. water)	သောက်ရေ	thau' jei
fresh (~ water)	ရေချို	jei gjou
ice	ရေခဲ	jei ge:
to freeze over (ab. river, etc.)	ရေခဲသည်	jei ge: de

203. Rivers' names

Seine	ဆိန်မြစ်	sein mji'
Loire	လောဲရီမြစ်	lo ji mji'
Thames	သိမ်းမြစ်	thain: mji'
Rhine	ရိုင်းမြစ်	rain: mji'
Danube	ဒင်နယုမြစ်	din na. ju mji'

Volga	ဗော်လဂါမြစ်	bo la. ga mja'
Don	ဒွန်မြစ်	dun mja'
Lena	လီနာမြစ်	li na mji'

Yellow River	မြစ်ဝါ	mji' wa
Yangtze	ရန်ဇီးမြစ်	jan zi: mji'
Mekong	မဲခေါင်မြစ်	me: gaun mji'
Ganges	ဂင်္ဂါမြစ်	gan ga. mji'

Nile River	နိုင်းမြစ်	nain: mji'
Congo River	ကွန်ဂိုမြစ်	kun gou mji'
Okavango River	အိုကာဗန်ဂိုမြစ်	ai' hou ban
Zambezi River	ဇမ်ဘီဇီးမြစ်	zan bi zi: mji'
Limpopo River	လင်ပိုပိုမြစ်	lin po pou mji'
Mississippi River	မစ်စစ္စပီမြစ်	mi' si. si. pi. mji'

204. Forest

forest, wood	သစ်တော	thi' to:
forest (as adj)	သစ်တောနှင့်ဆိုင်သော	thi' to: hnin. zain de.

thick forest	ထူထပ်သောတော	htu da' te. do:
grove	သစ်ပင်အုပ်	thi' pin ou'
forest clearing	တောတွင်းလဟာပြင်	to: dwin: la. ha bjin

thicket	ချုံဗိုက်ပေါင်း	choun bei' paun:
scrubland	ချုံထနောင်းတော	choun hta naun: de.

footpath (troddenpath)	လူသွားလမ်းကလေး	lu dhwa: lan: ga. lei:
gully	လျှို	shou

tree	သစ်ပင်	thi' pin
leaf	သစ်ရွက်	thi' jwe'
leaves (foliage)	သစ်ရွက်များ	thi' jwe' mja:

fall of leaves	သစ်ရွက်ကြွေခြင်း	thi' jwe' kjwei gjin:
to fall (ab. leaves)	သစ်ရွက်ကြွေသည်	thi' jwe' kjwei de
top (of the tree)	အဖျား	ahpja:

branch	အကိုင်းခွဲ	akain: khwe:
bough	ပင်မကိုင်း	pin ma. gain:
bud (on shrub, tree)	အဖူး	ahpu:
needle (of pine tree)	အပ်နှင့်တူသောအရွက်	a' hnin. bu de. ajwe'
pine cone	ထင်းရှူးသီး	htin: shu: dhi:

tree hollow	အခေါင်းပေါက်	akhaun: bau'
nest	ငှက်သိုက်	hnge' thai'
burrow (animal hole)	မြေတွင်း	mjei dwin:
trunk	ပင်စည်	pin ze
root	အမြစ်	amji'

| bark | သစ်ခေါက် | thi' khau' |
| moss | ရေညှို | jei hnji. |

to uproot (remove trees or tree stumps)	အမြစ်မှဆွဲနှုတ်သည်	amji' hma zwe: hna' te
to chop down	ခုတ်သည်	khou' te
to deforest (vt)	တောပြုန်းစေသည်	to: bjoun zei de
tree stump	သစ်ငုတ်တို	thi' ngou' tou

campfire	မီးပုံ	mi' boun
forest fire	မီးလောင်ခြင်း	mi: laun gjin:
to extinguish (vt)	မီးသတ်သည်	mi: tha' de

forest ranger	တောခေါင်း	to: gaun:
protection	သစ်တောဝန်ထမ်း	thi' to: wun dan:
to protect (~ nature)	ထိန်းသိမ်းစောင့်ရှောက်သည်	htein: dhein: zaun. shau' te
poacher	ခိုးယူသူ	khou: ju dhu
steel trap	သံမဏိထောင်ချောက်	than mani. daun gjau'

to gather, to pick (vt)	ရှူးသည်	khu: de
to pick (mushrooms)	ဆွတ်သည်	hsu' te
to pick (berries)	ရှူးသည်	khu: de
to lose one's way	လမ်းပျောက်သည်	lan: bjau' de

205. Natural resources

natural resources	သယံဇာတ	thajan za da.
minerals	တွင်းထွက်ပစ္စည်း	twin: htwe' pji' si:
deposits	နန်း	noun:
field (e.g., oilfield)	ဓာတ်သတ္တုထွက်ရာမြေ	da' tha' tu dwe' ja mjei

to mine (extract)	တူးဖော်သည်	tu: hpo de
mining (extraction)	တူးဖော်ခြင်း	tu: hpo gjin:
ore	သတ္တုရိုင်း	tha' tu. jain:
mine (e.g., for coal)	သတ္တုတွင်း	tha' tu. dwin:
shaft (mine ~)	မိုင်းတွင်း	main: dwin:
miner	သတ္တုတွင်း အလုပ်သမား	tha' tu. dwin: alou' thama:

| gas (natural ~) | ဓာတ်ငွေ့ | da' ngwei. |
| gas pipeline | ဓါတ်ငွေ့ပိုက်လိုင်း | da' ngwei. bou' lain: |

oil (petroleum)	ရေနံ	jei nan
oil pipeline	ရေနံပိုက်လိုင်း	jei nan bou' lain:
oil well	ရေနံတွင်း	jei nan dwin:
derrick (tower)	ရေနံစင်	jei nan zin
tanker	လောင်စာတင်သင်္ဘော	laun za din dhin bo:

sand	သဲ	the:
limestone	ထုံးကျောက်	htoun: gjau'
gravel	ကျောက်စရစ်	kjau' sa. ji'

peat	မြေ‌‌ဆွေး‌ခဲ	mjei zwei: ge:
clay	မြေ‌စေး	mjei zei:
coal	‌ကျောက်မီးသွေး	kjau' mi dhwei:
iron (ore)	သံ	than
gold	‌ရွှေ	shwei
silver	‌ငွေ	ngwei
nickel	နီကယ်	ni ke
copper	‌ကြေးနီ	kjei: ni
zinc	သွပ်	thu'
manganese	မဂ္ဂနီးစ်	ma' ga. ni:s
mercury	ပြဒါး	bada:
lead	ခဲ	khe:
mineral	သတ္တုရား	tha' tu. za:
crystal	သလင်းကျောက်	thalin: gjau'
marble	စကျင်ကျောက်	zagjin kjau'
uranium	ယူရေနီယမ်	ju rei ni jan

The Earth. Part 2

206. Weather

weather	ရာသီဥတု	ja dhi nja. tu.
weather forecast	မိုးလေဝသသန့်မှန်းချက်	mou: lei wa. dha. gan. hman: gje'
temperature	အပူရှိန်	apu gjein
thermometer	သာမိုမီတာ	tha mou mi ta
barometer	လေဖိအားတိုင်းကိရိယာ	lei bi. a: dain: gi. ji. ja
humid (adj)	စိုထိုင်းသော	sou htain: de
humidity	စိုထိုင်းမှု	sou htain: hmu.
heat (extreme ~)	အပူရှိန်	apu shein
hot (torrid)	ပူလောင်သော	pu laun de.
it's hot	ပူလောင်ခြင်း	pu laun gjin:
it's warm	နွေးခြင်း	nwei: chin:
warm (moderately hot)	နွေးသော	nwei: de.
it's cold	အေးခြင်း	ei: gjin:
cold (adj)	အေးသော	ei: de.
sun	နေ	nei
to shine (vi)	သာသည်	tha de
sunny (day)	နေသာသော	nei dha de.
to come up (vi)	နေထွက်သည်	nei dwe' te
to set (vi)	နေဝင်သည်	nei win de
cloud	တိမ်	tein
cloudy (adj)	တိမ်ထူသော	tein du de
rain cloud	မိုးတိမ်	mou: dain
somber (gloomy)	ညို့မှိုင်းသော	njou. hmain: de.
rain	မိုး	mou:
it's raining	မိုးရွာသည်	mou: jwa de.
rainy (~ day, weather)	မိုးရွာသော	mou: jwa de.
to drizzle (vi)	မိုးဖွဲဖွဲရွာသည်	mou: bwe: bwe: jwa de
pouring rain	သည်းထန်စွာရွာသောမိုး	thi: dan zwa jwa dho: mou:
downpour	မိုးပုထိန်	mou: bu. zain
heavy (e.g., ~ rain)	မိုးသည်းသော	mou: de: de.
puddle	ရေအိုင်	jei ain
to get wet (in rain)	မိုးမိသည်	mou: mi de
fog (mist)	မြူ	mju

foggy	မြူထူထပ်သော	mju htu hta' te.
snow	နှင်း	hnin:
it's snowing	နှင်းကျသည်	hnin: gja. de

207. Severe weather. Natural disasters

thunderstorm	မိုးသက်မုန်တိုင်း	mou: dhe' moun dain:
lightning (~ strike)	လျှပ်စီး	hlja' si:
to flash (vi)	လျှပ်ပြက်သည်	hlja' pje' te

thunder	မိုးကြိုး	mou: kjou:
to thunder (vi)	မိုးကြိုးပစ်သည်	mou: gjou: pi' te
it's thundering	မိုးကြိုးပစ်သည်	mou: gjou: pi' te

| hail | မိုးသီး | mou: dhi: |
| it's hailing | မိုးသီးကြွေသည် | mou: dhi: gjwei de |

| to flood (vt) | ရေကြီးသည် | jei gji: de |
| flood, inundation | ရေကြီးမှု | jei gji: hmu. |

earthquake	ငလျင်	nga ljin
tremor, shoke	တုန်ခါခြင်း	toun ga gjin:
epicenter	ငလျင်ဗဟိုချက်	nga ljin ba hou che'

| eruption | မီးတောင်ပေါက်ကွဲခြင်း | mi: daun pau' kwe: gjin: |
| lava | ချော်ရည် | cho ji |

twister	လေဆင်နှာမောင်	lei zin hna maun
tornado	လေဆင်နှာမောင်	lei zin hna maun:
typhoon	တိုင်ဖွန်းမုန်တိုင်း	tain hpun moun dain:

hurricane	ဟာရီကိန်းမုန်တိုင်း	ha ji gain: moun dain:
storm	မုန်တိုင်း	moun dain:
tsunami	ဆူနာမိ	hsu na mi

cyclone	ဆိုင်ကလုန်းမုန်တိုင်း	hsain ga. loun: moun dain:
bad weather	ဆိုးရွားသော ရာသီဥတု	hsou: jwa: de. ja dhi u. tu.
fire (accident)	မီးလောင်ခြင်း	mi: laun gjin:

| disaster | ဘေးအန္တရာယ် | bei: an daje |
| meteorite | ဥက္ကာခဲ | ou' ka ge: |

| avalanche | ရေခဲနှင့်ကျောက်တုံးများထိုးကျခြင်း | jei ge: hnin kjau' toun mja: htou: gja. gjin: |
| snowslide | လေတိုက်ပြီးဖြစ်နေသောနှင်းပုံ | lei dou' hpji: bi' nei dho: hnin: boun |

| blizzard | နှင်းမုန်တိုင်း | hnin: moun dain: |
| snowstorm | နှင်းမုန်တိုင်း | hnin: moun dain: |

208. Noises. Sounds

silence (quiet)	တိတ်ဆိတ်မှု	tei' hsei' hmu.
sound	အသံ	athan
noise	ဆူညံသံ	hsu. njan dhan.
to make noise	ဆူညံသည်	hsu. njan de
noisy (adj)	ဆူညံသော	hsu. njan de.

loudly (to speak, etc.)	ကျယ်လောင်စွာ	kje laun zwa
loud (voice, etc.)	ကျယ်လောင်သော	kje laun de
constant (e.g., ~ noise)	ဆက်တိုင်ဖြစ်သော	hse' dain bja' de.

cry, shout (n)	အော်သံ	o dhan
to cry, to shout (vi)	အော်သည်	o de
whisper	တီးတိုးပြောသံ	ti: dou: bjo dhan
to whisper (vi, vt)	တီးတိုးပြောသည်	ti: dou: bjo de

barking (dog's ~)	ဟောင်သံ	han dhan
to bark (vi)	ဟောင်သည်	han de

groan (of pain, etc.)	တကျိကျိမြည်သံ	ta kjwi. kjwi. mji dhan
to groan (vi)	တကျိကျိမြည်သည်	ta kjwi. kjwi. mji de
cough	ချောင်းဆိုးခြင်း	gaun: zou: gjin:
to cough (vi)	ချောင်းဆိုးသည်	gaun: zou: de

whistle	လေချွန်သံ	lei gjun dhan
to whistle (vi)	လေချွန်သည်	lei gjun de
knock (at the door)	တံခါးခေါက်သံ	daga: khau' than
to knock (on the door)	တံခါးခေါက်သည်	daga: khau' te

to crack (vi)	တိုက်သည်	tai' te
crack (cracking sound)	ဒိုင်းခနဲမြည်သံ	dein: ga. ne: mji dhan.

siren	အချက်ပေးညံသံ	ache' pei ou' o: dhan
whistle (factory ~, etc.)	ညှုလ္လဲသံ	udhja zwe: dhan
to whistle (ab. train)	ညှုလ္လဲသည်	udhja zwe: de
honk (car horn sound)	ဟွန်းသံ	hwun: dhan
to honk (vi)	ဟွန်းတီးသည်	hwun: di: de

209. Winter

winter (n)	ဆောင်းရာသီ	hsaun: ja dhi
winter (as adj)	ဆောင်းရာသီနှင့်ဆိုင်သော	hsaun: ja dhi hnin. zain de.
in winter	ဆောင်းရာသီမှာ	hsaun: ja dhi hma

snow	နှင်း	hnin:
it's snowing	နှင်းကျသည်	hnin: gja. de
snowfall	ဆီးနှင်းကျခြင်း	hsi: hnin: gja gjin:
snowdrift	နှင်းခဲပုံ	hnin: ge: boun

snowflake	ဆီးနှင်းပွင့်	hsi: hnin: bwin.
snowball	နှင်းဆုပ်လုံး	hnin: zou' loun:
snowman	နှင်းခဲလူရုပ်	hnin: ge: lu jou'
icicle	ရေခဲပန်းဆွဲ	jei ge: ban: zwe:
December	ဒီဇင်ဘာလ	di zin ba la.
January	ဇန်နဝါရီလ	zan na. wa ji la.
February	ဖေဖော်ဝါရီလ	hpei bo wa ji la
frost (severe ~, freezing cold)	နှင်းခဲခြင်း	hnin: ge: gjin:
frosty (weather, air)	နှင်းခဲသော	hnin: ge: de.
below zero (adv)	သုညအောက်	thoun nja. au'
first frost	နှင်းခဲ့	hnin: ga:
hoarfrost	နှင်းပေါက်ခဲဖြူ	hnin: bau' khe: bju
cold (cold weather)	အေးခြင်း	ei: gjin:
it's cold	အေးသည်	ei: de
fur coat	သားမွေးအနွေးထည်	tha: mwei: anwei: de
mittens	နှစ်ကန့်လက်အိတ်	hni' kan. le' ei'
to get sick	အဖျားဝင်သည်	ahpja: win de
cold (illness)	အအေးမိခြင်း	aei: mi. gjin:
to catch a cold	အအေးမိသည်	aei: mi. de
ice	ရေခဲ	jei ge:
black ice	ရေခဲပြင်ပါး	jei ge: bjin ba:
to freeze over (ab. river, etc.)	ရေခဲသည်	jei ge: de
ice floe	ရေခဲမျော	jei ge: mjo:
skis	နှင်းလျှောစီးစက်တိတ်	hnin: sho: zi: zakei'
skier	နှင်းလျှောစီးစက်တသမား	hnin: sho: zi: zakei' dhama:
to ski (vi)	နှင်းလျှောစီးသည်	hnin: sho: zi: de
to skate (vi)	ရေခဲပြင်စက်တိတ်စီးသည်	jei ge: bjin za. gei' si: de

Fauna

210. Mammals. Predators

predator	သားရဲ	tha: je:
tiger	ကျား	kja:
lion	ခြင်္သေ့	chin dhei.
wolf	ဝံပုလွေ	wun bu. lwei
fox	မြေခွေး	mjei gwei:
jaguar	ဂျက္ဂွာကျားသစ်မျိုး	gja gwa gja: dhi' mjou:
leopard	ကျားသစ်	kja: dhi'
cheetah	သစ်ကျွတ်	thi' kjou'
black panther	ကျားသစ်နက်	kja: dhi' ne'
puma	ပျူမားတောင်ခြင်္သေ့	pju. ma: daun gjin dhei.
snow leopard	ရေခဲတောင်ကျားသစ်	jei ge: daun gja: dhi'
lynx	လင့်ကြောင်မြီးတို	lin. gjaun mji: dou
coyote	ဝံပုလွေငယ်တစ်မျိုး	wun bu. lwei nge di' mjou:
jackal	ခွေးအ	khwei: a.
hyena	ဟိုင်းအီးနား	hain i: na:

211. Wild animals

animal	တိရစ္ဆာန်	tharei' hsan
beast (animal)	ခြေလေးချောင်းသတ္တဝါ	chei lei: gjaun: dhadawa
squirrel	ရှဉ့်	shin.
hedgehog	ဖြူကောင်	hpju gaun
hare	တောယုန်ကြီး	to: joun gji:
rabbit	ယုန်	joun
badger	ခွေးတူဝက်တူကောင်	khwei: du we' tu gaun
raccoon	ရက်ကွန်းဝံ	je' kwan: wan
hamster	မြီးတိုပါးတွဲကြွက်	mji: dou ba: dwe: gjwe'
marmot	မားမွတ်ကောင်	ma: mou. t gaun
mole	ပွေး	pwei:
mouse	ကြွက်	kjwe'
rat	မြေကြွက်	mjei gjwe'
bat	လင်းနို့	lin: nou.
ermine	အားမင်ကောင်	a: min gaun
sable	ဆေသာယ်	hsei be

marten	အသားစားအကောင်ငယ်	atha: za: akaun nge
weasel	သားစားဖျံ	tha: za: bjan
mink	မင့်ခ်မွေပါ	min kh mjwei ba
beaver	ဖျံကြီးတစ်မျိုး	hpjan gji: da' mjou:
otter	ဖျံ	hpjan
horse	မြင်း	mjin:
moose	ဦးချိုပြားသော သမင်ကြီး	u: gjou bja: dho: thamin gji:
deer	သမင်	thamin
camel	ကုလားအုတ်	kala: ou'
bison	အမေရိကန်ပြောင်	amei ji kan pjaun
wisent	အောရက်စ်	o: re' s
buffalo	ကျွဲ	kjwe:
zebra	မြင်းကျား	mjin: gja:
antelope	အပြေးမြန်သော တောဆိတ်	apjei: mjan de. hto: zei'
roe deer	ဒရယ်ငယ်တစ်မျိုး	da. je nge da' mjou:
fallow deer	ဒရယ်	da. je
chamois	တောင်ဆိတ်	taun zei'
wild boar	တောဝက်ထီး	to: we' hti:
whale	ဝေလငါး	wei la. nga:
seal	ပင်လယ်ဖျံ	pin le bjan
walrus	ဝေါရုစ်ဖျံ	wo: ra's hpjan
fur seal	အမွေးပါသောပင်လယ်ဖျံ	amwei: pa dho: bin le hpjan
dolphin	လင်းပိုင်	lin: bain
bear	ဝက်ဝံ	we' wun
polar bear	ဝိုလာဝက်ဝံ	pou la we' wan
panda	ပန်ဒါဝက်ဝံ	pan da we' wan
monkey	မျောက်	mjau'
chimpanzee	ချင်ပင်ဇီမျောက်ဝံ	chin pin zi mjau' wan
orangutan	အော်ရန်အူတန်လုဝံ	o ran u tan lu wun
gorilla	ဂေါ်ရီလာမျောက်ဝံ	go ji la mjau' wun
macaque	မာကာတွေမျောက်	ma ga gwei mjau'
gibbon	မျောက်လွှဲကျော်	mjau' hlwe: gjo
elephant	ဆင်	hsin
rhinoceros	ကြံ့	kjan.
giraffe	သစ်ကုလားအုတ်	thi' ku. la ou'
hippopotamus	ရေမြင်း	jei mjin:
kangaroo	သားပိုက်ကောင်	tha: bai' kaun
koala (bear)	ကိုအာလာဝက်ဝံ	kou a la we' wun
mongoose	မွေပါ	mwei ba
chinchilla	ချင်းချီလာ	chin: chi la
skunk	စကန့်ဖျံ	sakan. kh hpjan
porcupine	ဖြူ	hpju

212. Domestic animals

cat	ကြောင်	kjaun
tomcat	ကြောင်ထီး	kjaun di:
dog	ခွေး	khwei:
horse	မြင်း	mjin:
stallion (male horse)	မြင်းထီး	mjin: di:
mare	မြင်းမ	mjin: ma.
cow	နွား	nwa:
bull	နွားထီး	nwa: di:
ox	နွားထီး	nwa: di:
sheep (ewe)	သိုး	thou:
ram	သိုးထီး	thou: hti:
goat	ဆိတ်	hsei'
billy goat, he-goat	ဆိတ်ထီး	hsei' hti:
donkey	မြည်း	mji:
mule	လား	la:
pig, hog	ဝက်	we'
piglet	ဝက်ကလေး	we' ka lei:
rabbit	ယုန်	joun
hen (chicken)	ကြက်	kje'
rooster	ကြက်ဖ	kje' pha.
duck	ဘဲ	be:
drake	ဘဲထီး	be: di:
goose	ဘဲငန်း	be: ngan:
tom turkey, gobbler	ကြက်ဆင်	kje' hsin
turkey (hen)	ကြက်ဆင်	kje' hsin
domestic animals	အိမ်မွေးတိရစ္ဆာန်များ	ein mwei: ti. ji. swan mja:
tame (e.g., ~ hamster)	ယဉ်ပါးသော	jin ba: de.
to tame (vt)	ယဉ်ပါးစေသည်	jin ba: zei de
to breed (vt)	သားပေါက်သည်	tha: bau' te
farm	စိုက်ပျိုးမွေးမြူ ရေးခြံ	sai' pjou: mwei: mju jei: gjan
poultry	ကြက်ငှက်တိရိစ္ဆာန်	kje' ti ji za hsan
cattle	ကျွဲနွားတိရစ္ဆာန်	kjwe: nwa: tarei. zan
herd (cattle)	အုပ်	ou'
stable	မြင်းဇောင်း	mjin: zaun:
pigpen	ဝက်ခြံ	we' khan
cowshed	နွားတင်းကုပ်	nwa: din: gou'
rabbit hutch	ယုန်အိမ်	joun ein
hen house	ကြက်လှောင်အိမ်	kje' hlaun ein

213. Dogs. Dog breeds

dog	ခွေး	khwei:
sheepdog	သိုးကျောင်းခွေး	thou: kjaun: gwei:
German shepherd	ဂျာမနီလိုး ကျောင်းခွေး	gja ma, ni hnin, gjaun: gwei:
poodle	ပူဒယ်လ်ခွေး	pu de l gwei:
dachshund	ဒတ်ရှန်းခွေး	da' shan: gwei:
bulldog	ခွေးဘီလူး	khwei: bi lu:
boxer	ဘောက်ဆာခွေး	bo' hsa gwei:
mastiff	အိန်စောင့်ခွေး ကြီးတစ်မျိုး	ein zaun. gwei: gji: di' mjou:
Rottweiler	ရော့ဝိလာခွေး	ro. wi la gwei:
Doberman	ဒိုဘာမင်းခွေး	dou ba min: gwei:
basset	ခြေတိုတိုအမဲ လိုက်ခွေး	chei dan dou ame: lai' gwei:
bobtail	ခွေးပုတစ်မျိုး	khwei: bu di' mjou:
Dalmatian	ဒယ်မေးရှင်းခွေး	de mei: shin gwe:
cocker spaniel	ကိုကာစပန်နီရယ်ခွေး	kou ka sa. pan ni je khwei:
Newfoundland	နယူးဖောင်လန်ခွေး	na. ju: hpaun lan gwe:
Saint Bernard	ကျက်ခြေနီခွေး	kje' chei ni khwei:
husky	စွတ်ဖားဆွဲခွေး	su' hpa: zwe: gwei:
Chow Chow	တရုတ်ပြည်ပေါက် အမွေး ထူခွေး	tajou' pji bau' amwei: htu gwei:
spitz	စပစ်ဇ်ခွေး	sapi's khwei:
pug	ပတ်ခွေး	pa' gwei:

214. Sounds made by animals

barking (n)	ဟောင်သံ	han dhan
to bark (vi)	ဟောင်သည်	han de
to meow (vi)	ကြောင်အော်သည်	kjaun o de
to purr (vi)	ညိမ့်ညိမ့်လေးမြည် သံပေးသည်	njein. njein. le: mje dhan bei: de
to moo (vi)	နွားအော်သည်	nwa: o de
to bellow (bull)	တိရစ္ဆာန်အော်သည်	tharei' hsan o de
to growl (vi)	မာန်ဖီသည်	man bi de
howl (n)	အူသံ	u dhan
to howl (vi)	အူသည်	u de
to whine (vi)	ရှည်လျားစူးရှစွာအော်သည်	shei lja: zu: sha. zwa o de
to bleat (sheep)	သိုးအော်သည်	thou: o de
to oink, to grunt (pig)	တအီအီမြည်သည်	ta. i i mji de

to squeal (vi)	တစစီအော်မြည်သည်	ta. zi. zi. jo mje de
to croak (vi)	ဖားအော်သည်	hpa: o de
to buzz (insect)	တစစီအော်သည်	ta. wi wi o de
to chirp (crickets, grasshopper)	ကျည်ကျည်ကျာကျာအော်သည်	kji kji kja kja o de

215. Young animals

cub	သားပေါက်	tha: bau'
kitten	ကြောင်ပေါက်ကလေး	kjaun bau' ka. lei:
baby mouse	ကြွက်ပေါက်ကလေး	kjwe' bau' ka. lei:
puppy	ခွေးကလေး	khwei: galei:

leveret	ယုန်ပေါက်ကလေး	joun bau' kalei:
baby rabbit	ယုန်ကလေး	joun galei:
wolf cub	ဝံပုလွေပေါက်ကလေး	wun lwei bau' ka. lei:
fox cub	မြေခွေးပေါက်ကလေး	mjei gwei: bau' kalei:
bear cub	ဝက်ဝံပေါက်ကလေး	we' wun bau' ka. lei:

lion cub	ခြင်္သေ့ပေါက်ကလေး	chin dhei. bau' kalei:
tiger cub	ကျားပေါက်ကလေး	kja: bau' ka. lei:
elephant calf	ဆင်ပေါက်ကလေး	hsin bau' ka. lei:

piglet	ဝက်ကလေး	we' ka lei:
calf (young cow, bull)	နွားပေါက်ကလေး	nwa: bau' ka. lei:
kid (young goat)	ဆိတ်ပေါက်ကလေး	hsei' pau' ka. lei:
lamb	သိုးပေါက်ကလေး	thou: bau' kalei:
fawn (young deer)	သမင်ပေါက်ကလေး	thamin bau' kalei:
young camel	ကုလားအုတ်ပေါက်ကလေး	mjin: bau' kalei:

| snakelet (baby snake) | မြွေပေါက်ကလေး | mwei bau' kalei: |
| froglet (baby frog) | ဖားပေါက်ကလေး | hpa: bau' ka. lei: |

baby bird	ငှက်ပေါက်ကလေး	hnge' pau' ka. lei:
chick (of chicken)	ကြက်ပေါက်ကလေး	kje' pau' ka. lei:
duckling	ဘဲပေါက်ကလေး	pe: bau' ga. lei:

216. Birds

bird	ငှက်	hnge'
pigeon	ခို	khou
sparrow	စာကလေး	sa ga. lei:
tit (great tit)	စာဝတီးငှက်	sa wadi: hnge'
magpie	ငှက်ကျား	hnge' kja:

raven	ကျီးနက်	kji: ne'
crow	ကျီးကန်း	kji: kan:
jackdaw	ဥရောပကျီးတစ်မျိုး	u. jo: pa gji: di' mjou:

rook	ကျီးအ	kji: a.
duck	ဘဲ	be:
goose	ဘဲငန်း	be: ngan:
pheasant	ရစ်ငှက်	ji' hnge'
eagle	လင်းယုန်	lin: joun
hawk	သိမ်းငှက်	thain: hnge'
falcon	အမဲလိုက်သိမ်းငှက် တစ်မျိုး	ame: lai' thein: hnge' ti' mjou:
vulture	လင်းတ	lin: da.
condor (Andean ~)	တောင်အမေရိကာလင်းတ	taun amei ri. ka. lin: da.
swan	ငန်း	ngan:
crane	ငှက်ကုလား	hnge' ku. la:
stork	ချည်ခင်စွပ်ငှက်	che gin zu' hnge'
parrot	ကြက်တူရွေး	kje' tu jwei:
hummingbird	ငှက်ပိတုန်း	hnge' pi. doun:
peacock	ဥဒေါင်း	u. daun:
ostrich	ငှက်ကုလားအုတ်	hnge' ku. la: ou'
heron	ဗျာစ်ငှက်	nga hi' hnge'
flamingo	ကြိုးကြာနီ	kjou: kja: ni
pelican	ငှက်ကြီးဝန်ပို	hnge' kji: wun bou
nightingale	တေးဆိုငှက်	tei: hsou hnge'
swallow	ပျံလွှား	pjan hlwa:
thrush	မြေလူးငှက်	mjei lu: hnge'
song thrush	တေးဆိုမြေလူးငှက်	tei: hsou mjei lu: hnge'
blackbird	ငှက်မည်း	hnge' mji:
swift	ပျံလွှားတစ်မျိုး	pjan hlwa: di' mjou:
lark	ဘီလုံးငှက်	bi loun: hnge'
quail	ငုံး	ngoun:
woodpecker	သစ်တောက်ငှက်	thi' tau' hnge'
cuckoo	ဥဩငှက်	udhja hnge'
owl	ဇီးကွက်	zi: gwe
eagle owl	သိမ်းငှက်အနွယ် ဝင်ဇီးကွက်	thain: hnge' anwe win zi: gwe'
wood grouse	ရစ်	ji'
black grouse	ရစ်နက်	ji' ne'
partridge	ခါ	kha
starling	ကျွဲဆက်ရက်	kjwe: hse' je'
canary	စာဝါငှက်	sa wa hnge'
hazel grouse	ရစ်ညို	ji' njou
chaffinch	စာကျွဲခေါင်း	sa gjwe: gaun:
bullfinch	စာကျွဲခေါင်းငှက်	sa gjwe: gaun: hngwe'
seagull	စင်ရော်	sin jo
albatross	ပင်လယ်စင်ရော်ကြီး	pin le zin jo gji:
penguin	ပင်ဝွင်း	pin gwin:

217. Birds. Singing and sounds

to sing (vi)	ဂုက်တေးဆိုသည်	hnge' tei: zou de
to call (animal, bird)	အော်သည်	o de
to crow (rooster)	တွန်သည်	tun de
cock-a-doodle-doo	ကြက်တွန်သံ	kje' twan dhan
to cluck (hen)	ကြက်မကာတော်သည်	kje' ma. ka. do de
to caw (crow call)	ကျီးအောသည်	kji: a de
to quack (duck call)	တဂက်ဂက်အောင်သည်	ta. ge' ge' aun de
to cheep (vi)	ကျည်ကျည်ကျာကျာမြည်သည်	kji kji kja kja mji de
to chirp, to twitter	တွတ်ထိုးသည်	tu' htou: de

218. Fish. Marine animals

bream	ငါးကြင်းတစ်မျိုး	nga: gjin: di' mjou
carp	ငါးကြင်း	nga gjin:
perch	ငါးပြဲမတစ်မျိုး	nga: bjei ma, di' mjou:
catfish	ငါးခူ	nga: gu
pike	ပိုက်ငါး	pai' nga
salmon	ဆော်လမွန်ငါး	hso: la. mun nga:
sturgeon	စတာဂျင်ငါးကြီးမျိုး	sata gjin nga: gji: mjou:
herring	ငါးသလောက်	nga: dha. lau'
Atlantic salmon	ဆော်လမွန်ငါး	hso: la. mun nga:
mackerel	မက်ကာရယ်ငါး	me' ka. je nga:
flatfish	ဥရောပ ငါးခွေး လျှာတစ်မျိုး	u. jo: pa nga: gwe: sha di' mjou:
zander, pike perch	ငါးပြဲမအနွှယ် ဝင်ငါးတစ်မျိုး	nga: bjei ma. anwe win nga: di' mjou:
cod	ငါးကြီးဆီထုတ်သောငါး	nga: gji: zi dou' de. nga:
tuna	တူနာငါး	tu na nga:
trout	ထရောက်ငါး	hta. jau' nga:
eel	ငါးရှည့်	nga: shin.
electric ray	ငါးလက်ထု	nga: le' htoun
moray eel	ငါးရှည့်ကြီးတစ်မျိုး	nga: shin. gji: da' mjou:
piranha	အသွားစားငါးငယ် တစ်မျိုး	atha: za: nga: nge ti' mjou:
shark	ငါးမန်း	nga: man:
dolphin	လင်းပိုင်	lin: bain
whale	ဝေလငါး	wei la. nga:
crab	ကကာန်း	kanan:
jellyfish	ငါးဖန်ခွက်	nga: hpan gwe'
octopus	ရေဘဝဲ	jei ba. we:

starfish	ကြယ်ငါး	kje nga:
sea urchin	သိပဘချို	than ba. gjou'
seahorse	ရေနဂါး	jei naga:

oyster	ကမာကောင်	kama kaun
shrimp	ပုစွန်	bazun
lobster	ကျောက်ပုစွန်	kjau' pu. zun
spiny lobster	ကျောက်ပုစွန်	kjau' pu. zun

219. Amphibians. Reptiles

| snake | မြွေ | mwei |
| venomous (snake) | အဆိပ်ရှိသော | ahsei' shi. de. |

viper	မြွေပွေး	mwei bwei:
cobra	မြွေပေါက်	mwei hau'
python	စပါးအုံးမြွေ	saba: oun: mwei
boa	စပါးကြီးမြွေ	saba: gji: mwei

grass snake	မြက်လျှောမြွေ	mje' sho: mwei
rattle snake	ခလောက်ဆွဲမြွေ	kha. lau' hswe: mwei
anaconda	အနာကွန်ဒါမြွေ	ana kun da mwei

lizard	တွားသွားသတ္တဝါ	twa: dhwa: tha' tawa
iguana	ဖွတ်	hpu'
monitor lizard	ပုတ်သင်	pou' thin
salamander	ရေပုတ်သင်	jei bou' thin
chameleon	ပုတ်သင်ညို	pou' thin njou
scorpion	ကင်းမြီးကောက်	kin: mji: kau'

turtle	လိပ်	lei'
frog	ဖား	hpa:
toad	ဖားပြုပ်	hpa: bju'
crocodile	မိကျောင်း	mi. kjaun:

220. Insects

insect, bug	ပိုးမွာ:	pou: hmwa:
butterfly	လိပ်ပြာ	lei' pja
ant	ပုရွက်ဆိတ်	pu. jwe' hsei'
fly	ယင်ကောင်	jin gaun
mosquito	ခြင်	chin
beetle	ပိုးတောင်မာ	pou: daun ma

wasp	နကျယ်ကောင်	na. gje gaun
bee	ပျား	pja:
bumblebee	ဝိတုန်း	pi. doun:
gadfly (botfly)	မှက်	hme'

spider	ပင့်ကူ	pjin. gu
spiderweb	ပင့်ကူအိမ်	pjin gu ein
dragonfly	ပုစဉ်း	bazin
grasshopper	နံကောင်	hnan gaun
moth (night butterfly)	ပိုးဖလံ	pou: ba. lan
cockroach	ပိုးဟပ်	pou: ha'
tick	မွှား	hmwa:
flea	သန်း	than:
midge	မျက်အသေးစား	hme' athei: za:
locust	ကျိုင်းကောင်	kjain: kaun
snail	ခရု	khaju.
cricket	ပုရစ်	paji'
lightning bug	ပိုးစုန်းကြူး	pou: zoun: gju:
ladybug	လေဒီဘာ့ပိုးတောင်မာ	lei di ba' pou: daun ma
cockchafer	အုန်းပိုး	oun: bou:
leech	မျှော	hmjo.
caterpillar	ပေါက်ဖက်	pau' hpe'
earthworm	တီကောင်	ti gaun
larva	ပိုးတုံးလုံး	pou: doun: loun:

221. Animals. Body parts

beak	ငှက်နုတ်သီး	hnge' hnou' thi:
wings	တောင်ပံ	taun pan
foot (of bird)	ခြေထောက်	chei htau'
feathers (plumage)	အမွေး	ahmwei
feather	ငှက်မွေး	hnge' hmwei:
crest	အမောက်	amou'
gills	ပါးဟက်	pa: he'
spawn	ငါးဥ	nga: u.
larva	ပိုးလောက်လန်း	pou: lau' lan:
fin	ဆူးတောင်	hsu: daun
scales (of fish, reptile)	ကြေးခွံ	kjei: gwan
fang (canine)	အစွယ်	aswe
paw (e.g., cat's ~)	ခြေသည်းရှည်ပါ သောဖဝါး	chei dhi: shi ba dho: ba. wa:
muzzle (snout)	နှုတ်သီး	hnou' thi:
maw (mouth)	ပါးစပ်	pa: zi'
tail	အမြီး	ami:
whiskers	နှုတ်ခမ်းမွေး	hnou' khan: hmwei:
hoof	ခွာ	khwa
horn	ဦးချို	u: gjou
carapace	လိပ်ကျောခွံ	lei' kjo: ghwan

| shell (of mollusk) | အခွံ | akhun |
| eggshell | ဥခွံ | u. gun |

| animal's hair (pelage) | အမွေး | ahmwei |
| pelt (hide) | သားရေ | tha: ei |

222. Actions of animals

to fly (vi)	ပျံသည်	pjan de
to fly in circles	ဝဲသည်	we: de
to fly away	ပျံတွက်သွားသည်	pjan dwe' dwa: de
to flap (~ the wings)	အတောင်ခတ်သည်	ataun khai' te

to peck (vi)	နှုတ်သီးဖြင့်ဆိတ်သည်	hnou' thi: bjin. zei' te
to sit on eggs	ဝပ်သည်	wu' te
to hatch out (vi)	ဥမှသားပေါက်သည်	u. hma. dha: bau' te
to build a nest	အသိုက်ပြုလုပ်သည်	athai' pju. lou' dhe

to slither, to crawl	တွားသွားသည်	twa: dhwa: de
to sting, to bite (insect)	တုပ်သည်	tou' te
to bite (ab. animal)	ကိုက်သည်	kou' de

to sniff (vt)	အနံ့ခံနှာရှူ.သည်	anan. khan hna shun. de
to bark (vi)	ဟောင်သည်	han de
to hiss (snake)	ရှူးရှူးရဲရဲ	shu: shu: she: she:
	အသံပြုသည်	athan bju. de

| to scare (vt) | ခြောက်လှန့်သည် | chau' hlan. de |
| to attack (vt) | တိုက်ခိုက်သည် | tai' khai' te |

to gnaw (bone, etc.)	ကိုက်ဖြတ်သည်	kou' hpja' te
to scratch (with claws)	ကုတ်သည်	kou' te
to hide (vi)	ပုန်းသည်	poun: de

to play (kittens, etc.)	ကစားသည်	gaza: de
to hunt (vi, vt)	အမဲလိုက်သည်	ame: lai' de
to hibernate (vi)	ဆောင်းခိုသည်	hsaun: gou de
to go extinct	မျိုးသုဉ်းသည်	mjou: dhou: de

223. Animals. Habitats

| habitat | ကျက်စားရာဒေသ | kje' za: ja dei dha. |
| migration | ပြောင်းရွှေ့နေထိုင်ခြင်း | pjaun: shwei nei dain gjin: |

mountain	တောင်	taun
reef	ကျောက်တန်း	kjau' tan:
cliff	ကျောက်ဆောင်	kjau' hsain
forest	သစ်တော	thi' to:
jungle	တောရိုင်း	to: jain:

savanna	အပူပိုင်းမြင်ခင်းလွင်ပြင်	apu bain: gjin gin: lwin pjin
tundra	တန်ဒြာ-ကျောက်တီးမြေ	tun dra kje' bi: mjei
steppe	မြက်ခင်းလွင်ပြင်	mje' khin: lwin bjin
desert	သဲကန္တာရ	the: gan da ja.
oasis	အိုအေစစ်	ou ei zi'
sea	ပင်လယ်	pin le
lake	ရေကန်	jei gan
ocean	သမုဒ္ဒရာ	thamou' daja
swamp (marshland)	ရွှံ့ ညွန်	shwan njun
freshwater (adj)	ရေချို	jei gjou
pond	ရေကန်ငယ်	jei gan nge
river	မြစ်	mji'
den (bear's ~)	သားရဲလျှောင်အိမ်တွင်း	tha: je: hlaun ein twin:
nest	ငှက်သိုက်	hnge' thai'
tree hollow	အခေါင်းပေါက်	akhaun: bau'
burrow (animal hole)	မြေတွင်း	mjei dwin:
anthill	ခြတောင်ပို့	cha. daun bou.

224. Animal care

zoo	တိရိစ္ဆာန်ဥယျာဉ်	tharei' hsan u. jin
nature preserve	စားကျက်	sa: gja'
breeder (cattery, kennel, etc.)	တိရိစ္ဆာန်မျိုး ဖောက်သူ	tharei' hsan mjou: hpau' thu
open-air cage	လှောင်အိမ်	hlaun ein
cage	လှောင်အိမ်	hlaun ein
doghouse (kennel)	ခွေးအိမ်	khwei: ein
dovecot	ခိုအိမ်	khou ein
aquarium (fish tank)	အလှမွေးငါးကန်	ahla. mwei: nga: gan
dolphinarium	လင်းပိုင်မွေးကန်	lin: bain mwei kan
to breed (animals)	သားပေါက်သည်	tha: bau' te
brood, litter	သားပေါက်အုပ်စု	tha: bau' ou' zu.
to tame (vt)	ယဉ်ပါးစေသည်	jin ba: zei de
to train (animals)	လေ့ကျင့်ပေးသည်	lei. kjin. bei: de
feed (fodder, etc.)	အစာ	asa
to feed (vt)	အစာကျွေးသည်	asa gjwei: de.
pet store	အိမ်မွေးတိရိစ္ဆာန်ဆိုင်	ein mwei: ti. ji. swan zain
muzzle (for dog)	နှတ်သီးစွပ်	hnou' thi: zu'
collar (e.g., dog ~)	လည်ပတ်	le ba'
name (of animal)	အမည်	amji
pedigree (of dog)	ခွေးမျိုးရိုးမှတ်တမ်း	khwei: mjou: jou: hma' tan:

225. Animals. Miscellaneous

pack (wolves)	အုပ်	ou'
flock (birds)	အုပ်	ou'
shoal, school (fish)	အုပ်	ou'
herd (horses)	အုပ်	ou'
male (n)	အထီး	a hti:
female (n)	အမ	ama.
hungry (adj)	ဆာလောင်သော	hsa laun de.
wild (adj)	တောရိုင်း	to: jain:
dangerous (adj)	အန္တရာယ်ရှိသော	an dare shi. de.

226. Horses

horse	မြင်း	mjin:
breed (race)	အမျိုးအစားကောင်း သော်မြင်း	amjou: asa: gaun: dho: mjin:
foal	မြင်းပေါက်	mjin: bau'
mare	မြင်းမ	mjin: ma.
mustang	မာစတန်မြင်း	ma za. dan mjin:
pony	မြင်းပု	mjin: bu.
draft horse	ခိုင်းမြင်း	khain: mjin:
mane	လည်ဆံမွေး	le zan hmwei:
tail	အမြီး	ami:
hoof	ခွာ	khwa
horseshoe	မြင်းသံခွာ	mjin: dhan gwa
to shoe (vt)	မြင်းသံခွာရိုက်သည်	mjin: dhan gwa jai' te
blacksmith	ပန်းပဲသမား	pan: be: dhama:
saddle	မြင်းကုန်းနှီး	mjin: goun: ni:
stirrup	ခြေနင်းကွင်း	chei nin: gwin:
bridle	မြင်းဇက်ကြိုး	mjin: ze' kjou:
reins	မြင်းထိန်းကြိုး	mjin: dein: gjou:
whip (for riding)	ကြာပွတ်	kja bu'
rider	မြင်းစီးသူ	mjin: zi: dhu
to saddle up (vt)	မြင်းကုန်းနှီးချုပ်သည်	mjin: goun: ni: gjou' te
to mount a horse	မြင်းပေါ်တက်သည်	mjin: bo da' te
gallop	မြင်းဒန်းစိုင်းစီးခြင်း	mjin: oun: zain: zi: gjin:
to gallop (vi)	မြင်းဒန်းစိုင်းစီးသည်	mjin: oun: zain: zi: de
trot (n)	ရွရွပြေးသည်	jwa. jwa. bjei: de
at a trot (adv)	ရွရွပြေးသည့်ခြေလှမ်း	jwa. jwa. bjei: de. gjei hlan:

to go at a trot	ရှုစီးသသည်	jwa. jwa. zi: de
racehorse	ပြိုင်မြင်း	pjain mjin:
horse racing	မြင်းပြိုင်ခြင်း	mjin: bjain gjin:
stable	မြင်းဆောင်း	mjin: zaun:
to feed (vt)	အစာကျွေးသည်	asa gjwei: de.
hay	မြက်ခြောက်	mje' khau'
to water (animals)	ရေတိုက်သည်	jei dai' te
to wash (horse)	ရေချိုးပေးသည်	jei gjou bei: de
horse-drawn cart	မြင်းသည်လှည်း	mjin: de hli:
to graze (vi)	စားကျက်တွင်းလွှတ်ထားသည်	sa: gja' twin hlu' hta' de
to neigh (vi)	မြင်းဟီသည်	mjin: hi de
to kick (to buck)	မြင်းကန်သည်	mjin: gan de

Flora

227. Trees

tree	သစ်ပင်	thi' pin
deciduous (adj)	ရွက်ပြတ်	jwe' pja'
coniferous (adj)	ထင်းရှူးပင်နှင့်ဆိုင်သော	htin: shu: bin hnin. zain de.
evergreen (adj)	အဲဗားဂရင်းပင်	e ba: ga rin: bin
apple tree	ပန်းသီးပင်	pan: dhi: bin
pear tree	သစ်တော်ပင်	thi' to bin
sweet cherry tree	ချယ်ရီသီးအချိုပင်	che ji dhi: akjou bin
sour cherry tree	ချယ်ရီသီးအချဉ်ပင်	che ji dhi: akjin bin
plum tree	ဆီးပင်	hsi: bin
birch	ဘုဇဝတ်ပင်	bu. za. ba' pin
oak	ဝက်သစ်ချပင်	we' thi' cha. bin
linden tree	လင်ဒန်ပင်	lin dan pin
aspen	ပေါ်ပလာပင်တစ်မျိုး	po. pa. la bin di' mjou:
maple	မေပယ်ပင်	mei pe bin
spruce	ထင်းရှူးပင်တစ်မျိုး	htin: shu: bin ti' mjou:
pine	ထင်းရှူးပင်	htin: shu: bin
larch	ကတောပုံထင်းရှူးပင်	ka dau. boun din: shu: pin
fir tree	ထင်းရှူးပင်တစ်မျိုး	htin: shu: bin ti' mjou:
cedar	သစ်ကတိုးပင်	thi' gadou: bin
poplar	ပေါ်ပလာပင်	po. pa. la bin
rowan	ရာအန်ပင်	ra an bin
willow	မိုးမခပင်	mou: ma. ga. bin
alder	အိုလ်ဒါပင်	oun da bin
beech	ယင်းသစ်	jin: dhi'
elm	အမ်ပင်	an bin
ash (tree)	အက်ရှ်အပင်	e' sh apin
chestnut	သစ်အယ်ပင်	thi' e
magnolia	တတိုင်းမွှေးပင်	ta tain: hmwei: bin
palm tree	ထန်းပင်	htan: bin
cypress	စိုက်ပရက်စ်ပင်	sai' pa. je's pin
mangrove	လမုပင်	la. mu. bin
baobab	ကုန္ဘာရဗေပါက်ပင်တစ်မျိုး	kan ta ja. bau' bin di' chju:
eucalyptus	ယူကလစ်ပင်	ju kali' pin
sequoia	ဆီကွိုလာပင်	hsi gwou la pin

228. Shrubs

bush	ချုံပုတ်	choun bou'
shrub	ချုံ	choun
grapevine	စပျစ်	zabji'
vineyard	စပျစ်ခြံ	zabji' chan
raspberry bush	ရက်စဘယ်ရီ	re' sa be ji
blackcurrant bush	ဘလက်ကားရန့်	ba. le' ka: jan.
redcurrant bush	အနီရောင်ဘယ်ရီသီး	ani jaun be ji dhi:
gooseberry bush	ကုလားဆီးခြူပင်	kala: zi: hpju pin
acacia	အကေရှားပင်	akei sha: bin:
barberry	ဘားဘယ်ရီပင်	ba: be' ji bin
jasmine	စံပယ်ပင်	san be bin
juniper	ဂျူနီပါပင်	gju ni ba bin
rosebush	နှင်းဆီချုံ	hnin: zi gjun
dog rose	တောရိုင်းနှင်းဆီပင်	to: ein: hnin: zi bin

229. Mushrooms

mushroom	မို့	hmou
edible mushroom	စားသုံးနိုင်သောမို့	sa: dhoun: nein dho: hmou
poisonous mushroom	အဆိပ်ရှိသောမို့	ahsei shi. de. hmou
cap (of mushroom)	မို့ပွင့်	hmou bwin.
stipe (of mushroom)	မို့ခြေထောက်	hmou gjei dau'
cep (Boletus edulis)	မို့ခြင်ထောင်	hmou gjin daun
orange-cap boletus	ထိပ်အ၀ါရောင်ရှိ သောမို့	htei' awa jaun shi. de. hmou
birch bolete	ခြေထောက်ရှည်မို့ တစ်မျိုး	chei htau' shi hmou di' mjou:
chanterelle	ချန်တရယ်မို့	chan ta. je hmou
russula	ရာဆယ်လာမို့	ja. ze la hmou
morel	ထိပ်ပုလဲးသောမို့ တစ်မျိုး	htei' loun: dho: hmou di' mjou:
fly agaric	အနီရောင်ရှိသော မို့တစ်မျိုး	ani jaun shi. dho: hmou di' mjou:
death cap	ဒက်ကုပ်မို့	de' ke. p hmou

230. Fruits. Berries

fruit	အသီး	athi:
fruits	အသီးများ	athi: mja:

apple	ပန်းသီး	pan: dhi:
pear	သစ်တော်သီး	thi' to dhi:
plum	ဆီးသီး	hsi: dhi:
strawberry (garden ~)	စတော်ဘယ်ရီသီး	sato be ri dhi:
cherry	ချယ်ရီသီး	che ji dhi:
sour cherry	ချယ်ရီချဉ်သီး	che ji gjin dhi:
sweet cherry	ချယ်ရီချိုသီး	che ji gjou dhi:
grape	စပျစ်သီး	zabji' thi:
raspberry	ရက်စဘယ်ရီ	re' sa be ji
blackcurrant	ဘလက်ကားရန့်	ba. le' ka: jan.
redcurrant	အနီရောင်ဘယ်ရီသီး	ani jaun be ji dhi:
gooseberry	ကလားဆီးဖြူ	ka. la: his: hpju
cranberry	ကရမ်ဘယ်ရီ	ka. jan be ji
orange	လိမ္မော်သီး	limmo dhi:
mandarin	ပျားလိမ္မော်သီး	pja: lein mo dhi:
pineapple	နာနတ်သီး	na na' dhi:
banana	ငှက်ပျောသီး	hnge' pjo: dhi:
date	စွန်ပလွံသီး	sun palun dhi:
lemon	သံပုယိုသီး	than bu. jou dhi:
apricot	တရုတ်ဆီးသီး	jau' hsi: dhi:
peach	မက်မွန်သီး	me' mwan dhi:
kiwi	ကီဝီသီး	ki wi dhi
grapefruit	ဂရိတ်ဖရူးသီး	ga. ri' hpa. ju dhi:
berry	ဘယ်ရီသီး	be ji dhi:
berries	ဘယ်ရီသီးများ	be ji dhi: mja:
cowberry	အနီရောင်ဘယ်ရီသီးတစ်မျိုး	ani jaun be ji dhi: di: mjou:
wild strawberry	စတော်ဘယ်ရီရိုင်း	sato be ri jain:
bilberry	ဘီလ်ဘယ်ရီအသီး	bi' l be ji athi:

231. Flowers. Plants

flower	ပန်း	pan:
bouquet (of flowers)	ပန်းစည်း	pan: ze:
rose (flower)	နှင်းဆီပန်း	hnin: zi ban:
tulip	ကျူးလစ်ပန်း	kju: li' pan:
carnation	ဇော်မွှာပန်း	zo hmwa: bin:
gladiolus	သစ္စာပန်း	thi' sa ban:
cornflower	အပြာရောင်တောပန်းတစ်မျိုး	apja jaun dho ban: da' mjou:
harebell	ခေါင်းရန်းအပြာပန်း	gaun: jan: apja ban:
dandelion	တောပန်းအဝါတစ်မျိုး	to: ban: awa ti' mjou:
camomile	မေပြိုပန်း	mei. mjou. ban:
aloe	ရှားစောင်းလက်ပတ်ပင်	sha: zaun: le' pa' pin

229

cactus	ရှားစောင်းပင်	sha: zaun: bin
rubber plant, ficus	ရော်ဘာပင်	jo ba bin
lily	နှင်းပန်း	hnin: ban:
geranium	ကြွေပန်းတစ်မျိုး	kjwei ban: da' mjou:
hyacinth	ဗေဒါပန်း	bei da ba:
mimosa	ထိကရှုံးကြီးပင်	hti. ga. joun: gji bin
narcissus	နားစီဆော်စ်ပင်	na: zi ze's pin
nasturtium	တောင်ကြာကလေး	taun gja galei:
orchid	သစ်ခွပင်	thi' khwa. bin
peony	စနုပန်း	san dapan:
violet	ဝိုင်းအိုးလက်	bain: ou le'
pansy	ပေါင်ဒါပန်း	paun da ban:
forget-me-not	ခင်မမေ့ပန်း	khin ma. mei: pan:
daisy	ဒေစီပန်း	dei zi bin
poppy	ဘိန်းပင်	bin: bin
hemp	ဆေးခြောက်ပင်	hsei: chau' pin
mint	ပူစီန	pu zi nan
lily of the valley	နှင်းပန်းတစ်မျိုး	hnin: ban: di' mjou:
snowdrop	နှင်းခေါင်းလောင်းပန်း	hnin: gaun: laun: ban:
nettle	ဖက်ယားပင်	hpe' ja: bin
sorrel	မှော်ရှဉ်ပင်	hmjo gji bin
water lily	ကြာ	kja
fern	ဖန်းပင်	hpan: bin
lichen	သစ်ကပ်မှော်	thi' ka' hmo
conservatory (greenhouse)	ဖန်လုံအိမ်	hpan ain
lawn	မြက်ခင်း	mje' khin:
flowerbed	ပန်းစိုက်ခင်း	pan: zai' khan:
plant	အပင်	apin
grass	မြက်	mje'
blade of grass	ရွက်ရှွန်း	jwe' chun:
leaf	အရွက်	ajwa'
petal	ပွင့်ချပ်	pwin: gja'
stem	ပင်စည်	pin ze
tuber	ဥမြစ်	u. mi'
young plant (shoot)	အစို့အညှောက်	asou./a hnjau'
thorn	ဆူး	hsu:
to blossom (vi)	ပွင့်သည်	pwin: de
to fade, to wither	ညှိုးနွမ်းသည်	hnjou: nun: de
smell (odor)	အနံ့	anan.
to cut (flowers)	ရိတ်သည်	jei' te
to pick (a flower)	ခူးသည်	khu: de

232. Cereals, grains

grain	နံစားပင်တို့၏ အစေ့အဆံ	hnan za: bin dou. i. asei. ahsan
cereal crops	ကောက်ပဲသီးနံ	kau' pe: dhi: nan
ear (of barley, etc.)	အနံ	ahnan
wheat	ဂျုံ	gja. mei: ka:
rye	ဂျုံရိုင်း	gjoun jain:
oats	မျြင်းစားဂျုံ	mjin: za: gjoun
millet	ကောက်ပဲသီးနံပင်	kau' pe: dhi: nan bin
barley	မူယောစပါး	mu. jo za. ba:
corn	ပြောင်းဖူး	pjaun: bu:
rice	ဆန်စပါး	hsan zaba
buckwheat	ပန်းဂျုံ	pan: gjun
pea plant	ပဲစေ့	pe: zei.
kidney bean	ဘိုလ်စားပဲ	bou za: be:
soy	ပဲပုပ်ပဲ	pe: bou' pe
lentil	ပဲနီဂလေး	pe: ni ga. lei:
beans (pulse crops)	ပဲအမျိုးမျိုး	pe: amjou: mjou:

233. Vegetables. Greens

vegetables	ဟင်းသီးဟင်းရွက်	hin: dhi: hin: jwe'
greens	ဟင်းခတ်အမွေးရွက်	hin: ga' ahmwei: jwe'
tomato	ခရမ်းချဉ်သီး	khajan: chan dhi:
cucumber	သခွါးသီး	thakhwa: dhi:
carrot	မုန်လာဥနီ	moun la u. ni
potato	အာလူး	a lu:
onion	ကြက်သွန်နီ	kje' thwan ni
garlic	ကြက်သွန်ဖြူ	kje' thwan bju
cabbage	ဂေါ်ဖီ	go bi
cauliflower	ပန်းဂေါ်ဖီ	pan: gozi
Brussels sprouts	ဂေါ်ဖီထုပ်အသေးစား	go bi dou' athei: za:
broccoli	ပန်းဂေါ်ဖီအစိမ်း	pan: gozi asein:
beet	မုန်လာဥနီလုံး	moun la u. ni loun:
eggplant	ခရမ်းသီး	khajan: dhi:
zucchini	ဘူးသီး	bu: dhi:
pumpkin	ဖရုံသီး	hpa joun dhi:
turnip	တရုတ်မုန်လာဥ	tajou' moun la u.
parsley	တရုတ်နံနံပင်	tajou' nan nan bin
dill	စမြိတ်ပင်	samjei: pin
lettuce	ဆလပ်ရွက်	hsa. la' jwe'

celery	တရုတ်နံနံကြီး	tajou' nan nan gji:
asparagus	ကညွတ်မာပင်	ka. nju' ma bin
spinach	ဒေါက်ခွ	dau' khwa.

pea	ပဲပင်	pe: bin
beans	ပဲအမျိုးမျိုး	pe: amjou: mjou:
corn (maize)	ပြောင်းဖူး	pjaun: bu:
kidney bean	စိုလ်စားပဲ	bou za: be:

pepper	ငရုတ်သီး	nga jou' thi:
radish	မုန်လာဥသေး	moun la u. dhei:
artichoke	အာတိချော	a ti cho.

REGIONAL GEOGRAPHY

Countries. Nationalities

Europe	ဥရောပ	u. jo: pa
European Union	ဥရောပသမဂ္ဂ	u. jo: pa dha: me' ga.
European (n)	ဥရောပသား	u. jo: pa dha:
European (adj)	ဥရောပနှင့်ဆိုင်သော	u. jo: pa hnin. zain de

Austria	သြစတြီးယား	o. sa. tji: ja:
Austrian (masc.)	သြစတြီးယန်းအမျိုးသား	o. sa. tji: jan: amjou: dha:
Austrian (fem.)	သြစတြီးယန်းအမျိုးသမီး	o. sa. tji: jan: amjou: dhami:
Austrian (adj)	သြစတြီးယားနှင့်ဆိုင်သော	o. sa. tji: ja: hnin. zain de.

Great Britain	အင်္ဂလန်	angga. lan
England	အင်္ဂလန်	angga. lan
British (masc.)	အင်္ဂလန်နိုင်ငံသား	angga. lan nain ngan dha:
British (fem.)	အင်္ဂလန်နိုင်ငံသူ	angga. lan nain ngan dhu
English, British (adj)	အင်္ဂလန်နှင့်ဆိုင်သော	angga. lan hnin. zein dho:

Belgium	ဘယ်လ်ဂျီယံ	be l gji jan
Belgian (masc.)	ဘယ်လ်ဂျီယံအမျိုးသား	be l gji jan dha:
Belgian (fem.)	ဘယ်လ်ဂျီယံအမျိုးသမီး	be l gji jan dhami:
Belgian (adj)	ဘယ်လ်ဂျီယံနှင့်ဆိုင်သော	be l gji jan hnin. zain de.

Germany	ဂျာမန်	gja man
German (masc.)	ဂျာမန်အမျိုးသား	gja man amjou: dha:
German (fem.)	ဂျာမန်အမျိုးသမီး	gja man amjou: dhami:
German (adj)	ဂျာမန်နှင့်ဆိုင်သော	gja man hnin. zain de.

Netherlands	နယ်သာလန်	ne dha lan
Holland	ဟော်လန်	ho lan
Dutch (masc.)	ဒတ်ချ်အမျိုးသား	da' ch amjou: dha:
Dutch (fem.)	ဒတ်ချ်အမျိုးသမီး	da' ch amjou: dhami:
Dutch (adj)	ဒတ်ချ်နှင့်ဆိုင်သော	da' ch hnin. zain de

Greece	ဂရိ	ga. ri.
Greek (masc.)	ဂရိအမျိုးသား	ga. ri. amjou: dha:
Greek (fem.)	ဂရိအမျိုးသမီး	ga. ri. amjou: dhami:
Greek (adj)	ဂရိနှင့်ဆိုင်သော	ga. ri. hnin. zain de.
Denmark	ဒိန်းမတ်	dein: ma'

Dane (masc.)	ဒိန်းမတ်သား	dein: ma' dha:
Dane (fem.)	ဒိန်းမတ်သူ	dein: ma' dhu
Danish (adj)	ဒိန်းမတ်နှင့်ဆိုင်သော	dein: ma' hnin. zain de.

Ireland	အိုင်ယာလန်	ain ja lan
Irish (masc.)	အိုင်ယာလန်အမျိုးသား	ain ja lan amjou: dha:
Irish (fem.)	အိုင်ယာလန်အမျိုးသမီး	ain ja lan amjou: dha. mi:
Irish (adj)	အိုင်ယာလန်နှင့်ဆိုင်သော	ain ja lan hnin. zain de.

Iceland	အိုက်စလန်း	ai' sa lan:
Icelander (masc.)	အိုက်စလန်းသား	ai' sa lan: dha:
Icelander (fem.)	အိုက်စလန်းသူ	ai' sa lan: dhu
Icelandic (adj)	အိုက်စလန်းနှင့်ဆိုင်သော	ai' sa lan: hnin. hsain de.

Spain	စပိန်	sapein
Spaniard (masc.)	စပိန်အမျိုးသား	sapein mjou: dha:
Spaniard (fem.)	စပိန်အမျိုးသမီး	sapein mjou: dhami:
Spanish (adj)	စပိန်နှင့်ဆိုင်သော	sapein hnin. zain de.

Italy	အီတလီ	ita. li
Italian (masc.)	အီတလီအမျိုးသား	ita. li amjou: dha:
Italian (fem.)	အီတလီအမျိုးသမီး	ita. li amjou: dhami:
Italian (adj)	အီတလီနှင့်ဆိုင်သော	ita. li hnin. zain de.

Cyprus	ဆွ်းပရက်စ်	hsu: pa. je' s te.
Cypriot (masc.)	ဆွ်းပရက်စ်သား	hsu: pa. je' s tha:
Cypriot (fem.)	ဆွ်းပရက်စ်သူ	hsu: pa. je' s thu
Cypriot (adj)	ဆွ်းပရက်စ်နှင့်ဆိုင်သော	hsu: pa. je' s hnin. zain de.

Malta	မာတာ	ma ta
Maltese (masc.)	မာတာသား	ma ta dha:
Maltese (fem.)	မာတာသူ	ma ta dhami:
Maltese (adj)	မာတာနှင့်ဆိုင်သော	ma ta hnin. zain de.

Norway	နော်ဝေး	no wei:
Norwegian (masc.)	နော်ဝေးအမျိုးသား	no wei: amjou: dha:
Norwegian (fem.)	နော်ဝေးအမျိုးသမီး	no wei: amjou: dhami:
Norwegian (adj)	နော်ဝေးနှင့်ဆိုင်သော	no wei: hnin. zain de.

Portugal	ပေါ်တူဂီ	po tu gi
Portuguese (masc.)	ပေါ်တူဂီအမျိုးသား	po tu gi amjou: dha:
Portuguese (fem.)	ပေါ်တူဂီအမျိုးသမီး	po tu gi amjou: dhami:
Portuguese (adj)	ပေါ်တူဂီနှင့်ဆိုင်သော	po tu gi hnin. zain de.

Finland	ဖင်လန်	hpin lan
Finn (masc.)	ဖင်လန်အမျိုးသား	hpin lan dha:
Finn (fem.)	ဖင်လန်အမျိုးသမီး	hpin lan dhami:
Finnish (adj)	ဖင်လန်နှင့်ဆိုင်သော	hpin lan hnin. zain de.

France	ပြင်သစ်	pjin dhi'
French (masc.)	ပြင်သစ်အမျိုးသား	pjin dhi' amjou: dha:
French (fem.)	ပြင်သစ်အမျိုးသမီး	pjin dhi' amjou: dhami:

French (adj)	ပြင်သစ်နှင့်ဆိုင်သော	pjin dhi' hnin. zain de.
Sweden	ဆွီဒင်	hswi din
Swede (masc.)	ဆွီဒင်အမျိုးသား	hswi din amjou: dha:
Swede (fem.)	ဆွီဒင်အမျိုးသမီး	hswi din amjou: dhami:
Swedish (adj)	ဆွီဒင်နှင့်ဆိုင်သော	hswi din hnin. zain de.
Switzerland	ဆွစ်ဇာလန်	hswa' za lan
Swiss (masc.)	ဆွစ်ဇာလန်အမျိုး သား	hswa' za lan amjou: dha:
Swiss (fem.)	ဆွစ်ဇာလန်အမျိုး သမီး	hswa' za lan amjou: dhami:
Swiss (adj)	ဆွစ်ဇာလန်နှင့်ဆိုင်သော	hswa' za lan hnin. zain de.
Scotland	စကော့တလန်	sa. ko: talan
Scottish (masc.)	စကော့တလန်အမျိုးသား	sa. ko: talan mjou: dha:
Scottish (fem.)	စကော့တလန်အမျိုးသမီး	sa. ko: talan mjou: dha:
Scottish (adj)	စကော့တလန်နှင့်ဆိုင်သော	sa. ko: talan hnin. zain de.
Vatican	ဗာတီကန်	ba di gan
Liechtenstein	ဗာတီကန်လူမျိုး	ba di gan dhu mjo:
Luxembourg	လျူဆန်ဘော့	lju hsan bo.
Monaco	မိုနာကို	mou na kou

235. Central and Eastern Europe

Albania	အယ်လ်ဘေးနီးယား	e l bei: ni: ja:
Albanian (masc.)	အယ်လ်ဘေးနီးယား အမျိုးသား	e l bei: ni: ja amjou: dha:
Albanian (fem.)	အယ်လ်ဘေးနီးယား အမျိုးသမီး	e l bei: ni: ja: amjou: dhami:
Albanian (adj)	အယ်လ်ဘေးနီးယား နှင့်ဆိုင်သော	e l bei: ni: ja: hnin. zain de.
Bulgaria	ဘူလ်ဂေးရီးယား	bou gei: ji: ja
Bulgarian (masc.)	ဘူလ်ဂေးရီးယား အမျိုးသား	bou gei: ji: ja amjou: dha:
Bulgarian (fem.)	ဘူလ်ဂေးရီးယား အမျိုးသမီး	bou gei: ji: ja amjou: dhami:
Bulgarian (adj)	ဘူလ်ဂေးရီးယားနှင့်ဆိုင်သော	bou gei: ji: ja hnin. zain de.
Hungary	ဟန်ဂေရီ	han gei ji
Hungarian (masc.)	ဟန်ဂေရီအမျိုးသား	han gei ji amjou: dha:
Hungarian (fem.)	ဟန်ဂေရီအမျိုးသမီး	han gei ji amjou: dhami:
Hungarian (adj)	ဟန်ဂေရီနှင့်ဆိုင်သော	han gei ji hnin. zain de.
Latvia	လတ်ဗီယန်	la' bi jan
Latvian (masc.)	လတ်ဗီယန်အမျိုးသား	la' bi jan amjou: dha:
Latvian (fem.)	လတ်ဗီယန်အမျိုးသမီး	la' bi jan amjou: dhami:
Latvian (adj)	လတ်ဗီယန်နှင့်ဆိုင်သော	la' bi jan hnin. zein de.
Lithuania	လစ်သူနီယံ	li' thu ni jan

Lithuanian (masc.)	လစ်သူနိယံအမျိုးသား	li' thu ni jan amjou: dha:
Lithuanian (fem.)	လစ်သူနိယံအမျိုးသမီး	li' thu ni jan amjou: dhami:
Lithuanian (adj)	လစ်သူနိယံနှင့်ဆိုင်သော	li' thu ni jan hnin. zain de.

Poland	ပိုလန်	pou lan
Pole (masc.)	ပိုလန်အမျိုးသား	pou lan amjou: dha:
Pole (fem.)	ပိုလန်အမျိုးသမီး	pou lan amjou: dhami:
Polish (adj)	ပိုလန်နှင့်ဆိုင်သော	pou lan hnin. zain de.

Romania	ရူမေးနီးယား	ru mei: ni: ja:
Romanian (masc.)	ရူမေးနီးယားအမျိုးသား	ru mei: ni: ja: amjou: dha:
Romanian (fem.)	ရူမေးနီးယားအမျိုးသမီး	ru mei: ni: ja: amjou: dha:
Romanian (adj)	ရူမေးနီးယားနှင့်ဆိုင်သော	ru mei: ni: ja: hnin. zain de.

Serbia	ဆယ်ဗီယံ	hse bi jan.
Serbian (masc.)	ဆာဗီယံအမျိုးသား	hsa bi jan amjou: dha:
Serbian (fem.)	ဆာဗီယံအမျိုးသမီး	hsa bi jan amjou: dhami:
Serbian (adj)	ဆာဗီယံနှင့်ဆိုင်သော	hsa bi jan hnin. zain de.

Slovakia	ဆလိုဗာကီယာ	hsa. lou ba ki ja
Slovak (masc.)	ဆလိုဗာကီယာ အမျိုးသား	hsa. lou ba ki ja amjou: dha:
Slovak (fem.)	ဆလိုဗာကီယာ အမျိုးသမီး	hsa. lou ba ki ja amjou: dhami:
Slovak (adj)	ဆလိုဗာကီယာ နှင့်ဆိုင်သော	hsa. lou ba ki ja hnin. zain de.

Croatia	ခရိုအေးရှား	kha. jou ei: sha:
Croatian (masc.)	ခရိုအေးရှား အမျိုးသား	kha. jou ei: sha: amjou: dha:
Croatian (fem.)	ခရိုအေးရှား အမျိုးသမီး	kha. jou ei: sha: amjou: dhami:
Croatian (adj)	ခရိုအေးရှား နှင့်ဆိုင်သော	kha. jou ei: sha: hnin. zain de.

Czech Republic	ချက်	che'
Czech (masc.)	ချက်အမျိုးသား	che' amjou: dha:
Czech (fem.)	ချက်အမျိုးသမီး	che' amjou: dhami:
Czech (adj)	ချက်နှင့်ဆိုင်သော	che' hnin. zain de.

Estonia	အက်စ်တိုးနီးယား	e's to' ni: ja:
Estonian (masc.)	အက်စ်တိုးနီးယံအမျိုးသား	e's to' ni: ja: dha:
Estonian (fem.)	အက်စ်တိုးနီးယံအမျိုးသမီး	e's to' ni: ja: dhami:
Estonian (adj)	အက်စ်တိုးနီးယားနှင့်ဆိုင်သော	e's to' ni: ja: hnin. zain de

Bosnia and Herzegovina	ဘော့စ်နီးယားနှင့်ဟာ ဇီဂိုဗီနာ	bo'. ni: ja: hnin. ha zi gou bi na
Macedonia (Republic of ~)	မက်ဆီဒိုးနီးယား	me' hsi: dou: ni: ja:
Slovenia	ဆလိုဗီနီးယား	hsa. lou bi ni: ja:
Montenegro	မွန်တန်နီဂရို	mun dan ni ga. jou

236. Former USSR countries

Azerbaijan	အာဇာဘိုင်ဂျန်း	a za bain gjin:
Azerbaijani (masc.)	အာဇာဘိုင်ဂျန်းအမျိုးသား	a za bain gjin: dha:
Azerbaijani (fem.)	အာဇာဘိုင်ဂျန်းအမျိုးသမီး	a za bain gjin: dhami:
Azerbaijani, Azeri (adj)	အာဇာဘိုင်ဂျန်းနှင့် ဆိုင်သော	a za bain gjin: hnin. zain de.

Armenia	အာမေးနီးယား	a me: ni: ja:
Armenian (masc.)	အာမေးနီးယားအမျိုးသား	a me: ni: ja: amjou: dhami:
Armenian (fem.)	အာမေးနီးယားအမျိုးသမီး	a me: ni: ja: amjou: dhami:
Armenian (adj)	အာမေးနီးယားနှင့်ဆိုင်သော	a me: ni: ja: hnin. zain de.

Belarus	ဘီလာရုစ်	bi la ju'
Belarusian (masc.)	ဘီလာရုစ်အမျိုးသား	bi la ju' amjou: dha:
Belarusian (fem.)	ဘီလာရုစ်အမျိုးသမီး	bi la ju' amjou: dhami:
Belarusian (adj)	ဘီလာရုစ်နှင့်ဆိုင်သော	bi la ju' hnin. zain de.

Georgia	ဂျော်ဂျီယာ	gjo gji ja
Georgian (masc.)	ဂျော်ဂျီယာအမျိုးသား	gjo gji ja amjou: dhami:
Georgian (fem.)	ဂျော်ဂျီယာအမျိုးသမီး	gjo gji ja amjou: dha:
Georgian (adj)	ဂျော်ဂျီယာနှင့်ဆိုင်သော	gjo gji ja hnin. zain de.

Kazakhstan	ကာဇက်စတန်	ka ze' satan
Kazakh (masc.)	ကာဇက်စတန်အမျိုးသမီး	ka ze' satan amjou: dhami:
Kazakh (fem.)	ကာဇက်စတန်အမျိုးသမီး	ka ze' satan amjou: dhami:
Kazakh (adj)	ကာဇက်စတန်နှင့်ဆိုင်သော	ka ze' satan hnin. zain de.

Kirghizia	ကစ်ရှိကစ္စတန်	ki' ji ki' za. tan
Kirghiz (masc.)	ကစ်ရှိကစ္စတန် အမျိုးသား	ki' ji ki' za. tan amjou: dha:
Kirghiz (fem.)	ကစ်ရှိကစ္စတန် အမျိုးသမီး	ki' ji ki' za. tan amjou: dhami:
Kirghiz (adj)	ကစ်ရှိကစ္စတန် နှင့်ဆိုင်သော	ki' ji ki' za. tan hnin. zain de.

Moldova, Moldavia	မိုဒိုဗာ	mou dou ja
Moldavian (masc.)	မိုဒိုဗာအမျိုးသား	mou dou ja amjou: dha:
Moldavian (fem.)	မိုဒိုဗာအမျိုးသမီး	mou dou ja amjou: dhami:
Moldavian (adj)	မိုဒိုဗာနှင့်ဆိုင်သော	mou dou ja hnin. zain de.

Russia	ရုရှား	ru. sha:
Russian (masc.)	ရုရှားအမျိုးသား	ru sha: amjou: dha:
Russian (fem.)	ရုရှားအမျိုးသမီး	ru. sha: amjou: dhami:
Russian (adj)	ရုရှားနှင့်ဆိုင်သော	ru. sha: hnin. zain de.

Tajikistan	တာဂျစ်ကစ္စတန်	ta gji' ki' sa. tan
Tajik (masc.)	တာဂျစ်အမျိုးသား	ta gji' amjou: dha:
Tajik (fem.)	တာဂျစ်အမျိုးသမီး	ta gji' amjou: dhami:
Tajik (adj)	တာဂျစ်နှင့်ဆိုင်သော	ta gji' hnin. zain de.
Turkmenistan	တာ်မင်နီစ္စတန်	ta' min ni' sa. tan

Turkmen (masc.)	တပ်မင်နစ္စတန်အမျိုးသား	ta' min ni' sa. tan amjou: dha:
Turkmen (fem.)	တပ်မင်နစ္စတန်အမျိုးသမီး	ta' min ni' sa. tan amjou: dhami:
Turkmenian (adj)	တပ်မင်နစ္စတန်နှင့်ဆိုင်သော	ta' min ni' sa. tan hnin. zain de.

Uzbekistan	ဥဇဘက်ကစ္စတန်	u. za. be' ki' sa. tan
Uzbek (masc.)	ဥဇဘက်အမျိုးသား	u. za. be' amjou: dha:
Uzbek (fem.)	ဥဇဘက်အမျိုးသမီး	u. za. be' amjou: dha:
Uzbek (adj)	ဥဇဘက်ကစ္စတန်နှင့်ဆိုင်သော	u. za. be' ki' sa. tan hnin. zain de.

Ukraine	ယူကရိန်း	ju ka. jein:
Ukrainian (masc.)	ယူကရိန်းအမျိုးသား	ju ka. jein: amjou: dha:
Ukrainian (fem.)	ယူကရိန်းအမျိုးသမီး	ju ka. jein: amjou: dhami:
Ukrainian (adj)	ယူကရိန်းနှင့်ဆိုင်သော	ju ka. jein: hnin. zain de.:

237. Asia

| Asia | အာရှ | a sha. |
| Asian (adj) | အာရှနှင့်ဆိုင်သော | a sha. hnin. zain de. |

Vietnam	ဗီယက်နမ်	bi je' nan
Vietnamese (masc.)	ဗီယက်နမ်အမျိုးသား	bi ja' nan amjou: dha:
Vietnamese (fem.)	ဗီယက်နမ်အမျိုးသမီး	bi je' nan amjou dha mi:
Vietnamese (adj)	ဗီယက်နမ်နှင့်ဆိုင်သော	bi je' nan hnin. zain de.

India	အိန္ဒိယ	indi. ja
Indian (masc.)	အိန္ဒိယအမျိုးသား	indi. ja amjou: dha:
Indian (fem.)	အိန္ဒိယအမျိုးသမီး	indi. ja amjou: dhami:
Indian (adj)	အိန္ဒိယနှင့်ဆိုင်သော	indi. ja hnin. zain de.

Israel	အစ္စရေး	a' sa. jei:
Israeli (masc.)	အစ္စရေးအမျိုးသား	a' sa. jei: amjou: dha:
Israeli (fem.)	အစ္စရေးအမျိုးသမီး	a' sa. jei: amjou: dhami:
Israeli (adj)	အစ္စရေးနှင့်ဆိုင်သော	a' sa. jei: hnin. zain de.

Jew (n)	ဂျူး	gju:
Jewess (n)	ဂျူးအမျိုးသမီး	gju: amjou: dhami:
Jewish (adj)	ဂျူးအမျိုးသား	gju: amjou: dha:

China	တရုတ်	tajou'
Chinese (masc.)	တရုတ်အမျိုးသား	tajou' amjou: dha:
Chinese (fem.)	တရုတ်အမျိုးသမီး	tajou' amjou: dhami:
Chinese (adj)	တရုတ်နှင့်ဆိုင်သော	tajou' hnin. zain de.

Korean (masc.)	ကိုးရီးယားအမျိုးသား	kou: ji: ja: amjou: dha:
Korean (fem.)	ကိုးရီးယားအမျိုးသမီး	kou: ji: ja: amjou: dhami:
Korean (adj)	ကိုးရီးယားနှင့်ဆိုင်သော	kou: ji: ja: hnin. zain de.

Lebanon	လက်ဘနွန်	le' ba. nun
Lebanese (masc.)	လက်ဘနွန်အမျိုးသား	le' ba. nun amjou: dha:
Lebanese (fem.)	လက်ဘနွန်အမျိုးသမီး	le' ba. nun amjou: dhami:
Lebanese (adj)	လက်ဘနွန်နှင့်ဆိုင်သော	le' ba. nun hnin zain de

Mongolia	မွန်ဂိုလီးယား	mun gou li: ja:
Mongolian (masc.)	မွန်ဂိုလီးယားအမျိုးသား	mun gou li: ja: amjou: dha:
Mongolian (fem.)	မွန်ဂိုလီးယားအမျိုးသမီး	mun gou li: ja: amjou: dhami:
Mongolian (adj)	မွန်ဂိုလီးယားနှင့်ဆိုင်သော	mun gou li: ja: hnin. zain de.

Malaysia	မလေးရှား	ma. lei: sha:
Malaysian (masc.)	မလေးရှားအမျိုးသား	ma. lei: sha: amjou: dha:
Malaysian (fem.)	မလေးရှားအမျိုးသမီး	ma. lei: sha: amjou: dhami:
Malaysian (adj)	မလေးရှားနှင့်ဆိုင်သော	ma. lei: sha: hnin. zain de.

Pakistan	ပါကစ္စတန်	pa ki' sa. tan
Pakistani (masc.)	ပါကစ္စတန်အမျိုးသား	pa ki' sa. tan dha:
Pakistani (fem.)	ပါကစ္စတန်အမျိုးသမီး	pa ki' sa. tan dhami:
Pakistani (adj)	ပါကစ္စတန်နှင့်ဆိုင်သော	pa ki' sa. tan hnin. zain de

Saudi Arabia	ဆော်ဒီအာရေ့ဗီးယား	hso: di a jei. bi: ja:
Arab (masc.)	အာရပ်အမျိုးသား	a ra' amjou: dha:
Arab (fem.)	အာရပ်အမျိုးသမီး	a ra' amjou: dhami:
Arab, Arabic (adj)	အာရပ်နှင့်ဆိုင်သော	a ra' hnin. zain de.

Thailand	ထိုင်း	htain:
Thai (masc.)	ထိုင်းအမျိုးသား	htain: amjou: dha:
Thai (fem.)	ထိုင်းအမျိုးသမီး	htain: amjou: dhami:
Thai (adj)	ထိုင်းနှင့်ဆိုင်သော	htain: hnin. zain de.

Taiwan	ထိုင်ဝမ်	htain wan
Taiwanese (masc.)	ထိုင်ဝမ်အမျိုးသား	htain wan amjou: dha:
Taiwanese (fem.)	ထိုင်ဝမ်အမျိုးသမီး	htain wan amjou: dhami:
Taiwanese (adj)	ထိုင်ဝမ်နှင့်ဆိုင်သော	htain wan hnin. zain de.

Turkey	တူရကီ	tu ra. ki
Turk (masc.)	တူရကီအမျိုးသား	tu ra. ki amjou: dha:
Turk (fem.)	တူရကီအမျိုးသမီး	tu ra. ki amjou: dhami:
Turkish (adj)	တူရကီနှင့်ဆိုင်သော	tu ra. ki hnin. zain de

Japan	ဂျပန်	gja pan
Japanese (masc.)	ဂျပန်အမျိုးသား	gja pan amjou: dha:
Japanese (fem.)	ဂျပန်အမျိုးသမီး	gja pan amjou: dhami:
Japanese (adj)	ဂျပန်နှင့်ဆိုင်သော	gja pan hnin. zain de

Afghanistan	အာဖဂန်နစ္စတန်	apha. gan na' tan
Bangladesh	ဘင်္ဂလားဒေ့ရှ်	bang la: dei. sh
Indonesia	အင်ဒိုနီးရှား	in do ni: sha:
Jordan	ဂျော်ဒန်	gjo dan

Iraq	အီရတ်	ira'
Iran	အီရန်	iran
Cambodia	ကမ္ဘောဒီးယား	ga khan ba di: ja:
Kuwait	ကူဝိတ်	ku wi'

Laos	လာအို	la ou
Myanmar	မြန်မာ	mjan ma
Nepal	နီပေါ	ni po:
United Arab Emirates	အာရပ်နိုင်ငံများ	a ra' nain ngan mja:

Syria	ဆီးရီးယား	hsi: ji: ja:
Palestine	ပါလက်စတိုင်း	pa le' sa tain:
South Korea	တောင်ကိုရီးယား	taun kou ri: ja:
North Korea	မြောက်ကိုရီးယား	mjau' kou ji: ja:

238. North America

United States of America	အမေရိကန် ပြည်ထောင်စု	amei ji kan pji htaun zu
American (masc.)	အမေရိကန်အမျိုးသား	amei ji kan amjou: dha:
American (fem.)	အမေရိကန်အမျိုးသမီး	amei ji kan amjou: dhami:
American (adj)	အမေရိကန်	amei ji kan

Canada	ကနေဒါနိုင်ငံ	ka. nei da nain gan
Canadian (masc.)	ကနေဒါအမျိုးသား	ka. nei da amjou: dha:
Canadian (fem.)	ကနေဒါအမျိုးသမီး	ka. nei da amjou: dhami:
Canadian (adj)	ကနေဒါနိုင်ငံ နှင့် ဆိုင်သော	ka. nei da nain gan hnin. zain de.

Mexico	မက္ကစီကို နိုင်ငံ	me' ka. hsi kou nain ngan
Mexican (masc.)	မက္ကစီကို အမျိုးသား	me' ka. hsi kou amjou: dha:
Mexican (fem.)	မက္ကစီကို အမျိုးသမီး	me' ka. hsi kou amjou: dhami:
Mexican (adj)	မက္ကစီကိုနိုင်ငံနှင့် ဆိုင်သော	me' ka. hsi kou hnin. zain de.

239. Central and South America

Argentina	အာဂျင်တီးနား	agin ti: na:
Argentinian (masc.)	အာဂျင်တီးနားအမျိုးသား	agin ti: na: amjou: dha:
Argentinian (fem.)	အာဂျင်တီးနားအမျိုးသမီး	agin ti: na: amjou: dhami:
Argentinian (adj)	အာဂျင်တီးနားနှင့်ဆိုင်သော	agin ti: na: hnin. zain de.

Brazil	ဘရာဇိL	ba. ra zi'l
Brazilian (masc.)	ဘရာဇီလိယံအမျိုးသား	ba. ra zi'l amjou: dha:
Brazilian (fem.)	ဘရာဇီလိယံအမျိုးသမီး	ba. ra zi'l amjou: dhami:
Brazilian (adj)	ဘရာဇိLနှင့်ဆိုင်သော	ba. ra zi'l hnin. zain de.

Colombia	ကိုလမ်ဘီးယား	kou lan: bi: ja:
Colombian (masc.)	ကိုလမ်ဘီးယား အမျိုးသား	kou lan: bi: ja: amjou: dha:
Colombian (fem.)	ကိုလမ်ဘီးယား အမျိုးသမီး	kou lan: bi: ja: amjou: dhami:
Colombian (adj)	ကိုလမ်ဘီးယား နှင့်ဆိုင်သော	kou lan: bi: ja: hnin. lain de.
Cuba	ကျူးဘား	kju: ba:
Cuban (masc.)	ကျူးဘားအမျိုးသား	kju: ba: amjou: dha:
Cuban (fem.)	ကျူးဘားအမျိုးသမီး	kju: ba: amjou: dhami:
Cuban (adj)	ကျူးဘားနှင့်ဆိုင်သော	kju: ba: hnin. zain de.
Chile	ချီလီ	chi li
Chilean (masc.)	ချီလီအမျိုးသား	chi li amjou: dha:
Chilean (fem.)	ချီလီအမျိုးသမီး	chi li amjou: dhami:
Chilean (adj)	ချီလီနှင့်ဆိုင်သော	chi li hnin. zain de.
Bolivia	ဘိုလစ်ဗီးယား	bou la' bi: ja:
Venezuela	ဗယ်နီဇွဲလား	be ni zwe: la:
Paraguay	ပါရာဂွေး	pa ja gwei:
Peru	ပီရူး	pi ju:
Suriname	ဆူရီနိမ်း	hsu. ji nei:
Uruguay	အုရုဂွေး	ou. ju gwei:
Ecuador	အီကွေဒေါ	i kwei: do:
The Bahamas	ဘာဟာမက်	ba ha me'
Haiti	ဟိုင်တီ	hain ti
Dominican Republic	ဒိုမီနီကန်	dou mi ni kan
Panama	ပနားမား	pa. na: ma:
Jamaica	ဂျမေးကား	g'me:kaa:

240. Africa

Egypt	အီဂျစ်	igji'
Egyptian (masc.)	အီဂျစ်အမျိုးသား	igji' amjou: dha:
Egyptian (fem.)	အီဂျစ်အမျိုးသမီး	igji' amjou: dhami:
Egyptian (adj)	အီဂျစ်နှင့်ဆိုင်သော	igji' hnin. zain de.
Morocco	မော်ရိုကို	mo jou gou
Moroccan (masc.)	မော်ရိုကို အမျိုးသား	mou jou gou amjou: dha:
Moroccan (fem.)	မော်ရိုကို အမျိုးသမီး	mou jou gou amjou: dhami:
Moroccan (adj)	မော်ရိုကိုနှင့်ဆိုင်သော	mou jou gou hnin. zain de.
Tunisia	တူနစ်ရှား	tu ni' sha:
Tunisian (masc.)	တူနစ်ရှားအမျိုးသား	tu ni' sha: amjou: dha:
Tunisian (fem.)	တူနစ်ရှာအမျိုးသမီး	tu ni' sha: amjou: dhami:

Tunisian (adj)	တူနစ်ရှားနှင့်ဆိုင်သော	tu ni' sha: hnin. zain de.
Ghana	ဂါနာ	ga na
Zanzibar	ဇန်ဇီဗာ	zan zi ba
Kenya	ကင်ညာ	kin nja
Libya	လီဗီယာ	li bi ja
Madagascar	မာဒဂက်ကာစကာ	ma de' ka za ga

Namibia	နမီမီးဘီးယား	nami: bi: ja:
Senegal	ဆယ်နီဂေါ်	hse ni go
Tanzania	တန်ဇားနီးယား	tan za: ni: ja:
South Africa	တောင်အာဖရိက	taun a hpa. ji. ka.

African (masc.)	အာဖရိကတိုက်သား	apha. ri. ka. dhai' tha:
African (fem.)	အာဖရိကသူ	apha. ri. ka. dhu
African (adj)	အာဖရိကန်နှင့်ဆိုင်သော	apha. ri. kan hnin. zain de.

241. Australia. Oceania

Australia	သြစတြေးလျ	thja za djei: lja
Australian (masc.)	သြစ္စတြေးလျား အမျိုးသား	o. sa. tjei: lja: amjou: dha:
Australian (fem.)	သြစ္စတြေးလျား အမျိုးသမီး	o. sa. tjei: lja: amjou: dhami:
Australian (adj)	သြစ္စတြေးလျနှင့် ဆိုင်သော	o. sa. tjei: lja: hnin. zain de.

New Zealand	နယူးဇီလန်	na. ju: zi lan
New Zealander (masc.)	နယူးဇီလန်အမျိုးသား	na. ju: zi lan dha:
New Zealander (fem.)	နယူးဇီလန်အမျိုးသမီး	na. ju: zi lan dhami:
New Zealand (as adj)	နယူးဇီလန်နှင့်ဆိုင်သော	na. ja: zi lan hnin. zain de

| Tasmania | တာ့စ်မေးနီးယား | ta. s mei: ni: ja: |
| French Polynesia | ပြင်သစ် ပေါ်လီးနီးရှား | pjin dhi' po li: ni: sha: |

242. Cities

Amsterdam	အမ်စတာဒမ်မြို့	an za ta dan mjou.
Ankara	အင်ကာရာမြို့	an ga ja mjou.
Athens	အေသင်မြို့	e thin mjou.
Baghdad	ဘဂ္ဂဒတ်မြို့	ba' ga. da mjou.
Bangkok	ဘန်ကောက်မြို့	ban gou' mjou.
Barcelona	ဘာစီလိုနာမြို့	ba zi lou na mjou.

Beijing	ဝီကျင်းမြို့	pi gin: mjou.
Beirut	ဘီရာရုမြို့	bi ja ju. mjou.
Berlin	ဘာလင်မြို့	ba lin mjou.
Mumbai (Bombay)	မွန်ဘိုင်းမြို့	mun bain mjou.
Bonn	ဘွန်းမြို့	bwun: mjou.

Bordeaux	ဘော်ဒိုးမြို့	bo dou: mjou.
Bratislava	ဘရာတတ်ဆလာဗာမြို့	ba. ra ta' hsa. la ba mjou.
Brussels	ဘရပ်ဆဲလ်မြို့	ba. ja' hse:' mjou.
Bucharest	ဗူးဆရက်မြို့	bu: ga. ja' mjou.
Budapest	ဘူဒါပက်စ်မြို့	bu da pa' s mjou.
Cairo	ကိုင်ရိုမြို့	kain jou mjou.
Kolkata (Calcutta)	ကာလကတ္တားမြို့	ka la ka' ta mjou.
Chicago	ရှီကာဂိုမြို့	chi ka gou mjou.
Copenhagen	ကိုပင်ဟေးဂင်မြို့	kou pin hei: gin mjou.
Dar-es-Salaam	ဒါရှုစလမ်မြို့	da ju za. lan mjou.
Delhi	ဒေလီမြို့	dei li mjou.
Dubai	ဒူဘိုင်းမြို့	du bain mjou.
Dublin	ဒဗ္ဗလင်မြို့	da' ba lin mjou.
Düsseldorf	ဂျူဆက်ဒွေါ့ဖ်မြို့	gju hse' do. hp mjou.
Florence	ဖလောရန့်စ်မြို့	hpa. lau jan s mjou.
Frankfurt	ဖရန့်ဖွာ့တ်မြို့	hpa. jan. hpa. t. mjou.
Geneva	ဂျန်ဗာမြို့	gja. ni ba mjou.
The Hague	ဒဟာဂူးမြို့	da. ha gu: mjou.
Hamburg	ဟန်းဘာဂ်မြို့	han: ba. k mjou.
Hanoi	ဟနွိုင်းမြို့	ha. noin: mjou.
Havana	ဟာဗားနားမြို့	ha ba: na: mjou.
Helsinki	ဟယ်လ်ဆင်ကီမြို့	he l hsin ki mjou.
Hiroshima	ဟီရိုရှီးမားမြို့	hi jou si: ma: mjou.
Hong Kong	ဟောင်ကောင်မြို့	haun: gaun: mjou.
Istanbul	အစ္စတန်ဘူလ်မြို့	a' sa. tan bun mjou.
Jerusalem	ဂျေရုဆလင်မြို့	gjei jou hsa. lin mjou.
Kyiv	ကီးယက်မြို့	ki: je' mjou.
Kuala Lumpur	ကွာလာလမ်ပူမြို့	kwa lan pu mjou.
Lisbon	လစ်ဘွန်းမြို့	li' sa bun: mjou.
London	လန်ဒန်မြို့	lan dan mjou.
Los Angeles	လော့အိန်ဂျလီမြို့	lau in gja. li mjou.
Lyons	လိုင်ယွန်မြို့	lain jun mjou.
Madrid	မတ်ဒရစ်မြို့	ma' da. ji' mjou.
Marseille	မာရ်ဆေးမြို့	ma zei: mjou.
Mexico City	မက္ကဆီကိုမြို့	me' ka. hsi kou mjou.
Miami	မီရာမီမြို့	mi ja mi mjou.
Montreal	မွန်ထရရယ်မြို့	mun da. ji je mjou.
Moscow	မော်စကိုမြို့	ma sa. kou mjou.
Munich	မြူးနစ်မြို့	mju: ni' mjou.
Nairobi	နိုင်ရိုဘီမြို့	nain jou bi mjo.
Naples	နီပေါမြို့	ni po: mjou.
New York	နယူးယောက်မြို့	na. ju: jau' mjou.
Nice	နိုက်စ်မြို့	nai's mjou.
Oslo	အော်စလိုမြို့	o sa lou mjou.
Ottawa	အော့တဝါမြို့	o. ta wa mjou.

Paris	ပဲရစ်မြို့	pe: ji' mjou.
Prague	ပရက်မြို့	pa. ra' mjou.
Rio de Janeiro	ရီရိုဒေးဂျန်နိုမြို့	ri jou dei: gjan ni jou mjou.
Rome	ရောမမြို့	ro: ma. mjou.

Saint Petersburg	စိန့်ပီတာစဘတ်မြို့	sein. pi ta za ba' mjou.
Seoul	ဆိုးလ်မြို့	hsou: l mjou.
Shanghai	ရှန်ဟိုင်းမြို့	shan hain: mjou.
Singapore	စကၤပူ	sin ga pu
Stockholm	စတော့ဟုမ်းမြို့	sato. houn: mjou.
Sydney	စစ်ဒနေမြို့	si' danei mjou.

Taipei	တိုင်ပေမြို့	tain bei mjou.
Tokyo	တိုကျိုမြို့	tou gjou mjou.
Toronto	တိုရွန်တိုမြို့	tou run tou mjou.

Venice	ဗင်းနစ်စ်မြို့	bin: na' s mjou.
Vienna	ဗီယင်နာမြို့	bi jin na mjou.
Warsaw	ဝါဆောမြို့	wa so mjou.
Washington	ဝါရှင်တန်မြို့	wa shin tan mjou.

243. Politics. Government. Part 1

politics	နိုင်ငံရေး	nain ngan jei:
political (adj)	နိုင်ငံရေးနှင့်ဆိုင်သော	nain ngan jei: hnin. zain de
politician	နိုင်ငံရေးသမား	nain ngan jei: dhama:

state (country)	နိုင်ငံ	nain ngan
citizen	နိုင်ငံသား	nain ngan dha:
citizenship	နိုင်ငံသားအဖြစ်	nain ngan dha: ahpji'

| national emblem | နိုင်ငံတော်တံဆိပ် | nain ngan da dan zei' |
| national anthem | နိုင်ငံတော်သီချင်း | nain ngan do dhi gjin: |

government	အစိုးရ	asou: ja. hpja' te.
head of state	နိုင်ငံခေါင်းဆောင်	nain ngan gaun zaun
parliament	ပါလီမန်	pa li man
party	ပါတီ	pa ti

| capitalism | အရင်းရှင်ဝါဒ | ajin: hjin wa da. |
| capitalist (adj) | အရင်းရှင် | ajin: shin |

| socialism | ဆိုရှယ်လစ်ဝါဒ | hsou she la' wa da. |
| socialist (adj) | ဆိုရှယ်လစ် | hsou she la' |

communism	ကွန်မြူနစ်ဝါဒ	kun mu ni' wa da.
communist (adj)	ကွန်မြူနစ်	kun mu ni'
communist (n)	ကွန်မြူနစ်ဝါဒ	kun mu ni' wa da.
	ယုံကြည်သူ	joun kji dhu

| democracy | ဒီမိုကရေစီဝါဒ | di mou ka jei zi wa da. |

democrat	ဒီမိုကရေစီ ယုံကြည်သူ	di mou ka jei zi joun gji dhu
democratic (adj)	ဒီမိုကရေစီ နှင့်ဆိုင်သော	di mou ka jei zi hnin zain de.
Democratic party	ဒီမိုကရေစီပါတီ	di mou ka jei zi pa ti
liberal (n)	လစ်ဘရယ်	li' ba. je
liberal (adj)	လစ်ဘရယ်နှင့်ဆိုင်သော	li' ba. je hnin. zain de.
conservative (n)	ကွန်ဆာဗေးတစ်လိုလားသူ	kun sa bei: ti' lou la: dhu:
conservative (adj)	ကွန်ဆာဗေးတစ်နှင့် ဆိုင်သော	kun sa bei: ti' hnin. zain de.
republic (n)	သမ္မတနိုင်ငံ	thamada. nain ngan
republican (n)	သမ္မတစနစ်လိုလားသူ	thamada. zani' lou la: dhu
Republican party	သမ္မတစနစ်လိုလားသော	thamada. zani' lou la: de.
elections	ရွေးကောက်ပွဲ	jwei: kau' pwe:
to elect (vt)	မဲပေးရွေးချယ်သည်	me: bei: jwei: gje de
elector, voter	မဲဆန္ဒရှင်	me: hsan da. shin
election campaign	မဲဆွယ်ပွဲ	me: hswe bwe:
voting (n)	ဆန္ဒမဲပေးခြင်း	hsan da. me: pwei: gjin
to vote (vi)	ဆန္ဒမဲပေးသည်	hsan da. me: pwei: de
suffrage, right to vote	ဆန္ဒမဲပေးခွင့်	hsan da. me: khwin.
candidate	ကိုယ်စားလှယ်လောင်း	kou za: hle laun:
to be a candidate	ရွေးကောက်ပွဲဝင်သည်	jwei: kau' pwe: win de
campaign	လုပ်ဆောင်မှုများ	lou' zaun hmu. mja:
opposition (as adj)	အတိုက်အခံဖြစ်သော	atoi' akhan hpja' tho:
opposition (n)	အတိုက်အခံပါတီ	atoi' akhan ba di
visit	အလည်အပတ်	ale apa'
official visit	တရားဝင်အလည်အပတ်	taja: win alei apa'
international (adj)	အပြည်ပြည်ဆိုင်ရာဖြစ်သော	apji pji zain ja bja' de.
negotiations	ဆွေးနွေးပွဲ	hswe: nwe: bwe:
to negotiate (vi)	ဆွေးနွေးသည်	hswe: nwe: de

244. Politics. Government. Part 2

society	လူထု	lu du
constitution	ဖွဲ့စည်းပုံအခြေ ခံဥပဒေ	hpwe. zi: boun akhei gan u. ba. dei
power (political control)	အာဏာ	a na
corruption	ခြစားမှု	cha. za: hmu.
law (justice)	ဥပဒေ	u. ba. dei
legal (legitimate)	တရားဥပဒေဘောင် တွင်းဖြစ်သော	taja: u ba dei baun twin: bji' te.

| justice (fairness) | တရားမျှတခြင်း | taja: hmja. ta. gjin: |
| just (fair) | တရားမျှတသော | taja: hmja. ta. de. |

committee	ကော်မတီ	ko ma. din
bill (draft law)	ဥပဒေကြမ်း	u. ba. dei gjan:
budget	ဘတ်ဂျက်	ba' gje'
policy	မူဝါဒ	mu wa da.
reform	ပြုပြင်ပြောင်းလဲမှု	pju. bjin bjaun: le: hmu.
radical (adj)	အစွန်းရောက်သော	aswan: jau' de.

power (strength, force)	အား	a:
powerful (adj)	အင်အားကြီးသော	in a: kji: de.
supporter	ထောက်ခံအားပေးသူ	htau' khan a: bei: dhu
influence	သြဇာ	o: za

regime (e.g., military ~)	အစိုးရစနစ်	asou: ja. za. na'
conflict	အငြင်းပွားမှု	anjin: bwa: hmu.
conspiracy (plot)	လျှို့ဝှက်ပူးပေါင်း ကြံစည်ချက်	shou. hwe' pu: baun: kjan ze gje'
provocation	ရန်စခြင်း	jan za gjin:

to overthrow (regime, etc.)	ဖြုတ်ချသည်	hpjou' cha. de
overthrow (of government)	ဖြုတ်ချခြင်း	hpjou' cha. chin:
revolution	တော်လှန်ရေး	to hlan jei:
coup d'état	အာဏာသိမ်းခြင်း	a na thein: gjin:
military coup	လက်နက်နှင့် အာဏာ သိမ်းခြင်း	le' ne' hnin.a na dhain: gjin:

crisis	အခက်အခဲကာလ	akhe' akhe: ga la.
economic recession	စီးပွားရေးကျဆင်းခြင်း	si: bwa: jei: gja zin: gjin:
demonstrator (protester)	ဆန္ဒပြသူ	hsan da. bja dhu
demonstration	ဆန္ဒပြပွဲ	hsan da. bja bwe:
martial law	စစ်အခြေအနေ	si' achei anei
military base	စစ်စခန်း	si' sakhan

stability	တည်ငြိမ်မှု	ti njein hnu
stable (adj)	တည်ငြိမ်သော	ti njein de.
exploitation	ခေါင်းပုံဖြတ်ခြင်း	gaun: boun bja' chin:
to exploit (workers)	ခေါင်းပုံဖြတ်သည်	gaun: boun bja' te

racism	လူမျိုးကြီးဝါဒ	lu mjou: gji: wa da.
racist	လူမျိုးရေးခွဲခြားသူ	lu mjou: jei: gwe: gjal dhu
fascism	ဖက်ဆစ်ဝါဒ	hpe' hsi' wa da.
fascist	ဖက်ဆစ်ဝါဒီ	hpe' hsi' wa di

245. Countries. Miscellaneous

| foreigner | နိုင်ငံခြားသား | nain ngan gja: dha: |
| foreign (adj) | နိုင်ငံခြားနှင့် ဆိုင်သော | nain ngan gja: hnin. zain de. |

abroad (in a foreign country)	နိုင်ငံရပ်ခြား	nain ngan ja' cha:
emigrant	အခြားနိုင်ငံတွင် အခြေချသူ	apja: nain ngan dwin agjei gja dhu
emigration	အခြားနိုင်ငံ့တွင် အခြေချခြင်း	apja: nain ngan dwin agjei gja gjin:
to emigrate (vi)	အခြားနိုင်ငံတွင် အခြေချသည်	apja: nain ngan dwin agjei gja de
the West	အနောက်အရပ်	anau' aja'
the East	အရှေ့အရပ်	ashei. aja'
the Far East	အရှေ့ဖျား	ashei. bja:
civilization	လူ့နေမှုစနစ် ထွန်းကားခြင်း	lu nei hma za ni' htun: ga: gjin:
humanity (mankind)	လူသားခြင်းစာနာမှု	lu dha: gjin: za na hmu
the world (earth)	ကမ္ဘာ	ga ba
peace	ငြိမ်းချမ်းရေး	njein: gjan: jei:
worldwide (adj)	ကမ္ဘာတခွင်ဖြစ်နေသော	ga ba ta khwin hpji' nei de.
homeland	မွေးရပ်မြေ	mwei: ja' mjei
people (population)	ပြည်သူလူထု	pji dhu lu du.
population	လူဦးရေ	lu u: ei
people (a lot of ~)	လူများ	lu mja:
nation (people)	လူမျိုး	lu mjou:
generation	မျိုးဆက်	mjou: ze'
territory (area)	နယ်မြေ	ne mjei
region	အပိုင်း	apain:
state (part of a country)	ပြည်နယ်	pji ne
tradition	အစဉ်အလာ	asin ala
custom (tradition)	ဓလေ့	da lei.
ecology	ဂေဟာဗေဒ	gei ha. bei da.
Indian (Native American)	အိန္ဒိယလူမျိုး	indi. ja thu amjou:
Gypsy (masc.)	ဂျစ်ပစီ	gji' pa. si
Gypsy (fem.)	ဂျစ်ပစီမိန်းကလေး	gji' pa. si min: ga. lei
Gypsy (adj)	ဂျစ်ပစီနှင့်ဆိုင်သော	gji' pa. si hnin. zain de.
empire	အင်ပါယာ	in pa jaa
colony	ကိုလိုနီ	kou lou ni
slavery	ကျွန်ဘဝ	kjun: ba. wa.
invasion	ကျူးကျော်ခြင်း	kju: gjo gjin:
famine	ငတ်မွတ်ခြင်းဘေး	nga' mwa' khin: dhei:

246. Major religious groups. Confessions

religion	ဘာသာအယူဝါဒ	ba dha alu wa da.
religious (adj)	ဘာသာရေးကိုင်းရှိုင်းသော	ba dha jei: gain: shin: de.

faith, belief	ယုံကြည်ကိုးကွယ်မှု	joun kji gou: gwe hmu.
to believe (in God)	ယုံကြည်ကိုးကွယ်သည်	joun kji gou: gwe de
believer	ယုံကြည်ကိုးကွယ်သူ	joun kji gou: gwe dhu
atheism	ဖန်ဆင်းရှင်ဘုရား မွဲဝါဒ	hpan zin: shin bu ja: me. wa da.
atheist	ဖန်ဆင်းရှင်ဘုရား မွဲဝါဒ	hpan zin: shin bu ja: me. wa di
Christianity	ခရစ်ယာန်ဘာသာ	khari' jan ba dha
Christian (n)	ခရစ်ယာန်	khari' jan
Christian (adj)	ခရစ်ယာန်နှင့်ဆိုင်သော	khari' jan hnin. zain de
Catholicism	ရှိုမန်ကတ်သလစ်ဝါဒ	jou man ga' tha. li' wa da.
Catholic (n)	ကတ်သလစ်ဝိုက်းဝင်	ka' tha li' goun: win
Catholic (adj)	ကတ်သလစ်နှင့်ဆိုင်သော	ka' tha li' hnin zein de
Protestantism	ပရိုတက်စတင့်ဝါဒ	pa. jou te' sa tin. wa da.
Protestant Church	ပရိုတက်စတင့်အသင်းတော်	pa. jou te' sa tin athin: do
Protestant (n)	ပရိုတက်စတင့်ဝိုက်းဝင်	pa. jou te' sa tin gain: win
Orthodoxy	အော်သိုဒေါ့ဝါဒ	o dhou do. athin wa da.
Orthodox Church	အော်သိုဒေါ့အသင်းတော်	o dhou do. athin: do
Orthodox (n)	အော်သိုဒေါ့နှင့်ဆိုင်သော	o dhou do. athin: de.
Presbyterianism	ပရက်စ်ဘိုင်တီးရီး ယန်းဝါဒ	pa. je's bain di: ji: jan: wa da.
Presbyterian Church	ပရက်စ်ဘိုင်တီးရီး ယန်အသင်းတော်	pa. je's bain di: ji: jan athin: do
Presbyterian (n)	ပရက်စ်ဘိုင်တီးရီး ယန်းဝိုက်းဝင်	pa. je's bain di: ji: jan: gain: win
Lutheranism	လူသာရင်ဝါဒ	lu dha jin wa da.
Lutheran (n)	လူသာရင်ဝိုက်းဝင်	lu dha jin gain: win
Baptist Church	နှစ်ခြင်းအသင်းတော်	hni' chin: a thin: do
Baptist (n)	နှစ်ခြင်းဝိုက်းဝင်	hni' chin: gain: win
Anglican Church	အင်္ဂလိကန်အသင်းတော်	angga. li kan - athin: do
Anglican (n)	အင်္ဂလိကန်ဝိုက်းဝင်	angga. li kan gain win
Mormonism	မောမောန်ဝါဒ	mo maun wa da.
Mormon (n)	မော်မောန်ဝိုက်းဝင်	mo maun gain: win
Judaism	ဂျူးဘာသာ	gju: ba dha
Jew (n)	ဂျူးဘာသာဝင်	gju: ba dha win
Buddhism	ဗုဒ္ဓဘာသာ	bou' da. ba dha
Buddhist (n)	ဗုဒ္ဓဘာသာဝင်	bou' da. ba dha win
Hinduism	ဟိန္ဒူဘာသာ	hin du ba dha
Hindu (n)	ဟိန္ဒူဘာသာဝင်	hin du ba dha win

Islam	အစ္စလမ်ဘာသာ	a' sa. lan ba dha
Muslim (n)	မွတ်စလင်ဘာသာဝင်	mu' sa lin ba dha win
Muslim (adj)	မွတ်စလင်နှင့်ဆိုင်သော	mu' sa lin hnin. zain de.

| Shiah Islam | ရှီးအိုက်အစ္စလာမ်ဂိုဏ်း | shi: ai' asa. lan gain: |
| Shiite (n) | ရှီးအိုက်ထောက်ခံသူ | shi: ai' htau' khan dhu |

| Sunni Islam | ဆွန်နီအစ္စလာမ်ဂိုဏ်း | sun ni i' sa lan gain: |
| Sunnite (n) | ဆွန်နီထောက်ခံသူ | sun ni dau' khan dhu |

247. Religions. Priests

| priest | ခရစ်ယာန်ဘုန်းကြီး | khari' jan boun: gji: |
| the Pope | ပုပ်ရဟန်းမင်းကြီး | pou' ja. han: min: gji: |

monk, friar	ဘုန်းကြီး	hpoun: gji:
nun	သီလရှင်	thi la shin
pastor	သင်းအုပ်ဆရာ	thin: ou' zaja

abbot	ကျောင်းထိုင်ဆရာတော်	kjaun: dain zaja do
vicar (parish priest)	ဗီကာဘုန်းတော်ကြီး	bi ka boun: do kji:
bishop	ဘစ်ရှော့ပ်ဘုန်းကြီး	ba' shau' hpoun: gja:
cardinal	ကာဒီနယ်ဘုန်းကြီး	ka di ne boun: gji:

preacher	ခရစ်ယာန်တရားဟောဆရာ	khari' jan da. ja ho: zaja
preaching	တရာဟောခြင်း	taja ho: gjin:
parishioners	အသွင်းတော်နှင့်သက် ဆိုင်သူများ	athin: do hnin. dha' hsain: dhu mja:

| believer | ယုံကြည်ကိုးကွယ်သူ | joun kji gou: gwe dhu |
| atheist | ဖန်ဆင်းရှင်မရှိ ယုံကြည်သူ | hpan zin: shin ma. shi. joun gji dhu |

248. Faith. Christianity. Islam

| Adam | အာဒံ | adan |
| Eve | ဝဝ | ei wa. |

God	ဘုရား	hpaja:
the Lord	ဘုရားသခင်	hpaja: dha gin
the Almighty	ထာဝရဘုရားသခင်	hta wa. ja. bu. ja: dha. gin

sin	အပြစ်	apja'
to sin (vi)	မကောင်းမှုပြုသည်	ma. gaun: hmu. bju de
sinner (masc.)	မကောင်းမှုပြု လုပ်သူ	ma. gaun: hmu. bju. lou' thu
sinner (fem.)	မကောင်းမှုပြု လုပ်သူ	ma. gaun: hmu. bju. lou' thu

| hell | ငရဲ | nga. je: |
| paradise | ကောင်းကင်ဘုံ | kaun: gin boun |

| Jesus | ယေရှု | jei shu |
| Jesus Christ | ယေရှုခရစ်တော် | jei shu khari' to |

the Holy Spirit	သန့်ရှင်းသော ဝိညာဉ်တော်	than. shin: dho: bein njin do
the Savior	ကယ်တင်ရှင်သခင်	ke din shin dhakhin
the Virgin Mary	ဘုရားသခင်၏ မိခင်အပျိုစင်မာရိ	hpaja: dha gin i. amjou za' ma ji.

the Devil	မကောင်းဆိုးဝါး	ma. gaun: zou: wa:
devil's (adj)	မကွင်းဆိုးဝါးနှင့်ဆိုင်သော	ma. gaun: zou: wa: hnin. zain de.
Satan	စာတန်မာရ်နတ်	hsa tan ma na'
satanic (adj)	စေတန်မာရ်နတ်ဖြစ်သော	sei tan man na' hpji te.

angel	ဘုရားသခင်၏တမန်	hpaja: dha gin i. da man
guardian angel	ကိုယ်စောင့်ကောင်းကင်တမန်	kou zaun. kan: kin da. man
angelic (adj)	အပြစ်ကင်းစင်သော	apja' kin: zin de.

apostle	တမန်တော်	taman do
archangel	ကောင်းကင်တမန်မင်း	kaun: gin da. man min:
the Antichrist	အန္တိခရစ်-ခရစ်တော်ကိုဆန့်ကျင်သူ	anti khari' - khari' to kou zin. kjin dhu

Church	အသင်းတော်	athin: do
Bible	ခရိယာန်သမ္မာကျမ်းစာ	khari' jan dhan ma gjan: za
biblical (adj)	သမ္မာကျမ်းလာ	than ma gjan: la

Old Testament	ဓမ္မဟောင်းကျမ်း	dama. hain gjan:
New Testament	ဓမ္မသစ်ကျမ်း	dama. dha' kjan:
Gospel	ခရစ်ဝင်ကျမ်း	khari' win gjan:
Holy Scripture	သန့်ရှင်းမြင့်မြတ်သော သမ္မာကျမ်းစာ	than. shin: mjin. mja' te. than ma gjan: za

| Heaven | ကောင်းကင်ဘုံ | kaun: gin boun |

Commandment	ကျင့်စောင့်ရမည့် ပညတ်တရား	kjin. zain. ja. mji. ba. nja' ta ja:
prophet	ပရောဖက်	pa. jo. hpe'
prophecy	ကြိုတင်ဟောကိန်း	kjou din ho: kein:

Allah	အလ္လာဟ်	al la'
Mohammed	မိုဟာမက်	mou ha ma'
the Koran	ကိုရန်ကျမ်း	kou jan kjein:

mosque	ဗလီ	bali
mullah	ဗလီဆရာ	bali zaja
prayer	ဆုတောင်းစကား	hsu. daun: zaga:
to pray (vi, vt)	ရှိခိုးသည်	shi. gou: de
pilgrimage	ဘုရားဖူးခရီး	hpaja: hpu: ga ji:

pilgrim	ဘုရားဖူး	hpaja: hpu:
Mecca	မက္ကာမြို့	me' ka mjou.
church	ခရစ်ယာန်ဘုရားကျောင်း	khari' jan bu. ja: gjaun:
temple	ဘုရားကျောင်း	hpaja: gjaun:
cathedral	ဘုရားရှိခိုးကျောင်းတော်	hpaja: gjaun: do:
Gothic (adj)	ဂေါ့သစ်ခံ ဗိသုကာဖြစ်သော	go. dhi' kh bi. dhou ka bji' de
synagogue	ဂျူးဘုရားရှိ မိုးကျောင်း	gju: bou ja: shi. gou: kjaun:
mosque	ဗလီ	bali
chapel	ဝတ်ပြုဆုတောင်းရာနေရာ	wa' pju. u. daun: ja nei ja
abbey	ခရစ်ယာန်ကျောင်းတိုက်	khari' jan gjaun: dai'
convent	သီလရှင်ကျောင်း	thi la shin kjaun:
monastery	ဘုန်းကြီးကျောင်း	hpoun: gji: gjaun:
bell (church ~s)	ခေါင်းလောင်း	gaun: laun:
bell tower	ခေါင်းလောင်းစင်	gaun: laun: zin
to ring (ab. bells)	တီးသည်	ti: de
cross	လက်ဝါးကပ်တိုင်	le' wa: ka' tain
cupola (roof)	လိပ်ခုံးပုံအမိုး	lei' khoun: boun amou:
icon	ခရစ်ယာန်သူတော်စင်ပုံ	khari' jan dhu do zin boun
soul	အသက်ဝိညည်	athe'
fate (destiny)	ကံတရား	kan daja:
evil (n)	အဆိုး	ahsou:
good (n)	ကောင်းမှု	kaun: hma.
vampire	သွေးစုပ်ဖုတ်ကောင်	thwei: zou' hpou' kaun
witch (evil ~)	စုန်းမ	soun: ma.
demon	နတ်ဆိုး	na' hsou:
spirit	ဝိညာဉ်	wi. njan
redemption (giving us ~)	အပြစ်မှကယ်နှုတ် ခံရခြင်း	apja' hma. ge hnou' knan ja. gjin:
to redeem (vt)	အပြစ်မှကယ်နုတ်သည်	apja' hma. ge nou' te
church service, mass	အသင်းတော်ဝတ်ပြုစည်းဝေး	athin: do wu' pju zi: wei:
to say mass	ဝတ်ပြုသည်	wa' pju. de
confession	ဝန်ခံခြင်း	wun khan gjin:
to confess (vi)	အပြစ်ဝန်ခံသည်	apja' wun gan de
saint (n)	သူတော်စင်	thu do zin
sacred (holy)	မြင့်မြတ်သော	mjin. mja' te.
holy water	သန့်ရှင်းမြင့်မြတ်သောရေ	than. shin: mjin. mja' te. jei
ritual (n)	ထုံးတမ်းဓလေ့	htoun: dan: dalei.
ritual (adj)	ထုံးတမ်းဓလေ့ဖြစ်သော	htoun: dan: dalei. bji' te.
sacrifice	ယဇ်ပူဇော်ခြင်း	ji' pu zo gjin:
superstition	အယူသီးခြင်း	aju dhi: gjin:

superstitious (adj)	အယူသီးသော	aju dhi: de
afterlife	တမလွန်	tamalun
eternal life	ထာဝရ ရှင်သန်	hta wa. ja. shin dhan
	ရှင်းဘဝ	gjin: ba. wa.

MISCELLANEOUS

background (green ~)	နောက်ခံ	nau' khan
balance (of situation)	ဟန်ချက်ညီမျှမှု	han gje' nji hma. hmu.
barrier (obstacle)	အတားအဆီး	ata: ahsi;
base (basis)	အခြေခံ	achei khan
beginning	အစ	asa.
category	အမျိုးအစား	amjou: asa:
cause (reason)	အကြောင်း	akjaun:
choice	ရွေးချယ်မှု	jwei: che hmu.
coincidence	တိုက်ဆိုင်မှု	tai' hsain hmu.
comfortable (~ chair)	သက်သောင့်သက်သာရှိသော	the' thaun. dhe' tha shi. de
comparison	နိုင်းယှဉ်ခြင်း	hnain: shin gjin:
compensation	လျော်ကြေး	jo kjei:
degree (extent, amount)	အတိုင်းအတာ	atain: ata
development	ဖွံ့ဖြိုးတိုးတက်မှု	hpjun. bjou: dou: de' hmu.
difference	ကွာဟချက်	kwa ha. che'
effect (e.g., of drugs)	အကျိုးဆက်	akjou: amja' hse'
effort (exertion)	အားထုတ်ကြိုးပမ်းမှု	a: htou' kjou: ban: hmu.
element	အစိတ်အပိုင်း	asei' apain:
end (finish)	အဆုံး	ahsoun:
example (illustration)	နမူနာ	na. mu na
fact	အချက်အလက်	ache' ale'
frequent (adj)	မကြာခဏဖြစ်သော	ma. gja gan bji' de.
growth (development)	ကြီးထွားမှု	kji: htwa: hmu.
help	အကူအညီ	aku anji
ideal	စံပြ	san bja.
kind (sort, type)	အမျိုးအစား	amjou: asa:
labyrinth	ဝင်္ကပါ	win gaba
mistake, error	အမှား	ahma:
moment	အခိုက်	akhai'
object (thing)	အရာ	aja
obstacle	အဟန့်အတား	ahan. ata:
original (original copy)	မူရင်း	mu jin:
part (~ of sth)	အပိုင်း	apain:
particle, small part	အမှုန့်	ahmoun.
pause (break)	ရပ်ခြင်း	ja' chin:

position	နေရာ	nei ja
principle	အခြေခံသဘောတရား	achei khan dha. bo da. ja:
problem	ပြဿနာ	pjadhana
process	ဖြစ်စဉ်	hpji' sin
progress	တိုးတက်မှု	tou: te'
property (quality)	အရည်အချင်း	aji achin:
reaction	တုံ့ပြန်မှု	toun. bjan hmu
risk	စွန့်စားခြင်း	sun. za: gjin:
secret	လျှို့ဝှက်ချက်	shou. hwe' che'
series	အစဉ်	asin
shape (outer form)	ပုံသဏ္ဍာန်	poun thadan
situation	အခြေအနေ	achei anei
solution	ဖြေရှင်းချက်	hpjei shin: gje'
standard (adj)	စံဖြစ်သော	san bji' te.
standard (level of quality)	စံ	san
stop (pause)	ရပ်နားခြင်း	ja' na: gjin:
style	ပုံစံ	poun zan
system	စနစ်	sani'
table (chart)	ဇယား	za ja:
tempo, rate	အရှိန်	ashein
term (word, expression)	ဝေါဟာရ	wo: ha ra.
thing (object, item)	ပစ္စည်း	pji' si:
truth (e.g., moment of ~)	အမှန်တရား	ahman da ja:
turn (please wait your ~)	အလှည့်	ahle.
type (sort, kind)	အမျိုးအစား	amjou: asa:
urgent (adj)	အမြန်လိုသော	aman lou de.
urgently (adv)	အမြန်	aman
utility (usefulness)	အကျိုး	akjou:
variant (alternative)	အမျိုးကွဲ	amjou: asa: gwe:
way (means, method)	နည်းလမ်း	ne: lan:
zone	ဇုန်	zoun

250. Modifiers. Adjectives. Part 1

additional (adj)	ထပ်ဖြည့်သော	hta' hpi. de.
ancient (~ civilization)	ရှေးကျသော	shei: gja. de
artificial (adj)	သဘာဝအတိုင်း မဟုတ်သော	tha. bawa ahtain: ma. hou' te.
back, rear (adj)	နောက်ကျောဖြစ်သော	nau' kjo: bji' te.
bad (adj)	ဆိုးသော	hsou: de.
beautiful (~ palace)	လှပသော	hla. ba. de.
beautiful (person)	လှပသော	hla. ba. de.

big (in size)	ကြီးသော	kji: de.
bitter (taste)	ခါးသော	kha: de.
blind (sightless)	မမြင်ရသော	ma. mjin ja. de.
calm, quiet (adj)	အေးဆေးသော	ei: hsei: de.
careless (negligent)	နမော်နမဲ့နိုင်သော	na. mo na. me nain de.
caring (~ father)	ဂရုစိုက်သော	ga ju. sai' te.
central (adj)	အလယ်ဗဟိုဖြစ်သော	ale ba hou hpji' te.
cheap (low-priced)	ဈေးပေါသော	zei: po: de.
cheerful (adj)	ပျော်ရွှင်သော	pjo shwin de.
children's (adj)	ကလေးများနှင့်ဆိုင်သော	kalei: mja: hnin.zain de.
civil (~ law)	အများပြည်သူနှင့်ဆိုင်သော	amja: pji dhu hnin. zain de.
clandestine (secret)	လျှို့ဝှက်စွာလုပ်သော	shou. hwe' swa lou' te.
clean (free from dirt)	သန့်ရှင်းသော	than. shin: de.
clear (explanation, etc.)	ရှင်းလင်းသော	shin: lin: de.
clever (smart)	သွက်လက်ထက်မြက်သော	thwe' le' the' mja' te.
close (near in space)	နီးသော	ni: de.
closed (adj)	ပိတ်ထားသော	pei' ta: de.
cloudless (sky)	တိမ်ကင်းစင်သော	tain gin: dhin de.
cold (drink, weather)	အေးသော	ei: de.
compatible (adj)	လိုက်ဘက်ညီသော	lai' be' nji de.
contented (satisfied)	ကျေနပ်သော	kjei na' de.
continuous (uninterrupted)	နားချိန်မရှိသော	na: gjein ma. shi. de.
cool (weather)	အေးမြသော	ei: mja. de.
dangerous (adj)	အန္တရာယ်ရှိသော	an dare shi. de.
dark (room)	မှောင်သော	hmaun de.
dead (not alive)	သေနေသော	thei nei de.
dense (fog, smoke)	ထူထပ်သော	htu da' te.
destitute (extremely poor)	ခိုကိုးရာမဲ့သော	khou gou: ja me. de.
different (not the same)	ကွဲပြားခြားနားသော	kwe: bja: gja: na: de.
difficult (decision)	ခက်ခဲသော	khe' khe: de.
difficult (problem, task)	ခက်ခဲသော	khe' khe: de.
dim, faint (light)	မှိန်ဖျသော	hmein bja de.
dirty (not clean)	ညစ်ပတ်သော	nji' pa' te.
distant (in space)	ဝေးသော	wei: de.
dry (clothes, etc.)	ခြောက်သော	chau' de.
easy (not difficult)	လွယ်ကူသော	lwe gu de.
empty (glass, room)	ဘာမျှမရှိသော	ba hmja. ma. shi. de.
even (e.g., ~ surface)	ညီညာပြန့်ပြူးသော	nji nja bjan. bju: de.
exact (amount)	တိကျသော	ti. gja. de.
excellent (adj)	အလွန်ကောင်းသော	alun kaun: de.
excessive (adj)	လွန်ကဲသော	lun ge: de.
expensive (adj)	ဈေးကြီးသော	zei: kji: de.
exterior (adj)	အပြင်ပန်းဖြစ်သော	apjin ban hpja' te.
far (the ~ East)	ဝေးကွာသော	wei: kwa de.

fast (quick)	မြန်သော	mjan de.
fatty (food)	အဆီများသော	ahsi mja: de.
fertile (land, soil)	အကျိုးဖြစ်ထွန်းသော	akjou: hpji' htun. de.
flat (~ panel display)	ညီညာပြန့်ပြူးသော	nji nja bjan. bju: de.
foreign (adj)	နိုင်ငံခြားနှင့်	nain ngan gja: hnin.
	ဆိုင်သော	zain de.
fragile (china, glass)	ကွဲလွယ်သော	kwe: lwe de.
free (at no cost)	အခမဲ့	akha me.
free (unrestricted)	လွတ်လပ်သော	lu' la' de.
fresh (~ water)	ရေချို	jei gjou
fresh (e.g., ~ bread)	လတ်ဆတ်သော	la' hsa' te.
frozen (food)	အေးခဲနေသော	ei: khe: nei de.
full (completely filled)	ပြည့်သော	pjei. de.
gloomy (house, forecast)	မှုန်မှိုင်းနေသော	hmoun hmain: nei de.
good (book, etc.)	ကောင်းသော	kaun: de.
good, kind (kindhearted)	သဘောကောင်းသော	thabo: kaun: de.
grateful (adj)	ကျေးဇူးတင်သော	kjei: zu: din de.
happy (adj)	ပျော်ရွှင်သော	pjo shwin de.
hard (not soft)	မာကြောသော	ma gjo: de.
heavy (in weight)	လေးလံသော	lei: lan de.
hostile (adj)	ရန်လိုသော	jan lou de.
hot (adj)	ပူသော	pu dho:
huge (adj)	အလွန်ကြီးမားသော	alun gji: ma: de.
humid (adj)	စိုထိုင်းသော	sou htain: de
hungry (adj)	ဆာလောင်သော	hsa laun de.
ill (sick, unwell)	နေမကောင်းသော	nei ma. kaun: de.
immobile (adj)	လုပ်ရှားမှုကင်းသော	hlou' sha: hmu. gin: de.
important (adj)	အရေးကြီးသော	ajei: akji: de.
impossible (adj)	မဖြစ်နိုင်သော	ma. bji' nain de.
incomprehensible	နားမလည်နိုင်သော	ma: ma. le nain de.
indispensable (adj)	မရှိမဖြစ်သော	ma. shi ma. bji' te.
inexperienced (adj)	အတွေ့အကြုံမရှိသော	atwei. akjoun ma. shi. dho:
insignificant (adj)	အရေးမပါသော	ajei: ma. ba de.
interior (adj)	အတွင်းပိုင်းဖြစ်သော	atwin: bain: bji' tho:
joint (~ decision)	ပူးတွဲဖြစ်သော	pu: twe: bji' te.
last (e.g., ~ week)	လွန်ခဲ့သော	lun ge. de.
last (final)	နောက်ဆုံးဖြစ်သော	nau' hsoun: bji' te.
left (e.g., ~ side)	ဘယ်	be
legal (legitimate)	ဥပဒေနှင့် ညီညွတ်သော	u. ba. dei hnin. nji nju' te.
light (in weight)	ပေါ့ပါးသော	po. ba: de.
light (pale color)	ဖျော့သော	hpjo. de.
limited (adj)	အကန့်အသတ်ရှိသော	akan. atha' shi. de.
liquid (fluid)	အရည်ဖြစ်သော	aja hpja' te.

long (e.g., ~ hair)	ရှည်လျားသော	shei lja: de.
loud (voice, etc.)	ကျယ်လောင်သော	kje laun de
low (voice)	တိုးသော	tou: dho:

251. Modifiers. Adjectives. Part 2

main (principal)	အဓိက	adi. ka.
matt, matte	မှိုင်းသော	main: dho:
meticulous (job)	စေ့စပ်သော	sei. sa' te.
mysterious (adj)	လျှို့ဝှက်ဆန်းကြယ်သော	shou. hwe' hsan: gje de.
narrow (street, etc.)	ကျဉ်းသော	kjin de.
native (~ country)	မွေးရာဇာတိဖြစ်သော	mwei: ja za di. bji' te.
nearby (adj)	အနီးအနားတွင်ရှိသော	ani: ana: dwin shi. de
nearsighted (adj)	အဝေးမှုန်သော	awei: hmun de.
needed (necessary)	လိုအပ်သော	lou a' de.
negative (~ response)	ဆန့်ကျင်ဘက်ဖြစ်သော	hsan. gjin ba' hpja' te.
neighboring (adj)	အိမ်နီးချင်းဖြစ်သော	ein ni: na: gjin: hpji' tho:
nervous (adj)	စိတ်လှုပ်ရှားသော	sei' hlou' sha: de.
new (adj)	အသစ်ဖြစ်သော	athi' hpji' te.
next (e.g., ~ week)	နောက်ရောက်လာ	nau' jau' la
	မည်ဖြစ်သော	me bji' te.
nice (agreeable)	ချစ်စရာကောင်းသော	chi' saja kaun: de.
pleasant (voice)	သာယာသော	tha ja de.
normal (adj)	ပုံမှန်ဖြစ်သော	poun hman gji' te.
not big (adj)	မကြီးသော	ma. gji: de.
not difficult (adj)	မခက်ခဲသော	ma. ge' khe: de.
obligatory (adj)	မလုပ်မနေဖြစ်သော	ma. lou' ma. nei bji' te.
old (house)	ဟောင်းသော	haun: de.
open (adj)	ဖွင့်ထားသော	hpwin. da: de.
opposite (adj)	ဆန့်ကျင်ဘက်ဖြစ်သော	hsan. gjin ba' hpja' te.
ordinary (usual)	သာမန်ဖြစ်သော	tha man bji' te.
original (unusual)	မူရင်းဖြစ်သော	mu jin: bji' te.
past (recent)	အတိတ်ကဖြစ်သော	ati' ka. hpja' te.
permanent (adj)	အမြဲတမ်းဖြစ်သော	amje: dan: bji' te.
personal (adj)	ကိုယ်ပိုင်	kou bain
polite (adj)	ယဉ်ကျေးသော	jin gjei: de.
poor (not rich)	ဆင်းရဲသော	hsin: je: de.
possible (adj)	ဖြစ်နိုင်သော	hpji' nein de.
present (current)	ပစ္စုပ္ပန်ဖြစ်သော	pji' sou' pan bji' te.
previous (adj)	အရင်ကဖြစ်သော	ajin ka. hpja' de.
principal (main)	အဓိက	adi. ka.
private (~ jet)	ကိုယ်ပိုင်	kou bain
probable (adj)	ဖြစ်နိုင်ခြေရှိသော	hpji' nain gjei shi. de.

prolonged (e.g., ~ applause)	ရှည်ကြာသော	shei gja de.
public (open to all)	အများပြည်သူနှင့်ဆိုင်သော	amja: pji dhu hnin. zain de.
punctual (person)	အချိန်မှန်ကန်ဝီ ကျသော	achein hman kan ti. gja. de.
quiet (tranquil)	တိတ်ဆိတ်သော	tei' hsei' te
rare (adj)	ရှားပါးသော	sha: ba: de.
raw (uncooked)	အစိမ်းသက်သက်ဖြစ်သော	asain: dhe' dhe' hpja' te.
right (not left)	ညာဘက်	nja be'
right, correct (adj)	မှန်ကန်သော	hman gan de.
ripe (fruit)	မှည့်သော	hme. de.
risky (adj)	အန္တရာယ်များသော	an dare mja: de.
sad (~ look)	ဝမ်းနည်းသော	wan: ne: de.
sad (depressing)	ဝမ်းနည်းသော	wan: ne: de.
safe (not dangerous)	လုံခြုံသော	loun gjoun de.
salty (food)	ငန်သော	ngan de.
satisfied (customer)	အားရကျေနပ်သော	a: ei kjei nin de.
second hand (adj)	သုံးပြီးသားဖြစ်သော	thoun: bji: dha: bji' te.
shallow (water)	တိမ်သော	tein de
sharp (blade, etc.)	ရှုန်ထက်သော	chwan de' te.
short (in length)	တိုသော	tou de.
short, short-lived (adj)	တိုတောင်းသော	tou daun: de.
significant (notable)	အရေးရောက်သော	aja jau' de.
similar (adj)	တူညီသော	tu nji de.
simple (easy)	လွယ်ကူသော	lwe gu de.
skinny	ပိန်ကပ်ကပ်ဖြစ်သော	pein ga' ka' hpji' te.
small (in size)	သေးသော	thei: de.
smooth (surface)	ချောမွတ်သော	cho: mu' te.
soft (~ toys)	နူးညံ့သော	nu: njan. de.
solid (~ wall)	အစိုင်အခဲဖြစ်သော	asoun akhe:
sour (flavor, taste)	ချဉ်သော	q'useaa
spacious (house, etc.)	ကျယ်ဝန်းသော	kje wan de.
special (adj)	အထူးဖြစ်သော	a htu: hpja' te.
straight (line, road)	ဖြောင့်တန်းသော	hpjaun. dan: de.
strong (person)	သန်မာသော	than ma de.
stupid (foolish)	မိုက်မဲ ထုံထိုင်းသော	mai' me: doun dain: de.
suitable (e.g., ~ for drinking)	အသုံးဝင်သော	athoun: win de.
sunny (day)	နေသာသော	nei dha de.
superb, perfect (adj)	ထိပ်တန်းဖြစ်သော	htei' tan: hpi' te.
swarthy (adj)	ညိုသော	njou de.
sweet (sugary)	ချိုသော	chou de.
tan (adj)	အသားညိုသော	atha: njou de.

tasty (delicious)	အရသာရှိသော	aja. dha shi. de.
tender (affectionate)	ကြင်နာသနားတတ်သော	kjin na dha. na: da' de.
the highest (adj)	အမြင့်ဆုံးဖြစ်သော	amjin. zoun: bje' te.
the most important	အရေးအကြီးဆုံးသော	ajei: akji: zoun: de.
the nearest	အနီးဆုံး	ani: zoun:
the same, equal (adj)	တူညီသော	tu nji de.
thick (e.g., ~ fog)	ထူထပ်သော	htu da' te.
thick (wall, slice)	ထူသော	htu de.
thin (person)	ပိန်သော	pein de.
tight (~ shoes)	ကျပ်သော	kja' te.
tired (exhausted)	ပင်ပန်းသော	pin ban: de.
tiring (adj)	ပင်ပန်းနေသော	pin ban: nei de
transparent (adj)	ဖောက်ထွင်းမြင်နိုင်သော	hpau' htwin: mjin nain de.
unclear (adj)	မရှင်းလင်းသော	ma. shin: lin: de.
unique (exceptional)	ပြိုင်ဘက်ကင်းသော	pjain be' kin: de.
various (adj)	အမျိုးစုံသော	amjou: zoun de.
warm (moderately hot)	နွေးထွေးသော	nwei: dwei: de.
wet (e.g., ~ clothes)	စိုစွတ်သော	sou zu' te.
whole (entire, complete)	အားလုံးဖြစ်သော	a: loun: bji' te.
wide (e.g., ~ road)	ကျယ်သော	kje de.
young (adj)	ငယ်ရွယ်သော	ngwe jwe de.

MAIN 500 VERBS

252. Verbs A-C

to accompany (vt)	လိုက်ပို့သည်	lai' pou. de
to accuse (vt)	စွပ်စွဲသည်	su' swe: de
to acknowledge (admit)	ဝန်ခံသည်	wun khan de
to act (take action)	ပြုလုပ်သည်	pju. lou' te
to add (supplement)	ထည့်သည်	hte de.
to address (speak to)	အမည်တပ်သည်	amji din te
to admire (vi)	ရှိးကျူးသည်	chi: kju: de
to advertise (vt)	ကြော်ငြာသည်	kjo nja de
to advise (vt)	အကြံပေးသည်	akjan bei: de
to affirm (assert)	အခိုင်အမာပြောဆိုသည်	akhain ama pjo hsou de
to agree (say yes)	သဘောတူသည်	dhabo: tu de
to aim (to point a weapon)	ချိန်သည်	chein de
to allow (sb to do sth)	ခွင့်ပြုသည်	khwin bju. de
to amputate (vt)	ဖြတ်တောက်ကုသသည်	hpja' tau' ku. dha de
to answer (vi, vt)	ဖြေသည်	hpjei de
to apologize (vi)	တောင်းပန်သည်	thaun: ban de
to appear (come into view)	ပေါ်လာသည်	po la de
to applaud (vi, vt)	လက်ခုပ်ဩဘာပေးသည်	le' khou' thja ba bei: de
to appoint (assign)	ခန့်အပ်သည်	khan. a' te
to approach (come closer)	ချဉ်းကပ်သည်	chan: ga' te
to arrive (ab. train)	လာရောက်သည်	la jau' te
to ask (~ sb to do sth)	တောင်းဆိုသည်	taun: hsou: de
to aspire to ...	ရည်မှန်းသည်	ji hman: de
to assist (help)	ကူညီသည်	ku nji de
to attack (mil.)	တိုက်ခိုက်သည်	tai' hsai' te
to attain (objectives)	ရရှိသည်	ja. hji. de
to avenge (get revenge)	လက်စားရှေသည်	le' sa: gjei de
to avoid (danger, task)	ရှောင်သည်	shaun de
to award (give medal to)	ရီးမြှင့်သည်	chi: hmjin. de
to battle (vi)	တိုက်သည်	tai' te
to be (~ a teacher)	ဖြစ်သည်	hpji' te
to be (~ on a diet)	ဖြစ်နေသည်	hpji' nei de
to be a cause of ...	အကြောင်းရင်းဖြစ်သည်	akjaun: jin: hpji' te
to be afraid	ကြောက်သည်	kjau' te

to be angry (with …)	စိတ်ဆိုးသည်	sei' hsou: de
to be at war	စစ်ပွဲတွင်ပါဝင်ဆင် နွဲသည်	si' pwe: dwin ba win zin hnwe: de
to be based (on …)	အခြေခံသည်	achei khan dhe
to be bored	ပျင်းသည်	pjin: de
to be convinced	လက်ခံယုံကြည်စေသည်	le' khan joun gji zei de
to be enough	လုံလောက်သည်	loun lau' te
to be envious	မနာလိုဖြစ်သည်	ma. na lou bji' te
to be indignant	မခံမရပ်နိုင်ဖြစ်သည်	ma. gan ma. ja' nain bji' te
to be interested in …	စိတ်ဝင်စားသည်	sei' win za: de
to be lost in thought	တွေးသည်	twei: de
to be lying (~ on the table)	တည်ရှိသည်	ti shi. de
to be needed	အလိုရှိသည်	alou' shi. de
to be perplexed (puzzled)	စိတ်ရှုပ်ထွေးသည်	sei' shou' htwei: de
to be preserved	မပျက်မစီးဖြစ်နေသည်	ma. bje: ma. zi: bji' nei de
to be required	လိုအပ်သည်	lou a' te
to be surprised	အံ့ဩသည်	an. o. de
to be worried	စိတ်ပူသည်	sei' pu de
to beat (to hit)	ရိုက်သည်	jai' te
to become (e.g., ~ old)	ဖြစ်လာသည်	hpji' la de
to behave (vi)	ပြုမူဆက်ဆံသည်	pju. hmu. ze' hsan de
to believe (think)	ယုံကြည်သည်	joun kji de
to belong to …	ပိုင်ဆိုင်သည်	pain zain de
to berth (moor)	ဆိုက်ကပ်သည်	hseu' ka' de
to blind (other drivers)	ကန်းစေသည်	kan: zei de
to blow (wind)	တိုက်ခတ်သည်	tai' hsai' te
to blush (vi)	မျက်နှာနီသည်	mje' hna ni de
to boast (vi)	ကြွားသည်	kjwa: de
to borrow (money)	ရေးယူသည်	chei: dhu de
to break (branch, toy, etc.)	ဖျက်ဆီးသည်	hpje' hsi: de
to breathe (vi)	အသက်ရှူသည်	athe' shu de
to bring (sth)	ယူလာသည်	ju la de
to burn (paper, logs)	မီးရှို့သည်	mi: shou. de
to buy (purchase)	ဝယ်သည်	we de
to call (~ for help)	ခေါ်သည်	kho de
to call (yell for sb)	ခေါ်သည်	kho de
to calm down (vt)	ငြိမ်သက်စေသည်	njein dhe' sei de
can (v aux)	တတ်နိုင်သည်	ta' nain de
to cancel (call off)	ပယ်ဖျက်သည်	pe hpje' te
to cast off (of a boat or ship)	စွန့်ပစ်သည်	sun. bi' de
to catch (e.g., ~ a ball)	ဖမ်းသည်	hpan: de
to change (~ one's opinion)	ပြောင်းလဲသည်	pjaun: le: de

English	Burmese	Pronunciation
to change (exchange)	ပြောင်းလဲသည်	pjaun: le: de
to charm (vt)	ညှို့သည်	hnjou. de
to choose (select)	ရွေးသည်	jwei: de
to chop off (with an ax)	ခုတ်ဖြတ်သည်	khou' bja' te
to clean (e.g., kettle from scale)	သန့်ရှင်းရေးလုပ်သည်	than. shin: jei: lou' te
to clean (shoes, etc.)	သန့်ရှင်းအောင်လုပ်သည်	than. shin: aun: lou' te
to clean up (tidy)	သန့်ရှင်းရေးလုပ်သည်	than. shin: jei: lou' te
to close (vt)	ပိတ်သည်	pei' te
to comb one's hair	ဖြီးသည်	hpji: de
to come down (the stairs)	အောက်ဆင်းသည်	au' hsin: de
to come out (book)	ထွက်သည်	htwe' te
to compare (vt)	နှိုင်းယှဉ်သည်	hnain: shin de
to compensate (vt)	လျော်ကြေးပေးသည်	jo kjei: bei: de
to compete (vi)	ပြိုင်ဆိုင်သည်	pjain zain de
to compile (~ a list)	ရေးဆွဲသည်	jei: zwe: de
to complain (vi, vt)	တိုင်ပြောသည်	tain bjo: de
to complicate (vt)	ခဲနက်စေသည်	khe: ga' sei de
to compose (music, etc.)	ရေးဖွဲ့သီကုံးသည်	jei: bwe dhi goun: de
to compromise (reputation)	နာမည်ဖျက်သည်	na me bje' te
to concentrate (vi)	အာရုံစူးစိုက်သည်	a joun su: zai' dhi
to confess (criminal)	ဝန်ခံသည်	wun khan de
to confuse (mix up)	ရောထွေးသည်	jo: dwei: de
to congratulate (vt)	ဂုဏ်ပြုသည်	goun bju de
to consult (doctor, expert)	တိုင်ပင်သည်	tain bin de
to continue (~ to do sth)	ဆက်လုပ်သည်	hse' lou' te
to control (vt)	ထိန်းချုပ်သည်	htein: gjou' te
to convince (vt)	လက်ခံယုံကြည်စေသည်	le' khan joun gji zei de
to cooperate (vi)	ပူးပေါင်းဆောင်ရွက်သည်	pu: baun: zaun jwe' te
to coordinate (vt)	ညှိနှိုင်းဆောင်ရွက်သည်	hnji. hnain: zaun jwe' te
to correct (an error)	အမှားပြင်သည်	ahma: pjin de
to cost (vt)	ကုန်ကျသည်	koun kja de
to count (money, etc.)	ရေတွက်သည်	jei dwe' te
to count on …	အားကိုးသည်	a: kou: de
to crack (ceiling, wall)	အက်ကွဲသည်	e' kwe: de
to create (vt)	ဖန်တီးသည်	hpan di: de
to crush, to squash (~ a bug)	ဖိသတ်သည်	hpi. dha' te
to cry (weep)	ငိုသည်	ngou de
to cut off (with a knife)	ဖြတ်သည်	hpja' te

253. Verbs D-G

to dare (~ to do sth)	လုပ်ရဲသည်	lou' je: de
to date from …	ရက်စွဲတပ်သည်	je' swe: da' te
to deceive (vi, vt)	လိမ်ပြောသည်	lain bjo: de
to decide (~ to do sth)	ဆုံးဖြတ်သည်	hsoun: hpja' te
to decorate (tree, street)	အလှဆင်သည်	ahla. zin dhe
to dedicate (book, etc.)	ရည်ညွှန်းသည်	ji hman: de
to defend (a country, etc.)	ကာကွယ်သည်	ka gwe de
to defend oneself	ခုခံသည်	khu. gan de
to demand (request firmly)	တိုက်တွန်းသည်	tai' tun: de
to denounce (vt)	လူသိရှင်ကြားစွပ် စွဲရှတ်ချသည်	lu dhi shin gja: zu' swe: sha' khja. de
to deny (vt)	ငြင်းပယ်သည်	njin: be de
to depend on …	မူတည်သည်	mu de de
to deprive (vt)	ပိတ်ပင်ထားသည်	pei' hsou. da: de
to deserve (vt)	ထိုက်တန်သည်	htai' tan de
to design (machine, etc.)	ပုံစံဆွဲသည်	poun zan zwe: de
to desire (want, wish)	လိုချင်သည်	lou gjin de
to despise (vt)	အထင်သေးသည်	a htin dhei: de
to destroy (documents, etc.)	ဖျက်ဆီးသည်	hpje' hsi: de
to differ (from sth)	ခြားနားသည်	hpja: na: de
to dig (tunnel, etc.)	တူးသည်	tu: de
to direct (point the way)	ဦးတည်သည်	u: te de
to disappear (vi)	ပျောက်ကွယ်သည်	pjau' kwe de
to discover (new land, etc.)	ရှာဖွေတွေ့ရှိသည်	sha hpwei dwei. shi. de
to discuss (vt)	ဆွေးနွေးသည်	hswe: nwe: de
to distribute (leaflets, etc.)	ဖြန့်ဝေသည်	hpjan. wei de
to disturb (vt)	နောင့်ယှက်သည်	hnaun. hje' te
to dive (vi)	ရေငုပ်သည်	jei ngou' te
to divide (math)	စားသည်	sa: de
to do (vt)	ပြုလုပ်သည်	pju lou' te
to do the laundry	လျှော်ဖွပ်သည်	sho ba' de
to double (increase)	နှစ်ဆဖြစ်စေသည်	hni' has. bji' sei de
to doubt (have doubts)	သံသယဖြစ်သည်	than thaja. bji' te
to draw a conclusion	ကောက်ချက်ချသည်	kau' che' cha. de
to dream (daydream)	စိတ်ကူးယဉ်သည်	sei' ku: jin de
to dream (in sleep)	အိပ်မက်မက်သည်	ei' me' me' te
to drink (vi, vt)	သောက်သည်	thau' te
to drive a car	ကားမောင်းသည်	ka: maun: de
to drive away (scare away)	မောင်းထုတ်သည်	maun: dou' te
to drop (let fall)	ဖြုတ်ချသည်	hpjou' cha. de

to drown (ab. person)	ရေနစ်သည်	jei ni' te
to dry (clothes, hair)	အခြောက်လှန်းသည်	a chou' hlan: de
to eat (vi, vt)	စားသည်	sa: de
to eavesdrop (vi)	ချောင်းပြီးနားထောင်သည်	gaun: bji: na: daun de
to emit (diffuse - odor, etc.)	ပြန့်သည်	pjan. de
to enjoy oneself	ပျော်ရွှင်သည်	pjo shwin de
to enter (on the list)	ထည့်သွင်းရေးထားသည်	hte dhwin: jei: da: de
to enter (room, house, etc.)	ဝင်သည်	win de
to entertain (amuse)	ဖျော်ဖြေသည်	hpjo bjei de
to equip (fit out)	တပ်ဆင်သည်	ta' hsin de
to examine (proposal)	စဉ်းစားသည်	sin: za: de
to exchange (sth)	အပြန်အလှန်လဲသည်	apjan a hlan le: de
to excuse (forgive)	ခွင့်လွှတ်သည်	khwin. hlu' te
to exist (vi)	တည်ရှိသည်	ti shi. de
to expect (anticipate)	မျှော်လင့်သည်	hmjo. lin. de
to expect (foresee)	ကြိုမြင်သည်	kjou mjin de
to expel (from school, etc.)	ထုတ်သည်	tou' te
to explain (vt)	ရှင်းပြသည်	shin: bja. de
to express (vt)	ဖော်ပြသည်	hpjo bja. de
to extinguish (a fire)	မီးငြိမ်းသတ်သည်	mi: njein: dha' te
to fall in love (with …)	ချစ်မိသည်	chi' mi. de
to feed (provide food)	အစာကျွေးသည်	asa gjwei: de.
to fight (against the enemy)	တိုက်ခိုက်သည်	tai' hsai' te
to fight (vi)	ခိုက်ရန်ဖြစ်သည်	khai' jan bji' te
to fill (glass, bottle)	ဖြည့်သည်	hpjei. de
to find (~ lost items)	ရှာတွေ့သည်	sha dwei. de
to finish (vt)	ပြီးသည်	pji: de
to fish (angle)	ငါးဖမ်းသည်	nga: ban: de
to fit (ab. dress, etc.)	သင့်တော်သည်	thin. do de
to flatter (vt)	မြှောက်သည်	hmjau' de
to fly (bird, plane)	ပျံသည်	pjan de
to follow … (come after)	လိုက်သည်	lai' te
to forbid (vt)	တားမြစ်သည်	ta: mji' te
to force (compel)	အတင်းလုပ်ခိုင်းသည်	atin: lou' khain: dhe
to forget (vi, vt)	မေ့သည်	mei. de
to forgive (pardon)	ခွင့်လွှတ်သည်	khwin. hlu' te
to form (constitute)	ဖွဲ့စည်းသည်	hpwe. zi: de
to get dirty (vi)	ညစ်ပေသွားသည်	nji' pei dhwa: de
to get infected (with …)	ကူးစက်သည်	ku: ze' te
to get irritated	ဒေါသထွက်သည်	do: dha. dwe' de

| to get married | မိန်းမယူသည် | mein: ma. ju de |
| to get rid of … | ရှင်းပစ်သည် | shin: ba' te |

to get tired	ပင်ပန်းသည်	pin ban: de
to get up (arise from bed)	အိပ်ရာထသည်	ei' ja hta. de
to give (vt)	ပေးသည်	pei: de
to give a bath (to bath)	ရေချိုးပေးသည်	jei gjou bei: de

to give a hug, to hug (vt)	ဖက်သည်	hpe' te
to give in (yield to)	အလျှော့ပေးသည်	asho. bei: de
to glimpse (vt)	လျပ်တပျက်မြင်သည်	lja' ta bje' mjin de
to go (by car, etc.)	သွားသည်	thwa: de

to go (on foot)	သွားသည်	thwa: de
to go for a swim	ရေကူးသည်	jei ku: de
to go out (for dinner, etc.)	ထွက်သည်	htwe' te
to go to bed (go to sleep)	အိပ်ရာဝင်သည်	ei' ja win de

to greet (vt)	နှုတ်ဆက်သည်	hnou' hsei' te
to grow (plants)	စိုက်ပျိုးသည်	sai' pjou: de
to guarantee (vt)	အာမခံပေးသည်	a ma. gan bei: de
to guess (the answer)	မှန်းဆသည်	hman za de

254. Verbs H-M

to hand out (distribute)	ဝေငှသည်	wei hnga. de
to hang (curtains, etc.)	ချိတ်သည်	chei' te
to have (vt)	ရှိသည်	shi. de
to have a try	စမ်းကြည့်သည်	san: kji. de
to have breakfast	နံနက်စာစားသည်	nan ne' za za: de

to have dinner	ညစာစားသည်	nja. za za: de
to have lunch	နေ့လယ်စာစားသည်	nei. le za za de
to head (group, etc.)	ဦးဆောင်သည်	u: zaun de
to hear (vt)	ကြားသည်	ka: de
to heat (vt)	နွေးသည်	hnwei: de

to help (vt)	ကူညီသည်	ku nji de
to hide (vt)	ဖုံးကွယ်သည်	hpoun: gwe de
to hire (e.g., ~ a boat)	ငှါးရမ်းသည်	hna: jan: de
to hire (staff)	လုပ်အားငှါးသည်	lou' a: hnga: de
to hope (vi, vt)	မျှော်လင့်သည်	hmjo. lin. de

to hunt (for food, sport)	အမဲလိုက်သည်	ame: lai' de
to hurry (vi)	အလျင်စလိုပြုသည်	aljin za lou pju. de
to imagine (to picture)	စိတ်ကူးသည်	sei' ku: de
to imitate (vt)	အတုလုပ်သည်	atu. lou' te
to implore (vt)	အနူးအညွတ်တောင်းပန်သည်	anu: anwi' taun: ban de
to import (vt)	တင်သွင်းသည်	tin dhwin: de
to increase (vi)	မြင့်တက်သည်	mjin. da' te

to increase (vt)	မြှင့်တင်သည်	hmja. din de
to infect (vt)	ရောဂါကူးသည်	jo ga gu: de
to influence (vt)	သြဇာလွှမ်းသည်	o: za hlan: de
to inform (e.g., ~ the police about …)	အကြောင်းကြားသည်	akjaun: kja: de
to inform (vt)	အကြောင်းကြားသည်	akjaun: kja: de
to inherit (vt)	အမွေဆက်ခံသည်	amwei ze' khan de
to inquire (about …)	စုံစမ်းသည်	soun zan: de
to insert (put in)	ထည့်သည်	hte de.
to insinuate (imply)	စောင်းပြောသည်	saun: bjo: de
to insist (vi, vt)	တိုက်တွန်းပြောဆိုသည်	tou' tun: bjo: zou de
to inspire (vt)	အားပေးသည်	a: bei: de
to instruct (teach)	ညွှန်ကြားသည်	hnjun gja: de
to insult (offend)	စော်ကားသည်	so ga: de
to interest (vt)	စိတ်ဝင်စားစေသည်	sei' win za: zei de
to intervene (vi)	ကြားဝင်သည်	ka: win de
to introduce (sb to sb)	မိတ်ဆက်ပေးသည်	mi' hse' pei: de
to invent (machine, etc.)	တီထွင်သည်	ti htwin de
to invite (vt)	ဖိတ်သည်	hpi' de
to iron (clothes)	မီးပူတိုက်သည်	mi: bu tai' te
to irritate (annoy)	ဒေါသထွက်အောင်လုပ်သည်	do: dha. dwe' aun lou' te
to isolate (vt)	ခွဲခြားထားသည်	khwe: gja: da: de
to join (political party, etc.)	ပေါင်းစပ်သည်	paun: za' te
to joke (be kidding)	စနောက်သည်	sanau' te
to keep (old letters, etc.)	သိမ်းဆည်းသည်	thain: zain: de
to keep silent, to hush	နှုတ်ဆိတ်သည်	hnou' hsei' te
to kill (vt)	သတ်သည်	tha' te
to knock (on the door)	တံခါးခေါက်သည်	daga: khau' te
to know (sb)	သိသည်	thi. de
to know (sth)	သိသည်	thi. de
to laugh (vi)	ရယ်သည်	je de
to launch (start up)	စတင်သည်	sa. tin de
to leave (~ for Mexico)	ထွက်ခွာသည်	htwe' kha de
to leave (forget sth)	ချန်သည်	chan de
to leave (spouse)	ပစ်ထားသည်	pi' hta: de
to liberate (city, etc.)	လွတ်မြောက်စေသည်	lu' mjau' sei de
to lie (~ on the floor)	လှဲသည်	hle: de
to lie (tell untruth)	လိမ်ပြောသည်	lain bjo: de
to light (campfire, etc.)	မီးညှိသည်	mi: hnji de
to light up (illuminate)	မီးထွန်းသည်	mi: dwan: de
to like (I like …)	ကြိုက်သည်	kjai' de
to limit (vt)	ချုပ်ချယ်သည်	chou' che de
to listen (vi)	နားထောင်သည်	na: daun de
to live (~ in France)	နေထိုင်သည်	nei dain de

to live (exist)	ေနသည်	nei de
to load (gun)	ကျည်ထိုးသည်	kji dou: de
to load (vehicle, etc.)	ကုန်တင်သည်	koun din de

to look (I'm just ~ing)	ကြည့်သည်	kji. de
to look for ... (search)	ရှာသည်	sha de
to look like (resemble)	တူသည်	tu de
to lose (umbrella, etc.)	ပျောက်သည်	pjau' te
to love (e.g., ~ dancing)	ကြိုက်သည်	kjai' de

to love (sb)	ချစ်သည်	chi' te
to lower (blind, head)	အောက်ချသည်	au' cha. de
to make (~ dinner)	ချက်ပြုတ်သည်	che' pjou' te
to make a mistake	မှားသည်	hma: de
to make angry	စိတ်ဆိုးအောင်လုပ်သည်	sei' hsou: aun lou' te

to make easier	လွယ်စေသည်	lwe zei de
to make multiple copies	မိတ္တူကူးသည်	mi' tu gu: de
to make the acquaintance	မိတ်ဆက်သည်	mi' hse' te
to make use (of ...)	သုံးစွဲသည်	thoun: zwe: de
to manage, to run	ညွှန်ကြားသည်	hnjun gja: de

to mark (make a mark)	မှတ်သည်	hma' te
to mean (signify)	ဆိုလိုသည်	hsou lou de
to memorize (vt)	မှတ်ထားသည်	hma' hta: de
to mention (talk about)	ဖော်ပြသည်	hpjo bja. de
to miss (school, etc.)	ပျက်ကွက်သည်	pje' kwe' te

to mix (combine, blend)	ရောသည်	jo: de
to mock (make fun of)	သရော်သည်	thajo: de
to move (to shift)	ရွှေ့သည်	shwei. de
to multiply (math)	မြှောက်သည်	hmjau' de
must (v aux)	ရမည်	ja. me

255. Verbs N-R

to name, to call (vt)	အမည်ပေးသည်	amji bei: de
to negotiate (vi)	စေ့စပ်ညှိနှိုင်းသည်	sei. sa' njou hmain: de
to note (write down)	ရေးမှတ်သည်	jei: hma' te
to notice (see)	သတိထားမိသည်	dhadi. da: mi. de

to obey (vi, vt)	လိုက်နာသည်	lai' na de
to object (vi, vt)	ငြင်းသည်	njin: de
to observe (see)	စောင့်ကြည့်သည်	saun. gji. de
to offend (vt)	စိတ်ထိခိုက်စေသည်	sei' hti. gai' sei de
to omit (word, phrase)	ပယ်သည်	pe de

to open (vt)	ဖွင့်သည်	hpwin. de
to order (in restaurant)	မှာသည်	hma de
to order (mil.)	အမိန့်ပေးသည်	amin. bei: de

to organize (concert, party)	ကျင်းပသည်	kjin: ba. de
to overestimate (vt)	တန်ဖိုးပြန်ဖြတ်သည်	tan bou: bjan bja' te
to own (possess)	ပိုင်ဆိုင်သည်	pain zain de
to participate (vi)	ပါဝင်ဆင်နွှဲသည်	pa win zin hnwe: de
to pass through (by car, etc.)	ဖြတ်သွားသည်	hpja' thwa: de
to pay (vi, vt)	ပေးချေသည်	pei: gjei de
to peep, spy on	ချောင်းကြည့်သည်	chaun: gje. de
to penetrate (vt)	ထိုးဖောက်သည်	tou: bau' te
to permit (vt)	ခွင့်ပြုသည်	khwin bju. de
to pick (flowers)	ခူးသည်	khu: de
to place (put, set)	နေရာချသည်	nei ja gja de
to plan (~ to do sth)	စီစဉ်သည်	si zin de
to play (actor)	သရုပ်ဆောင်သည်	thajou' hsaun de
to play (children)	ကစားသည်	gaza: de
to point (~ the way)	ညွှန်ပြသည်	hnjun bja. de
to pour (liquid)	လောင်းထဲ့သည်	laun: de. de
to pray (vi, vt)	ရှိခိုးသည်	shi. gou: de
to prefer (vt)	ပိုကြိုက်သည်	pou gjai' te
to prepare (~ a plan)	ပြင်ဆင်သည်	pjin zin de
to present (sb to sb)	မိတ်ဆက်ပေးသည်	mi' hse' pei: de
to preserve (peace, life)	ထိန်းသည်	htein: de
to prevail (vt)	လွှမ်းမိုးသည်	hlwan: mou: de
to progress (move forward)	တိုးတက်သည်	tu: te' te
to promise (vt)	ကတိပေးသည်	gadi pei: de
to pronounce (vt)	အသံထွက်သည်	athan dwe' te
to propose (vt)	အဆိုပြုသည်	ahsou bju. de
to protect (e.g., ~ nature)	ကာကွယ်စောင့်ရှောက်သည်	ka gwe zaun. sha' te
to protest (vi)	ကန့်ကွက်သည်	kan gwe' te
to prove (vt)	သက်သေပြသည်	the' thei pja. de
to provoke (vt)	ရန်စသည်	jan za de
to pull (~ the rope)	ဆွဲသည်	hswe: de
to punish (vt)	အပြစ်ပေးသည်	apja' pei: de
to push (~ the door)	တွန်းသည်	tun: de
to put away (vt)	သိမ်းဆည်းသည်	thain: zain: de
to put in order	အစီအစဉ်တကျထားသည်	asi asin da. gja. da: de
to put, to place	ထားသည်	hta: de
to quote (cite)	ကိုးကားသည်	kou: ga: de
to reach (arrive at)	ရောက်သည်	jau' te
to read (vi, vt)	ဖတ်သည်	hpa' te
to realize (a dream)	ဆောင်ရွက်သည်	hsaun jwe' te
to recognize (identify sb)	မှတ်မိသည်	hma' mi. de

to recommend (vt)	အကြံပြုထောက်ခံသည်	akjan pju htau' khan de
to recover (~ from flu)	ရောဂါပျောက်သည်	jo ga bjau' te
to redo (do again)	ပြန်ပြင်သည်	pjan bjin de
to reduce (speed, etc.)	လျှော့သည်	sho. de

to refuse (~ sb)	ငြင်းဆန်သည်	njin: zan de
to regret (be sorry)	နောင်တရသည်	naun da. ja. de
to reinforce (vt)	ခိုင်မာစေသည်	khain ma zei de
to remember (Do you ~ me?)	မှတ်မိသည်	hma' mi. de

to remember (I can't ~ her name)	သတိရသည်	dhadi. ja. de
to remind of …	သတိပေးသည်	dhadi. pei: de
to remove (~ a stain)	ဖယ်ရှားသည်	hpe sha: de
to remove (~ an obstacle)	ဖယ်ရှားသည်	hpe sha: de

to rent (sth from sb)	ငှားသည်	hnga: de
to repair (mend)	ပြင်သည်	pjin de
to repeat (say again)	ထပ်လုပ်သည်	hta' lou' te
to report (make a report)	သတင်းပို့သည်	dhadin: bou. de

to reproach (vt)	အပြစ်တင်သည်	apja' tin te
to reserve, to book	မှာသည်	hma de
to restrain (hold back)	တားဆီးသည်	ta: zi: de
to return (come back)	ပြန်သည်	pjan de

to risk, to take a risk	စွန့်စားသည်	sun. za: de
to rub out (erase)	ဖျက်ပစ်သည်	hpje' pa' te
to run (move fast)	ပြေးသည်	pjei: de
to rush (hurry sb)	လောသည်	lo de

256. Verbs S-W

to satisfy (please)	ကျေနပ်စေသည်	kjei na' sei de
to save (rescue)	ကယ်ဆယ်သည်	ke ze de
to say (~ thank you)	ပြောသည်	pjo: de
to scold (vt)	ဆူသည်	hsu. de

to scratch (with claws)	ကုတ်သည်	kou' te
to select (to pick)	ရွေးချယ်သည်	jwei: che de
to sell (goods)	ရောင်းသည်	jaun: de
to send (a letter)	ပို့သည်	pou. de

to send back (vt)	ပြန်ပို့သည်	pjan bou. de
to sense (~ danger)	အာရုံခံစားသည်	a joun gan za: dhi
to sentence (vt)	ပြစ်ဒဏ်ပေးသည်	pji' dan bei: de
to serve (in restaurant)	တာဝန်ခင်းသည်	ti khin: de
to settle (a conflict)	ဖြေရှင်းသည်	hpjei shin: de
to shake (vt)	လှုပ်ခါသည်	hlou' kha de

to shave (vi)	ရိတ်သည်	jei' te
to shine (gleam)	မီးရောင်ထွက်သည်	mi: jaun htwe' te
to shiver (with cold)	တုန်သည်	toun de
to shoot (vi)	ပစ်သည်	pi' te
to shout (vi)	အော်သည်	o de
to show (to display)	ပြသည်	pja. de
to shudder (vi)	သိမ့်သိမ့်တုန်သည်	thein. dhein. doun de
to sigh (vi)	သက်ပြင်းချသည်	the' pjin: gja. de
to sign (document)	လက်မှတ်ထိုးသည်	le' hma' htou: de
to signify (mean)	ဆိုလိုသည်	hsou lou de
to simplify (vt)	လွယ်ကူစေသည်	lwe gu zei de
to sin (vi)	မကောင်းမှုပြုသည်	ma. gaun: hmu. bju. de
to sit (be sitting)	ထိုင်သည်	htain de
to sit down (vi)	ထိုင်သည်	htain de
to smell (emit an odor)	အနံ့ထွက်သည်	anan. htwei de
to smell (inhale the odor)	ရှုကြည့်သည်	shu gjei. de
to smile (vi)	ပြုံးသည်	pjoun: de
to snap (vi, ab. rope)	ပြတ်သည်	pja' te
to solve (problem)	ဖြေရှင်းသည်	hpjei shin: de
to sow (seed, crop)	မျိုးကြဲသည်	mjou: gje: de
to spill (liquid)	ဖိတ်ကျသည်	hpi' kja de
to spill out, scatter (flour, etc.)	သွန်မိသည်	thun mi. de
to spit (vi)	ထွေးသည်	htwei: de
to stand (toothache, cold)	သည်းခံသည်	thi: khan de
to start (begin)	စတင်သည်	sa. tin de
to steal (money, etc.)	ခိုးသည်	khou: de
to stop (for pause, etc.)	ရပ်သည်	ja' te
to stop (please ~ calling me)	ရပ်သည်	ja' te
to stop talking	နှုတ်ဆိတ်သွားသည်	hnou' hsei' thwa: de
to stroke (caress)	ပွတ်သပ်သည်	pu' tha' te
to study (vt)	သင်ယူလေ့လာသည်	thin ju lei. la de
to suffer (feel pain)	နာကျင်ခံစားသည်	na gjin hmu. gan za: de
to support (cause, idea)	ထောက်ခံသည်	htau' khan de
to suppose (assume)	ယူဆသည်	ju za. de
to surface (ab. submarine)	ပေါ်လာသည်	po la de
to surprise (amaze)	အံ့သြစေသည်	an. o: sei: de
to suspect (vt)	သံသယရှိသည်	than thaja. shi. de
to swim (vi)	ရေကူးသည်	jei ku: de
to take (get hold of)	ယူသည်	ju de
to take a bath	ရေချိုးသည်	jei gjou: de
to take a rest	အနားယူသည်	ana: ju de

to take away (e.g., about waiter)	ယူသွားသည်	ju dhwa: de
to take off (airplane)	ပျံတက်သည်	pjan de' te
to take off (painting, curtains, etc.)	ဖြုတ်ချသည်	hpjou' cha. de
to take pictures	ဓာတ်ပုံရိုက်သည်	da' poun jai' te
to talk to …	ပြောသည်	pjo: de
to teach (give lessons)	သင်ပေးသည်	thin bei: de
to tear off, to rip off (vt)	ဆွတ်ဖြဲသည်	hsou' hpje: de
to tell (story, joke)	ပြောပြသည်	pjo: bja. de
to thank (vt)	ကျေးဇူးတင်သည်	kjei: zu: din de
to think (believe)	ထင်သည်	htin de
to think (vi, vt)	ထင်သည်	htin de
to threaten (vt)	ခြိမ်းခြောက်သည်	chein: gjau' te
to throw (stone, etc.)	ပစ်သည်	pi' te
to tie to …	ချည်နှောင်သည်	che naun de
to tie up (prisoner)	တုတ်နှောင်သည်	tou' hnaun de
to tire (make tired)	ပင်ပန်းစေသည်	pin ban: zei de
to touch (one's arm, etc.)	ထိသည်	hti. de
to tower (over …)	မိုးနေသည်	mou: nei de
to train (animals)	လေ့ကျင့်ပေးသည်	lei. kjin. bei: de
to train (sb)	လေ့ကျင့်ပေးသည်	lei. kjin. bei: de
to train (vi)	လေ့ကျင့်သည်	lei. kjin. de
to transform (vt)	ပုံစံပြောင်းလဲသည်	poun zan bjaun: le: de
to translate (vt)	ဘာသာပြန်သည်	ba dha bjan de
to treat (illness)	ကုသည်	ku. de
to trust (vt)	ယုံကြည်သည်	joun kji de
to try (attempt)	ကြိုးစားသည်	kjou: za: de
to turn (e.g., ~ left)	ကွေ့သည်	kwei. de
to turn away (vi)	နောက်ကိုလှည့်သည်	nau' kou hle. de
to turn off (the light)	မီးပိတ်သည်	mi: pi' te
to turn on (computer, etc.)	ဖွင့်သည်	hpwin. de
to turn over (stone, etc.)	မှောက်သည်	hmau' de
to underestimate (vt)	လျှော့တွက်သည်	sho. dwe' de
to underline (vt)	အလေးထားဖော်ပြသည်	a lei: da: hpo pja. de
to understand (vt)	နားလည်သည်	na: le de
to undertake (vt)	ပြုလုပ်ဆောင်ရွက်သည်	pju. lou' hsaun jwe' te
to unite (vt)	ပေါင်းစည်းသည်	paun: ze: de
to untie (vt)	ဖြေသည်	hpjei de
to use (phrase, word)	အသုံးပြုသည်	athoun: bju. de
to vaccinate (vt)	ကာကွယ်ဆေးထိုးသည်	ka gwe hsei: dou: de
to vote (vi)	ဆန္ဒမဲပေးသည်	hsan da. me: pwei: de
to wait (vt)	စောင့်သည်	saun. de

to wake (sb)	နှိုးသည်	hnou: de
to want (wish, desire)	လိုချင်သည်	lou gjin de
to warn (of the danger)	သတိပေးသည်	dhadi. pei: de
to wash (clean)	ဆေးသည်	hsei: de
to water (plants)	ရေလောင်းသည်	jei laun: de
to wave (the hand)	လက်ပြသည်	le' pja de
to weigh (have weight)	အလေးချိန်ရှိသည်	a lei: chein shi. de
to work (vi)	အလုပ်လုပ်သည်	alou' lou' te
to worry (make anxious)	စိတ်ပူအောင်လုပ်သည်	sei' pu aun lou' te
to worry (vi)	စိတ်ပူသည်	sei' pu de
to wrap (parcel, etc.)	ထုပ်သည်	htou' te
to wrestle (sport)	နပန်းလုံးသည်	naban: loun: de
to write (vt)	ရေးသည်	jei: de
to write down	ရေးထားသည်	jei: da: de

www.ingramcontent.com/pod-product-compliance
Lightning Source LLC
Chambersburg PA
CBHW071318090426
42738CB00012B/2721